THE CULTURE

AND COMMERCE

OF PUBLISHING

IN THE 21ST CENTURY

ALBERT N. GRECO,

CLARA E. RODRÍGUEZ,

AND ROBERT M. WHARTON

STANFORD BUSINESS BOOKS
An Imprint of Stanford University Press
Stanford, California 2007

.

PREFACE

The one question that has sparked more debate in U.S. book publishing circles, ever since the first book was printed and published in what is now Massachusetts in 1639, has been, Is publishing a cultural or a commercial endeavor?

That question prodded us to spend almost three years investigating the eclectic, dynamic book-publishing industry. We profited from innumerable discussions, some in person and some on the telephone, with hundreds of editors, publishers, sales representatives, and other people in book publishing. We visited commercial and scholarly publishing houses and publishing executives in New York City, Boston, Chicago, San Francisco, Los Angeles, Washington, D.C., Kansas City, Atlanta, San Antonio, Austin, Denver, and in many other cities. We visited book warehouses, printing plants (both lithographic and print on demand), and hundreds (and at times it seemed as if it were thousands) of bookstores. We talked with reporters from major newspapers in New York, Chicago, Los Angeles, and Washington, D.C., etc. We discussed book publishing with reporters at the Associated Press, Reuters, Bloomberg, and elsewhere. We had numerous discussions with individuals who covered this industry at various Wall Street financial firms and hedge funds. We talked with authors, agents, book industry trade association leaders, and researchers at a number of book industry firms.

We also had the opportunity to read substantive papers and books about publishing, leading to frequent discussions with fellow academics in the United States, Canada, Europe, and Asia who were also interested in this industry.

It has been quite an education, filled with probing analyses of a myriad of statistical data sets (sometimes a bit daunting), great talks with really interesting people (who were eager to talk on and sometimes off the record—in one instance, an individual insisted on taping our discussion), and a few disappointments. This is a complex, adaptive business, evolving with Google initiatives, new e-books, and a changing consumer marketplace. And after three years, we just ran out of time. We really wanted to spend more time on technological issues; but since technology is changing so rapidly, anything relevant in 2006 will probably become old hat in 2007. So maybe it was time to close the book, or perhaps leave the book open for a few new chapters in the coming months.

THE CULTURE
AND COMMERCE
OF PUBLISHING
IN THE 21ST CENTURY

1 CHANGES IN THE BOOK-PUBLISHING INDUSTRY, 1945–2005

The U.S. book-publishing industry in 1945 was an established, cozy world of editors, authors, publishers, booksellers, and readers (Tebbel 1987). Traditions inextricably bound these participants together, and publishing was for the most part a cultural institution dominated by the great trade houses. Publishers and editors, whether an Alfred A. Knopf or a Maxwell Perkins, were keenly aware of their role in the literary life of this nation. Yet financial matters often took a back seat when issues of literary importance and taste were discussed. They were, after all, independent publishers and editors, the guardians of the intellectual life of the United States.

It was a small world where everyone knew someone who knew someone. In 1947 (the first postwar year with reliable data) there were 648 book-publishing firms in the United States. The vast majority of these book houses were in New York City, with important clusters in Boston and Philadelphia. They published 9,182 new titles and saw revenues of $435.1 million (Bowker Annual 1974). In that year, 1,307 new fiction hardcovers were published with an average retail price of $2.66. The number one national fiction best seller in 1947 was *Miracle of the Bells* by Russell Janney (Korda 2001). Consumer books (or trade books, comprising mass-market, religious, book-club, and mail-order books) were sold in independent bookstores, department stores, and book clubs. The new 25¢ mass-market paperback book was also available at transportation terminals and newsstands. In 1947 consumer books battled for media usage and discretionary dollars against a small number of competitors, including magazines, newspapers, newsletters, AM radio, motion pictures, and various sporting and recreational activities. See table 1.1 for detailed information about title output after 1940.

By 2005 publishing had changed. The U.S. Department of Commerce, Bureau of the Census (1992, 1997, 2000–2004) tracked annually more than 3,500 publishing firms, although the R. R. Bowker Company (which issues all the International Standard Book Numbers [ISBNs] in the United States) counted more than 81,000 publishers (Bowker 2005). While still centered in New York City, publishing had active centers located in the Midwest, in the Sunbelt, and on the West Coast, and these houses published 195,000 new titles in

TABLE 1.4

Top-selling fiction and nonfiction hardcover books, 1945–2005

Year	Fiction	Nonfiction
1945	*Forever Amber* (Winsor)	*Brave Men* (Pyle)
1946	*The King's General* (du Maurier)	*The Egg and I* (MacDonald)
1947	*The Miracle of the Bells* (Janney)	*Peace of Mind* (Liebman)
1948	*The Big Fisherman* (Douglas)	*Crusade in Europe* (Eisenhower)
1949	*The Egyptian* (Waltari)	*White Collar Zoo* (Barnes)
1950	*The Cardinal* (Robinson)	*Betty Crocker's Picture Cook Book* (Crocker)
1951	*From Here to Eternity* (Jones)	*Look Younger, Live Longer* (Hauser)
1952	*The Silver Chalice* (Costain)	*The Holy Bible* (revised standard version)
1953	*The Robe* (Douglas)	*The Holy Bible* (revised standard version)
1954	*Not as a Stranger* (Thompson)	*The Holy Bible* (revised standard version)
1955	*Marjorie Morningstar* (Wouk)	*Gift from the Sea* (Morrow)
1956	*Don't Go Near the Water* (Brinkley)	*Arthritis and Common Sense* (Alexander)
1957	*By Love Possessed* (Cozzens)	*Kids Say the Darndest Things!* (Linkletter)
1958	*Doctor Zhivago* (Pasternak)	*Kids Say the Darndest Things!* (Linkletter)
1959	*Exodus* (Uris)	*'Twixt Twelve and Twenty* (Boone)
1960	*Advise and Consent* (Drury)	*Folk Medicine* (Jarvis)
1961	*The Agony and the Ecstasy* (Stone)	*The New English Bible* (The New Testament)
1962	*Ship of Fools* (Porter)	*Calories Don't Count* (Taller)
1963	*The Shoes of the Fisherman* (West)	*Happiness Is a Warm Puppy* (Schultz)
1964	*The Spy Who Came in from the Cold* (LeCarre)	*Four Days* (American Heritage)
1965	*The Source* (Michener)	*How to Be A Jewish Mother* (Greenberg)
1966	*Valley of the Dolls* (Susann)	*How to Avoid Probate* (Dacey)
1967	*The Arrangement* (Kazan)	*Death of a President* (Manchester)
1968	*Airport* (Hailey)	*Better Homes and Gardens New Cook Book*
1969	*Portnoy's Complaint* (Roth)	*American Heritage Dictionary* (Morris)
1970	*Love Story* (Segal)	*Everything You Always Wanted to Know about Sex, but Were Afraid to Ask* (Reuben)
1971	*Wheels* (Hailey)	*The Sensuous Man* ("M")
1972	*Jonathan Livingston Seagull* (Bach)	*The Living Bible* (Taylor)
1973	*Jonathan Livingston Seagull* (Bach)	*The Living Bible* (Taylor)
1974	*Centennial* (Michener)	*The Total Woman* (Morgan)
1975	*Ragtime* (Doctorow)	*Angels: God's Secret Agents* (Graham)
1976	*Trinity* (Uris)	*The Final Days* (Woodward & Bernstein)
1977	*The Silmarillion* (Tolkien)	*Roots* (Haley)
1978	*Chesapeake* (Michener)	*If Life Is a Bowl of Cherries, What Am I Doing in the Pits?* (Bombeck)
1979	*The Matarese Circle* (Ludlum)	*Aunt Erma's Cope Book* (Bombeck)
1980	*The Covenant* (Michener)	*Crisis Investing* (Casey)
1981	*Noble House* (Clavell)	*The Beverly Hills Diet* (Mazel)
1982	*E.T.: The Extra-Terrestrial* (Kotzwinkle)	*Jane Fonda's Workout Book* (Fonda)
1983	*Return of the Jedi* (Vinge)	*In Search of Excellence* (Peters & Waterman)
1984	*The Talisman* (King & Straub)	*Iacocca: An Autobiography* (Iacocca)
1985	*The Mammoth Hunters* (Auel)	*Iacocca: An Autobiography* (Iacocca)
1986	*It* (King)	*Fatherhood* (Cosby)
1987	*The Tommyknockers* (King)	*Times Flies* (Cosby)
1988	*The Cardinal of the Kremlin* (Clancy)	*The 8-Week Cholesterol Cure* (Kowalski)
1989	*Clear and Present Danger* (Clancy)	*All I Really Need to Know I Learned in Kindergarten* (Fulghum)
1990	*The Plains of Passage* (Auel)	*A Life on the Road* (Kuralt)
1991	*Scarlett: The Sequel to Margaret Mitchell's Gone with the Wind* (Ripley)	*Me: Stories of My Life* (Hepburn)
1992	*Dolores Clairborne* (King)	*The Way Things Ought to Be* (Limbaugh)
1993	*The Bridges of Madison County* (Waller)	*See, I Told You So* (Limbaugh)
1994	*The Chamber* (Grisham)	*In the Kitchen with Rosie* (Daley)
1995	*The Rainmaker* (Grisham)	*Men Are from Mars, Women Are from Venus* (Gray)
1996	*The Runaway Jury* (Grisham)	*Make the Connection* (Winfrey & Greene)
1997	*The Partner* (Grisham)	*Angela's Ashes* (McCourt)
1998	*The Street Lawyer* (Grisham)	*The 9 Steps to Financial Freedom* (Orman)
1999	*The Testament* (Grisham)	*Tuesdays with Morrie* (Albom)

TABLE 1.4
(Continued)

Year	Fiction	Nonfiction
2000	*The Brethren* (Grisham)	*Who Moved My Cheese?* (Johnson)
2001	*Desecration* (Jenkins & LaHaye)	*The Prayer of Jabez* (Wilkinson)
2002	*The Summons* (Grisham)	*Self Matters* (McGraw)
2003	*The Da Vinci Code* (Brown)	*The Purpose-Driven Life* (Warren)
2004	*The Da Vinci Code* (Brown)	*The Purpose-Driven Life* (Warren)
2005	*Harry Potter and the Half-Blood Prince* (Rowling)	*Natural Cures "They" Don't Want You to Know About* (Trudeau)

SOURCE: *Publishers Weekly*, various issues.

TABLE 1.5
Average hardcover U.S. book price by category, 1947–1966 (dollars)

Category	1947–1949	1956	1958	1960	1961	1962	1963	1964	1965	1966
Agriculture	3.23	5.09	6.95	—	7.66	6.39	7.60	7.69	8.04	8.37
Art	7.06	9.97	11.35	12.61	10.63	8.57	10.32	10.68	10.60	1.73
Biography	3.89	4.47	5.20	4.98	5.49	5.94	6.56	6.65	7.65	7.57
Business	4.72	6.30	7.98	6.83	7.36	8.70	9.47	9.74	9.68	9.47
Juvenile	2.11	2.50	2.73	2.74	2.77	2.77	2.94	3.06	3.11	3.46
Economics	4.03	5.97	6.16	6.19	6.75	6.59	8.70	7.63	8.43	9.08
Education	3.39	4.47	4.75	4.97	4.89	5.64	5.71	5.50	5.78	5.61
History	4.76	5.88	6.46	5.91	6.01	6.72	6.75	7.73	8.83	8.56
Law	4.84	7.17	8.12	8.01	7.59	10.60	9.09	9.96	10.64	10.95
Literature—general	3.52	2.63	3.54	3.97	3.78	4.76	5.31	5.16	6.90	6.67
Literature—fiction	2.66	3.49	3.52	3.40	3.59	3.97	4.17	4.14	4.34	4.52
Literature—poetry	2.42	2.40	3.49	3.31	3.46	4.03	4.37	4.11	3.92	4.74
Literature—drama	3.09	3.60	4.03	4.48	4.86	4.62	6.38	5.91	5.47	6.67
Medicine	6.39	7.73	7.97	8.41	9.40	9.87	10.98	11.22	11.88	12.37
Music	4.06	4.56	5.53	5.56	5.10	6.74	7.79	6.98	8.04	8.15
Religion	2.84	3.74	3.69	4.05	3.98	4.42	4.48	4.63	6.72	5.38
Science	5.52	8.46	9.16	10.21	9.06	10.30	11.22	10.99	12.13	11.72
Sports & recreation	3.91	4.57	4.68	4.80	5.41	5.12	5.59	6.13	6.58	6.28
Technology	4.86	7.52	8.09	8.89	10.38	10.46	10.69	11.02	12.30	12.51
Average price for all categories	3.59	4.61	5.12	5.24	5.81	5.90	6.55	6.93	7.64	7.94

SOURCE: *Bowker Annual*, various issues.

TABLE 1.6
Average hardcover U.S. book price by category, 1967–1976 (dollars)

Category	1967	1968	1969	1970	1971	1972	1973	1974	1975	1976
Agriculture	8.90	10.23	8.97	10.42	13.64	10.94	11.79	13.21	13.72	15.40
Art	12.32	12.00	12.65	16.16	16.41	14.94	15.42	14.46	17.90	20.29
Biography	8.52	9.03	10.63	11.49	11.64	12.80	12.70	12.65	14.09	15.05
Business	9.77	10.00	10.47	12.45	12.60	12.45	13.23	14.97	16.54	18.28
Juvenile	3.41	3.47	3.85	4.05	4.23	4.37	4.65	5.01	5.82	6.01
Economics	8.65	9.68	9.65	—	—	—	—	—	—	—
Education	5.61	6.22	6.99	10.75	7.81	10.26	9.67	10.33	10.81	12.91
History	9.02	9.03	10.64	14.75	12.97	14.92	15.56	15.69	15.85	16.74
Law	12.52	12.79	13.39	16.41	18.37	17.15	16.78	18.24	23.22	20.65
Literature—fiction	4.80	4.93	5.14	5.51	5.98	6.47	7.37	7.43	8.31	9.96
Literature—poetry	5.49	5.97	7.26	—	—	—	—	—	—	—
Literature—drama	6.49	8.14	9.13	—	—	—	—	—	—	—
Literature—poetry & drama	—	—	—	9.35	9.15	10.62	10.50	9.93	10.76	12.66

(*Continued*)

DOMINANT TRENDS SINCE 1945

Eight substantive business and economic trends directly affected the growth of the U.S. book-publishing industry since 1945:

1. A large increase in and concomitant growth of the number of publishing firms, the sale of family-owned establishments, and consolidation in the consumer book-publishing industry, the largest (and in many ways the most important) component of the entire industry

2. A pattern of overall modest annual increases in the consumer price index (CPI)

3. A period of economic growth and sharp increases in the gross domestic product (GDP), the gross national product (GNP), disposable personal income, the unemployment rate, median and mean household incomes, and the population of the country

4. An expansion in consumer credit and disposable personal income

5. Changes in the channels of distribution, the marketing of books, the best-seller phenomenon, and the electronic distribution of content

6. The price sensitivity of consumer books

7. The importance of the book export market

8. Uncertainty in the marketplace

Consolidation in the Book-Publishing Industry

While the total number of publishing establishments after 1945 experienced sharp growth, the number of mergers and acquisitions in the U.S. also saw an extraordinary increase. They involved some of the industry's best-known firms (e.g., Random House, Dial Press, New American Library, Bantam Books, Simon & Schuster, Pocket Books, Harper & Row) as well as large media and nonmedia corporations (e.g., the American Broadcasting Company, Bertelsmann AG, Gulf & Western, the Music Corporation of America, News Corporation, Pearson PLC, and the Radio Corporation of America; Greco 2005).

Clearly, consolidation within book publishing occurred for a number of disparate reasons. Some entrepreneurs had children who were unable or unwilling to succeed them. Others either had severe cash flow problems or lacked access to enough capital to remain competitive. A few publishers were visionaries, able to handle adroitly the pains and challenges associated with a start-up but unable to manage a company on the upswing. Managing growth requires a different skill set than the one needed to launch a firm. The potential impact of inheritance taxes compelled some individuals to sell in order to maximize the estate they left to their family. Lastly, as the value of their content (backlist and new titles) increased, some publishers sold their companies to cash in on sizable profits (Connors, Henry, and Reader 1985–1986; Dessauer 1985–1986; Tebbel 1987).

Was something lost, some intangible asset associated with privately owned publishing firms? These publishers, ranging from Alfred A. Knopf to Bennett Cerf, operated in what was, and still is, a market economy. One must assume they made a voluntary business decision to sell, and a few made sizable profits from these transactions. Did they select mammon over culture? Only they can answer that question. What is known, however, is that this consolidation pattern paralleled developments in other industries.

Many observers were dismayed with this consolidation. Bagdikian remarked in *The Media Monopoly* that "for the first time in U.S. history, the country's most widespread news, commentary, and daily entertainment are controlled by six firms that are among the world's largest corporations, two of them foreign." He also addressed events in book publishing. "In books, as in other media, there is the growing presence of corporations that dominate in other media. . . . The six companies are: Paramount Communications (Simon & Schuster, Ginn & Company, and others), Harcourt Brace Jovanovich (Academic Press and others), Time Warner (Little, Brown; Scott, Foresman; and others), Bertelsmann, A.G. (Doubleday, Bantam Books, and others), Reader's Digest Association (Condensed Books and others), Newhouse (Random House and others)" (Bagdikian 2000).

Schiffrin, in *The Business of Books: How International Conglomerates Took Over Publishing and Changed the Way We Read*, commented on what he perceived to be a lack of editorial independence at Random House after its purchase by Sy Newhouse. "Despite his early promises of editorial independence, Newhouse soon became personally involved in acquiring titles. He insisted that Random House pay a huge advance to Donald Trump, the New York real estate speculator." Schiffrin, publisher of Pantheon Books, a Random House imprint at the time of its purchase by Newhouse, also alleged that Vitale, president of Random House, told him to "stop publishing 'so many books on the left' and instead publish more on the right" (Schiffrin 2000).

McChesney, in *Rich Media, Poor Democracy: Communication Politics in Dubious Times*, argued, "The striking structural features of the U.S. media system in the 1990s are concentration and conglomeration." The end result in book publishing, according to McChesney, was a "situation in which a handful of global firms dominate the market," which he believed changed the way publishers operated in the marketplace of ideas. "In addition to shaping what manuscripts are considered market-worthy and what authors 'bankable,' there is increased pressure to publish and record writers and artists whose work complements products produced in other branches of these far-flung empires" (McChesney 1999).

Epstein wrote in *Book Business: Publishing Past, Present, and Future* about the "golden age of publishing." Epstein remarked that "for many of them Random House was their family as much as it was ours . . . [an enterprise run by individuals who] risked their personal fortunes and disapproved of their elders by aggressively promoting the literature and ideas of modernism." Epstein insisted that this world of letters and authors was undermined by a vast transformation. "Book publishing has deviated from its true nature by assuming, under duress from unfavorable market conditions and the misconceptions of remote managers, the posture of a conventional business . . . book publishing is not a conventional business. It more closely resembles a vocation" (Epstein 2001).

In essence, these critics insisted that the mergers had created a real or de facto media monopoly (i.e., a restraint of free trade) that threatened and undermined the marketplace of ideas, culture, and democracy itself. A few writers insisted that the U.S. Department of Justice (Justice) or the Federal Trade Commission (FTC), the two agencies empowered to investigate

TABLE 1.11
Top 10 U.S. consumer (trade) book publishers, 1997–1998

Publisher	1997 net revenues ($ millions)	1997 market share (%)	1997 HHI	1998 net revenues ($ millions)	1998 market share (%)	1998 HHI
Random House	1,250	12.49	156.00	1,580	14.79	218.74
Simon & Schuster	975	9.75	95.06	932	8.72	76.04
Pearson	845	8.45	71.40	975	9.13	83.36
HarperCollins	737	7.37	54.32	750	7.02	49.28
Bantam Doubleday	660	6.60	43.56	330	3.09	9.55
Time Warner	310	3.10	9.61	310	2.90	8.41
Holtzbrinck	300	3.00	9.00	285	2.67	7.13
Hearst Books	170	1.70	2.89	180	1.69	2.86
Andrews McMeel	100	1.00	1.00	87	0.81	0.66
Houghton Mifflin	88	0.88	0.77	89	0.83	0.69
Total Top 10	5,435	—	—	5,418	—	—
Industry Total	10,004.7	—	—	10,682.0	—	—
C4	—	—	376.78	—	—	427.42
C8	—	—	441.84	—	—	455.37
HHI Top 10	—	—	443.61	—	—	456.72

SOURCE: *Subtext*, various issues, and author's calculations. All percentages were rounded off and may not add up to 100%.
NOTE: HHI = Herfindahl-Hirschman index; C4 = the top four firms; C8 = the top eight firms.

TABLE 1.12
Top 10 U.S. consumer (trade) book publishers, 1999–2000

Publisher	1999 net revenues ($ millions)	1999 market share (%)	1999 HHI	2000 net revenues ($ millions)	2000 market share (%)	2000 HHI
Random House	1,410	12.36	152.77	1,612	14.34	205.64
HarperCollins	780	6.84	46.79	1,029	9.15	83.72
Penguin Putnam	705	6.18	38.19	1,141	10.15	103.02
Simon & Schuster	590	5.17	26.73	596	5.30	28.09
Holtzbrinck	300	2.63	6.92	280	2.49	6.20
Scholastic	—	—	—	325	2.89	8.35
Time Warner	298	2.61	6.81	300	2.67	7.13
John Wiley	—	—	—	162	1.44	2.07
Thomas Nelson	183	1.60	2.56	168	1.49	2.22
IDG Books	165	1.45	2.10	—	—	—
Houghton Mifflin	89	0.78	0.61	103	0.92	0.85
Andrews McMeel	85	0.75	0.56	—	—	—
Total Top 10	4,605	—	—	5,716.0	—	—
Industry Total	11,409.1	—	—	11,242.1	—	—
C4	—	—	264.48	—	—	420.47
C8	—	—	282.87	—	—	441.22
HHI Top 10	—	—	284.04	—	—	444.29

SOURCE: *Subtext*, various issues, and author's calculations. All percentages were rounded off and may not add up to 100%.
NOTE: HHI = Herfindahl-Hirschman index; C4 = the top four firms; C8 = the top eight firms.

If the empirical data do not indicate any monopolistic levels, is it possible some firms employed other monopolistic practices, including predatory pricing practices, creating stiff or impenetrable market entry barriers, or reducing output (to create scarcity in the market to push up prices)? A review of data (in tables 1.1–1.9) on prices, the increase in the number of firms between 1947 and 2005, the apparent ease of access into the industry by new

TABLE 1.13
Top 10 U.S. consumer (trade) book publishers, 2001–2002

Publisher	2001 net revenues ($ millions)	2001 market share (%)	2001 HHI	2002 net revenues ($ millions)	2002 market share (%)	2002 HHI
Random House	1,350	12.15	147.62	1,463	12.90	166.41
Harper Collins	790	7.11	50.55	835	7.86	61.78
Penguin	787	7.08	50.13	810	7.14	50.98
Simon & Schuster	625	5.63	31.70	660	5.82	33.87
Holtzbrinck	300	2.70	7.29	320	2.82	7.95
Time Warner	297	2.67	7.13	350	3.09	9.55
Scholastic	210	1.89	3.57	208	1.83	3.35
Thomas Nelson	202	1.82	3.31	188	1.66	2.76
John Wiley	162	1.46	2.19	322	2.84	8.07
Houghton Mifflin	110	0.99	0.98	145	1.28	1.64
Total Top 10	4,833	—	—	5,301	—	—
Industry Total	11,108.6	—	—	11,304.7	—	—
C4	—	—	280.0	—	—	313.04
C8	—	—	301.30	—	—	341.96
HHI Top 10	—	—	304.47	—	—	346.36

SOURCE: *Subtext*; various issues, and author's calculations. All percentages were rounded off and may not add up to 100%.
NOTE: HHI = Herfindahl-Hirschman index; C4 = the top four firms; C8 = the top eight firms.

TABLE 1.14
Top 10 U.S. consumer (trade) book publishers, 2003–2004

Publisher	2003 net revenues ($ millions)	2003 market share (%)	2003 HHI	2004 net revenues ($ millions)	2004 market share (%)	2004 HHI
Random House	1,400	11.98	143.52	1,330	16.5	272.25
HarperCollins	920	7.87	61.94	920	11.4	129.96
Penguin	902	7.72	59.60	900	11.2	125.44
Simon & Schuster	640	5.48	30.03	640	7.9	62.41
Time Warner	350	3.00	9.00	350	4.3	18.49
John Wiley	340	2.91	8.47	340	4.2	17.64
Holtzbrinck	322	2.76	7.62	280	3.4	11.56
Scholastic	320	2.74	7.51	170	2.1	4.41
Thomas Nelson	195	1.67	2.79	195	2.4	5.76
Houghton Mifflin	125	1.07	1.14	138	1.7	2.89
Total Top 10	5,514	—	—	5,263	—	—
Industry Total	10,194	—	—	8,503	—	—
C4	—	—	295.09	—	—	590.06
C8	—	—	327.69	—	—	643.51
HHI Top 10	—	—	331.62	—	—	650.81

SOURCE: *Subtext*; various issues, and our calculations. All percentages were rounded off and may not add up to 100%.
NOTE: HHI = Herfindahl-Hirschman index; C4 = the top four firms; C8 = the top eight firms.

firms, and increases in the total output of new titles shows no indication of monopolistic practices.

It appears that the allegations of Bagdikian, Schiffrin, and McChesney about the creation of a real or de facto media monopoly cannot be substantiated using standard empirical analysis or analyzing the structure, title output, ease of entry into the marketplace, prices, etc.

TABLE 1.15
(*Continued*)

Year	Book title output	CPI all items	Gross domestic product ($ billions)	Gross national product ($ billions)	Personal income	Population (thousands)
2001	141,703*	177.1	10,128.0	10,135.9	26,236	285,321
2002	147,120*	179.9	10,487.0	10,502.3	27,159	288,205
2003	171,061*	184.0	11,004.0	11,031.5	28,034	291,049
2004	195,000*	189.0	11,735.0	—	29,034	292,801
2005	200,000**	193.5**	12,487.1	—	—	295,507

SOURCE: U.S. Department of Commerce, various agencies and departments; Bowker Annual, various issues.

*Starting in 1997, Bowker changed its methodology, incorporating more data sets, resulting in an increase in totals.

**Estimate.

***Commerce changed the index year. Gross domestic product plus income receipts from the rest of the world less income payments to the rest of the world equals the gross national product.

Overall, the GDP surged 5,159.97 percent between 1945 and 2004. See table 1.15 for details.

The Gross National Product

The GNP is the total market value of all of the final goods and services produced in a month, quarter, or year. In 1945 the GNP of the United States stood at $211.9 billion (U.S. Department of Commerce, Bureau of the Census 1959). Because of the postwar conversion of industries and the return of veterans, the GNP was expected to decline in 1946 and in subsequent years. Although 1946's GNP was off a modest 0.61 percent, positive gains were posted in 1947 and 1948. While the tallies for 1949 were disappointing, this was the last decline in the GNP recorded in the 20th century (U.S. Department of Commerce, Bureau of the Census 1999).

Overall, the GNP increased between 1945 and 2003, topping $11.03 trillion (+5,205.99 percent). See table 1.15 for information about the GNP for 1945–2003.

Personal Income

Personal income (PI) is the income households receive, including interest income and governmental transfer programs (e.g., Social Security). PI statistics were unavailable for 1945–1959, and five-year tallies were available for certain years (1960, 1965, 1970, and 1975). Consistently reliable data were available between 1980 and 2002.

PI stood at $2,277.00 in 1960 and $2,860.00 in 1965, for a growth rate of 25.60 percent. The CPI, on the other hand, grew at a slower pace of 7.55 percent during those years. This pattern was also evident in subsequent years: in 1965–1970 PI increased 43.00 percent and the CPI increased 21.90 percent, in 1970–1975 PI increased 51.12 percent and the CPI increased 38.60 percent. A change in the CPI index in 1980 negated any opportunity to compare data for 1975 with 1980. However, annual data were available after 1980.

In the 1980s PI surged 82.99 percent while the CPI lagged at 50.49 percent. As for the 1990s, PI experienced a far more moderate pattern, an increase of 30.93 percent, barely exceeding the CPI's 27.49 percent increase.

Overall, personal income increased sharply, influencing a number of discretionary consumer expenditures, including book purchases.

The Unemployment Rate

The U.S. government considers individuals employed if they spent most of the previous week working at a paid job. Individuals are considered unemployed if they are laid off, looking for a job, or waiting to start a new job. A third classification is "not in the work force," that is, an individual who is a full-time student, retired, etc. Unemployment statistics exist for all years since 1980 and for certain preceding years (1950, 1960, 1970). See table 1.16 for details.

The unemployment rate stood at 5.3 percent in 1950, increasing to 5.5 percent in 1960 and declining to 4.9 percent in 1970. The nation withstood a period of high unemployment rates starting in 1980 (7.1 percent), growing sharply to 9.7 percent in 1982. Declines were posted between 1984 and 1989, bottoming out at 5.3 percent in 1989.

The economy sustained a period of uncertainty in the early part of the 1990s, and increases in unemployment mirrored these trends, reaching 7.5 percent in 1992. Yet a period of relative prosperity marked the years after 1993, with better employment rates the norm. Unemployment dropped annually, reaching a low of 4.2 percent in 1999.

While the tallies for 2000 were impressive, a recession and the impact of 9/11 triggered yet another round of higher unemployment rates, reaching 6.0 percent in 2003. The only positive feature was an increase in the total number of Americans working between 2000 and 2003, paced by increases in the overall population.

Median and Mean Household Income

Median and mean household income statistics (for all races) were evaluated for 1967–2004. See table 1.16 for details.

In 1967 the median household income stood at $34,234.00, reaching $39,688 by 1979 (+15.93 percent). During the next 10 years, median household income increased a sluggish 10.59 percent, a pattern also evident in the 1990s (income +9.93 percent) and between 2000 and 2004 (income −3.62 percent).

A review of data on mean household income during those same years revealed a radically different pattern. While the mean for 1967 was below the median (off $1,945), the mean's growth rate when compared to the median's was startling.

Between 1967 and 1979, mean income grew 46.01 percent. During the 1980s, the mean (+17.48 percent) again exceeded the median, as it did in the 1990s (mean +18.36 percent) and between 2000 and 2004 (−3.42 percent).

Overall, the median household income grew 29.66 percent between 1967 ($34,234) and 2004 ($44,389), with the mean up 87.46 percent during those years (1967: $32,289; 2004: $60,528). Ultimately, an increase in household income, and the concomitant increase in discretionary income, helped trigger a strong increase in consumer expenditures, including book sales, especially after 1985.

TABLE 1.16
(*Continued*)

Year	Number of banks	Consumer credit ($ millions)	Disposable personal income ($ billions)	Unemployment in labor force (%)	Median household income all races ($)	Mean household income all races ($)
2000	9,908	153,150	7,194.0	4.0	46,058	62,671
2001	n.d.	n.d.	7,469.4	4.7	45,062	62,114
2002	n.d.	n.d.	7,857.2	5.8	44,546	60,768
2003	n.d.	n.d.	n.d.	6.0	44,482	60,654
2004	n.d.	n.d.	n.d.	n.d.	44,389	60,528

SOURCE: U.S. Department of Commerce, Bureau of the Census, *The Statistical Abstract of the United States*, various years (1955–2004); U.S. Department of Commerce, Economics and Statistics Administration 2004; *Economic Indicators*, various years (1945–2003).

NOTE: n.d. = no data available.

Population Growth Patterns

The U.S. population stood at 133.4 million in 1945. Hefty growth rates (+11.89 percent) were posted between 1946 and 1949 because of births and immigration from Europe (U.S. Department of Commerce, Bureau of the Census 1959). Between 1950 and 1959 (+16.79 percent) and between 1960 and 1969 (+12.18 percent) increases were on the upswing, triggering the well-documented baby boom. Slower growth rates were evident in the 1970s (+9.76 percent) and 1980s (+8.61 percent) because of a number of socioeconomic factors, although the pace increased in the 1990s (+11.66 percent). The population topped 295,507,000 (+4.65 percent) between 2000 and 2005 (U.S. Department of Commerce, Bureau of the Census 2004). See table 1.15 for additional details.

Banks and Consumer Credit

In 1945 the U.S. banking system was fragmented and the vast majority of banks (14,598 of them) were small, local (e.g., in some states banks were allowed to operate branch offices in only one county), and undercapitalized. By 2000 the total number of banks had declined to 9,908; however, that number is misleading since there was a period of rapid consolidation and sharp increases in the number of branch offices beyond the restriction to a single county or a single state.

In addition, the launch of effective national (and international) credit cards after 1970 allowed consumers the luxury of buying consumer goods and services anywhere without the limitations of a check. The launch of the World Wide Web in the 1980s and the emergence of a vast number of Web-based companies offering a plethora of goods and services (specifically Amazon.com, eBay, etc.) changed the consumer marketing landscape, including the sale of books.

An expansion in the availability of consumer credit also had a profound impact on consumer marketing trends. Consumer credit stood at $5.66 billion in 1945 (U.S. Department of Commerce, Economic Indicators 1945). By 1949 the nation experienced a 104.59 percent increase in consumer credit because of the expansion of the nation's banks, reaching

$11.59 billion. This pace continued unabated throughout the 1950s and 1960s and into the 21st century. Table 1.16 lists this growth pattern.

Consumers purchase consumer books with disposable personal income (DPI). In 1945 the total amount of DPI was $154.1 billion. It grew 23.10 percent between 1945 and 1949, followed by periods of growth in subsequent decades: 1950–1959, up 62.5 percent; 1960–1969, up 80.11 percent; 1970–1979, up 152.12 percent; 1980–1989, up 93.92 percent; 1990–1999, up 65.29 percent; and 2000–2002, up 9.22 percent. Between 1945 and 2002, DPI surged 4,998.77 percent, topping $7.86 trillion. (See table 1.16 for complete details.)

Summary of U.S. Economic Growth Patterns

Consumer expenditures account for approximately 66 percent of the GDP. However, consumer expenditures accounted for approximately 72 percent of all consumer book purchases in the U.S. between 1985 (the first year of reliable data from BISG's *Book Industry Trends 1985–2005*) and 2005. The U.S. book industry was positioned for growth in the years and decades after the end of World War II.

In retrospect, between 1945 and 2005, the U.S. economy exhibited great strength and resiliency. The strong increase in the GDP (+5,159.97 percent) and GNP (+5,205.99 percent), when coupled with a strong surge in PI (+1,139.66 percent between 1960 and 2002), the growth in median and mean household incomes, a significant increase in the population (+121.46 percent), and the overall growth of consumer credit (+2,603.44 percent) and PI (+4,998.77 percent), provided the nation with positive business conditions and expanding markets that sparked growth in many sectors of the economy, including the book-publishing industry.

These increases, and the growth in the book-publishing industry, took place despite 11 periods of economic contractions (i.e., recessions) during those years. The following list (with quarters in parentheses) outlines the business cycle of contractions as defined by the National Bureau of Economic Research (2005):

- February 1945 (I) to October 1945 (IV): 8 months
- November 1948 (IV) to October 1949 (IV): 11 months
- July 1953 (II) to May 1954 (II): 10 months
- August 1957 (III) to April 1958 (II): 8 months
- April 1960 (II) to February 1961 (I): 10 months
- December 1969 (IV) to November 1970 (IV): 11 months
- November 1973 (IV) to March 1975 (I): 16 months
- January 1980 (I) to July 1980 (III): 6 months
- July 1981 (III) to November 1982 (IV): 16 months
- July 1990 (III) to March 1991 (I): 8 months
- March 2001 (I) to November 2001 (IV): 8 months

CHANGES IN DISTRIBUTION CHANNELS
AND BOOK MARKETING

The Channels of Distribution

For most of the 20th century, books were sold as they had been in the 19th century. There was a fall and spring list, dictated originally by the inability to ship titles because of harsh winters and a fragile transportation network. Editors and not publishers held sales conferences describing the new list, and sales personnel traveled throughout the nation talking to bookstore owners about new books. Catalogs circulated, and the mail delivered orders to publishers. It was a world with Dickensian overtones, where accountants worked in cages with green visors, editors were hired all too frequently because of old college connections, and publishers and editors held the hands of aspiring and well-established authors. Maxwell Perkins's ability to craft a novel out of the morass of papers submitted by Hemingway, Fitzgerald, and Wolfe became legendary.

Books were sold at suggested retail prices in 1945 in a limited number of independent retail bookstores and department stores. Book clubs functioned, but their market penetration excluded millions, and used-book and antiquarian bookstores played a small role. It was a marginally functioning distribution system (Tebbel 1987).

This structure was transformed with the emergence of large chain bookstores in the 1970s (e.g., B. Dalton, Brentano's). These chains, located in shopping malls or strip shopping centers, stocked 8,000 to 12,000 titles, many of which were discounted (mainly best sellers) at 10–30 percent off the suggested retail price. As the chains expanded, more books were available to more Americans than ever before at lower prices. Publishers responded enthusiastically. A sale of 25,000 paperback copies of *Jaws* to B. Dalton in 1975 was more cost efficient than calling on 2,500 bookstores, each purchasing 10 copies.

The second major event was the creation in the late 1980s of superstores (Barnes & Noble, Borders, etc.) with approximately 60,000 square feet of space and stocking between 150,000 and 170,000 distinct titles (Greco 2005). Many general titles and best sellers were offered at a discount (generally 10–20 percent), and more books were being purchased than ever before. By 1985, 1.9 billion books were sold in the United States. By 1999 the total reached 2.4 billion, with superstores accounting for about 25 percent of the trade book total.

There was a downside, however. Independent bookstores were hard-pressed to compete with superstores in terms of title selection, prices, and ambiance (e.g., Starbucks coffee, comfortable chairs). They relied, instead, on knowing what their customers liked and superb service, strategies that sometimes failed to stem the growth of superstores. In 1991 the independents accounted for about 33 percent of all book sales; by 2005 this total receded to about 17 percent, thousands of independent bookstores having closed their doors during the 1990s. The American Booksellers Association, which represents the vast majority of independent bookstores, had 5,100 members in 1991; by 2004 that total declined to about 1,900.

The third major development was the emergence of mass-merchandise discount stores (e.g., Wal-Mart, Kmart, Target) and price clubs (or warehouse clubs; e.g., Costco, Sam's Club) as major book-retailing channels. These establishments sold best sellers and reference books at deep discounts (often for pennies above wholesale prices) to attract customers. Some independent bookstore owners found it more profitable to buy books from price clubs (rather than directly from publishers or distributors) and then resell them to their customers.

The fourth development was the emergence of the Internet as a book-selling channel. In the summer of 1995, Amazon.com was launched. It offered detailed data on millions of books (many at discounted prices), a user-friendly environment, book reviews, used books, and other services that revolutionized bookselling. Amazon.com attracted repeat customers and the attention of Wall Street. Other competing sites were launched, including BN.com, but Amazon.com became the brand name in Internet bookselling. While some industry observers initially questioned whether Amazon.com could survive because of its massive debt, most individuals recognized that the Internet had become a major marketing and distribution channel. Many industry experts insisted that traditional bookstores (the brick-and-mortar variety) would have to offer Internet services (in a brick-and-click environment) to survive in a changing retail environment.

The fifth event was the expansion of book distribution networks. Ingram, Baker & Taylor, etc., operated large regional warehouses (with up to one million books) supplying titles to libraries and retail establishments and handling orders from Internet sites (Greco 2000, 2005). Another major trend was the emergence of handheld electronic reading devices (called "e-books"). While plagued with a small screen, limited batteries, and high prices, these devices had the potential to revolutionize reading and publishing. By 2005 between 30,000 and 50,000 e-book units were in use in the United States, with several million advanced Palm Pilot devices capable of storing book content. This was a new, emerging market waiting for consumers to adopt these devices at the expense of printed books. Yet it appears unlikely that e-books will capture a sizable portion of the conventional book market by 2010; in 2005 total e-book sales were in the $12 million range. Microsoft predicts it will take until 2017 to attain a 51 percent market share because of technological issues, pricing, title availability, and inertia among consumers.

Another development was the emergence of sophisticated computerized print-on-demand (POD) equipment capable of producing small book runs (as low as one copy) at an economical price. POD technology allowed publishers to keep titles "in print," effectively reaching new audiences for decades. Lastly, as the cost of computers and software declined and with the emergence of viable enterprise software systems capable of tracking everything from book orders to royalty payments, publishing firms adopted modern technologies and created electronic ordering systems, toll-free telephone services, and other telemarketing systems, increasing their operating efficiency and the bottom line.

Marketing Books

Distribution changes affected book marketing. Between 1945 and the late 1970s, publishing houses had large sales forces in the field servicing independent bookstores (with costly field sales managers and corporate staff employees supporting these operations). This was an expensive way to do business since a sales representative could visit only two or three stores each day. This changed in the 1980s. Sales and marketing teams started calling on book buyers at large chains and eventually superstores (Greco 2005). Now publishers sold more books with smaller staffs at lower costs. In addition, promotion campaigns and marketing budgets (generally cooperative dollars) were targeted to specific clusters of superstores in designated regions and author tours were arranged more efficiently. Better tracking of point-of-purchase sales occurred, especially with the emergence of BookScan, which aggregates and analyzes 70–75 percent of all weekly U.S. book sales. Carefully designed co-op advertisements were placed in newspapers and magazines; radio (especially National Public Radio) and cable television (especially book coverage on C-Span) became useful platforms to target specific demographic groups; and advance reading copies were sent to a large and growing number of newspaper and magazine reviewers and television and radio hosts. These procedures allowed publishers to reduce costly field staffs in the early to mid-1990s.

Consumer Purchasing Trends

Reliable consumer research on trade book purchasing trends was unavailable for 1945–1989. However, data gathered by the market research organization the NPD Group on the 1990s revealed a number of substantive facts (NPD 1991, 1992, 1993). The largest number of book purchases occurred in the fall (October through December). The other three seasons shared almost equally the remaining book sales.

By 2005 mass-market paperbacks accounted for an impressive share of all book sales, with an average suggested retail price of $7.99.

The NPD data (released by the BISG) revealed that consumers purchased books for a number of disparate reasons, including (in ranked order) the book's cover art, its price, a review they had read or seen, a recommendation by someone they knew, advertisements, the book's being prominently displayed in the store, endorsements of the book, an interview of the book's author they saw or heard on television or radio, the book's inclusion on a bestseller list, they had seen a motion picture or television show based on the book, the book was recommended by a salesperson, they had seen or heard the author in person, the book was recommended by a media personality, or another reason. Around 55 percent of all purchased books were planned (and not impulse) purchases (NPD 1994, 1995, 1996). Fifty-eight percent of all books were bought by people older than age 45; and 21 percent of these people had annual incomes between $50,000 and $74,999, with an additional 28 percent above $75,000. Twenty percent of book buyers graduated from college, and 18 percent had some graduate studies. The largest number of book buyers who bought more than the average lived in the Pacific region (NPD 1997, 1998, 1999).

Most books (about 70 percent) were purchased in person. By 2005 Internet bookselling sites accounted for about 10 percent of all sales. Almost one of out every four books was purchased at a superstore; book clubs were a distant second at 17 percent; and small chains and independents held a 15 percent share. The rest of the market was shared by price and warehouse clubs (6.5 percent), mass merchandisers (6 percent), mail order (4 percent and declining), food and drug stores (3 percent), discount stores (3 percent), and used-book stores (3 percent); small retail operations accounted for the remaining balance. More than one out of every two books purchased in the United States was a fiction title. Cooking-craft books, at a 10 percent share, were the second-most-purchased group. The other major categories included religion (9 percent); nonfiction (8 percent); technical, science, and educational titles (almost 6 percent); psychology and recovery books (5 percent); art, literature, and poetry (3 percent); reference (2 percent); and travel and regional (about 1 percent; NPD 2000, 2001, 2002).

The Price Sensitivity of Consumer Books

Did suggested retail prices keep pace with the CPI? Are consumers sensitive to book price changes?

Average suggested retail prices are available for books, but not for every year or for every category. Hardcover prices are of primary importance since mass-market paperback prices increased in small increments, remaining at 25¢ between 1945 and 1950, and then slowly inching up to 35¢ and then 50¢. Accordingly, we used the average prices for hardcover history and fiction books and the average price for all categories of hardcover books to gauge increases since these are major trade book categories (U.S. Department of Commerce, Bureau of the Census 2004).

Average hardcover prices in 1947 (the first year totals were available) were history, $4.76; fiction, $2.66; and all hardcover books, $3.59. In 1956 the averages stood at history, $5.88 (+23.53 percent since 1947); fiction, $3.49 (+31.20 percent since 1947); and all hardcover books, $4.61 (+28.41 percent since 1947). The increase in the CPI between 1947 and 1956 was 16.06 percent; books in these three categories exceeded the CPI by healthy margins (Bowker Annual 1963, 1968, 1969, 1971, 1979–1981, 1983, 1989, 1991, 1993, 1995, 1996, 2000, 2005).

As of 1960, averages are available for the entire decade. During those 10 years, the price for history titles jumped 80.03 percent; fiction, 51.18 percent; and all hardcover books, 78.82 percent. All three categories surpassed the CPI's 10-year increase of 23.89 percent. A different pattern was evident in the 1970s, a period of tremendous CPI changes (+86.93 percent). History was up 34.17 percent, fiction posted a 126.13 percent gain, and all hardcover titles were up 105.49 percent. More realistic book price increases were posted for the 1980s. While the CPI increased 50.49 percent, history's increase stood at 66.59 percent, making up for lost ground in the 1970s. Fiction's 50 percent increase matched the CPI, while all hardcover books generated a rate of 64.81 percent.

As for the 1990s (CPI +27.47 percent), history inched up 21.51 percent, fiction's 47.65 percent exceeded the CPI, and all hardcover books increased 18.71 percent. Ironically, while the CPI increased 19.54 percent between 2000 and 2005, history prices fell 2 percent, as did fiction (−7.51 percent; Bowker Annual 1997–2005).

Overall, between 1945 and 2005, book prices exceeded the CPI. However, are books price sensitive? Did price increases act as a disincentive to book purchases? Reliable data on unit prices and sales are available only for 1985–2005 in the following trade book categories: total trade, adult trade, juvenile, mass market, book clubs, mail order, and religion (BISG 2005).

Between 1985 and 2005, adult trade books posted a 108.46 percent increase in prices with a 32.41 percent increase in units sold. Mass market's track record was more depressing, an increase of 73.26 percent in price and 0.86 percent in units, a pattern followed by book clubs and mail order. Negative calculations were recorded for mail order; religious titles were up (price +204 percent; units +22.76 percent). These data indicated that consumer book unit sales, with the exception of juvenile titles (price +77.73 percent, quantity +103.55 percent), lagged behind price, indicative that consumer books exhibited some pronounced price sensitivity characteristics.

Book Exports

U.S. book exports grew in the last half of the 20th century; *exports* refers to exported books (i.e., titles) and not foreign rights revenues. By 1945 U.S. book exports totaled $12.5 million, reaching $36.4 million in 1955 (Grannis 1952; Bowker Annual 1961, 1971). Exports continued to grow during the rest of the 1950s because U.S. publishers developed new lines in the professional and textbook fields (especially in the burgeoning scientific, technical, medical, and business areas) and issued a sizable number of fiction titles, categories with strong export appeal. By the late 1950s and early 1960s, exports garnered a larger share of total net publisher revenues. As English became the lingua franca of business and commerce, the U.S. export market matured; many major publishers established subsidiaries or sales offices in Canada, Europe, the Pacific Rim, etc., to solidify their presence in these markets. International sales representatives based in the United States called on customers abroad semiannually as air travel became more manageable in the early 1960s.

By 1970 exports reached $174.9 million, easily outpacing imports ($92 million), for an impressive export-to-import ratio of 1.90:1. This trend continued into 1975 (exports $269.3 million, imports $147.6 million, a ratio of 1.82) and on into 1990 (exports topped $1.41 billion, imports stood at $855.1 million, a ratio of 1.65:1).

However, currency conversion issues, inflationary pressures, and political uncertainty plagued exports from the 1960s into the mid-1980s and well into the 1990s (Greco 1999, 2000b; Bowker Annual 2005). However, the constant outpouring of titles, a more aggressive international sales operation, and the use of new communications technologies generated stunning export results for U.S. firms in the 1990s, reaching $1.87 billion in exports by 1999. Yet these econometric trends stimulated book imports, which topped $1.44 billion in 1999; and the important export-to-import ratio fell annually in the 1990s, reaching 1.30:1 by 1999.

Export totals vacillated after 2000, dropping from an industry high of $1.88 billion in 2000 to $1.74 billion in 2004. Imports continued to grow, reaching $1.93 billion in 2004; and the export-to-import ratio fell annually, reaching an all-time low of 0.90 in 2004. Table 1.17 outlines these trends.

In terms of the relative importance of exports to total net publisher revenues, the industry experienced steady growth between 1970 and 1980, accounting for 8.5 percent of all revenues in 1980. After a sharp drop in 1985, exports surged in 1990, with strong results posted for 1995 (9.1 percent), 1996 (8.8 percent), and 1997 (9.0 percent).

However, exports experienced a period of decline starting in 1998 (8.2 percent), eventually reaching a 6.6 percent market share in 2004. Table 1.18 outlines this downward spiral.

Canada was the United States' primary market for books from the late 1940s through 2004, followed by the United Kingdom and Australia.

TABLE 1.17
U.S. book exports and imports, 1970–2004 (millions of dollars)

Year	Book exports	Book imports	Ratio of exports to imports
1970	174.9	92.0	1.90
1975	269.3	147.6	1.82
1980	518.9	306.5	1.69
1985	591.2	564.2	1.05
1990	1,415.1	855.1	1.65
1995	1,779.5	1,184.5	1.50
1996	1,775.6	1,240.1	1.43
1997	1,896.6	1,297.5	1.46
1998	1,841.8	1,383.7	1.33
1999	1,871.1	1,441.4	1.30
2000	1,877.0	1,590.5	1.18
2001	1,712.3	1,627.8	1.05
2002	1,681.2	1,661.2	1.01
2003	1,693.6	1,755.9	0.96
2004	1,740.5	1,934.4	0.90

SOURCE: U.S. Department of Commerce, International Trade Administration (various issues).

TABLE 1.18
U.S. book industry shipments compared to U.S. book exports,
1970–2004 (millions of dollars)

Year	Total publisher net publishing revenues	Total book exports	Exports as a percentage of publisher net publishing revenues
1970	2,434.2	174.9	7.2
1975	3,536.5	269.3	7.6
1980	6,114.4	518.9	8.5
1985	10,165.7	591.2	5.8
1990	14,982.6	1,415.1	9.4
1995	19,471.0	1,779.5	9.1
1996	20,285.7	1,775.6	8.8
1997	21,131.9	1,896.6	9.0
1998	22,507.0	1,841.8	8.2
1999	23,926.9	1,871.1	7.8
2000	24,749.0	1,877.0	7.6
2001	24,742.6	1,712.3	6.9
2002	25,270.2	1,681.2	6.7
2003	25,998.5	1,693.6	6.5
2004	26,450.9	1,740.5	6.6

SOURCE: U.S. Department of Commerce, International Trade Administration; Book Industry Study Group, Book Industry Trends 2005.

Overall, exports jumped 13,824 percent between 1945 and 2004. However, U.S. exports did not keep pace with imports during 2002–2004, a harbinger of potential balance-of-trade problems.

Uncertainty in the Consumer Marketplace

Uncertainty in the consumer marketplace was the one theme consistently evident in the U.S. book-publishing industry between 1945 and 2005. To combat uncertainty and to minimize risk, executives in some industries employed mathematical models to understand the vagaries of the business cycle and predict sales on the basis of prices, advertising, promotions, placements, seasonality, weather conditions, brands, competition, new entries into the marketplace, changes in regulatory agency guidelines, discounts, coupons, foreign currency problems, etc.

Two economists, De Vany and Walls (1996, 1999) studied the motion picture industry, and they remarked that book publishing exhibited many of the same characteristics, an observation supported by our research on the book-publishing industry. In the following section, we apply the theories developed by De Vany and Walls to books.

Selling books is not the same as selling cornflakes. Each book is unique, a new product in the marketplace of ideas, and supply and demand in book publishing operates in a profoundly different manner than in other industries. As De Vany and Walls explained, readers select or reject a new book not by revealing preferences they already have but by discovering what they like or dislike about a new book. They do not know in advance whether they will enjoy a book before it is published (De Vany and Walls 1996). Of course, publishers do not know if readers will like a book, a phenomenon economists call the "dual-sided uncertainty factor." This means consumers constantly search for and update information about new books from reviews, advertisements, word of mouth, cover art, displays in bookstores, television (the Oprah factor), author speaking engagements, the Internet, reading groups, etc. They use this informational model, called the "information cascade" by economists and "buzz" by marketers, to decide which book to purchase. A positive information cascade makes a book a hit; a negative information cascade almost certainly triggers failure and removal from bookstore shelves in a matter of weeks.

This informational search and updating process has always been random. Although publishers have been trying since 1945 to manage this exchange of information through a variety of extensive (and often costly) marketing and promotion techniques (especially in the 1950s and 1960s when advertising costs became more reasonable), in reality they could not control it. So publishing executives realized in the late 1940s that their business was inherently a complex and semichaotic enterprise because of the intricate nature of their distributional dynamics (De Vany and Walls 1996). The way readers responded determined the fate of a single book as well as the success or failure of other books not chosen. Even a small difference in what readers preferred grew into larger differences at the cash register. A review of bestsellers between 1945 and 2005 revealed that a small proportion of authors accounted for a high percentage of all sales. See table 1.4 for a list of best-selling books and authors.

So if book publishing was a semichaotic industry, does that mean that editors and publishers were hopelessly adrift, unable to do anything to help spark purchases? By the 1980s, sophisticated computer systems generated sales data on a daily and weekly basis, providing publishers with information on how a specific title sold in certain stores, in specific geographical regions, and nationally. However, every new book (called a "frontlist" book) was in a survival, or tournament in De Vany and Walls's terminology, mode, battling for sales against other frontlist and backlist books; generally a frontlist book becomes a backlist book about nine months after its initial publication date (De Vany and Walls 1996). Weekly sales revenues were viewed as a random variable, often depending on the number and quality of competing frontlist and backlist books (which changed daily). Traditionally, total revenues fell as a book exhausted its audience.

By the mid-1980s, because of the emergence of mall bookstores, editors and publishers started to rely on sales tallies and information to make adaptive decisions on which book became a survivor (i.e., received additional attention, advertisements, and marketing-promotional push) and which book did not. This adaptive process, depending on flexible responses, captured success and cast out failure (De Vany and Walls 1996).

Could editors and publishers predict what a new book by a star would do in the market-place? Star authors (e.g., John Grisham, Mary Higgins Clark) generated attention, the sought-after buzz that sparked the interest of potential readers, large advertisement and promotional campaigns, Web sites, television appearances, and articles in newspapers and the popular press. These events generated large initial orders by bookstores. However, stars represented only an exceptionally small portion of all new titles published annually in the United States since 1945. De Vany and Walls insisted that "the strong evidence . . . points to the stark uncertainty . . . [that] neither genre nor stars can guarantee success" (De Vany and Walls 1996).

Clearly, the knowledge needed to predict in advance which new book will or will not be successful is unknown and unknowable; and anything can happen once a book is placed on sale, and something often did. This is a prime example of what economists call "infinite variance." The bottom line is stark: there are no formulas for success, and most books since 1945 failed to generate substantial profits for publishers and authors. Our research indicates that 7 out of every 10 frontlist hardbound books fail financially (i.e., they do not earn enough to cover the author's advance and other editorial, marketing, and overhead costs), 2 books break even, and 1 is a hit. Coincidentally, this is precisely the same ratio found in the motion picture industry. Consequently, even a carefully managed and expensive marketing promotion campaign cannot control the information cascade. It has always been a stochastic (i.e., random), complex process that can go anywhere.

Publishers understood the unnerving uncertainty of the marketplace, and they tried to minimize risks. Yet this cautious approach, while understandable, triggered the blockbuster and hit mentality that permeated, and in many ways undermined, much of trade publishing in the years after 1980.

CONCLUSION

In spite of this uncertainty, as well as a series of recessions, the U.S. book industry grew. A number of factors directly influenced this growth. The U.S. population increased sharply between 1945 and 2004, as did GDP, GNP, PI, median and mean household incomes, and the amount and availability of consumer credit. The number of children registered in elementary and secondary schools shot up, as did registration in junior colleges, four-year colleges, and graduate and professional schools (U.S. Department of Commerce, Bureau of the Census 2004).

Because of constitutional protections, no licenses were needed to enter this business. In addition, market entry barriers, as defined by Porter, were negligible in this industry since capital requirements were low, all services could be subcontracted out, and there was a constant source of new publishable manuscripts (Porter 1979).

The intrinsic value of many publishing firms increased with fluctuations in the value of the dollar, the emergence of English as an international language in business and trade, and the rising economic importance of the backlist. Some media corporations viewed publishing as supplying valuable content (and synergy) for their diverse media and entertainment operations.

There were also intangible reasons to own a publishing house. Ownership allowed some individuals access to what had been a rather exclusive club. Having lunch with Mary Higgins Clark at the tony Four Seasons restaurant or taking John Grisham to Wimbledon seemed more exciting than opening a new department store. Lastly, book-publishing revenues were on the upswing, growing from $435.1 million in 1947 to $26.45 billion in 2005. Because of major demographic changes, trade and professional books and college textbooks were the market drivers through the 1990s and into 2004.

Robert Solow's neoclassical growth model is an exceptionally useful tool to evaluate growth in advanced economies. Solow, who won the Noble Prize in 1990 for his work on growth theories, maintained that the size of the economy is determined by inputs and technology; and growth was due specifically to capital accumulation, a process economists term "capital deepening" (i.e., the availability of adequate sources of capital and the concomitant belief that the supply of capital grows more rapidly than the labor force; Solow 1997, 1956, 1994; Solow, Tobin, von Weizacker, and Yaari 1966; Solow, Dertouzos, and Lester 1989). Consequently, firms with access to capital have a distinct competitive advantage over undercapitalized corporations.

This pattern was evident in book publishing after 1945. Firms able to acquire capital, by the capital-deepening process, had the ability to acquire, publish, and market the best authors, establish efficient domestic and foreign sales and marketing procedures, and adopt new technologies. So the emergence of large, diversified firms as owners of the major houses (including Bertelsmann AG, Pearson PLC, News Corporation, Viacom, Time Warner) with large pools of capital or the ability to acquire capital should not be viewed as an unusual event. It was in keeping with trends found throughout the business community, both domestically and globally. It was to Solow the sine qua non of growth and survival.

With capital accumulation and the ability to grow the company, managers had fiduciary responsibilities to maximize revenues for stockholders. This meant executives had to make prudent investment decisions to ascertain which projects were supported. While not commenting directly on the tournament theory developed by De Vany and Walls, Solow's theory supports their notion; and the merger and acquisition phenomenon in publishing offers data showing that acquisitions were a major obligation and requirement for growth.

Clearly, mergers, capital deepening, technological advancements, etc., improved book-publishing operating efficiencies. Some individuals heavily criticized this process. However, this growth provided publishers with scarce resources that allowed them (1) to find and develop editors and authors; (2) to expand title output and channels of distribution; (3) to bring to the market intriguing and conflicting ideas and opinions; (4) to ensure that the critically important marketplace of ideas remained a vital component of this nation; (5) to publish genres formerly excluded during the golden age of publishing (e.g., books on feminism or African American, Hispanic American, and Asian American issues and themes); and (6) to pay dividends to stockholders, wages to hundreds of thousands of employees, and taxes to myriad governmental agencies.

These were laudable achievements for an enterprise caught inextricably between its cultural and commercial orientation.

CASE STUDY: CHANGES IN TITLE OUTPUT AND EMERGENCE OF MASS-MARKET PAPERBACK BOOKS

Title Output

Between 1945 and 2005, slightly more than 3.05 million new hardbound and paperback books were published in the United States.

In 1945 total new book output reached 6,548 titles. In the next four years, totals increased rapidly, generating 44,254 new titles (Bowker Annual 1963, 1968). During the 1950s, publishers released 124,675 new titles; and the 1960s experienced an even larger surge, with 256,584 new books. This velocity continued unabated in the 1970s (402,911 titles), the 1980s (510,206 titles), and the 1990s (634,412 titles; Bowker Annual 1981, 1988, 1995, 1999, 2005).

By 2005 Bowker reported there were approximately 3,200,000 titles in print and more than 5,000,000 out-of-print titles available from used-book and antiquarian bookstores and Internet "bookstores." These totals excluded imported books.

Data on title output by book category revealed the diversity of U.S. publishing. Totals are listed for decades (starting with 1940; 1945 data were unavailable); annual totals were available for 1991–2005. These tallies include hardcover and paperback books. Fiction was the traditional leader in title output. In 1940 it accounted for 1,736 titles and 14.59 percent of all new output. Juvenile literature was a distant second, followed closely by history and religion. This pattern was also evident in the 1950s and 1960s, with fiction again number one and juvenile books in second place (Bowker Annual 1981). Changes took place in the ranking of other categories, indicative of shifts in interests, taste, and the impact of political and economic trends. Biographies posted impressive market share numbers in the 1950s and 1960s, with the number of religion titles increasing and history lagging. Overall, nonfiction titles dominated title output, although fiction remained the largest-selling category (statistical data on these categories can be found in chapter 2).

In 1970 Bowker revised its book cataloging system and created more subcategories, making comparisons with prior years difficult. The most notable change centered on the sociology and economics category, which emerged as the largest category in 1970 (Bowker Annual 1983). After 1970, fiction settled into its secure second-place ranking, although juvenile titles occasionally displaced it. Biographies, history, and religion posted impressive tallies, as did business, medical, art, and technology books.

While there was an ebb and flow to title output, adult fiction remained exceptionally popular (Bowker Annual 2005). So when Americans read books, they tended to read fiction, the vast majority written by U.S. authors. Imported and translated fiction generally failed to make best-seller lists.

The Paperbacking of America

One of the most dramatic events in publishing history was the emergence of the paperback book (Davis 1984). During the summer of 1945, Ian and Betty Ballantine launched Bantam Books, publishing 25¢ mass-market paperback books. Capitalizing on a market eager for inexpensive books, Bantam published Westerns, mysteries, and books by Mark Twain, F. Scott Fitzgerald (putting Fitzgerald back into print after a five-year hiatus), and other authors (Davis 1984; Tebbel 1987). Ballantine developed an innovative network of distributors (who also handled newspapers and magazines). Motion picture and eventually television tie-ins aided paperback sales. These marketing procedures allowed paperbacks to reach nontraditional retail establishments (e.g., transportation terminals, newsstands, candy stores). A new book market was created and sales flourished, with Bantam's print runs often tipping the 200,000 mark (Davis 1984).

Other publishers entered this niche, including Dell, Fawcett, New American Library, Popular Library, Signet, Avon, and Berkley. Unfortunately, business and legal problems surfaced by the early 1950s. The market was glutted with too many titles, warehouses were flooded with returns, and massive write-offs occurred. Concerns were expressed about both the editorial content and cover art of many paperbacks (Davis 1984).

As economic conditions worsened, some of the houses, including Bantam Books, replaced top managers, including Ballantine. Publishers responded with innovative strategies in the mid-1950s and 1960s. They launched paperback books in new categories at attractive prices and with sturdier bindings. Distribution channels were expanded, and sales were spurred by school and college adoptions of paperbacks as required readings (Davis 1984; Tebbel 1987). By the late 1960s and 1970s, paperbacks were an entrenched part of the publishing scene, with many titles selling more than one million copies, a pattern that continued into the 1980s. In 1985 publishers had net revenues of $10.08 billion. Paperbacks accounted for $3.39 billion of that total. By 1999 publishers' total net revenues stood at $23.26 billion and paperbacks generated $7.33 billion. In 2005 paperbacks accounted for 39.75 percent of all books sold ($27.74 billion) in the United States.

Paperbacks changed the reading habits of millions of Americans because of the availability of inexpensive titles, the accessibility of first-rate literary works (classics, contemporary works, poetry), attractive popular genres (especially romance novels), and the portability of these books.

REFERENCES

Bagdikian, Ben H. 2000. *The Media Monopoly*. Boston: Beacon.

Book Industry Study Group. 1990–2005. Book Industry Trends. New York: Book Industry Study Group. [Published annually.]

The Book Standard. 2005. http://www.thebookstandard.com.

Bowker. 2005. http://www.bowker.com.

Bowker Annual Library and Book Trade Almanac. 1961–2005. New Providence, NJ: Information Today. [Published annually.]

Connors, Linda E., Sara Lynn Henry, and Jonathan W. Reader. 1985–1986. "From Art to Corporation: Harry N. Abrams, Inc., and the Cultural Effects of Merger." *Book Research Quarterly* 1, no. 4 (Winter): 28–59.

Davis, Kenneth C. 1984. *Two-Bit Culture: The Paperbacking of America*. Boston: Houghton Mifflin.

De Vany, Arthur, and W. D. Walls. 1996. "Bose-Einstein Dynamics and Adaptive Contracting in the Motion Picture Industry." *Economic Journal* 106, no. 439 (November): 1493–1514.

De Vany, Arthur, and W. D. Walls. 1999. "Uncertainty in the Movie Industry: Does Star Power Reduce the Terror of the Box Office?" *Journal of Cultural Economics* 23, no. 4 (November): 285–318.

Dessauer, John P. 1985–1986. "Coming Full Circle at Macmillan: A Publishing Merger in Economic Perspective." *Book Publishing Quarterly* 1, no. 4 (Winter): 60–72.

Epstein, Jason. 2001. *Book Business: Publishing Past, Present, and Future*. New York: Norton.

Grannis, Chandler B., ed. 1952. *What Happens in Book Publishing*. New York: Columbia University Press.

Greco, Albert N. 1999. "The Impact of Horizontal Mergers and Acquisitions on Corporate Concentration in the U.S. Book Publishing Industry: 1989–1994." *Journal of Media Economics* 12, no. 3: 165–80.

———. 2000. "U.S. Book Exports and Imports: 1999." In Bowker Annual 2000: 516–27.

———. 2000a. "Market Concentration Levels in the U.S. Consumer Book Industry: 1995–1996." *Journal of Cultural Economics* 24, no. 4 (November): 321–36.

———, ed. 2000b. *The Media and Entertainment Industries*. Boston: Allyn & Bacon.

———. 2005. *The Book Publishing Industry*. Mahwah, NJ: Erlbaum.

Korda, Michael. 2001. *Making the List: A Cultural History of the American Bestseller 1900–1999*. New York: Barnes & Noble.

McChesney, Robert W. 1999. *Rich Media, Poor Democracy: Communication Politics in Dubious Times*. Urbana: University of Illinois Press.

National Bureau of Economic Research. 2005. http://www.nber.org.

NPD Group. 1991–2002. Consumer Research Study on Book Purchasing. New York: Book Industry Study Group. [Published annually.]

Porter, Michael. 1979. "How Competitive Forces Shape Strategy." *Harvard Business Review* 57 (March–April): 137.

Schiffrin, Andre. 2000. *The Business of Books: How International Conglomerates Took Over Publishing and Changed the Way We Read*. New York: Verso.

Solow, Robert M. 1956. "A Contribution to the Theory of Economic Growth." *Quarterly Journal of Economics Perspectives* 70:65–94.

———. 1994. "Perspectives on Growth Theory." *Journal of Economic Perspectives* 8, no. 1 (Winter): 45–54.

———. 1997. *Learning from "Learning by Doing": Lessons for Economic Growth*. Stanford, CA: Stanford University Press.

Solow, Robert M., Michael Dertouzos, and Richard K. Lester. 1989. *Made in America*. Cambridge, MA: MIT Press.

Solow, Robert M., James Tobin, C. C. von Weizacker, and M. Yaari. 1966. "Neoclassical Growth with Fixed Proportions." *The Review of Economic Studies* 33, no. 2 (April): 88.

Subtext. 1995–2005. Perspective on Book Publishing: Numbers, Issues, and Trends. Darien, CT: Open Book Publishing. [Published annually.]

Tebbel, John. 1987. *Between Covers: The Rise and Transformation of American Book Publishing*. New York: Oxford University Press.

U.S. Department of Commerce, Bureau of the Census. 1945–2005. *Economic Indicators*. Washington, DC: GPO.

———. 1959–2004. *The Statistical Abstract of the United States*. Washington, DC: GPO.

U.S. Department of Commerce, Bureau of the Census. 1992–1999. *Economic Census Information* [Book Publishing]. Washington, DC: GPO.

U.S. Department of Justice. 1997. *The Department of Justice Manual*. Vol. 6. Englewood Cliffs, NJ: Aspen.

COMMERCIAL AND SCHOLARLY
BOOK PUBLISHING

Books are ubiquitous. They are found in bookstores, convenience stores, mass merchandisers, price clubs, and a plethora of other retail shops. They are found in libraries of all types, ranging from vast public library systems to small classroom libraries in elementary schools. They come in many different formats, including hardbound (cloth) books, trade books, and mass-market (rack-size) paperbacks. Some have a plastic spiral binding, others have a glued spine, and still others are Symth sewn.

In the United States, there are eight distinct types of books (Book Industry Study Group 2005):

1. Adult trade books (hardbound and paperback): titles written for adults, whether fiction (possibly the novels of John Grisham or Mary Higgins Clark) or nonfiction (perhaps the autobiography of actor Alan Alda). Other major adult book subcategories include food and cooking (possibly *Sparks in the Kitchen*); parenting and child care (such as *Help for Worried Kids: How Your Child Can Conquer Anxiety and Fear*), as well as beauty, health, and fitness (for example, *Superfoods Healthstyle: Proven Strategies for Lifelong Health*). This is the nation's largest book category, with 2005 sales of $5.2 billion (474 million units).

2. Juvenile trade books (hardbound and paperback): from titles written for young children (touch-and-feel and scratch books) to books for toddlers (perhaps a Sesame Street book about Elmo) and children in grades one through eight. This category also includes picture books, often hardbound titles with extensive illustrations, for example, *The Little Engine That Could* or *High in the Clouds*, and young adult (called "YA") books for boys and girls in their early teens. The immensely successful Harry Potter series is, by definition, a prime example of this type of book. This large book category had 2005 sales of $1.86 billion (484 million units).

3. Mass-market paperbacks: these books (approximately 4″ × 7″) are immensely popular (especially romance novels, mysteries, and thrillers) because of their size and price. Examples include the popular Janet Evanovich series about an intrepid

bounty hunter named Stephanie Plum; classic Greek and Latin literary and poetry titles; and the well-established book series by Louis L'Amour, Erle Stanley Garner, and Agatha Christie. In 2005 the average suggested retail price was $7.99, and net revenues reached $1.78 billion (540 million units).

4. Religious (hardbound and paperback) books: this is a broadly configured category including Bibles, testaments, hymnals, and prayer books as well as fiction and non-fiction titles dealing with religious inspirational (books by Rick Warren or M. Basil Pennington), prayer (*The Power of Prayer and Fasting: 21 Days That Can Change Your Life*) or historical issues (*World Religions: A Guide to the Essentials*), biographies, theological studies (*The Beatitudes for Today*). This category posted the most dramatic sales in the years after 1995, with revenues hovering near the $4.1 billion mark in 2005 (236 million units).

5. Professional and scholarly (hardbound and paperback) books: these highly specialized books (published by professional publishers including Thomson and McGraw-Hill, as well as commercial scholarly presses including Lawrence Erlbaum Associates and Elsevier) are in the fields of business (perhaps a study by Michael Porter); legal issues (Strong's *The Copyright Book*); medical, scientific, and technical (Brian Greene's *The Fabric of the Cosmos*); the humanities (*Heroes, Lovers and Others: The Story of Latinos in Hollywood*); and the social sciences (*The Book Publishing Industry*). Books in this category do not include textbooks. In 2005 professional and scholarly book sales reached $5.5 billion (176 million units).

6. University press (hardbound and paperback) books: these are important scholarly (and sometimes monographic) titles published by a relatively small number of major colleges and universities in the United States, including Stanford University Press (publisher of this book). Total university press revenues reached $450 million in 2005 (24 million units).

7. Elhi (elementary and high school) hardbound and paperback textbooks, workbooks, and supplements. Elhi sales topped $4.7 billion in 2005 (178 million units).

8. College (hardbound and paperback) textbooks for junior and four-year colleges, and graduate and professional-school students. In 2005 sales reached $3.9 billion (67 million units).

There are two other types of books: (a) Book-club books, which are titles published or released by various adult and juvenile book clubs. These books are viewed as a channel of distribution rather than a distinct book category; 2005 revenues exceeded $1 billion (110 million units). (b) Mail-order books, which are titles sold directly to consumers or institutions via direct marketing channels; 2005 revenues reached about $386 million (51 million units).

Detailed statistical data on these book categories can be found in various statistical tables in this book.

NETWORKS AND PUBLISHING CIRCLES

It has been said that book publishing is a business where everyone knows someone who knows someone. In reality more than 89,000 individuals are employed in this eclectic business. Publishing houses are found throughout the United States, with exceptionally important clusters in the large metropolitan areas in and near Boston, Chicago, and San Francisco. However, this business has long been centered in the New York City region.

One of the most intriguing facets of publishing is that individuals, whether seasoned fiction editors or well-entrenched agents or whether new sales and marketing managers at commercial publishing firms or university presses, quickly realize there are networks and publishing circles. As employees come and go from one house to another, they make acquaintances and friends in their circle, whether it is the big editorial circle or the relatively small production circles. They keep in contact with their old associates, often looking to them for guidance and advice, sometimes sharing gossip, frequently alerting someone about a job opening at their new house, and on occasion, referring an author to an old friend's new publishing house.

These circles are invisible, except for those individuals in them; and they are very difficult to enter, operating akin to college social clubs or fraternities and sororities.

Attempts were made in the past to study these circles from an anthropological standpoint. Coser, Kadushin, and Powell in their important study *Books: The Culture and Commerce of Publishing* (1985) analyzed circles and networks. However, in the years since the 1980s, little substantive research has been done since the individuals in the circles seem a bit reluctant to talk about how they operate; they are, after all, rather informal, with few rules and no bylaws. Yet in our interviews it was immensely clear that these circles often form the glue that keeps some houses and certain types of publishing companies (especially university presses) functioning at a relatively high level. Appendix 2A lists firms and organizations we contacted either in person or via telephone or various questionnaires (between 2000 and 2005) for our research.

Clearly, while circles and networks have helped countless thousands of industry employees seeking work and managers looking for topflight talent, there can be a dark side to these circles. The industry has made a sincere, concerted, and valiant effort to attract minorities to publishing, including active recruiting on college campuses (especially urban colleges and schools with large minority student populations). Yet anyone who has ever visited Book Expo America (BEA), toured trade or university press offices, talked before a publishing audience, or combed through detailed Commerce Department data sets, realizes that the number of minorities employed in the business is remarkably small, although the percentages of minorities employed in back-office operations (i.e., the mail department or the warehouse) can be substantial.

The inability to attract larger numbers of minorities, especially since executive-recruitment firms, or headhunters, often are hired to find individuals for fast-track positions (usually in editorial, sales, or marketing), is an issue the industry must confront.

TOP MANAGEMENT, TOP MANAGERS, AND THEIR FUNCTIONS IN A COMMERCIAL PUBLISHING HOUSE OR UNIVERSITY PRESS

The organizational structure of the typical trade, professional, or educational publishing firm and, in many instances, university presses resembles the configuration of most large corporations in the United States.

There is generally a company president (or a university press director). The basic job responsibilities of this chief executive officer include everything related to the smooth operation of the house:

- communicating constantly with the company's owners (perhaps a large conglomerate, private owners, or a university's administration)
- hiring (and often removing) top managers
- developing and implementing strategic plans
- approving and monitoring budgets of the house's departments and operations
- talking with key agents, authors, and the media (especially publications covering the industry)

This managerial leader is surrounded by a plethora of vice presidents (or assistant or associate directors at university presses) handling the following functions:

- Business operations: The responsible individual in this area generally handles warehouse, fulfillment, and book-return procedures, including processing credits for returned books. At a few of the largest U.S. trade publishing firms (e.g., Random House), this office handles "special sales," that is, third-party book distribution services for smaller publishing firms.
- Finance and accounting: The chief financial officer (an associate director at many university presses) has intricate financial and accounting responsibilities, especially post-Enron. This means this individual supervises all accounting functions, including budgets, cash flow statements, profit and loss documents, balance sheets, and consolidated statements of income and retained earnings. In addition, this office is responsible for quarterly and annual financial documents (as required by the Securities and Exchange Commission); public offerings (stocks and bonds); and working with investment bankers, any relevant stock exchange, etc. At many university presses, the majority of financial issues are handled by the university's vice president of finance or the treasury officer.
- Legal affairs: The general counsel and secretary of the corporation ensures that the corporate entity conforms to all appropriate federal, state, and local codes. In addition, the legal affairs officer reviews contracts, bids, etc. A significant responsibility involves working with members of the editorial department to ensure that all key elements are contained in the publisher's contract with an author. These elements include (a) terms and conditions related to an advance tendered to the author against future royalties earned by the author, the royalty rate, and the related

accounting procedures and royalty payment schedule; (b) the grant of rights from the author to the publisher and a noncompete clause; (c) the delivery of the manuscript (in an agreed-on format); (d) acceptance procedures and policies for the author's manuscript as well as a statement concerning revised editions and a possible option for the author's next book; (e) an appropriate book title and whether the publisher has the right (as stipulated in the contract) to provide the book's title and design the book jacket; (f) a clear statement related to the author's representations (i.e., the author is the creator and owner of the manuscript, the work does not contain anything libelous, etc.) and warranties; (g) a clear statement that provides indemnification of the publisher (in essence holding the publisher harmless against lawsuits); (h) the responsibility of the publisher to edit the manuscript and publish, promote, and market the book; (i) the standard copyright notice in the book's front matter; and (j) issues related to the possible bankruptcy of the publisher, placing a book in the out-of-print category, the reversion of the copyright from the publisher to the author, the jurisdiction where legal disputes will be handled, the choice of law (e.g., the Uniform Commercial Code), and the method to resolve disputes between the author and the publisher. In addition, this office works with outside counsel (especially if a matter is outside the realm of in-house legal expertise) to review (or vet) any manuscript to make sure the document does not contain words or statements that could be construed as defamatory or libelous. If the company is involved in international business ventures, the chief legal officer will review all pertinent policies to ensure they conform to a foreign nation's legal policies. At a university press, it is rare for a press to have a full-time legal affairs officer on its staff, relying instead on the university's legal affairs office.

- Human resources: The individual heading this department is responsible for the recruitment of new hires, training of supervisors, reviewing of compensation and benefits packages, and when necessary, reviewing decisions involving employee termination to ensure that all corporate and legal policies are followed. In some companies, certain classes of employees are covered by a collective bargaining agreement. The human resources department (with the assistance of legal affairs) negotiates the agreement and is held accountable (along with any manager) for fulfilling all its stipulations regarding wages, hours, and the terms and conditions of employment.

- Information technology: The information officer supervises a staff that installs, upgrades, and maintains all computer operations, software, etc. Most of the largest publishers rely on enterprise software, sophisticated software able to handle complex functions, including tracking manuscripts through the editorial and production offices, accounts payable and receivable, and inventory.

- Public relations and corporate communications: The vice president of this department issues all press releases and corporate communications, works with the news media (especially the financial press), and is the company's spokesperson whenever a major event (perhaps answering questions if the house signs a former chairman of the Federal Reserve to a book contract) or a crisis occurs.

- Publicity: The individual responsible for publicity supervises functions ranging from developing author tours, maintaining media contacts, and mailing out galleys to book reviewers and key people in the business.
- Strategic planning and development: While most university press directors handle these functions, the large publishing firms have a separate staff reviewing a number of areas, including reviewing a company for a possible merger or acquisition or developing strategic plans to enter or withdraw from a product line or a market.

THE EDITORIAL PROCESS

The complex editorial function, obtaining, editing, and processing manuscripts, is the heart and soul of any commercial or university press house. To many individuals, editing is a glamorous job, involving meetings with well-known personalities (perhaps a former president of the United States or a Hollywood star), lunch at the Four Seasons restaurant in New York City (the power-lunch location in book publishing), lavish expense accounts, and leisurely summers at the Hamptons on Long Island.

In reality, editing is all too frequently a cross between utter boredom and drudgery and a life committed to correcting poor grammar and untangling sentences, sifting through piles of yellow Post-it notes, and working with recalcitrant authors (especially academics) who believe their prose is filled with beauty and wisdom and that editorial changes are never needed much less permitted.

In publishing there are a number of different editors, each handling discrete parts of the editorial process. They include the following:

- Editorial director: This individual supervises all editorial functions and all of the editors, works with the house's major authors, and acquires manuscripts. At some university presses, the director is the editorial director. This is more of a managerial position than just an editorial job since financial issues are, in some ways, the paramount responsibility of the editorial director.
- Editor in chief, senior editor, or executive editor: These titles are often used interchangeably at commercial houses and university presses. If any job is glamorous, this one is since this individual is primarily responsible for acquiring manuscripts. Developing effective relations with major agents and authors is a responsibility critical to the effective handling of this tricky but, generally, highly lucrative position.
- Associate or assistant editors (AEs): While these individuals also acquire manuscripts, they often have actual line-editing responsibilities, the hard, gritty task.
- Editorial assistants (EAs): This is the entry job in the editorial office. EAs handle important but mundane tasks, including line editing and checking that all relevant documents (e.g., permission letters) are submitted.

No one is a born editor. It takes years, under the tutelage of a master editor, to learn the intricate but exciting responsibilities that form the framework of the editorial process.

BOOK SALES, BOOK MARKETING, AND RETAIL BOOKSELLING

The Sales Function

Book publisher sales representatives (sales reps) sell books directly at a discount to a wide variety of outlets, including large national-account bookstore chains (e.g., Barnes & Noble, Borders, Books-A-Million), online (Amazon.com, BN.com), jobbers (Baker & Taylor, Ingram), local- or regional-account small chains, and independent bookstores (Cody's, Powell's).

The discount rate varies significantly, but for trade books it is generally in the 42–48 percent range off the suggested retail price. Scholarly monographs (sometimes called "academic trade books," perhaps Thornton's *Markets from Culture: Institutional Logics and Organizational Decisions in Higher Education Publishing*, 2004) often have a lower rate, about 40 percent. Highly specialized books (perhaps books in the Loeb Classical Library published by Harvard University Press) generally are offered at a short discount rate (probably 20 percent). However, each publishing firm is free to charge whatever it wants (frequently posting charges in the "Weekly Exchange" section of *Publishers Weekly*); and a retailer is free to charge whatever he or she determines is the going rate.

In addition, some publishers (most of the largest ones) and a small number of university presses (mainly the largest ones) provide cooperative (or co-op) advertising dollars to retailers to pay for store displays in windows, on end caps, and on specially placed tables; arranging books face out rather than spine out; banners; point-of-purchase displays (POPs or dumps); and advertisements in local newspapers or book review sections, flyers, etc. The precise discount rates or co-op dollars are stated in the terms and conditions of sales, which are published and released (generally annually) by the publisher.

Sales are often made indirectly to independent distributors (IDs), companies, mass merchandisers (e.g., Wal-Mart, Kmart, Target), colleges, libraries and institutions, and general retailers. These sales are often handled by Baker & Taylor or Ingram. While the discount rate offered by Baker & Taylor or Ingram is often lower (often about 35 percent off the suggested discount rate) than that offered directly by a publisher, Baker & Taylor or Ingram provide myriad services, ranging from fast delivery (often within 24 hours) to a consolidated invoice (quite important to libraries and small independent bookstores) to library collection management (academic libraries often use the services of Yankee Book Peddler, another jobber, to build up their collection in a specific area, perhaps 18th century French poetry).

The typical large publisher will maintain three different sales forces. A national sales force sells frontlist and backlist books (generally titles more than 9 to 12 months old), as well as making "special sales" (to libraries, mail-order companies, premium sales, etc.). A regional sales force is also maintained, selling to bookstores in the Eastern, Central, and Western states. The large publishers have an international sales force selling books to bookstores or distributors in Asia, Africa, Latin America, Europe, and the Middle East. Small publishers, and most university presses, lack the resources of the largest publishers; they rely instead on independent sales reps selling domestically and internationally.

The Marketing, Promotion, and Publicity Functions

A publisher's diverse and complicated marketing and promotion operations handle many responsibilities. Personnel attend national (e.g., BEA) and regional (e.g., the Pacific Northwest Booksellers Association) book trade shows and exhibitions. Display booths are staffed, authors sign copies of books, and at BEA, international or rights sales are transacted. Academic publishers also attend scholarly conferences (e.g., the annual meeting of the Academy of Marketing Science) to inform college professors of existing or upcoming books. They also attend sessions where scholarly papers are presented to scout for possible authors and manuscripts.

The marketing, promotion, and publicity offices also arrange author tours, author signings, and radio and television interviews. In addition, the publicity department sends out uncorrected galley proofs (also called advance reading copies, or ARCs) to book reviewers at important newspapers, magazines, and television and radio stations.

Bookstores and Retail Sales

> In the depth of winter, I finally learned that within me there lay an invincible summer.
> —*Albert Camus*, L'été

Reliable monthly bookstore data, covering the years since January 1967, are available from the U.S. Department of Commerce, Bureau of the Census. Anyone using this data set should be aware that substantive changes took place in this retail environment since 1967.

First, between 1967 and 1984, retailing was dominated by independent bookstores, department stores, and small chains and eventually affected by the emergence of mall and strip-mall stores (notably B. Dalton and Waldenbooks). During those years, total bookstore receipts were modest; monthly sales in 1967 ranged from $37 million to $84 million (total sales topped $657 million that year). Growth rates were uneven at best, with both positive and negative growth patterns evident between 1967 and 1976. Table 2.1 outlines these trends. As the chains extended their reach, and their strong commitment to discounting books, sales took off. The billion-dollar plateau was achieved in 1970 (actually $1.35 billion); within a few years, sales exceeded $1.58 billion (1975) and then $2.27 billion (1978). Sales accelerated in the early 1980s as bigger stores (and big-selling books) made bookstores a destination point at many malls. By 1984 bookstore sales topped $4.1 billion. Table 2.2 lists the monthly and annual trends.

Second, starting in 1985 the big chains (notably Barnes & Noble and Borders) began to launch superstores, vast retail establishments crammed with titles (averaging about 170,000 unique titles), attractive amenities (coffee, tea, plush sofas, music, etc.), and heavily discounted books. Receipts skyrocketed, and negative annual totals (i.e., annual declines) were not recorded in the years after 1985. Total revenues surpassed $4.45 billion in 1985, $5.34 billion in 1987, and $6.54 billion in 1989, eventually breaking the $10 billion threshold in 1994. Tables 2.2 and 2.3 contain detailed data on these developments. By the end of the 1990s, bookstore sales topped $14 billion, reaching $16.2 billion by 2004. As the superstores grew in popularity and exerted an almost overwhelming influence on book sales, independent

TABLE 2.1
U.S. bookstore sales, 1967–1976 (millions of dollars)

Month	1967	1968	1969	1970	1971	1972	1973	1974	1975	1976
January	47	55	68	88	107	93	107	144	147	161
February	53	60	71	112	101	96	73	87	101	105
March	75	72	72	92	99	111	79	95	125	117
April	37	47	57	75	93	91	71	84	105	104
May	47	52	59	76	96	85	77	96	115	111
June	40	49	60	80	111	91	75	99	109	112
July	44	52	60	83	109	76	81	99	111	112
August	51	48	67	104	116	81	97	116	129	148
September	84	85	127	176	177	143	167	129	192	148
October	53	64	75	141	107	112	129	88	129	97
November	53	64	72	145	93	103	123	91	121	116
December	73	85	112	181	112	128	151	139	191	171
Annual total	657	733	900	1,353	1,321	1,210	1,230	1,267	1,575	1,502
Percentage change from previous year		11.57	22.78	50.33	−2.37	−8.04	1.65	3.01	24.31	−4.63

SOURCE: U.S. Department of Commerce, Bureau of the Census, various years.

TABLE 2.2
U.S. bookstore sales, 1977–1986 (millions of dollars)

Month	1977	1978	1979	1980	1981	1982	1983	1984	1985	1986
January	155	190	204	229	250	299	347	396	457	462
February	96	162	163	171	180	205	222	262	286	296
March	109	169	173	172	181	215	230	272	281	280
April	99	156	172	168	190	224	224	258	271	273
May	100	160	184	179	199	212	233	270	286	305
June	111	165	179	184	208	250	269	326	302	339
July	102	159	165	173	210	224	253	276	294	321
August	194	211	219	219	263	305	384	373	425	440
September	207	208	225	242	286	327	405	419	437	510
October	186	173	193	233	258	262	305	320	364	387
November	211	202	216	242	288	267	318	341	388	403
December	272	315	326	382	474	479	557	607	661	745
Annual total	1,842	2,270	2,419	2,594	2,987	3,269	3,747	4,120	4,452	4,761
Percentage change from previous year	22.64	23.24	6.56	7.23	15.15	9.44	14.62	9.95	8.06	6.94

SOURCE: U.S. Department of Commerce, Bureau of the Census, various years.

bookstores, long the backbone of book retailing, sustained deep declines. Table 2.4 lists data for 1997 through most of 2005.

Third, starting in the 1980s, and accelerating in the 1990s, mass merchandisers (Wal-Mart, Kmart, Target, etc.) and price (discount) clubs (Costco, Sam's Club, etc.) emerged as significant bookselling venues. Selling a selective number of frontlist titles at exceptionally deep discounts, these stores challenged the independents and some superstores for sales. Unfortunately, sales for these retail establishments are not included in the monthly data sets from the U.S. Department of Commerce. Commerce insists that a retail establishment must have at least 51 percent of its sales in books to be included as a bookstore. The mass merchandisers and price clubs do not (and in reality never will) reach that threshold.

TABLE 2.3
U.S. bookstore sales, 1987–1996 (millions of dollars)

Month	1987	1988	1989	1990	1991	1992	1993	1994	1995	1996
January	519	537	607	692	750	790	999	1,055	1,309	1,375
February	386	402	410	483	499	540	568	636	720	758
March	360	398	411	490	520	536	602	635	696	743
April	353	381	425	485	497	524	583	610	689	751
May	357	413	457	527	523	553	613	684	786	855
June	378	453	454	527	529	589	619	726	808	839
July	356	408	437	529	539	593	608	679	783	787
August	447	555	631	723	807	895	985	1,156	1,248	1,361
September	527	575	655	753	778	863	905	1,023	1,103	1,042
October	401	441	509	599	597	647	669	733	747	899
November	437	510	591	611	655	642	693	772	851	908
December	817	925	952	1,015	1,037	1,166	1,275	1,410	1,468	1,600
Annual total	5,338	5,998	6,539	7,434	7,731	8,338	9,119	10,119	11,208	11,918
Percentage change from previous year	12.12	12.36	9.02	13.69	4.00	7.85	9.37	10.97	10.76	6.33

SOURCE: U.S. Department of Commerce, Bureau of the Census, various years.

TABLE 2.4
U.S. bookstore sales, 1997–2005 (millions of dollars)

Month	1997	1998	1999	2000	2001	2002	2003	2004	2005
January	1,559	1,466	1,511	1,500	1,578	1,956	2,058	2,070	2,053
February	825	922	987	1,086	1,064	991	992	1,072	1,070
March	813	882	973	1,027	1,057	998	925	1,036	1,082
April	806	853	931	971	930	957	978	987	979
May	893	918	974	1,099	1,064	1,105	1,104	1,071	1,098
June	876	937	1,029	1,118	1,072	1,034	1,171	1,159	1,129
July	830	880	1,021	1,044	999	1,026	1,129	1,128	1,187
August	1,301	1,383	1,383	1,587	1,809	1,777	2,116	2,043	2,167
September	1,159	1,244	1,238	1,400	1,397	1,472	1,547	1,493	1,511
October	926	952	1,016	1,010	1,008	1,010	1,041	1,032	1,030
November	996	988	1,085	1,094	1,090	1,057	1,024	1,044	1,111
December	1,771	1,846	1,991	1,883	1,941	1,937	2,018	2,089	2,179
Annual total	12,755	13,271	14,139	14,819	15,009	15,320	16,103	16,224	16,596
Percentage change from previous year	7.02	4.05	6.54	4.81	1.28	2.07	5.11	0.75	

SOURCE: U.S. Department of Commerce, Bureau of the Census, various years.

Fourth, in the summer of 1995, a small, insignificant online book-retailing company was launched in cyberspace, changing book retailing perhaps forever. Amazon.com became the best-known online company (at least until Google and eBay opened for business), selling books, CDs, DVDs, and an assortment of products and offering consumers "frictionless" commerce. While many other book retailers entered online selling (notably BN.com and Bestbookbuys.com), Amazon.com became the lightning rod, the company to beat in online retailing.

Fifth, many objective observers of the book industry (but regrettably few book-publishing executives) realized that, by the late 1990s, books were, in the minds of most consumers, a consumer product, a product that had to be packaged, priced, and promoted.

To some industry leaders, these views were heretical. Books were cultural icons, the repositories of wisdom and truth, and precious objects to be read, reread, and prized. Those who accepted the former position were positioned to produce books (or at least some books) that consumers wanted; those who believed in the latter produced books (or at least some books) that languished on bookshelves, returned to the publisher after the obligatory 30 or 45 days in a bookstore.

Sixth, book retailing is seasonal; and since 1997 there are actually seven distinct book retailing cycles:

1. December and January: While one would assume that December would be a banner month because of the frenetic sales patterns associated with Christmas, Hanukah, and other religious or seasonal holidays, the strong, consistent pattern evident in January probably surprises some individuals. January's strong sales record is due to post-Christmas sales and the redemption of bookstore gift cards, which are counted as receipts not when they are sold but when they are redeemed by consumers. Overall, these two months account for (approximately) more than 25 percent of annual sales (25.3 percent in 2003; 25.7 percent in 2004), averaging slightly higher than $4 billion in sales.

2. February and March: These two months exhibit some resiliency and consistency; however, sales decline on average (approximately) 50 percent from the December-January cycle (2003: −52.9 percent; 2004: −49.3 percent). Since the early 1990s, February has been the month the new John Grisham novel was published, sparking sales and traffic in many bookstores. Overall, February and March account for about $2 billion and slightly more than 12 percent of annual book sales (2003: 11.9 percent; 2004: 12.9 percent).

3. April: Even though Easter generally occurs in April, this month has been an exceptionally slow month for book sales, averaging 6 percent of annual sales (2003: 6.1 percent; 2004: 6.1 percent). It is odd that book retailers do not craft some innovative marketing strategies to increase traffic and sales in what is the slowest month of the year (generally averaging in the mid-to-high $900 million range).

4. May, June, and July: Sun, surf, sand, and trade hardbound and mass-market paperback "beach reads" trigger strong late spring and early summer sales. These three months average more than $3.3 billion in annual sales, accounting for 21.1 percent of annual sales in 2003 and 20.7 percent in 2004.

5. August: In 2003, August generated the largest monthly sales (and 13.1 percent of annual sales); and in 2004 it was third (behind December and January; slipping to 12.6 percent). Without August, the book industry could experience the depth of winter Camus so aptly described.

6. September: Sales declines posted in September are draconian, falling 17.2 percent in 2002 from August's tallies, with additional declines in 2003 (−26.9 percent) and 2004 (−26.92 percent). However, September still generates more than $1.5 billion in monthly sales (9.6 percent annually in 2003; 9.2 percent in 2004).

7. October and November: These are two transitional months, with revenues generally smaller than September's. Yet tallies hover around the $1 billion mark, and collectively they account for almost 13 percent of annual sales (12.8 percent in 2003; 12.8 percent in 2004).

In 2006 there were approximately 22,321 U.S. retail establishments selling books, down from 25,137 in 2002 and 28,510 in 1995 (Bowker Annual 2005). These tallies include rare and antiquarian bookstores (more than 1,100), college bookstores (3,226), museum stores (539), computer stores (1,347), and department stores (1,673). The largest clusters are general retailers (5,238, a category dominated by a small number of chains).

The nation's largest bookstore chain is Barnes & Noble, with 820 stores (−2.6 percent in 2004) generating more than $4.45 billion dollars (+5.5 percent over 2004's $4.22 billion). Of the 2005 total, 673 stores are superstores with $4.1 billion in sales (i.e., $255.20/square foot). Same-store sales in 2005 were up 3.1 percent over 2004 totals. Of the total dollars, approximately 70 percent are in books, 6 percent in CDs and DVDs, with the balance (24 percent) from sidelines (newspapers, magazines, calendars, desk diaries, blank books, bookmarks, etc.). The company has an operating margin of 5 percent with an 11.6 percent return on invested capital. Strip-mall and mall stores account for the remaining revenue, and the company is in the process of reducing the number of mall stores because of the tremendous financial successes posted by superstores. The company does not have any international stores (Subtext 2005).

The second-largest bookstore chain is the Borders Group, with 2005 revenues of $3.88 billion (+4.9 percent; 2004, $3.7 billion). Borders has 1,167 stores (−0.9 percent from 2004). The company has 464 superstores generating $2.6 billion in annual sales ($226.30/square foot). The superstores posted a modest 0.7 percent increase in same-store sales in 2005, with 62 percent of total revenues from books, 22 percent in CDs and DVDs, and the balance (16 percent) in sidelines. Borders had an operating margin of 5.5 percent with an 8.9 percent return on invested capital. The company has 80 international stores.

The remaining chains are smaller: Books-A-Million ($475 million; 207 stores); Family Christian Stores ($317 million; 308 stores); Hastings ($125 million; 153 stores); Musicland ($50 million; 900 stores); and Berean Christian Stores ($47 million; 18 stores).

These seven chains generated $9.35 billion in sales in 2005 (+4.9 percent; $8.91 billion in 2004) with 3,573 stores (−3 percent; 3,683 in 2004). This meant that Barnes & Noble held a 47.65 percent share of total revenues with Borders' share hovering near the 41.5 percent mark. Their market share of stores was equally impressive: Barnes & Noble, 22.95 percent; Borders, 32.66 percent.

The very largest chains exhibit certain competitive advantages, including strong brand equity and a leadership position, a wide network of stores, and improved cash flows. Opportunities comprise (1) a growth in online shopping (capitalizing on their online ventures); (2) a growing consumer book market; (3) an expansion into the highly profitable self-publishing business; and (4) a growth in the older consumer market, the best cluster of readers and book buyers in the United States.

Yet an analysis of the expanding book retailing environment also reveals certain concerns. Weaknesses include (1) a dependence on the U.S. market by most of the major chains; (2) a cluster of underperforming mall and strip-mall stores; (3) the burden of costs to remodel some of the larger but older superstores; (4) a significant dependence on certain book publishers (suppliers) for new titles; and (5) the volatility of currency exchange rates (the dynamic changes that took place during the "Asian currency contagion" undermined sales and profits abroad for many companies) and some resentment toward globalization. Threats consist of (1) intense competition from other chains and all media and entertainment goods and services; (2) the piracy of products sold in these chains, including books, CDs, and DVDs; (3) deep declines in CD sales, an important revenue stream for some book retailers; (4) uneven quarterly growth rates for same-store sales; (5) a major difficulty in estimating the demand for frontlist books. The very largest chains began addressing these competitive advantages and threats (by doing what is known to marketing and management experts as a SWOT—strengths, weaknesses, opportunities, and threats—analysis), although results to date are somewhat uneven or, in some instances, sketchy, developments that do not go unnoticed by Wall Street analysts.

An ongoing concern, indeed dismay, for many Wall Street analysts is the tradition of buying books at a discount, with these books fully returnable for a complete refund (as long as the publisher's terms and conditions of sale are fulfilled). This policy of returns, which dates back to the Great Depression, means that book-return rates can be substantial. For example, in 2005, a typical year, the book-return rates were quite high: adult trade hardcovers, 35 percent; adult trade paperbacks, 22 percent; mass-market paperbacks, 47 percent; juvenile–young adult hardcovers, 13 percent; juvenile–young adult paperbacks, 18 percent; religious books, 18 percent; college books, 26 percent; university press hardcovers, 17 percent; university press paperbacks, 15 percent; and professional books, 20 percent.

Some industry observers believe that the returns policy helps stimulate sales, puts more books into the retail marketplace, and overall, is the cost of doing business. Others believe that the return policy undermines the fiscal strength of publishing houses and leads ultimately to waste in the value chain.

While both arguments have merit, it might be time for the entire industry to evaluate the wisdom of a policy that allows millions of books to be printed for a market that does not exist, a market that is shrinking (and certainly not expanding), and a policy that aids very few components of the vast publishing community of authors and agents, editors and marketers, bookstore managers, and the reading public.

Book Reviews

Sales and editorial managers in book publishing believe that book reviews in key publications and media outlets (e.g., *New York Times*, *USA Today*, *People*, *New York Review of Books*, *New Yorker*, *The Today Show*, National Public Radio's *All Things Considered*, Public Broadcasting Service's *The Charlie Rose Show*, C-Span's weekend book discussions) sell books. Do they?

The issue of a review's importance has been analyzed by a number of scholars. Reinstein and Snyder (2005), addressing the effect of reviews on motion pictures, remarked that "an inherent problem in measuring the influence of expert reviews on the demand for experience goods is that a correlation between good reviews and high demand may be spurious, induced by underlying correlation with unobservable quality signals." Desai and Basuroy (2005) also studied the effect of reviews on motion pictures, and they insisted that "academic research pertaining to the marketing of cultural products such as Broadway shows, books, music, and movies has identified a product's genre (or type), star power, and critics' reviews as important factors influencing the market performance of an individual product." Basuroy, Chatterjee, and Ravid (2003) investigated "how critics affect the box office performance and how the effects may be moderated by stars and budgets." Dellarocas, Awad, and Zhang (2004) evaluated the impact of online reviews in forecasting motion picture revenues, providing "encouraging evidence for the value of publicly available online forum information to firms for real-time forecasting and competitive analysis." Dellarocas (2003) studied the impact of word of mouth (sometimes called the "information cascade" or "buzz") as a feedback mechanism, which is "poised to have a much wider impact on organizations." Chevalier and Mayzlin (2003), after investigating the impact of word of mouth reviews on online book sales, argue, "Our methodology of comparing the sales and reviews of a given book across Internet retailers allows us to improve on the existing literature by better capturing a causal relationship between word of mouth [reviews] and sales since we are able to difference out factors that affect the sales and word of mouth of both retailers, such as a book's quality." Sorensen (2004) and Sorensen and Rasmussen (2004) incorporated "detailed weekly data on sales of hardcover fiction books to evaluate the impact of the *New York Times'* book reviews on sales." They concluded that "book reviews serve largely to inform consumers about books' content and characteristics (including the books' existence). However, positive reviews have a larger impact on sales than negative reviews, suggesting that reviews also have a persuasive effect." Timko (2001) studied the types of books reviewed in the *New York Times* book reviews and book purchases by libraries, believing that "the importance of the [*New York Times*] book review should not be overstated. It should be remembered that typically the large majority of the [book] selection decisions, at least in large research libraries, are made without any reference to any review. In fact, many selection decisions, especially at larger research libraries, are outsourced—in effect, they are made by book vendors."

In 2004 U.S. publishers released 195,000 new, unique titles in both hardbound and paperback formats. By 2005 that total exceeded 172,000; and projections for the years 2006 through 2010 are expected to increase on average 10 percent annually.

Unfortunately, only a small percentage of all new books are reviewed by the major media. As unlikely as it may seem, there has been a decline, and a relatively sharp decline, in the number of books reviewed annually in the United States, with draconian cuts in pages in book review sections (notably at the *New York Times*) and cutbacks in the total allocated space for reviews (called advertising lines) at many newspapers (including the *Los Angeles Times, Boston Globe, San Francisco Examiner*).

Booklist reviews more books than any other U.S. publication, with 8,729 reviews in 2003 and 8,674 in 2004 (approximately 4.45 percent of all new books; Bowker Annual 2005). *Publishers Weekly* (*PW*), for decades the leader in reviews, cut back on its reviews. In 2004 it published 8,303 reviews (4.26 percent; down from 9,055 in 2003); *PW* had additional declines in 2005. *Choice* was in third place with respect to number of book reviews in 2003 (6,520) and 2004 (7,538; 3.87 percent). The *New York Times Sunday Book Review*, long perceived as the most influential review in this country, held steady in both 2003 (1,196) and 2004 (1,190; 0.61 percent).

As for radio and television coverage of new books, while these broadcast formats are exceptionally important (especially NPR and PBS), neither radio nor television can provide access to more than a small number of reviews or author interviews.

In the late 1990s, a series of Internet weblogs (blogs) devoted to books and reading appeared, and they did have an impact on getting new books noticed in what is an exceptionally cluttered marketplace. One of the more interesting ones is the Bookreporter.com, which contains useful reviews, author profiles, book–motion picture tie-ins, a word of mouth feature ("Tell Us What You Are Reading—Two Prizes"), and a series of reports from writers (e.g., "The Fine Art of Small Talk").

Can a book become a best seller without a review in a major publication or media outlet? In fact, hundreds of books end up annually on bestseller lists with little or no substantive coverage.

Janet Evanovich is a mystery writer whose main character is Stephanie Plum, a bounty hunter (in reality a bond enforcement agent) for a bail bond company in Trenton, New Jersey. Her book *Eleven on Top* was released on Tuesday, June 21, 2005, and it was reviewed by that date by only two publications: a positive review in *Booklist* and a somewhat positive review in *PW*. The book sold 127,000 copies between June 21 and June 26, and it opened as the number one book in 78 of the 80 DMAs (distinct market areas) tracked by BookScan, including New York, Los Angeles, San Francisco, Boston, and Chicago. It was number two in the other two DMAs (Toledo, Ohio, and Baton Rouge, Louisiana).

How did this happen? Evanovich maintained a database of faithful fans, and she sent out newsletters and reminder postcards. She gave one radio interview on June 25, 2005 (to a Trenton, New Jersey, station), and she had a book signing in Trenton (the "Stephanie Plum Daze Festival"), also on the 25th, that attracted more than 5,000 fans. Evanovich is a star author, generally selling more than 500,000 hardbound copies of her Plum books, and she relies on word of mouth, not reviews at the *New York Times*, *Washington Post*, or *Los Angeles Times* (the book was also number one on the best-seller lists at all three newspapers).

Other authors achieved best-seller success with minimal and, in some instances, no reviews. It was only after books by Rick Warren and Joel Osteen topped various best-seller lists that the popular press or media reviewed their books, a situation that also occurred with Christopher Paolini's first book (see chapter 4) as well as many other authors. Cable television's Bill O'Reilly has had several books on the best-seller list, yet none of his books have ever been reviewed by the *New York Times*.

Will fame generate sales? A review of recent winners of the Nobel Prize in Literature indicated, overall, lackluster sales before and after winning this award. Elfriede Jelinek (the 2004 Nobel recipient) posted modest sales for *Lust* (ranked 147,362nd by Amazon.com [2005] one year after winning the prize); *The Piano Teacher* (ranking: 26,165th) and *Women as Lovers* (ranking: 56,801st) had better sales during the first week of October 2005 (literally days before the 2005 winner was announced). Gao Xingjian, the 2000 Nobel recipient, did not fare much better. During that same week in October 2005, *Soul Mountain* was ranked 65,665th. The results for some other Nobel winners include Dario Fo's (1997 Nobel) *Accidental Death of Anarchist* at 416,715th; Wislawa Szymborska's (1996 Nobel) *Poems New and Collected* ranked 68,831st; Imre Kertesz's (2002 Nobel) *Fateless* ranked 62,461st, *Liquidation* ranked 81,167th, and *Fatelessness* ranked 57,479th. Sales rankings at Amazon.com are done hourly, with changes regularly occurring.

J. M. Coetzee (the 2003 recipient), V. S. Naipaul (in 2001), Günter Grass (in 1999), and Toni Morrison (in 1993), on the other hand, traditionally achieved strong sales before and after winning the Nobel, but they remain the biggest exceptions in recent years. Laureates that seemed to flounder (at least in terms of book sales) include Kenzaburo Oe (1994), Camilo Jose Cela (1989), and Wole Soyinka (1986).

Will making the "Ten Best Book List" at the *New York Times* trigger sales? On December 11, 2005, the *New York Times* selected the following as the best books in fiction published in 2005: *Kafka on the Shore*, *On Beauty*, *Prep*, *Saturday*, and *Veronica*. The best nonfiction books included *The Assassins' Gate*, *De Kooning*, *The Lost Painting*, *Postwar*, and *The Year of Magical Thinking*. On that day, only 1 of these 10 books (*The Year of Magical Thinking*, winner of the 2005 National Book Award) was on any best-seller list (number 5 on the *New York Times* nonfiction list). During that same week, BookScan listed only *The Year of Magical Thinking* (at number 35 on its best-selling book list).

The results on Amazon.com were better, with the following sales ranking on December 11, 2005: for fiction, *Kafka on the Shore* (246), *On Beauty* (63), *Prep* (530), *Saturday* (145), and *Veronica* (385), and for nonfiction, *The Assassins' Gate* (97), *De Kooning* (1,094), *The Lost Painting* (29), *Postwar* (142), and *The Year of Magical Thinking* (11).

Reviews help a book's sales chances, but even exceptionally positive reviews or winning a major national or international award cannot guarantee success in what is an exceedingly crowded marketplace.

Oprah Winfrey

While authors come and go, and while book trends (hot issues and themes) vary with the seasons, the one constant force for the last 10 years in making Americans, regardless of age, gender, race, ethnicity, or religion, aware of books is Oprah Winfrey. She is committed to reading and informing the American people of books that she likes and admires, and she launched a series of book clubs in 1996 designed specifically to get Americans reading. Her procedure was quite informal. She would announce that on a certain day her club (in essence her television audience in the studio) would read and discuss a book with the book's author in attendance (or possibly taped). As soon as she selected a title, whether it was *The Deep End of the Ocean* or *A Million Little Pieces*, sales skyrocketed, generally topping the million-unit mark (and in some instances the two million level).

It worked. Americans became aware of books, including some obscure ones (*We Were the Mulvaneys*) and a few classics (*Anna Karenina*). Table 2.5 lists all of her selections.

TABLE 2.5
Oprah's book-club selections, 1996–2005

Year	Book title	Author
2005	*A Million Little Pieces*	James Frey
2005	*As I Lay Dying*	William Faulkner
2005	*The Sound and the Fury*	William Faulkner
2005	*A Light in August*	William Faulkner
2004	*One Hundred Years of Solitude*	Gabriel Garcia Marquez
2004	*The Heart Is a Lonely Hunter*	Carson McCullers
2004	*Anna Karenina*	Leo Tolstoy
2004	*The Good Earth*	Pearl Buck
2003	*East of Eden*	John Steinbeck
2003	*Cry, the Beloved Country*	Alan Paton
2002	*Sula*	Toni Morrison
2002	*Fall on Your Knees*	Ann-Marie MacDonald
2001	*A Fine Balance*	Rohinton Mistry
2001	*The Corrections*	Jonathan Franzen
2001	*Cane River*	Lalita Tedemy
2001	*Stolen Lives: Twenty Years in a Desert Jail*	Malika Oufkir
2001	*Icy Sparks*	Gwyn Hyman Rubio
2001	*We Were the Mulvaneys*	Joyce Carol Oates
2000	*House of Sand and Fog*	Andre Dubus III
2000	*Drowning Ruth*	Christina Schwarz
2000	*Open House*	Elizabeth Berg
2000	*The Poisonwood Bible*	Barbara Kingsolver
2000	*While I Was Gone*	Sue Miller
2000	*The Bluest Eye*	Toni Morrison
2000	*Back Roads*	Tawni O'Dell
2000	*Daughter of Fortune*	Isabel Allende
2000	*Gap Creek*	Robert Morgan
1999	*A Map of the World*	Jane Hamilton
1999	*Vinegar Hill*	A. Manette Ansay
1999	*River, Cross My Heart*	Breena Clarke
1999	*Tara Road*	Maeve Binchy
1999	*Mother of Pearl*	Melinda Haynes
1999	*White Oleander*	Janet Finch
1999	*The Pilot's Wife*	Anita Shreve
1999	*The Reader*	Bernard Schlink
1999	*Jewel*	Brett Lott
1998	*Where the Heart Is*	Billie Letts
1998	*Midwives*	Chris Bohjalian
1998	*What Looks like Crazy on an Ordinary Day*	Pearl Cledge
1998	*I Know This Much Is True*	Wally Lamb
1998	*Breath, Eyes, Memory*	Edwidge Danicat
1998	*Black and Blue*	Anna Quindlen
1998	*Here on Earth*	Alice Hoffman
1998	*Paradise*	Toni Morrison
1997	*The Meanest Thing to Say*	Bill Cosby
1997	*The Treasure Hunt*	Bill Cosby
1997	*The Best Way to Play*	Bill Cosby
1997	*Ellen Foster*	Kaye Gibbons
1997	*A Virtuous Woman*	Kaye Gibbons
1997	*A Lesson before Dying*	Ernest Gaines
1997	*Songs in Ordinary Time*	Mary McGarry Morris
1997	*The Heart of a Woman*	Maya Angelou
1997	*The Rapture of Canaan*	Sheri Reynolds
1997	*Stones from the River*	Ursula Hegi
1997	*She's Come Undone*	Wally Lamb
1996	*The Book of Ruth*	Jane Hamilton
1996	*Song of Solomon*	Toni Morrison
1996	*The Deep End of the Ocean*	Jacquelyn Mitchard

SOURCE: *Publishers Weekly*, various issues.

If all of the prodding of English teachers in high school, an outpouring of titles, the best library system on the planet, and reviews on television and in newspapers could not get Americans reading, how did a television personality do it? Perhaps it was her deep sincerity, her abiding interest in and love of books and reading. Perhaps she was able to select books that people really wanted to read (with the possible exception of three books by Faulkner that sold only 35,000 copies in the summer of 2005). So if Oprah can select books people want, why cannot publishers, editors, and book reviewers?

Global Sales

Global sales are very important revenue streams, and they take the form of two different types of "products." A publisher can sell foreign rights to an offshore publisher (perhaps a German or Mexican publisher) to translate and sell in a foreign language a book originally published in the United States. Or a publisher can sell the U.S. version of a book to a foreign distributor or a bookstore.

The U.S. Department of Commerce first started tracking rights sales in 2001. Commerce reported that rights generated $298 million in 2001, $274 million in 2002, and $230 million in 2003 (the last year Commerce reported data for this category).

However, exceptionally useful historical data on book exports (both units and dollars) were available from the U.S. Department of Commerce, International Trade Administration back to 1970 (but not for every year).

In that year exports tallied $174.9 million, representing 7.2 percent of net publisher revenues. In the following years, exports grew somewhat rapidly, reaching $269.3 million in 1975 (+53.97 percent; 7.6 percent of net sales). In subsequent years, the pace increased sharply, topping $1.4 billion in 1990 (9.4 percent of net sales) and $1.88 billion in 2000 (although the percentage of net sales declined to 7.6 percent). Yet exports slipped in the following years, bottoming out in 2002 and rebounding slightly by 2004. These fluctuations were often due to currency exchange problems. See Table 1.18.

Since 1996 Canada has remained the principal export destination for U.S. books (+9.8 percent between 1996 and 2004) with the United Kingdom a distant second (although in 2004 it posted a strong 27.8 percent increase in exports since 1996). Other nations on the top 10 export list included Japan (dropping 24 percent between 1996 and 2004), Australia (also experiencing a decline of 33.5 percent during those years), Mexico (up a modest 6.6 percent), Singapore (posting a sharp increase of almost 61 percent), Germany (off 35.9 percent), South Korea (down 21.5 percent), Hong Kong (up 4.5 percent), and India (up 29.9 percent). Ironically, China, the source of a significant amount of imports to the United States, did not make the top 10. Table 2.6 outlines these developments.

Other Sales and Marketing Issues and Book Industry Research

Consumer expenditures account for approximately two-thirds of the U.S. GDP. Consumer expenditures account for approximately 72 percent of all consumer book purchases in this nation.

Because of the development of linked computer checkout systems, enterprise software, as well as the emergence of sophisticated analytical tools, BookScan has the ability to tell us

TABLE 2.6
U.S. book exports to top 10 nations, 1996–2004 (millions of dollars)

Nation	1996	1997	1998	1999	2000	2001	2002	2003	2004	Percentage change 1996–2004
Canada	740.3	823.6	807.6	807.6	756.7	727.7	742.6	776.4	812.8	9.8
United Kingdom	226.3	254.4	237.0	253.6	264.2	250.0	270.6	274.6	289.2	27.8
Japan	129.5	120.3	133.3	101.1	123.1	129.3	100.8	95.8	98.4	−24.0
Australia	118.1	138.0	157.9	139.6	116.3	66.0	70.8	76.1	78.6	−33.5
Mexico	62.0	58.2	58.8	65.6	73.9	63.8	64.9	68.1	66.1	6.6
Singapore	36.0	36.9	26.5	41.1	60.7	49.0	49.6	48.4	58.0	60.9
Germany	42.3	48.9	40.7	43.1	34.3	34.0	29.1	34.1	24.1	−35.9
South Korea	34.0	21.2	16.1	24.6	36.8	35.5	29.1	24.7	26.7	−21.5
Hong Kong	22.0	23.9	21.3	20.7	32.5	29.4	31.6	19.2	22.9	4.5
India	14.6	17.8	12.3	12.0	14.4	16.0	19.5	16.8	19.0	29.9

SOURCE: U.S. Department of Commerce, International Trade Administration.

that, during a specific week, the number one best-selling fiction book was, for example, a title by John Grisham. BookScan also provides pivotal information: that Grisham's book was ranked (according to sales) number one in the Las Vegas DMA, number two in the Minneapolis DMA, and number six in the Providence–New Bedford, Massachusetts, DMA.

This information, unavailable just a few years ago, provides invaluable marketing data to publishers regarding the number of sales in distinct DMAs as well as the nation. Now marketers can attempt to position a title in the marketplace, targeting a specific segment of readers. The success of a specific book can assist publishers in the future when they make critically important decisions regarding price points, marketing campaigns, author tours, etc.

As important as the BookScan data are, and it is very important, these data are designed to tell us about unit sales in specific geographical regions. They do not tell us why an individual decided to purchase a specific title, or any title for that matter. Nor do the data provide a framework that marketers can use in assessing consumer intentions, attitudes, beliefs, or feelings. In essence, publishers are left to grapple with the issue of consumer behavior on both the macro and micro levels.

What is rather surprising is that publishers, armed with rather detailed geographical data, rarely have the time, personnel, or funds to capitalize on and use this data. For example, we investigated the book purchases of two towns on November 5, 2005 (using daily sales data from Amazon.com), for Trenton, New Jersey, and Morrisville, Pennsylvania (separated by only a few hundred yards by the Delaware River and connected by three bridges). The top 10 best-selling books on that day in Trenton were (1) *Safe Harbor*, (2) *Wicked*, (3) *Paige by Paige*, (4) *To the Nines* (a mass-market paperback written by Janet Evanovich and set in Trenton), (5) *Hard Eight*, (6) *Ransom*, (7) *Key of Knowledge*, (8) *Comfort Fools*, (9) *The Big Bad Wolf*, and (10) *The Twilight before Christmas*. In Morrisville the top 10 books were (1) *Beyond Belief*, (2) *1,000 Places to See before You Die*, (3) *The Da Vinci Code*, (4) *The Five People You Meet in Heaven*, (5) *Under the Banner of Heaven*, (6) *Benjamin Franklin*, (7) *Madam Secretary*, (8) *The World Almanac*, (9) *The Big Bad Wolf*, and (10) *The Time Traveler's Wife*.

The only book on both lists was *The Big Bad Wolf* (coincidentally ranked number 9 on both). These type of data are readily available; each week we track detailed weekly sales data for almost three dozen DMAs. We observed substantive regional preferences; but we also saw tremendous similarities. Why this type of analysis has not been done by publishers defies logic.

Publishers also have access to other exceptionally useful data sets. For example, detailed information exists for readers of romance, which is immensely popular: more than 2,000 new titles are produced annually, and consumers annually spend about $1.5 billion purchasing these books, almost exclusively released as mass-market paperbacks (Romance Writers of America 2005). Publishers have exhaustive demographic facts and figures regarding (1) marital status (49.5 percent of romance readers are married; 33 percent are single); (2) ethnicity (75 percent are white; 11 percent African American; 11 percent Hispanic American; 3 percent Asian American); (3) age (25 percent are ages 35–44; 21 percent ages 25–34; 17 percent ages 45–54); (4) educational levels (21 percent are college graduates with 10 percent possessing a post-college degree); (5) number of titles read annually (1–5 books, 57 percent; 6–10, 17 percent; 11–20, 8 percent; 21–50, 12 percent; 51–100, 4 percent; +100, 2 percent); (6) book purchases by channel of distribution (mass merchandisers, 31 percent; mall bookstores, 22 percent; free-standing bookstores, 16 percent); (7) new versus used copies (36 percent were new books; 5 percent, used); (8) literary genre (mystery or thriller, 30 percent); and (9) geographical distribution of romance readers (Northeast, 12.6 percent; South, 29 percent; Midwest, 26 percent; West, 27 percent; elsewhere, 8 percent).

Clearly, the book industry does not have access to the same amount of consumer marketing data that some other industries have, but some intriguing data do exist. Why publishers have failed to take advantage of this information is somewhat curious.

Econometric Influences

What are the key sales and marketing issues, theories, and econometric trends that affect book sales in major categories and in the United States?

After an intensive review of a significant number of econometric data sets and numerous detailed discussions with publishing executives, we believe the following ideas are pivotal in understanding consumer book buying behavior.

First, the average book consumer does not read the *Journal of Finance*, the *Journal of Marketing*, or the *Wall Street Journal*, but this consumer has an exceptional understanding of the state of the economy and prices. Spend some time in a supermarket and watch people shop or read Paco Underhill's *Why We Buy: The Science of Shopping* (1999), and you will become aware that the average consumer has tremendous knowledge about prices and product characteristics.

Second, these average consumers purchase books (and college textbooks for that matter) with discretionary dollars. They do not have to buy these consumer books, and recent data on college students indicate they are not buying textbooks (witness the 80 percent drop in unit sales between the release year and the second year).

Third, these consumers are affected by changes in the consumer price index (CPI), the GDP, personal income, median and mean household income patterns, interest rates, personal debt levels, the availability of consumer credit, employment and unemployment trends, and consumer confidence reports. They are buffeted constantly by what they perceive to be changes in the economy, and they pay attention to these data.

As for book sales, we believe the following are important marketing or economic indicators when analyzing book industry data:

- the U.S. population
- the elhi population
- the higher-education (college) population
- book title output
- media usage patterns of hours per person (older than 18) per year reading consumer books
- media expenditure patterns (dollars spent annually by individuals older than 18)
- changes in the channels of distribution, especially the emergence of shopbots (computerized Internet shopping robots) and the increase in used-book sales
- national bookstore sales (as tracked monthly by the U.S. Department of Commerce)
- the price sensitivity of books
- book exports (actual revenues and units tracked by Commerce and not just book rights)

So what does all of this tell us? Using 1999–2004 as a reference point, we observed a series of exceptionally positive econometric trends:

1. U.S. population: up 4.84 percent
2. Elhi population: up 0.91 percent
3. Higher-education population: up 8.67 percent
4. GDP: up 26.62 percent
5. Personal income: up 24.49 percent
6. Disposable personal income: up 29.41 percent
7. Bookstore sales: up 14.75 percent

Yet we also observed a series of unsettling statistics for those years:

	revenues	units
1. Media usage (hours per person per year consumer books):	down 10.08 percent	
2. Book title output:	up 63.32 percent	
3. Book exports (revenues):	down 6.95 percent	
4. Book exports (units):	down 31.38 percent	
5. Net publisher	revenues	units
Adult trade (total):	down 1.26 percent	down 15.46 percent
Juvenile trade (total):	up 3.57 percent	down 8.53 percent

Mass-market paperbacks:	up 0.88 percent	down 10.93 percent
Religious (total):	up 31.04 percent	up 10.10 percent
Professional-scholarly (total):	up 12.54 percent	down 1.35 percent
Elhi (total):	up 18.31 percent	up 11.35 percent
College (total):	up 24.61 percent	up 6.92 percent
All books:	up 10.55 percent	down 7.27 percent

BookScan (2005) data revealed that, in the first year of publication, 79 percent of all new ISBNs in the United States had sales of fewer than 99 copies. Results for all of the major book categories were equally depressing: (1) 70 percent of all new adult fiction books sold fewer than 99 copies; (2) 80 percent of all new adult nonfiction books sold fewer than 99 copies; (3) 68 percent of all new juvenile books solid fewer than 99 copies; and (4) almost 64 percent of all new hardcover books sold fewer than 99 copies.

Projections in *Book Industry Trends* for 2005 indicated a 4.9 percent increase in total book-industry net publisher revenues and a 2.1 percent increase in net publisher unit sales. Yet not all book categories will post increases in either category; and most will be razor thin.

Basically, it seems that some executives in the book-publishing industry have forgotten about the law of supply and demand:

If the supply of books continues to expand (195,000, +14 percent in 2004, and 172,000 in 2005);

if demand (book unit sales and hours per person per year) continues to decline;

if the majority of books sell fewer than 99 copies in the first year of publication;

if the U.S. population increases at 0.9–1 percent annually;

if book exports continue their lackluster trend; and

if used-book sales continue to grow;

then this industry could experience a shakeout, similar to the one adversely affecting many U.S. newspapers.

The purpose of a business, according to Peter Drucker and Philip Kotler, is to satisfy the wants and needs of a customer. If a company achieves this goal, then it has the opportunity (but not the guarantee) to make a profit.

Is the book-publishing industry in a crisis or a renaissance? Clearly, the book-publishing industry is releasing high-quality books, and the supply is certainly plentiful. So there is no crisis regarding output; in fact some could argue the industry is experiencing a renaissance regarding the number of high-quality books published in 2005.

It is the demand side of the equation that is unsettling. If the vast majority of new books do not sell and a flood of books is returned annually by book retailers to publishers or countless millions of titles are sitting in warehouses waiting for sales, one is not tempted to use the word *renaissance*.

IS THERE IRRATIONAL EXUBERANCE IN THE U.S. BOOK-PUBLISHING INDUSTRY? AN ANALYSIS OF UNIVERSITY PRESSES AND COMMERCIAL ACADEMIC PROFESSIONAL BOOK PUBLISHERS, 1989–2000

Introduction

In the 1970s, many observers of the higher-education scene began talking and writing about a crisis in scholarly communications.

Library purchases were declining; subventions from traditional sources, such as federal governmental agencies and private foundations, were drying up; and scholars in some fields seemed to be losing interest in buying academic books. Academic libraries, facing sharp increases in serials (journals), were compelled to reduce monograph purchases, which ultimately negatively affected university presses and their ability to hold down increases in the suggested price for monographic books.

Escalating production, warehousing, and distribution costs brought on by inflationary pressures and the realization that commercial scholarly publishers interested in broadly conceived academic studies were luring away a significant number of scholars from university presses by offering higher royalties, more promotion outlets, larger advertising budgets, and wider distribution contributed further to a sense of crisis in the university press publishing world.

These issues were first addressed in a series of major research papers published in the early to mid-1970s by Harvey et al. (1972); W. Becker (1973); Kerr (1975); S. Meyer (1978); Levant (1973); Bell (1970); and Brown (1970).

These developments produced a certain nervousness among publishers over the future of scholarly books (published by both university presses and commercial academic professional presses) that continued into the 1980s, the 1990s, and after the turn of the century. Some critics published jeremiads against a perceived disintegration of the university press world because of declining university subsidies, the exigencies of becoming break-even operations, and list trimming. Still others wrote that large commercial operations were driving out of the marketplace of ideas good, solid monographs (in essence, an academic example of Gresham's law—bad money drives out good).

As the crisis became more pronounced in the 1980s and especially in the 1990s, a number of major industry leaders and scholars addressed the fundamental structural issues, including important papers by Kerr (1987), Bailey (1988), Maguire (1991), Carrigan (1991), Parsons (1991), Moore (1993), Franklin (1993), and Rowson (1994).

By the early 1990s, uncertainty over the future of the scholarly monograph had, inevitably, coalesced into discussions about the impact on the tenure review process. For more than a century, university presses played a pivotal role (and in many ways *the* pivotal role) in furthering scholars' professional advancement by providing a trustworthy venue for the publication of highly specialized academic works, by employing the peer-review system to test the validity and soundness of studies and by maintaining high standards through its editorial development and production processes. In short, publication by a university could help to establish a scholar's credentials, and many industry observers were skeptical of the benefits of the changes taking place.

At the root of all of the turmoil was a fear that anti-intellectualism, an old tradition in certain circles in the United States addressed by Hofstadter (1966), had again reared its head. Serious academic research that customarily appeared as a monograph was inexorably doomed if university presses were compelled to modify their mission to publish for the academic community, balance the books, and ultimately, curtail their output. Some higher-education experts became very concerned that certain academic fields would be imperiled if cutting-edge research had no respectable publication outlet, resulting in an irrevocable loss to the entire intellectual community. Such fears, expressed across the full spectrum in the higher-education sector, led to a series of conferences in the 1990s, at which scholars, administrators, research librarians, and scholarly publishers met to explore the alleged death of the monograph and the impact a tectonic shift in academic communications would have on scholars and scholarship.

Major Issues

Many academics, especially in the humanities, alleged there was a crisis in scholarly communications, a viewpoint frequently heard at scholarly and professional conferences and evident in numerous articles in the *Chronicle of Higher Education*. Subsequently, academics posited that it had become far more difficult to get their first or second scholarly book published by university presses (especially in the fields of history and literature), undermining their ability for tenure, promotion, or merit pay increases.

In light of these critical concerns, the following questions were analyzed. A major review of statistical data on title output at university presses and commercial academic (i.e., scholarly and professional) publishing houses between 1989 and 2000 was conducted. Was there a crisis in scholarly publishing between 1989 and 2000? Did the number of new titles published by university presses and commercial academic presses decrease between 1989 and 2000, remain stable, or increase over this 12-year period? Was there a decrease or an increase in the number of books published in certain disciplines in the humanities, the social sciences, and the mathematics and science sectors? Was there evidence that irrational exuberance was present in book-publishing circles?

Book Categories: An Analysis of Marker Fields

The major academic areas at U.S. universities are the humanities, social sciences, and mathematics and science. Within these areas are hundreds of subfields. After a series of interviews with a cross section of publishers and editors, we selected for a detailed analysis 26 marker fields representative of the major scholarly fields.

The Humanities

- Philosophy
- Religion
- Archaeology

- North American history
- Western Hemisphere history
- Law (general)
- Literature of music

- Philology and linguistics
- Classical languages and literature
- Literary history
- English literature
- American literature
- Romance literature

The Social Sciences

- Psychology
- Anthropology
- Economics
- Finance

- Sociology
- Political theory
- Political science (United States)
- Political science (Europe)
- Political science (Asia and Africa)

Mathematics and Science

- Statistics
- Mathematics
- Physics
- Natural Science

Review of the Literature

The literature on output, markets, the supply and demand equilibrium, and the impact of the information cascade is exceptionally rich in the scholarly publishing arena.

Cronin (2002) argued that these presses "bring forth worthy scholarship of decidedly limited commercial appeal." Their goal to publish the best scholarship was critically important. "The publication of specialized monographs is culturally laudable in its own right, but for many scholars, humanists in particular, the university press performs an essential role." He posited that without university presses scholarship and "scholars would come to a sticky and premature end."

Steele (2003) analyzed the state of university press publishing, and he insisted, "Outlets for research monographs are drying up, print runs are being reduced, and monograph costs are increasing." His answer to some of these complex problems was intriguing. "The combination of the digital networked environment and open archived initiatives may, however, provide the opportunity, through institutional repositories, to rethink the role and nature of the distribution of research monographs in a university setting."

Owen (2002) also addressed problems associated with the dissemination of scholarship, and he also argued that "technological developments . . . are changing scholarly communications in fundamental ways." He posited that "scholarly communication is shifting from functional actors such as publishers and libraries to a more integral responsibility held by the academic community itself. Publishers and libraries would then change from product-oriented organizations to service-oriented organizations, supporting scholarly communications in an outsourcing relationship with the academic world." Mizzaro (2003) addressed similar issues, but he was pessimistic about relying exclusively on new technologies. "As the quantity of information available is constantly increasing, its quality is threatened since the traditional quality control mechanism of peer review is often not used" in online or electronic publications. Liu (2003) investigated similar issues. While he reviewed the purpose of scholarly communications and the various trends impacting scholars and publishers, he sought to "design more effective electronic scholarly publishing systems and digital libraries" that could serve more effectively the divergent needs of scholars.

Dowling (1997) analyzed in great detail what he called the "crisis of the monograph" in an article in the *Journal of Scholarly Publishing*. He quoted extensively from a letter to Hugh Kenner from John G. Ryden (then the director at Yale University Press): "Yale and every other university press in America has seen the sale of the scholarly monograph . . . decline by two-thirds. Where we once expected to sell perhaps 2,500 [copies], we now sell 800–900. Over the years smaller print runs pushed up the costs and therefore prices in an ongoing spiral. Scholars virtually stopped buying books." Yet the crisis had other parameters. Ryden remarked, "library budgets declined in the 70s; in the 80s they dropped again and serial purchases cut deeply into funds available to buy books." The remarks of Sanford G. Thatcher (the director at Penn State University Press) in the *Chronicle of Higher Education* were also quoted by Dowling. Thatcher reported that his press published 150 titles in literary studies. Of that amount 65 percent of the titles "sold fewer than 500 copies and 91 percent fewer than 800. The market for books of traditional literary criticism has now shrunk to the point that it is no longer possible for a small, unendowed press like Penn State to continue publishing such works."

Drawing on data for economics books in the *Journal of Economic Literature* in 1985 and 2000, Laband and Hudson (2003) examined university presses, commercial academic presses, and foreign presses to evaluate "the pricing decision, the hardback/paperback decision, the publication of joint editions in hardback and paperback, and the factors determining the length of a book." Their analyses revealed that "university presses are more likely to publish in paperback than commercial presses and to publish joint editions. They also tend to publish longer books, the estimate suggests some 13 percent longer in 2000. These results may reflect a more complex objective function for university presses." Their data on economics books prices revealed "university presses and other not-for-profit publishers sell at substantially lower prices than commercial publishing houses." The average university press price for economics books in 2000 was $47.71; our previous research paper on university press pricing indicated that economics books averaged $49.92, a difference of 4.85 percent.

Pavliscak, Ross, and Henry (1997) found that electronic technology has had an enormous effect on the delivery of information and communication among scholars and has profoundly influenced how research is conducted in the humanities. Their study indicated that in general humanists saw great positive potential in the use of electronic technology as a tool for increasing the dissemination of knowledge and research results.

Wissoker (1997) argued that the monograph was not dying, but that scholars who work in particular subfields may not find the route to publication as easy as it once was. Does this mean there has been a serious decline in monographic publishing in North America? Wissoker rejects the notion. Instead, he posits that anxiety over the demise of the monograph may stem from new directions in intellectual pursuits rather than a turn away from scholarship. He wondered if a feeling of uneasiness over the future of the scholarly monograph might be a reaction to a shift away from a concentration on publishing studies by elite scholars to giving equal consideration to works produced by junior scholars. Compounded with this shift to a meritocracy might be the presses' new emphasis on basing publishing decisions to a larger degree on self-interest; many of them needed to publish in areas that were likely to garner more reviews in the media and that were likely to result in a wider market for their books. These issues were also analyzed by Greco (2001a, 2001b, 2005).

Schiffrin (1999) was concerned about the penetration of commercial market forces into university press practices, especially the application of a business ideology to academic publishing. On the other hand, Hacken (1998), who evaluated European studies books issued in North America, was clearly optimistic about the state of scholarly publishing in this highly specialized niche.

Waters (2001), in an article that sparked heated debate in university press circles, insisted that the university tenure system had pushed reason to the margins. He wrote that, in a significant number of fields, tenure review committees now favor the countable quantity over the elusive quality as the criterion by which to judge a scholar's contribution to advancement of knowledge. Is there an answer to this perceived crisis? Waters developed a complex tripartite scenario: publish exciting books, free the monograph from the tyranny of tenure, and rethink who should evaluate scholars and scholarship. Waters concluded by pointing out the hidden costs of the existing scholarly publishing system that have not yet been considered.

Varian (2000) investigated market opportunities in the information sector. Information goods—which include books and journals—can be copied, shared, resold, or rented, and when such alternative opportunities to direct purchase exist, the producer will not profit from the distribution. He identified three circumstances under which profits can increase, including "when a sharing market provides a way to segment high-value and low-value users."

G. Becker (1991) was puzzled as to why many successful businesses did not raise prices even when faced with persistent excess demand for a particular product. He suggested that randomness, the famed argument put forward by Malkiel (1996), also applies to book sales. So he wondered, "Why does the price of a book not increase while it is experiencing a successful run?"

There were several developments in higher education in the 1990s (primarily at research universities) that had significant implications for scholarly publishing. The most important developments occurred in reappointment, tenure, promotion, and merit pay review systems. Many research universities reevaluated their strategies for assessing a scholar's fitness for reappointment, tenure, and promotion during the period under study in this research paper. Young scholars, who once might have expected to be promoted largely on the basis of their ability to teach effectively, were asked to show evidence of their worth by publishing in the best possible places—university presses or top-tier commercial presses.

At most research universities, scholars in the humanities are required to publish at least one book for tenure and promotion, and some humanities programs have recently raised the number to two for tenure and three for promotion to full professor.

The Modern Language Association (MLA; 2002) was concerned about these trends, and it created the MLA Ad Hoc Committee on the Future of Scholarly Publishing to "investigate and understand the widely perceived crisis in scholarly publishing and make recommendations to address the situation." This committee was created after Stephen Greenblatt (a professor at Harvard University and president of the MLA) sent his May 28, 2000, letter to the members of the MLA. In his letter, Greenblatt addressed what he termed "a serious problem in the publishing of scholarly books" and its impact on tenure and promotion.

Some of the key findings of the MLA ad hoc committee include the following:

- Library budgets for monographs in the humanities declined steadily, as did subsidies for university presses, described as more of a "chronic illness" than a crisis.

- "The apparent overproduction of book-length scholarly manuscripts in the humanities has led to widespread feelings of frustration among academics who are attempting to place their work with a publisher."

- Sales of scholarly books were "averaging 300 copies per title and failing fast. . . . Today the notion that university presses need not be concerned about the sales potential of the books they produce has increasingly given way to an emphasis on the bottom line."

- "Another matter of concern is the increasing emphasis that tenure and promotion committees place on the scholarly book, at a time when constraints on academic publishing make it more and more difficult to get such books published."

The committee also made a series of suggestions for tenure and promotion committees, deans, and other administrators at research universities. They include the following:

- "Colleges and universities need to reflect more carefully about appropriate models for tenure and promotion dossiers, with the aim of devising a variety of models that would do better justice to the different kinds of projects candidates may wish to undertake."

- "By ceasing to regard book publication as the gold standard for tenure and promotion, universities and colleges would be able to place more emphasis on the quality of publications."

- In essence, colleges and universities should emphasize quality over quantity and realize that "there is no ready or simple solution to the current crisis."

The situation in the social sciences is rather complex. Certain academic areas, notably sociology and to a lesser degree political theory and political science, remain heavily dependent on books in the scholarly communication process (and face the same problems as academics in the humanities). Other areas, including economics and finance, have been primarily dependent on journal articles.

Mathematics and science researchers are almost totally dependent on print journals to communicate scholarly developments to their colleagues, although the electronic dissemination of research papers is, perhaps, even more critically important than printed journals in certain scientific fields.

Overall, tenure in the humanities remains a book oriented system as it does in many areas of the social sciences; books are rarely a factor in the mathematics and science sectors since they emphasize publications in peer-reviewed scholarly or professional journals. Librarians also investigated these issues. R. Meyer (1996) compared the traditional role played by print journals with the increase in use of electronic journals and the impact on research libraries, issues also raised by Pascarelli (1990). Giles (1996) analyzed models of scholarly communication, investigating both econometric issues and the changing role of professional librarians. Network-based library systems received a great deal of attention, stimulated by the research of Lynch (1994), who also addressed the economic and organizational issues raised by the increased dependence of networks. The changing needs of faculty members, a pivotal issue at research universities, were investigated by a number of librarians, including Smith (2003); DeGroote and Dorsch (2003); and King, Tenopir, and Montgomery (2003). Library collections were the subject of many major studies. Miller-Francisco (2003) studied how librarians were managing electronic resources at a time of shrinking budgets. Edgar (2003) developed a theoretical framework for collection management.

Research Methodology: Book Industry Trends and the Yankee Book Peddler Data Sets

We reviewed net publisher unit sales from various issues of *Book Industry Trends*. This was done to ascertain sales in both (a) the professional and scholarly book sector and (b) university presses. Additional data on adult, juvenile, mass-market paperbacks, and religious books were evaluated. Table 2.7 lists this information.

The Yankee Book Peddler (YBP) database, listing university presses and commercial academic books for 1989–2000 in approximately 225 book subcategories, was evaluated. Its data, while extensive, presented certain methodological problems when we analyzed total title output.

First, between 1989 and 1996, YBP aggregated all title output data, combining cloth and paperback books into one total. We discussed this issue with Mr. Robert Nardini at YBP. He reviewed his data, and he estimated that approximately 50 percent of all new titles between 1989 and 1995 were paperbacks, with the number of new books published in paper increasing to 54 percent as of 1996. No data were available from Mr. Nardini on the cloth-paper ratios in any of the book subcategories. Second, Mr. Nardini estimated that, between 1989 and 2000, approximately 8 percent of all new titles in their database were textbooks, a percentage he believed remained constant between 1989 and 2000. Third, firm data on monograph publishing were unobtainable since YBP did not differentiate in their tallies between monographs and trade books intended for the general educated public.

Research Methodology: Bowker Data Sets

We also reviewed a data set from the R. R. Bowker Company. Bowker is one of the leading bibliographical information companies in North America. This firm issues all ISBNs in the United States, publishes a series of reference books (including *Books in Print* and *Paperback Books in Print*), and maintains an extensive database of books and approximately 85,000

TABLE 2.7

Net publisher book unit sales, 1985–2005 (millions of units)

Year	Adult trade total	Juvenile trade total	Mass-market paperbacks	Religious total	Professional and commercial scholarly total	University presses total
1985	376.7	199.9	429.8	141.5	125.7	16.1
1986	368.6	217.4	430.5	141.2	132.6	16.0
1987	373.5	226.7	441.4	135.5	135.9	14.7
1988	381.5	252.1	472.7	128.0	142.0	14.8
1989	421.2	289.6	497.5	131.7	145.3	15.4
1990	420.4	310.3	488.8	137.7	148.6	15.8
1991	429.7	335.0	499.6	143.4	147.0	16.6
1992	460.5	327.9	495.1	148.3	152.9	17.0
1993	482.5	307.4	510.0	147.2	155.9	17.1
1994	512.8	329.0	520.2	151.0	161.7	17.9
1995	484.7	357.1	529.9	156.5	165.4	17.7
1996	465.1	379.9	527.2	162.8	163.9	17.4
1997	476.5	342.3	473.2	166.6	165.2	28.3
1998	496.6	363.7	483.7	170.5	170.8	29.7
1999	548.5	524.9	601.3	200.9	178.3	26.5
2000	473.9	577.9	584.2	197.7	187.3	25.7
2001	458.3	520.7	564.0	201.1	168.6	24.5
2002	462.2	524.6	570.2	204.4	170.3	24.9
2003	449.9	514.8	562.6	203.9	172.1	24.6
2004	463.7	480.1	535.6	221.2	175.9	23.5
2005	473.9	484.1	540.1	236.4	176.4	23.7

SOURCE: Book Industry Trends, various years.

book publishers. For example, *Books in Print* alone contains more than 4.5 million listings of books in print, forthcoming books, out-of-print books, audio, and video titles.

Their university press tallies (covering 1992 and 1997 through 2000) were based on book production figures from what Andrew Grabois (2003) at Bowker termed the "56 largest university press publishers" regarding total output. Consequently, their smaller data set does not correspond precisely to the YBP university press data since (1) Bowker aggregated data into larger book categories (e.g., history) and (2) only 5 years' worth of data (rather than the YBP's 12 years' worth of data) was available. The Bowker data appears in table 2.8.

The Title Output Data

However, in spite of a significantly smaller sample of university presses, the Bowker data were exceptionally useful. Bowker reported 8,838 university press titles in 1992; YBP listed 7,728, a difference of 14.36 percent. By 1997 YBP listed 12,047, Bowker 10,336 (a difference of 16.55 percent); in 1998 YBP listed 12,306, Bowker 10,878 (13.13 percent); in 1999 YBP listed 12,763, Bowker 10,627 (20.1 percent); and in 2000 YBP listed 12,201, Bowker 10,938 (11.55 percent).

As for percentage increases, YBP posted a 1.28 percent change between 1997 and 2000; Bowker's change was 5.82 percent for those same years.

Overall, YBP listed 57,045 new titles for those four years while Bowker reported 51,617, a difference of 5,428 titles and 10.52 percent. So the discrepancy between the YBP and

TABLE 2.8

R. R. Bowker data on university press title output, 1992, 1997–2000

Book category	TITLE OUTPUT				
	1992	1997	1998	1999	2000
Agriculture	94	88	90	97	90
Arts	354	414	389	420	441
Biography	479	577	585	595	524
Business	105	141	138	111	142
Education	231	273	273	240	289
Fiction	147	215	243	252	231
General works	47	62	69	66	68
History	894	1,050	1,201	1,230	1,326
Home economics	42	31	53	47	43
Juveniles	45	91	77	95	131
Language	271	395	384	348	436
Law	217	251	303	296	285
Literature	792	847	871	820	735
Medicine	363	322	369	346	329
Music	161	177	194	195	208
Philosophy, psychology	662	720	798	830	756
Poetry, drama	372	387	442	347	310
Religion	401	485	558	475	551
Science	844	884	957	894	1,047
Sociology, economics	1,824	2,374	2,330	2,311	2,375
Sports, recreation	179	220	215	257	263
Technology	221	252	264	245	258
Travel	93	80	75	110	100
	—	—	—	—	—
Total	8,838	10,336	10,878	10,627	10,938

SOURCE: R. R. Bowker.

Bowker data averaged about 1,085 titles each year, with a percentage difference of slightly more than 2 percent annually.

All things considered, the Bowker data were statistically close to the YBP data during 1997–2000 in spite of its smaller sample.

Givler (2002) also reported on university press title output. "At this writing, ninety-two university presses in the United States and Canada belong to AAUP [Association of American University Presses]. Among them they publish on the order of 11,000 books a year." He also remarked, "AAUP has 121 members in all and includes scholarly societies, research institutions, museums, and international members. Only scholarly publishers affiliated with degree-granting institutions in the United States are counted here as university presses."

Since Givler's research was published in 2002, it is likely Givler used 2000 data. A review of *The Association of American University Presses Directory, 2002–2003* regarding title output for the "scholarly societies, research institutions, museums, and international members" in 2000 that Givler excluded from his total of 11,000 new titles revealed the following: in 2000 these excluded presses, as reported in the AAUP (2003) directory, published 5,740 titles; and data for 2001 indicated they published 5,760 new books.

Even if one (1) excluded all titles released by the Chinese University Press in 2000 (133); (2) excluded 80 percent of all the titles published by both Cambridge University Press

(2,376) and Oxford University Press (2,250) in 2000, using instead smaller totals for Cambridge (425) and Oxford (450); (3) assumed Givler rounded up his total to 11,000; and (4) assumed that most if not all of the titles published by the excluded presses were available in the United States and listed by both YBP and Bowker, then Givler's 11,000 total and the reduced excluded press total of 1,906 generates an estimated university press total of 12,906. The YBP university press estimate for 2000 was 12,201 (5.78 percent lower than the Givler-AAUP total) and close to Bowker's data.

Commercial Scholarly Academic (Professional) Presses

We were concerned, however, about the cluster of commercial academic press data in the YBP data set. While it is impossible to gauge the breadth of the presses listed by YBP, a review of various issues of the *Chronicle of Higher Education* shed some light on this issue.

Each week the *Chronicle of Higher Education* (2003) lists new scholarly books. For example, a review of the October 17, 2003, and the October 24, 2003, issues of the *Chronicle* revealed that a number of commercial academic presses were listed. They included Ashgate Publishing, Basic Books, Berg Publishers, Brill Academic Publishers, Carolina Academic Press, Edward Elgar Publishing, the Free Press, Alfred A. Knopf, Peter Lang Publishing, Palgrave Macmillan, Pluto Press, Praeger Publishers, Routledge, Rowman & Littlefield, Simon & Schuster, Society of Biblical Literature, and J. B. Tauris.

It appears that YBP's bibliographers and editorial personnel at the *Chronicle* felt it was reasonable to list these commercial academic presses, along with others, as publishers of scholarly books.

As for deleting some but not all commercial academic presses from the YBP data sets, one would have to go year by year, publisher by publisher, marker field by marker field, and determine, drawing on some pretested formula or methodology, which commercial academic publishers should be listed and which ones should be deleted. This task is clearly beyond the scope of this book.

Concluding Comments on Research Methodology

No data set is perfect, witness the changes made in balance-of-trade data released by the U.S. Department of Commerce during the span of a year. However, after a review of the available YBP university press data, the Bowker university press data, and the Givler-AAUP directory university press data, we believe the YBP data set on university presses, in spite of its aggregation of cloth and hardbound titles and the inclusion of textbooks, is the most extensive and only usable one available at this time.

The YBP data were remarkably close to the data released by Bowker and tallies in the Givler-AAUP directory; therefore, one is compelled to assume that its macro data on commercial academic presses also has relevance and usefulness.

Therefore, we urge readers to view all of the YBP tallies as ballpark statistics. The only available and reasonable alternative is to eschew all data from YBP, Bowker, and Givler-AAUP and rely exclusively on anecdotal comments, an alternative we believe is not in the best interest of academics, publishers, or the academic community.

TABLE 2.9
Total title output, 1989–2000

Year	University presses title output	Percentage change previous year	Commercial presses title output	Percentage change previous year	Total output	Percentage change previous year
1989	6,969	—	22,016	—	28,985	—
1990	7,254	4.09	23,300	5.83	30,554	5.41
1991	7,673	5.78	27,912	19.79	35,585	16.47
1992	7,728	0.72	29,597	6.04	37,325	4.89
1993	9,847	27.42	33,690	13.83	43,537	16.64
1994	10,353	5.14	35,004	3.90	45,357	4.18
1995	11,224	8.40	39,114	11.74	50,338	10.98
1996	11,428	1.82	40,626	3.87	52,054	3.41
1997	12,047	5.42	43,862	7.97	55,909	7.41
1998	12,306	2.15	41,035	−6.45	53,341	−4.59
1999	12,763	3.71	43,571	6.18	56,334	5.61
2000	12,201	−4.40	41,201	−5.44	53,402	−5.20
1989–2000	121,793	75.07	420,928	87.14	542,721	84.24

SOURCE: Yankee Book Peddler.

TITLE OUTPUT

According to bibliographical data released by the YBP, university presses published 121,793 books between 1989 and 2000. In 1989 new title output stood at 6,969 titles. By 2000 it had grown to 12,201. Table 2.9 shows an increase of more than 75 percent during those 12 years.

Commercial scholarly presses published 420,928 titles during those years. At 22,016 their output in 1989 was much larger than that of the university presses (+15,047 titles). By 2000 the gap between these two sectors of scholarly publishing had further widened. Commercial presses released 41,201 titles, 29,000 more than university presses. This represents an increase of 87.14 percent since 1989.

Output for both sectors totaled 28,985 in 1989 and climbed to 53,402 in 2000 (+84.24 percent). The 12-year total stood at 542,721 titles. University presses accounted for 34.43 percent of all scholarly titles in this period; commercial houses held a 65.57 percent share of total output. Unfortunately, the data did not reveal (a) how many of these titles were really new and distinctive and not merely simultaneously cloth and paperback issues or re-issues of the same title as second or revised editions or (b) how many were monographs, as opposed to trade or textbooks.

The Humanities, 1989–2000

To many observers, academics in the humanities faced major problems getting their research published, making them the most vulnerable among scholars in the humanities, the social sciences, and the math-science area. However, a review of YBP's new-book bibliographical data on title output indicated that all 13 humanities categories and subcategories posted robust totals between 1989 and 2000. During those years, scholarly presses published 42,328 books in the humanities. Table 2.10 reveals that the largest subcategory was American literature (7,814 titles), followed by English literature (6,132 titles). History also

TABLE 2.10
Title output in the humanities, 1989–2000

Category	University presses total title output	Percentage of total	Commercial presses total title output	Percentage of total	Total output	Percentage of total humanities
Philosophy	3,114	48.63	3,289	51.37	6,403	5.21
Religion	1,322	33.06	2,677	66.94	3,999	3.25
Archaeology	162	36.49	282	63.51	444	0.36
History—N. Am.	5,699	48.13	6,142	51.87	11,841	9.63
History—West. Hem.*	5,224	51.11	4,998	48.89	10,222	8.31
Law (general)	765	29.82	1,800	70.18	2,565	2.09
Literature of music	2,089	34.00	4,056	66.00	6,145	5.00
Philology & linguistics	1,741	31.79	3,736	68.21	5,477	4.45
Classical language & literature	1,150	54.32	967	45.68	2,117	1.72
Literary history	4,794	31.06	10,641	68.94	15,435	12.55
Eng. lit.	6,132	29.76	14,473	70.24	20,605	16.76
Am. lit.	7,814	24.47	24,122	75.53	31,936	25.98
Romance lit.	2,322	40.33	3,436	59.67	5,758	4.68
Total title output	42,328	34.43	80,619	65.57	122,947	—
Average annual title output	3,527.33	—	6,718.25	—	10,245.58	—

SOURCE: Yankee Book Peddler.

*"Western Hemisphere" refers to Latin America in this data set.

posted solid results: 5,699 titles on North America and 5,224 on Latin America ("Western Hemisphere" in the table). Two other subcategories posted sizable totals: literary history (4,794) and philosophy (3,114). Although religion (1,322), the literature of music (2,089), philology and linguistics (1,741), classical language and literature (1,150), and Romance literature (2,322) lagged behind, they made a respectable showing. Only two subcategories—archaeology (162) and general law (765)—tallied in the three-digit level.

University Presses, 1989–1994

The macro data on the humanities may look impressive, but they are inherently misleading. As we sifted slowly through the YBP data sets, we discovered that many individual subcategories exhibited sharp growth between 1989 and 1994, but then a distinct softening in the overall humanities market began in the late 1990s, with some subcategories posting jagged performance or dramatic declines.

University presses published 271 North American history titles in 1989 and 426 in 1994 (+57.2 percent). Even better results were posted for Western Hemisphere history: 285 in 1989 and 468 in 1994 (+64.21 percent). Literary history, with 243 in 1989 and 436 in 1994 (+79.42 percent), and Romance literature, with 129 in 1989 and 181 in 1994 (+40.3 percent), exhibited strength and resiliency during those years.

American and English literature also generated sizable increases between 1989 and 1994. American literature, at 447 in 1989, had jumped 42.28 percent by 1994 to 636. As for English literature, an increase of 30.41 percent had been achieved by 1994 (in 1989, 411; in 1994, 536).

The other fields all posted increases. The larger ones included philosophy (+49.75 percent), the literature of music (+41.44 percent), and philology and linguistics (+67.47 percent). Even three of the smaller categories grew: religion (+29.21 percent), archaeology

TABLE 2.11
Title output in the humanities, 1989–1994

Category	UNIVERSITY PRESSES						COMMERCIAL PRESSES					
	1989	1990	1991	1992	1993	1994	1989	1990	1991	1992	1993	1994
Philosophy	199	179	164	196	248	298	161	155	183	199	228	269
Religion	89	67	78	78	124	115	130	121	167	149	180	225
Archaeology	14	13	13	7	14	18	21	13	17	18	14	18
History—N. Am.	271	308	359	389	456	426	311	302	389	472	502	502
History—West. Hem.*	285	318	328	356	439	468	192	206	312	396	402	423
Law (general)	37	31	52	61	61	66	100	74	115	131	130	131
Literature of music	111	119	142	137	179	157	169	220	254	275	321	334
Philology & linguistics	83	96	94	88	115	139	191	188	208	226	294	297
Classical language & literature	91	90	85	75	93	86	32	46	46	58	65	73
Literary history	243	261	283	310	417	436	540	604	708	755	847	912
Eng. lit.	411	428	446	398	534	536	807	836	949	1,057	1,131	1,189
Am. lit.	447	422	464	471	617	636	1,257	1,218	1,685	1,847	2,066	2,116
Romance lit.	129	167	185	155	193	181	205	210	224	238	277	275

SOURCE: Yankee Book Peddler.

*"Western Hemisphere" refers to Latin America in this data set.

(+28.57 percent), and general law (+78.78 percent). Classical languages and literature was the only sector that declined (−5.49 percent).

Table 2.11 shows that, overall, university press title output in the humanities increased from 2,410 in 1989 to 3,562 in 1994 (+47.8 percent). The market share for university presses stood at 34.43 percent from 1989 to 1994.

Commercial Academic Presses, 1989–1994

Commercial academic publishers were even more active in the humanities between 1989 and 1994, outproducing university presses in 10 of the 13 subcategories. They published 502 titles in North American history in 1994, up from 311 in 1989 (+61.41 percent increase). Latin American ("Western Hemisphere" in the table) history posted equally interesting results, growing from 192 in 1989 to 423 in 1994 (+120.31 percent). Developments in literary history were also rather dramatic: 540 books were published in this category in 1989, and by 1994 total output had surged to 912 (+68.89 percent). Romance literature, however, did not fare as well: 205 in 1989 and 275 in 1994 (+34.15 percent).

American literature emerged as the largest category in the humanities in this six-year period: 1,257 titles in 1989 and 2,116 in 1994 (+68.34 percent). Philosophy surged 67.08 percent, from 161 in 1989 to 269 in 1994. Significant increases were posted by the literature of music—169 in 1989 and 334 in 1994 (+97.63 percent)—and philology and linguistics—191 in 1989 and 297 in 1994 (+55.5 percent). In terms of title output, archaeology is the smallest field, and it was squarely in the low double-digit range: 21 in 1989 and 18 in 1994 (−14.29 percent). General law—100 in 1989 and 131 in 1994 (+31 percent)—and classical language and literature—32 in 1989 and 73 in 1994 (+128.13 percent)—on the other hand, exhibited positive growth rates in those years.

Commercial publishers released 4,116 titles in 1989 and 6,764 in 1994, representing a vigorous increase of 64.33 percent. Impressive annual increases were posted in 12 of the 13 categories during those years.

University Presses, 1995–2000

A close review of 1995–2000 revealed an unsettling pattern at university presses. While total increases were positive in 11 of 13 subcategories, much of this growth was generated between 1995 and 1997 (and, in a few instances, by 1998). In 1998–1999 a downward spiral became evident. Five of the 13 subcategories sustained declines between 1999 and 2000; only modest increases, many in the single-digit range, were seen by 2000. Overall, the university press share of total output in scholarly publications declined to 24.31 percent from the previously held 34.43 percent between 1989 and 1994. Commercial houses, on the other hand, increased their share of the market from 65.57 percent in 1989–1994 to 75.69 percent in 1995–2000. These developments are significant because, as we noted earlier, the economy was undergoing an expansion. Unemployment rates had declined, and increases in the CPI were exceptionally small. Furthermore, student enrollment at institutions of higher learning was up.

University presses showed increases in their annual output of books on North American history from 1996 through 1999; then this field was whipsawed by a sharp decrease in title output in 2000. Overall, publishing in North American history was up a slim 14.06 percent between 1995 and 2000. The pattern for Latin American ("Western Hemisphere" in the table) history paralleled that of North American history, exhibiting some modest changes between 1995 and 1998. By 1999 a small decline was recorded, with another drop in 2000. The six-year totals indicated an unpretentious increase in titles of only 8.68 percent, lower than the North American history growth rate.

Literary history expanded at a slower pace, before sustaining a decline in annual output in 2000, up 8.52 percent between 1995 and 2000. Similar uneven—and in some instances, unimpressive—developments were evident in archaeology (−6.25 percent), English literature (−8.33 percent), American literature (+4.67 percent), general law (+12.86 percent), music (+3.9 percent), and classical languages and literature (−26.09 percent). However, religion (+58.59 percent) and philosophy (+20.43 percent) exhibited better than average results.

Total output in the 13 humanities categories increased from 3,961 in 1995 to 4,273 by 2000 (+7.88 percent), well below the 47.08 percent rate of the 1989–1994 years. Table 2.12 provides an overview of these developments. It is worth bearing in mind, though, that a one- or two-year decline might be an aberration and not indicative of major changes in this sector.

Commercial Academic Presses, 1995–2000

We discovered a similar but more significant title output pattern among the commercial academic presses up to 1999. These publishers' aggressive, expansionist policies of 1989–1994 were tempered by the end of the 1990s.

Still, most book categories exhibited a growth pattern between 1995 and 1997. This was most clearly evident in the literature triad and both history subcategories. By 1998 decreases in titles were evident in almost all categories. Only philosophy and Latin American ("Western Hemisphere" in the table) history showed increases, while literary history, American literature, and English literature experienced steep declines. During 1999 and 2000, fairly

TABLE 2.12
Title output in the humanities, 1995–2000

Category	UNIVERSITY PRESSES						COMMERCIAL PRESSES					
	1995	1996	1997	1998	1999	2000	1995	1996	1997	1998	1999	2000
Philosophy	279	281	310	278	346	336	291	363	350	361	379	350
Religion	99	140	120	120	135	157	272	282	313	298	247	293
Archaeology	16	14	14	16	8	15	17	28	25	24	43	44
History—N. Am.	512	512	601	629	652	584	587	640	630	611	593	603
History—West. Hem.*	461	489	483	554	542	501	453	512	515	560	512	515
Law (general)	70	75	77	84	72	79	137	191	205	168	207	211
Literature of music	205	209	205	197	215	213	396	392	461	420	436	378
Philology & linguistics	155	177	199	227	198	170	312	402	419	402	408	389
Classical language & literature	115	82	121	114	113	85	87	109	138	95	127	91
Literary history	457	446	454	459	530	496	966	1,030	1,147	1,034	1,040	1,058
Eng. lit.	600	545	545	486	653	550	1,238	1,442	1,427	1,363	1,570	1,463
Am. lit.	793	768	808	769	789	830	2,336	2,331	2,467	2,281	2,325	2,193
Romance lit.	199	207	224	203	222	257	325	332	357	326	368	299

SOURCE: Yankee Book Peddler.

*"Western Hemisphere" refers to Latin America in this data set.

modest increases were the norm, with many categories generating only single-digit increases, including North American history (2.73 percent), classical languages and literature (4.6 percent), literary history (9.52 percent), and Romance literature (8 percent). The literature of music (−4.55 percent) and American literature (−6.12 percent) posted negative results.

Respectable increases were recorded between 1995 and 2000 by only a handful of book categories, including philosophy (+20.27 percent), archaeology (+158.02 percent on a small number of titles), general law (+54.01 percent), philology and linguistics (+24.68 percent), and English literature (+18.17 percent).

Overall, commercial academic press title output increased from 7,414 to 7,887. This represents a 6.34 percent increase that was below the 7.88 percent of university presses in the same six years.

The Social Sciences, 1989–2000

While the social science category is smaller than the humanities category, accounting for 33,534 titles published between 1989 and 2000 (versus the humanities' 122,947), it is a vibrant component of scholarly communications.

Table 2.13 reveals that psychology represented 26.81 percent of the 8,991 titles released in this area. It easily surpassed finance's 6,313 titles (18.83 percent), the three political science areas at 4,743 (14.14 percent), and economics at 4,049 (12.07 percent). Sociology, with 3,899 titles (11.63 percent), and political theory, with 2,878 titles (8.58 percent), also exhibited strong results. University presses accounted for 24.31 percent of all social science books, but commercial presses captured 75.69 percent of the market. Again, the macro data on the social sciences exhibited the robust growth patterns seen in the humanities. What these data did not reveal, though, were the growing fissures in title output.

TABLE 2.13
Title output in the social sciences, 1989–2000

Category	University presses title output	Percentage of total	Commercial academic presses title output	Percentage of total	Total output	Percentage of total social sciences
Psychology	1,546	17.19	7,445	82.81	8,991	26.81
Anthropology	1,100	41.34	1,561	58.66	2,661	7.94
Economics	1,075	26.55	2,974	73.45	4,049	12.07
Finance	698	11.06	5,615	88.94	6,313	18.83
Sociology	924	23.70	2,975	76.30	3,899	11.63
Pol. theory	1,196	41.56	1,682	58.44	2,878	8.58
Poli-sci—U.S.	809	35.99	1,439	64.01	2,248	6.70
Poli-sci—Europe	503	29.16	1,222	70.84	1,725	5.14
Poli-sci—Asia & Africa	302	39.22	468	60.78	770	2.30
Total title output	8,153	24.31	25,381	75.69	33,534	—
Average annual title output	679.42	—	2,115.00	—	—	

SOURCE: Yankee Book Peddler.

TABLE 2.14
Title output in the social sciences, 1989–1994

Category	UNIVERSITY PRESSES						COMMERCIAL PRESSES					
	1989	1990	1991	1992	1993	1994	1989	1990	1991	1992	1993	1994
Psychology	90	100	97	80	123	135	372	404	473	468	557	605
Anthropology	66	58	65	71	110	72	54	67	56	78	102	129
Economics	83	87	82	80	92	88	197	193	217	260	232	242
Finance	45	39	46	44	54	57	249	236	449	412	439	436
Sociology	45	57	51	52	63	81	105	121	162	162	204	308
Pol. theory	63	56	50	79	91	83	63	64	76	95	112	123
Poli-sci—U.S.	39	38	42	42	58	67	80	66	87	101	99	117
Poli-sci—Europe	26	36	26	23	41	37	47	45	58	64	78	98
Poli-sci—Asia & Africa	20	13	21	14	20	29	10	19	27	18	29	34

SOURCE: Yankee Book Peddler.

University Presses, 1989–1994

Between 1989 and 1994, four of the nine social science subcategories sustained growth and then declined. Anthropology climbed from 66 titles in 1989 to 110 in 1993 before it dropped to 72 in 1994; economics, with 83 titles in 1989, jumped to 92 in 1993 but was down to 88 in 1994; political theory grew to 91 in 1993 from 63 in 1989 but then declined to 83 in 1994; and European political science, showing 26 titles in 1989 and then 41 in 1993, fell to 37 in 1994.

The remaining five niches experienced continuous growth rates, as shown in table 2.14. Sociology (+80 percent), U.S. political science (+71.79 percent), psychology (+50 percent), Asian and African political science (+45 percent), and finance (+26.67) all recorded very respectable tallies.

Commercial Academic Presses, 1989–1994

All nine subcategories in the commercial publishing sector experienced strong and, in some instances, exceptionally impressive totals. Asian and African political science grew

TABLE 2.15
Title output in the social sciences, 1995–2000

Category	UNIVERSITY PRESSES						COMMERCIAL PRESSES					
	1995	1996	1997	1998	1999	2000	1995	1996	1997	1998	1999	2000
Psychology	129	155	126	157	184	170	686	743	754	742	785	856
Anthropology	100	119	106	128	120	85	139	185	199	163	225	164
Economics	95	97	96	86	99	90	288	243	290	295	269	248
Finance	56	73	74	63	84	63	522	521	556	536	677	582
Sociology	94	86	83	100	103	109	279	290	337	317	333	357
Pol. theory	104	127	126	127	169	121	176	202	193	196	176	206
Poli-sci—U.S.	81	87	84	94	85	92	117	134	157	141	175	165
Poli-sci—Europe	46	55	40	47	72	54	112	149	142	135	157	137
Poli-sci—Asia & Africa	25	16	36	43	38	27	34	39	75	64	58	61

SOURCE: Yankee Book Peddler.

from 10 to 34 titles (+240 percent), eclipsing sociology (+193.33 percent), anthropology (+138.89 percent), and European political science (+108.51 percent). The others posted impressive numbers as well: psychology (+62.63 percent), finance (+75.10 percent, although it declined by three titles between 1993 and 1994), economics (+22.84 percent), political theory (+95.24 percent), and U.S. political science (+46.25 percent).

University Presses, 1995–2000

By 1995 most of the university presses had bounced back from the declines of the earlier year, but this upswing did not last long. Seven of the nine niches again experienced increases by 2000; decreases in annual output were seen only in anthropology and economics between 1995 and 2000. Table 2.15 outlines the trends in this area. These reductions paralleled developments in the humanities during 1999 and 2000.

Commercial Academic Presses, 1995–2000

In the commercial publishing area, eight of the nine social science book subcategories sustained increases. A decline was recorded only in economics.

In summary, between 1989 and 1994, university press social science title output grew from 477 titles to 649 (+36.06 percent). During those same six years commercial houses posted a 77.74 percent increase. Starting with 1,177 titles in 1989, they ended 1994 with 2,092 titles. However, following the path of the humanities, the commercial sector also experienced a slowdown in title output between 1995 and 2000. University presses recorded 730 titles in 1995 and inched up to 811 in 2000, an increase of only 11.01 percent, far off their tally in the 1989–1994 period. Commercial houses outpaced the university presses, growing from 2,353 in 1995 to 2,776 in 2000, but their rate was up only 17.98 percent, a staggering decline from its torrid 77.74 percent in 1989–1994.

Mathematics and the Sciences, 1989–2000

Only a handful of university presses are active in statistics, mathematics, physics, and natural science. In these categories, 42,192 books were released between 1989 and 2000. However, university presses accounted for a relatively small number of mathematics and science

TABLE 2.16
Title output in mathematics and science, 1989–2000

Category	University presses title output	Percentage of total	Commercial academic presses title output	Percentage of total	Total output	Percentage of total math-science
Statistics	69	15.16	386	84.84	455	1.08
Mathematics	2,134	7.63	25,844	92.37	27,978	66.31
Physics	1,163	13.65	7,358	86.35	8,521	20.20
Natural science	1,481	28.27	3,757	71.73	5,238	12.41
Total title output	4,847	11.49	37,345	88.51	42,192	—
Average annual output	403.92	—	3,112.08	—	3,516.00	—

SOURCE: Yankee Book Peddler.

TABLE 2.17
Title output in mathematics and science, 1989–1994

Category	UNIVERSITY PRESSES						COMMERCIAL PRESSES					
	1989	1990	1991	1992	1993	1994	1989	1990	1991	1992	1993	1994
Statistics	7	6	4	5	4	8	21	25	22	17	26	38
Mathematics	138	156	145	129	191	177	1,327	1,390	1,697	1,922	2,130	2,102
Physics	76	79	74	71	82	110	511	512	614	691	633	610
Natural science	83	79	88	78	110	147	260	256	269	272	289	302

SOURCE: Yankee Book Peddler.

titles (4,847) and only an 11.49 percent share of the market. Large commercial houses dominate in these four areas. With a formidable presence in the area, commercial presses released an outpouring of titles (37,345 titles) and commanded a staggering 88.51 percent market share. Table 2.16 shows the breakdown of title output in statistics, mathematics, physics, and natural science at university and commercial presses.

University Presses, 1989–2000

Statistics is the smallest of the four subcategories. Table 2.17, which records the totals, shows that it barely grew between 1989 and 1994. In 1994 only eight titles were published, but the number declined to only three titles in 2000. Mathematics, a more stable field, posted respectable increases, from 138 in 1989 to 177 in 1994. It experienced a surge between 1995 (203) and 1997 (220), but by 2000 it had sustained a steep decline (185).

Physics, exhibiting the same pattern, grew from 76 titles in 1989 to 147 in 1994; it then experienced an upward swing in 1997 (135) and a drop in 2000 (114). Natural science was somewhat unusual in that it grew sharply between 1989 (83) and 1994 (147) and then fell in 1995 (130). A fairly serious increase was recorded in 1998 (153) and again in 1999 (179) before this subcategory leveled off in 2000 (171). See table 2.18 for trends between 1995 and 2000.

Commercial Academic Presses, 1989–2000

Commercial presses were a little more active in statistics. They released 21 titles in 1989 and increased that number to 38 by 1994 (+80.95 percent). Their output in statistics

TABLE 2.18
Title output in mathematics and science, 1995–2000

Category	UNIVERSITY PRESSES						COMMERCIAL PRESSES					
	1995	1996	1997	1998	1999	2000	1995	1996	1997	1998	1999	2000
Statistics	6	5	6	5	10	3	41	35	37	42	50	32
Mathematics	203	207	220	198	185	185	2,298	2,356	2,730	2,602	2,689	2,601
Physics	106	112	135	102	102	114	695	625	588	650	649	580
Natural science	130	128	135	153	179	171	320	345	349	379	346	370

SOURCES: Yankee Book Peddler; Bowker 2005.

between 1995 and 2000 was exceptionally uneven: up to 41 in 1995, down to 37 in 1997, and bottoming out at 32 in 2000.

Commercial presses' share in mathematics, however, was extremely large. Starting with a base of 1,327 titles in 1989, they surged ahead (+58.4 percent), topping the 2,102 mark in 1994. They continued to increase their share of the market, so that by 2000 they had reached 2,601 titles. Physics, a subcategory with steep production costs, proved a dynamic niche for commercial publishers between 1989 and 1994. Titles published grew from 511 to 610. But the six-year pattern was really odd: 695 in 1995; 625 in 1996; 588 in 1997; 650 in 1998; 649 in 1999; and 580 in 2000. Natural science showed more consistent results, bounding from 260 in 1989 to 320 in 1995 and 370 in 2000.

Between 1989 and 1994, university press mathematics and science title output grew from 304 to 442 (+45.39 percent). Commercial houses essentially matched their pace, starting with 2,119 in 1989 and reaching 3,052 in 1994 (+44.03 percent). Total output of university presses and commercial presses for 1995 through 2000 were again remarkably close: up 6.29 percent for university presses and up 6.83 percent for commercial academic presses. While overall title output is small, this niche has strong domestic and foreign sales, and it is unlikely that output in these four subcategories is too large for the markets to absorb.

CONCLUSION

First, the bibliographical data on new title output do not indicate a substantive, long-term downward change in total scholarly book output, although declines were clearly evident in certain marker fields in certain years.

Second, the "crisis in scholarly communications" was triggered by the serials crisis, which negatively affected university book sales. Data released by the Association of Research Libraries (2005) unmistakably indicated this trend. Between 1989 and 2000, (a) libraries increased their serials budget by 109.6 percent because serials unit costs were up 135.56 percent; (b) monographic library expenditures, on the other hand, lagged at 50.41 percent with monographic unit costs growing only 23.81 percent.

Third, it is likely that, in spite of changes in the needs of scholars between 1989 and 2000, the book will remain the primary form of scholarly communication in the humanities and in many areas of the social sciences. Fourth, on the basis of discussions with a cross section of scholarly publishers, we believe the growth in title output by commercial academic publishers was due to a number of disparate events, centering on the increased reputation of these presses and their ability to provide advances and royalty schedules that rivaled, and in many instances exceeded, those offered by university presses. However, the data do not allow us to generate aggregated data on the number of academics publishing with commercial presses or university presses.

Fifth, it is possible that increased specialization had an impact on title output; but the available data are not clear on this point. Sixth, data in tables 2.10 through 2.18 reveal that university press titles increased between 1989 and 2000. What impact this had on the economics of these presses was not evident in these tables.

Seventh, one must recognize that the laws of supply and demand operate in all sectors of the economy, including scholarly communications. If title output increases and if demand is flat or declines, ultimately presses feel the impact of this situation. Since title output increased and demand declined, a trend line evident over a long period, one must question whether a sense of irrational exuberance permeated the university press community, prodding publishers and editors to publish books for a market that was clearly not expanding and was, in certain instances, declining.

Lastly, book title output statistics did not provide any information about how university presses responded to changes in higher education even though there were some major changes in higher education. The Association of Research Libraries (2005) found that the total student population increased 5.83 percent while graduate students surged 16.38 percent. Graduate students generally use scholarly books more than undergraduates.

REFERENCES

Amazon.com. 2005. http://www.amazon.com (accessed December 11, 2005).

Association of American University Presses. 2003. The Association of American University Presses Directory 2002–2003. New York: Association of American University Presses.

Association of Research Libraries. 2005. http://www.arl.org.

Bailey, Herbert S., Jr. 1988. "The Future of University Press Publishing." *Journal of Scholarly Publishing* 19:63–69.

Basuroy, Suman, Subimal Chatterjee, and S. Abraham Ravid. 2003. "How Critical Are Critical Reviews? The Box Office Effects of Film Critics, Star Power, and Budgets." *Journal of Marketing* 67 (October): 103–117.

Becker, Gary. 1991. "A Note on Restaurant Pricing and Other Examples of Social Influence on Price." *Journal of Political Economy* 99:1109, 1114, 1115.

Becker, William C. 1973. "The Crisis—One Year Later." *Journal of Scholarly Publishing* 4: 291–302.

Bell, J. G. 1970. "The Proper Domain of Scholarly Publishing." *Journal of Scholarly Publishing* 2:15.

Book Industry Study Group. 2005. *Book Industry Trends.* New York: Book Industry Study Group. [Published annually.]

BookScan. 2005. Working paper, September 25.

Bowker Annual Library and Book Trade Almanac. 2005. New Providence, NJ: Bowker. [Published annually.]

Brown, John. 1970. "University Press Publishing." *Journal of Scholarly Publishing* 1:133.

Carrigan, Dennis P. 1991. "Publish or Perish: The Troubled State of Scholarly Communication." *Journal of Scholarly Publishing* 22:131–42.

Chevalier, Judy, and Dina Mayzlin. 2003. "The Effect of Word of Mouth on Sales: Online Book Reviews." Yale School of Management working paper series ES & MK economics and marketing (ES 28, MK 15), pp. 1–34.

Coser, Lewis A., Charles Kadushin, and Walter W. Powell. 1985. *Books: The Culture and Commerce of Publishing.* Chicago: University of Chicago Press.

Cronin, Blaise. 2002. "The University Press." *Library Journal.* March 15, p. 60.

De Groote, Sandra, and Josephine L. Dorsch. 2003. "Measuring Use Patterns of Online Journals and Databases at the University of Chicago." *Journal of the Medical Library Association* 91 (2): 231–40.

Dellarocas, Chrysanthos. 2003. "The Digitization of Word of Mouth: Promise and Challenges of Online Feedback Mechanisms." *Management Science* 9, no. 10 (October): 1407–24.

Dellarocas, Chrysanthos, Neveen Farag Awad, and Xiaoquan (Michael) Zhang. 2004. "Exploring the Value of Online Reviews to Organizations: Implications for Revenue Forecasting and Planning." Working paper, Massachusetts Institute of Technology, pp. 1–34.

Desai, Kalpesh Kaushik, and Suman Basuroy. 2005. "Interactive Influence of Genre Familiarity, Star Power, and Critics' Reviews in the Cultural Goods Industry: The Case of Motion Pictures." *Psychology and Marketing* 22, no. 3 (March): 203–23.

Dowling, William C. 1997. "Saving Scholarly Publishing in the Age of Oprah: The Glastonbury Project." *Journal of Scholarly Publishing* 28 (3): 8.

Edgar, William B. 2003. "Toward a Theory of Collection Development: An Activities and Attributes Approach." *Library Collections* 27 (4): 393–423.

Franklin, Ursula M. 1993. "Does Scholarly Publishing Promote Scholarship or Scholars?" *Journal of Scholarly Publishing* 24:248–52.

Giles, Michael W. 1996. "From Gutenberg to Gigabytes: Scholarly Communication in the Age of Cyberspace." *Journal of Politics* 58 (3): 613–26.

Givler, Peter. 2002. "University Press Publishing in the United States." In *Scholarly Publishing: Books, Journals, Publishers, and Libraries in the Twentieth Century*, ed. Richard E. Abel and Lyman W. Newlin, 117. New York: Wiley.

Grabois, Andrew. 2003. "U.S. Book Production Tops 150,000 in 2002: Trade Publishing Down, University Presses Up." R. R. Bowker news release, 2.

Greco, Albert N. 2001a. "The General Reader Market for University Press Books in the United States, 1990–1999, with Projections for the Years 2000 through 2004." *Journal of Scholarly Publishing* 32:61–85.

———. 2001b. "The Market for University Press Books in the United States, 1985–1999." *Learned Publishing* 14:97–106.

———. 2005. *The Book Publishing Industry*. 2nd edition. Mahwah, NJ: Erlbaum, 26–50.

Hacken, Richard. 1998. "The Current State of European Studies in North America and Scholarly Publishing in Western Europe." *Journal of Academic Librarianship* 24:201–7.

Harvey, William B., Herbert S. Bailey, Jr., William C. Becker, and John B. Putnam. 1972. "The Impending Crisis in University Publishing." *Journal of Scholarly Publishing* 3: 195–97.

Hofstadter, Richard. 1966. *Anti-Intellectualism in American Life*. New York: Random House, 1–14.

Kerr, Chester. 1975. "A National Enquiry into the Production and Dissemination of Scholarly Knowledge." *Journal of Scholarly Publishing* 7 (October): 7.

———. 1987. "One More Time: American University Presses Revisited." *Journal of Scholarly Publishing* 18:214.

King, Donald W., Carol Tenopir, and Carol Hansen Montgomery. 2003. "Patterns of Journal Use by Faculty at Three Diverse Universities." *D-Lib Magazine* 9 (10): 1.

Laband, David, and John Hudson. 2003. "The Pricing of Economics Books." *Journal of Economic Education* 34 (4): 360.

Levant, Daniel J. 1973. "Marketing in the Crunch." *Journal of Scholarly Publishing* 4:302.

Liu, Ziming. 2003. "Trends in Transforming Scholarly Communication and Their Implications." *Information Processing and Management* 39 (6): 889.

Lynch, Clifford A. 1994. "Scholarly Communication in the Networked Environment: Reconsidering Economics and Organizational Missions." *Serials Review* 20 (3): 23–30.

Maguire, James H. 1991. "Publishing on a Rawhide Shoestring." *Journal of Scholarly Publishing* 22:78–82.

Malkiel, Burton G. 1996. *A Random Walk Down Wall Street*. New York: Norton.

Meyer, Richard W. 1996. "The Library in Scholarly Communication." *Social Science Quarterly* 77 (1): 210–17.

Meyer, Sheldon. 1978. "Publishing Trade Books." *Journal of Scholarly Publishing* 9:70.

Miller-Francisco, Emily. 2003. "Managing Electronic Resources in a Time of Shrinking Budgets." *Library Collections* 27 (4): 507–12.

Mizzaro, Stefano. 2003. "Quality Control in Scholarly Publishing: A New Proposal." *Journal of the American Society for Information Science and Technology* 54 (11): 989.

MLA Ad Hoc Committee on the Future of Scholarly Publishing. 2002. "The Future of Scholarly Publishing." *Profession*, 172.

Moore, Terrence W. 1993. "Believe It or Not, Academic Books Are a Bargain." *Journal of Scholarly Publishing* 24:161–65.

New York Times. *New York Times Book Review*. 2005. http://www.nytimes.com (accessed December 11, 2005).

Owen, John MacKenzie. 2002. "The New Dissemination of Knowledge: Digital Libraries and Institutional Roles in Scholarly Publishing." *Journal of Economic Methodology* 9 (3): 275.

Parsons, Paul. 1991. "The Evolving Publishing Agendas of University Presses." *Journal of Scholarly Publishing* 23:45–50.

Pascarelli, Anne M. 1990. "Coping Strategies for Libraries Facing the Serials Crisis." *Serials Review* 16 (1): 75–80.

Pavliscak, Pamela, Seamus Ross, and Charles Henry. 1997. "Information Technology in Humanities Scholarship: Achievements, Prospects, and Challenges—The United States Focus." American Council of Learned Societies, occasional paper, 37:1–2.

Reinstein, David A., and Christopher M. Snyder. 2005. "The Influence of Expert Reviews on Consumer Demand for Experience Goods: A Case of Movie Critics." *Journal of Industrial Economics* 53, no. 1 (March): 27–51.

Romance Writers of America. 2005. https://www.rwanational.org (accessed April 6, 2006).

Rowson, Richard C. 1994. "A Formula for Successful Scholarly Publishing." *Journal of Scholarly Publishing* 25:67–78.

Schiffrin, Andre. 1999. "Payback Time: University Presses as Profit Centers." *Chronicle of Higher Education*, June 18, B4.

Smith, Erin T. 2003. "Changes in Faculty Reading Behaviors: The Impact of Electronic Journals on the University of Georgia." *Journal of Academic Librarianship* 29 (3): 162–68.

Sorensen, Alan T. 2004. Bestseller Lists and Product Variety: The Case of Book Sales. Working paper; Stanford University; pp. 1–29.

Sorensen, Alan T., and Scott J. Rasmussen. 2004. "Is Any Publicity Good Publicity? A Note on the Impact of Book Reviews." Working paper, Stanford University, 1–16.

Steele, Colin. 2003. "Phoenix Rising: New Models for the Research Monograph?" *Learned Publishing* 16:111.

The Subtext *2003–2004 Perspective on Book Publishing: Numbers, Issues and Trends*. 2005. Darien, CT: Open Book Publishing.

Thornton, Patricia H. 2004. *Markets from Culture: Institutional Logics and Organizational Decisions in Higher Education Publishing*. Stanford, CA: Stanford University Press.

Timko, David A. 2001. "A Study of the Book Reviewing Habits of the *New York Times*, 1950–2000." Master's thesis, University of North Carolina, Chapel Hill, 1–78.

Underhill, Paco. 1999. *Why We Buy: The Science of Shopping*. New York: Simon & Schuster.

Varian, Hal R. 2000. "Buying, Sharing, and Renting Information Goods." *Journal of Industrial Economics* 48:473–88.

Waters, Lindsay. 2001. "Rescue Tenure from the Tyranny of the Monograph." *Chronicle of Higher Education*, April 20, B7.

Wissoker, Ken. 1997. "Scholarly Monographs Are Flourishing, Not Dying." *Chronicle of Higher Education*, September 12, B4.

Advertising Research Foundation

Allyn & Bacon

Amazon.com

American Antiquarian Society

American Booksellers Association

American Library Association

American Mathematical Society

Associated Press

Association of Research Libraries

Barnes & Noble

Bedford Books

Book Industry Study Group

Booknet Canada

The Book Standard

Borders Group

R. R. Bowker

British Columbia University Press

Brookings Institution Press

CALPIRG

Cambridge University

Cambridge University Press

Carnegie-Mellon University Press

Catholic University Press

Cato Institute

Caxton Press

CBS News

Chicago Sun-Times

Chicago Tribune

Columbia University Press

Congressional Quarterly

Cornell University Press

Crain's New York Business

Curriculum Associates

Denver Post

Dorchester Publishers

Duke University Book Warehouse

Duquesne University Press

Elsevier

EMC

Evangelical Christian Publishers
    Association

Farrar, Straus, Giroux

Follett

Fordham University Press

Foreword

W. H. Freeman Press / Worth

Frost Miller Group

Gallaudet University Press

Georgetown University Press

Getty Publications

Gibbs Smith Publishers

Globe and Mail

Goldman Sachs

Hacket Publishing Company

Hampton Press

Hampton-Brown Company

Harcourt

Harlequin Enterprises

HarperCollins Publishers

Harvard Business School Press

Harvard University Press

Harvard-Yale-MIT Book Warehouse

Harvest House Publishers

Henry Holt

Houghton Mifflin Company

Howard University Press

The Invus Group

Johns Hopkins University Press

Jones & Bartlett Publishers

Journal of Media Economics

Journal of Scholarly Publishing

Lawrence Erlbaum Associates

Leag Group LLC

Leapfrog School House

Lynne Rienner Publishers

Marakon Associates

Market Partners International

Marquette University Press

McGill Queens University Press

McGraw-Hill Companies

McKinsey & Company

Meredith Books

Minnesota Historical Society

MIT University Press

Modern Language Association

National Academy Press

National Public Radio

NBC News

New York Botanical Garden Press

New York Times

New York University Press

Newsday

Northeastern University Press

Northwestern University Press

W. W. Norton & Company

Ohio State University Press

Ohio University Press

Open EBook Forum

Oxford Brookes University

Oxford University

Oxford University Press

Palgrave

Pearson Education

Pennsylvania State University Press

Philadelphia Inquirer

Prentice-Hall

Princeton University Press

Publishers Marketing Association

Publishers Weekly

Random House

Renaissance Audio

Rockefeller University Press

Russell Sage Press

Rutgers University Press

Scholastic

Simon & Schuster

Smithsonian Institution Press

Southern Illinois University Press

St. Martin's Press

Stanford University Press

Subtext

SUNY University Press

Syracuse University Press

Teachers College Press

Temple University Press

Thames & Hudson

Thomson Learning

Time Warner Book Group

Tom Doherty Associates / Tor Books

United States Department of Commerce, Bureau of the Census

United States Department of Commerce, Bureau of Economic Research

United States Department of Commerce, Commercial Trade Service

United States Department of Commerce, International Trade Administration

University of Alabama Press

University of Alberta Press

University of California Press

University of Chicago Book Warehouse

University of Chicago Press

University of Florida Press

University of Illinois Press

University of Iowa Press

University of Kansas Press

University of Massachusetts Press

University of Michigan Press

University of Mississippi Press

University of Nebraska Press

University of New Mexico Press

University of Notre Dame Press

University of Pennsylvania Press

University of Pittsburgh Press

University Press of Colorado

University of Tennessee Press

University of Texas Press

University of Toronto Press

University of Washington Press

University of Wisconsin Press

USA Today

Vanderbilt University Press

Veronis Suhler Stevenson

Wall Street Journal

Washington Post

Washington State University Press

John Wiley & Sons

Workman Publishing

Yankee Book Peddler

3 ORGANIZATIONAL CHOICE IN THE U.S. BOOK-PUBLISHING INDUSTRY: STRATEGIES FOR DOMESTIC SUCCESS AND GLOBAL COMPETITIVENESS

The U.S. book-publishing industry is a classic example of the highly successful application of the basic principles of Michael E. Porter's five forces theory.

In his book *Competitive Strategy* (1980), Porter outlined the framework that models an industry and described in some detail the importance of the following forces:

1. The degree of rivalry between firms in an industry
2. The threat of substitutes
3. Buyer power
4. Supplier power
5. Barriers to entry and threat of entry

Porter insisted that a manager, seeking to craft a strategy designed to gain an edge over competitors, could follow his model to understand clearly the nature and scope of competition within an industry (Porter 1991; Porter and Stern 2001).

We will analyze the implication of these five forces to understand the organizational choices made by a selected number of large U.S. book publishers domestically and globally. While publishing firms developed disparate strategies to become and remain competitive in different market segments, the largest companies (and especially the eight major ones) all emphasized the following: (1) become bigger than your competitors, (2) focus on certain market segments, (3) sell domestically and globally, and (4) embrace technology (especially enterprise software).

However, because of space limitations, we will concentrate on substantive issues related to the three largest U.S. book categories (in terms of net publisher revenues and net publisher units) since they are the best and most interesting examples of Porter's five forces model (Greco 1997). These book categories are the following:

1. Trade or consumer books (i.e., adult, juvenile and young adult, mass-market paperbacks, and religious books)
2. Professional and scholarly books (i.e., books in the business, legal, medical, technical, and scientific fields that are not textbooks)

3. Educational textbooks (i.e., elementary and high school (elhi) textbooks and materials, and college textbooks)

RIVALRY

We have studied the U.S. book-publishing industry for the last 20 years and are familiar with the key industry statistical data sets (covering 1947–2004; Wharton and Greco 2001, 2003a, 2003b, 2004). For the last 7 years, we have collected, aggregated, analyzed, and prepared all of the historical data as well as ARIMA (i.e., autoregressive integrated moving average, or time series) projections for the Book Industry Study Group (BISG; 2004). See appendix 3A for details. In the last 5 years, we had detailed discussions with approximately 100 industry leaders in the consumer, professional, and educational market segments. Recently, we were involved in two major studies of the industry. The first one involved mailing more than 860 questionnaires to a random sample of industry leaders in the United States; the second one involved a complete census of more than 80,000 U.S. book publishers.

On the basis of our understanding of this industry, we believe there is intense rivalry within a small cluster of firms in each one of the market segments listed previously for domestic and global revenues and market shares.

The BISG (2005) reported that the U.S. book-publishing industry in 2004 had net publisher revenues of $26.45 billion dollars (i.e., gross revenues minus returns equals net revenues; all numbers are rounded off and may not add up to 100 percent). The adult trade category accounted for slightly more than $5 billion (18.98 percent of the total). Other major categories included juvenile trade books ($1.77 billion, or 6.69 percent), mass-market paperbacks ($1.7 billion, or 6.48 percent), religious books ($1.95 billion, or 7.36 percent), professional books ($5.3 billion, or 20.08 percent), elhi textbooks and related materials ($4 billion, or 15.32 percent), and college textbooks ($3.9 billion, or 14.74 percent). See table 3.1 for details on all book categories. Please note that this total (as well as those for units and domestic consumer end user) includes both domestic and export revenues.

Our prognosis for 2005–2009 is somewhat unsettling. Total net revenues are projected to increase 17.37 percent, topping the $31 billion mark. The Congressional Budget Office (CBO; 2004) projects 11.28 percent inflation during those years; so books are anticipated to exhibit slim annual growth rates, barely exceeding the projected inflation rate.

Net publisher units (again, gross sales minus returns yields net units) in 2004 stood at 2.29 billion, and we project units to reach 2.47 billion by 2009 (+7.45 percent), another modest increase for this industry. See table 3.2 for details.

Total domestic consumer end user expenditures for all books exceeded the $39.2 billion level in 2004. By 2009 this tally should increase 18.61 percent, reaching $46.5 billion. See table 3.3 for details.

Book returns continue to be a major concern for all publishers since books can be returned for full credit, assuming all of the terms and conditions of sale are followed (Raff 2000; Szenberg and Lee 1994–1995). This practice was developed during the Great Depression (1929–1941) to encourage bookstores to stock new authors and titles with limited

TABLE 3.1
Net publisher revenues, 2004–2009 (millions of dollars)

Category	2004	2005	2006	2007	2008	2009
Adult trade total	5,020.3	5,167.8	5,270.7	5,391.0	5,513.8	5,638.7
Hardbound	3,047.0	3,134.2	3,196.0	3,268.3	3,342.1	3,417.1
Paperback	1,973.3	2,033.6	2,074.7	2,122.7	2,171.7	2,221.6
Juvenile total	1,769.2	1,855.0	1,963.8	1,983.1	2,082.9	2,188.8
Hardbound	868.7	936.5	971.8	969.3	1,046.8	1,069.8
Paperback	900.5	918.5	992.0	1,013.8	1,036.1	1,119.0
Mass-market paperback	1,713.9	1,782.3	1,837.5	1,894.7	1,949.6	2,002.9
Book-club total	1,033.9	1,030.8	1,054.2	1,080.1	1,106.4	1,134.8
Hardbound	815.7	813.3	831.8	852.2	872.9	895.4
Paperback	218.2	217.5	222.4	227.9	235.5	239.4
Mail-order total	393.6	385.6	384.9	377.7	370.0	362.5
Religious total	1,946.3	2,121.5	2,301.8	2,497.4	2,697.2	2,913.0
Hardbound	1,165.8	1,270.8	1,378.8	1,495.9	1,615.6	1,744.9
Paperback	780.5	850.7	923.0	1,001.5	1,081.6	1,168.1
Professional total	5,312.1	5,449.6	5,554.3	5,676.6	5,801.7	5,929.2
Hardbound	3,775.3	3,873.0	3,947.4	4,034.4	4,123.3	4,213.9
Paperback	1,536.8	1,576.6	1,606.9	1,642.2	1,678.4	1,715.3
University press total	437.8	450.6	463.3	476.9	490.5	504.9
Hardbound	213.9	220.3	226.6	233.2	239.9	246.9
Paperback	223.9	230.3	236.7	243.7	250.6	258.0
Elhi total	4,051.7	4,659.0	4,815.5	4,936.9	5,059.3	5,185.8
Hardbound	2,022.9	2,326.2	2,404.4	2,464.5	2,526.1	2,589.3
Paperback	2,028.8	2,332.8	2,411.1	2,471.4	2,533.2	2,595.5
College total	3,899.1	3,948.1	3,992.5	4,059.4	4,134.3	4,215.1
Hardbound	2,612.8	2,645.6	2,675.4	2,720.2	2,770.4	2,824.5
Paperback	1,286.3	1,302.5	1,317.1	1,339.2	1,363.9	1,390.6
Subscription reference	873.0	889.7	906.9	926.4	946.5	968.4
Total	26,450.9	27,740.0	28,545.4	29,299.2	30,152.2	31,044.1

SOURCE: Book Industry Study Group, Book Industry Trends 2005.

NOTE: Net revenues is gross revenues minus returns; all numbers are rounded off and may not add up to 100 percent.

TABLE 3.2
Net publisher units, 2004–2009 (millions of units)

Category	2004	2005	2006	2007	2008	2009
Adult trade total	463.7	473.9	481.5	487.5	493.6	501.2
Hardbound	234.2	237.4	240.3	242.1	243.9	245.8
Paperback	229.5	236.5	241.2	245.4	249.6	255.4
Juvenile total	480.1	484.1	501.4	494.3	500.4	516.8
Hardbound	147.2	156.1	159.3	156.3	166.2	167.2
Paperback	333.5	328.0	342.1	337.9	334.2	349.7
Mass-market paperback	535.6	540.1	540.4	541.3	541.6	541.3
Book-club total	112.4	109.7	109.8	110.2	110.6	111.3
Hardbound	35.8	34.8	34.7	34.8	34.8	35.0
Paperback	76.6	74.9	75.2	75.4	75.9	76.3
Mail-order total	53.9	51.4	50.6	49.1	48.1	46.5
Religious total	221.2	236.4	251.4	267.4	283.2	300.3
Hardbound	78.2	84.2	90.1	95.5	101.6	107.7
Paperback	142.9	152.2	161.3	171.5	181.5	192.6
Professional total	175.9	176.4	176.3	176.8	177.4	178.6
Hardbound	70.0	69.9	69.5	69.2	65.6	65.4
Paperback	105.9	106.5	106.8	107.6	111.9	113.2
University press total	23.5	23.7	24.0	24.2	24.4	24.7
Hardbound	7.2	7.3	7.3	7.4	7.5	7.6
Paperback	16.3	16.5	16.6	16.8	17.0	17.1

(*Continued*)

TABLE 3.2
(*Continued*)

Category	2004	2005	2006	2007	2008	2009
Elhi total	158.9	178.2	179.7	179.7	179.7	179.7
Hardbound	55.9	62.7	63.2	63.2	63.2	63.2
Paperback	103.0	115.6	116.5	116.5	116.5	116.5
College total	68.0	67.1	66.1	65.4	64.9	64.4
Hardbound	30.2	29.8	29.3	29.0	28.8	28.6
Paperback	37.6	37.3	36.7	36.4	36.1	35.8
Subscription reference	1.2	1.2	1.2	1.2	1.2	1.2
Total	2,295.0	2,342.2	2,382.4	2,397.1	2,435.9	2,466.0

SOURCE: Book Industry Study Group, Book Industry Trends 2005.
NOTE: Net units is gross sales minus returns.

TABLE 3.3
Domestic consumer expenditures, 2004–2009 (millions of dollars)

Category	2004	2005	2006	2007	2008	2009
Adult trade total	8,823.8	9,035.5	9,207.2	9,409.8	9,616.8	9,828.4
Hardbound	5,333.5	5,461.5	5,565.2	5,687.7	5,812.8	5,940.7
Paperback	3,490.3	3,574.0	3,642.0	3,722.1	3,804.0	3,887.7
Juvenile total	3,120.1	3,268.1	3,371.2	3,381.3	3,542.5	3,664.2
Hardbound	1,446.4	1,567.2	1,528.1	1,497.6	1,617.4	1,585.1
Paperback	1,673.7	1,700.9	1,843.1	1,883.7	1,925.1	2,079.1
Mass-market paperback	2,946.1	2,899.3	2,870.7	2,923.1	2,982.0	3,071.6
Book-club total	1,753.1	1,704.0	1,689.9	1,703.8	1,722.6	1,743.3
Hardbound	1,383.2	1,334.9	1,297.6	1,284.8	1,297.6	1,311.9
Paperback	369.9	369.1	389.3	419.0	425.0	431.4
Mail-order total	518.6	517.6	492.4	482.5	472.6	462.8
Religious total	3,763.8	4,143.9	4,537.7	4,968.8	5,417.0	5,904.5
Hardbound	2,235.3	2,568.8	2,812.7	3,065.9	3,342.1	3,642.8
Paperback	1,528.5	1,575.1	1,725.0	1,902.9	2,074.9	2,261.7
Professional total	6,600.5	6,846.6	7,104.8	7,318.0	7,493.8	7,673.7
Hardbound	4,601.7	4,777.2	4,939.7	5,083.1	5,202.8	5,322.5
Paperback	1,998.8	2,087.4	2,165.1	2,234.9	2,291.0	2,351.2
University press total	547.1	567.7	580.9	599.0	619.9	642.5
Hardbound	267.4	275.9	284.6	295.8	304.7	313.9
Paperback	279.7	291.8	296.3	303.2	315.2	328.6
Elhi total	4,585.5	5,272.9	5,449.9	5,588.9	5,727.6	5,865.1
Hardbound	2,289.6	2,610.5	2,704.3	2,773.2	2,839.8	2,908.0
Paperback	2,295.9	2,662.4	2,745.6	2,815.7	2,887.8	2,957.1
College total	5,478.6	5,703.2	5,874.9	6,053.6	6,241.2	6,428.5
Hardbound	3,671.2	3,821.7	3,940.6	4,061.6	4,183.5	4,308.9
Paperback	1,807.4	1,881.5	1,934.3	1,992.0	2,057.7	2,119.6
Subscription reference	1,064.9	1,093.9	1,118.7	1,149.3	1,179.0	1,211.2
Total	39,202.1	41,070.7	42,295.3	43,578.1	45,015.0	46,495.8

SOURCE: Book Industry Study Group, Book Industry Trends 2005.

sales potential. While some attempts were made to abolish book returns, it appears that retailers will not accept any modification in this time-tested policy.

Adult trade hardbound book returns hovered near the 33 percent level between 1995 and 2004 (reliable data for the years before 1995 were not available). Mass-market paperbacks during those years generally exceeded the 42 percent mark, reaching 45.2 percent in 2001. Most of the other categories were in the 20 percent range. See table 3.4 for details.

TABLE 3.4
Average annual book returns as a percentage of gross sales

Category	1995	1996	1997	1998	1999	2000	2001	2002	2003	2004
Adult trade hardbound	32.3	35.1	36.3	31.5	30.8	34.3	35.2	32.6	33.5	33.6
Adult trade paperbound	23.5	25.0	23.6	23.6	22.7	23.1	22.0	19.9	22.9	23.1
Juvenile trade hardbound	17.1	18.7	17.3	16.9	15.6	12.6	21.0	24.9	20.2	20.9
Juvenile trade paperbound	15.0	18.9	26.4	21.1	24.5	19.8	13.5	20.4	22.0	21.4
Mass-market paperback	42.3	43.5	46.4	43.5	43.4	43.4	45.2	41.8	45.2	47.1
Mail-order total	21.8	20.7	25.2	24.7	26.4	27.1	—	—	—	—
Book-club total	—	19.6	20.0	19.6	20.5	19.7	—	—	—	—
Bibles, testaments, etc.	7.7	10.9	13.6	—	—	—	—	—	13.5	15.2
Technical, scientific, business, law, medical, etc.	15.1	17.2	15.5	15.1	16.2	20.5	19.8	19.0	21.4	19.6
University press hardbound	16.8	19.1	17.6	16.8	18.5	20.6	20.2	25.2	19.5	15.4
University press paperbound	19.5	22.9	20.3	21.4	20.9	26.4	24.6	25.3	23.8	14.0
College	21.6	23.1	23.2	23.6	22.8	24.7	23.0	21.9	22.7	22.9

SOURCE: Book Industry Study Group, Book Industry Trends, various years.

NOTE: Average annual book return rates are based on the submission of data from a broad number of book-publishing firms. Data not available for all book categories for every year.

TABLE 3.5
Concentration by largest U.S. book publishing firms, 2002

Number of largest firms	Revenues (thousands of dollars)	Percentage	Annual payroll of total (thousands of dollars)	Number of employees
4	11,362,672	41.8	1,635,985	28,648
8	15,372,994	56.6	2,158,031	34,947
20	19,547,635	72.0	2,969,833	49,032
50	21,800,921	80.3	3,448,937	57,842
All firms	27,162,866	100.00	4,879,506	95,175

SOURCE: U.S. Department of Commerce, Census of Information 2002.

While there are a sizable number of U.S. book-publishing houses, a relatively small number of them account for the majority of all net revenues. The U.S. Department of Commerce, Bureau of the Census (2004) collected detailed data on 3,570 book-publishing firms in 2002. While that is a relatively large number of establishments, Commerce's data revealed the level of concentration (concentration ratios, or CRs) held by eight houses.

The four largest firms accounted for 41.8 percent of all revenues, while the eight largest companies had a CR of 56.6 percent. See table 3.5 for details on revenues, payroll, and the number of employees.

The eight largest publishing establishments with a U.S. market share were the following:

1. Pearson PLC (its international headquarters is in the United Kingdom; trade and educational books)

2. Thomson (Canada; professional and educational books)

3. Reed Elsevier (United Kingdom and the Netherlands; professional and educational books)

4. Scholastic (United States; consumer and educational books)

T A B L E 3 . 6
Largest U.S. book publishers (millions of dollars)

Publisher	1997	1998	1999	2000	2001	2002	2003
Simon & Schuster	2,470	2,470	596	597	649	660	640
Pearson	1,796	2,033	4,145	4,086	4,901	3,900	4,006
Harcourt	1,481	1,860	2,408	2,409	1,197	—	—
Random House	1,250	1,730	1,995	1,612	1,805	1,463	1,400
McGraw-Hill	1,575	1,620	2,000	1,993	2,322	1,496	1,959
Thomson	1,580	1,530	1,600	1,601	1,781	3,400	1,457
Scholastic	1,058	1,165	1,962	1,961	1,917	1,639	1,864
Time Warner	1,120	1,115	990	300	310	350	355
Wolters Kluwer	930	1,020	1,590	1,591	1,610	1,300	973
Reader's Digest	1,110	756	831	757	670	604	536
Reed Elsevier	920	1,060	1,020	1,849	2,736	2,700	2,406
Houghton Mifflin	797	862	1,030	1,035	1,126	1,180	1,259
HarperCollins	737	764	1,029	1,029	1,078	855	920
Harlequin/Torstar	443	319	394	393	396	340	237
John Wiley	467	508	614	615	734	524	567
Bantam Doubleday Dell	960	480	—	—	—	—	—
Encyclopedias Britannica	370	360	340	341	370	280	273
Grolier	380	425	450	—	—	—	—
Tribune	226	349	340	—	—	—	—
Holtzbrinck	320	300	300	280	300	320	322
Rodale	—	230	270	260	247	215	290
Hungry Minds	—	230	202	—	—	—	—
WRC Media	—	219	219	232	—	210	203
BNA	—	—	250	260	—	263	267
Thomas Nelson	—	—	—	—	—	188	195

s o u r c e : *Subtext.*

n o t e : Data are not available for all publishers for all years. Fluctuations in revenues are due to a variety of factors, including currency exchange rates, mergers, and acquisitions. Some of the major acquisitions include (1) Bantam Doubleday Dell's of Random House, which acquired Golden Books; (2) HarperCollins' of the Hearst Book Group; (3) Pearson's of Putnam Berkeley; (4) Scholastic's of Grolier; (5) John Wiley's of IDG Books; (6) Reed Elsevier's of Harcourt.

5. McGraw-Hill (United States; professional and educational books)

6. Random House (Germany; consumer books)

7. Wolters Kluwer (Netherlands; professional books)

8. Houghton Mifflin (United States; consumer and educational books)

Additional analysis revealed that the 20 largest corporate entities had a CR of 72 percent; the 50 largest companies topped 80.3 percent. See table 3.6 for details.

All of the U.S. firms active in the domestic market, as well as the various global conglomerates that entered the U.S. market, for that matter, positioned themselves optimally by acquiring existing U.S. firms. Depending on their market niche (e.g., consumer, professional, or educational), they followed two different competitive strategies: (1) product differentiation (e.g., Random House focusing on consumer-book backlist and frontlist titles and various genres; Reed Elsevier, McGraw-Hill, Wolters Kluwer, and Thomson focusing on the professional book market; or Houghton Mifflin and McGraw-Hill focusing on the college textbook niche); or (2) a cost leadership position (e.g., Scholastic or Pearson, i.e., Penguin, in the adult trade paperbound or mass-market paperback niches).

TABLE 3.7
Trade publishers: global revenues (millions of dollars)

Rank	Publisher	Parent	FISCAL YEAR		
			2001–2002	2002–2003	2003–2004
1	Random House	Bertelsmann AG	2,137	1,975	2,000
2	Penguin Putnam	Pearson	1,320	1,500	1,504
3	HarperCollins	News Corp.	1,078	1,162	1,276
4	Simon & Schuster	Viacom	660	688	693
5	Time Warner	Time Warner	380	408	412
6	John Wiley	John Wiley	292	369	393
7	St. Martin's– Holt-Farrar-Straus-Giroux	Holtzbrinck	306	320	322
8	Scholastic	Scholastic	215	208	320
9	Thomas Nelson	Thomas Nelson	188	188	195
10	Houghton Mifflin	Houghton Mifflin	147	145	125
	Total		6,723	6,929	7,240

SOURCE: *Subtext.*

NOTE: The trade book category includes adult hardbound, adult paperbound, juvenile hardbound, juvenile paperbound, and mass-market paperback.

Many of these same companies were major players in the global market. See table 3.7 for details.

There was intense rivalry in the trade, or consumer, book segment. This U.S. market was dominated by Random House, long known for its strong frontlist and deep backlist; Bertelsmann AG consolidated its Bantam Doubleday Dell operations with Random House in March 1998. HarperCollins, Penguin (with an extensive paperback backlist), and Simon & Schuster round out the top four in 2003 (CR 14.85 percent); the next four firms were Time Warner, John Wiley & Sons, St. Martin's–Holt-Farrar-Straus-Giroux, and Scholastic, with a CR of 19.98 percent. See table 3.8 for details.

Reed Elsevier, Thomson, Wolters Kluwer, and John Wiley dominate the international professional book business (see table 3.9). Pearson, McGraw-Hill, Thomson, and Harcourt achieved impressive sales results in the global educational market (Thornton 2004). See table 3.10 for details.

Some mention is needed of the apparent (and perhaps unsettling) disparity between data sets. While the U.S. Department of Commerce does a superb job of collecting and aggregating data on the book-publishing industry, there is an inevitable lag between collection and publication (often two to three years). The end result is a bit of a challenge to researchers since the important U.S.-based reporting services (notably the BISG, Subtext, and Bowker) are able to gather and release their data at a faster pace than Commerce. For example, the BISG released its estimated data on 2002 in May 2003, approximately 18 months before Commerce published its 2002 data, in September 2004. So it is quite usual that Commerce's statistics on net revenues, for example, will differ from data released by the BISG and others. One must be somewhat cautious in using data from Commerce without comparing their results with other reliable statistical data sets. Accordingly, some of the data in our tables came from Commerce as well as other sources; and at times all of the data will not be in harmony.

TABLE 3.8
Trade publisher revenues: U.S. market (millions of dollars)

	YEAR								
Publisher	1995	1996	1997	1998	1999	2000	2001	2002	2003
Random House	1,255	1,220	1,250	1,580	1,410	1,685	1,350	1,463	1,400
Penguin Putnam	—	—	845	875	705	820	787	810	902
HarperCollins	—	754	737	750	780	800	790	835	920
Simon & Schuster	—	—	—	—	590	578	625	660	640
Time Warner	—	—	310	310	298	276	297	350	350
St. Martin's– Holt-Farrar-Straus-Giroux	260	242	300	285	300	280	300	320	322
Scholastic	136	160	—	—	—	325	210	208	320
Thomas Nelson	162	153	164	—	183	202	202	188	195
John Wiley	—	—	—	—	—	—	162	322	340
Houghton Mifflin	87	88	89	89	89	95	110	145	125
Bantam Doubleday Dell	670	670	680	—	—	—	—	—	—
Reader's Digest	556	561	—	—	—	—	—	—	—
Grolier	—	465	480	—	—	—	—	—	—
Macmillan	—	385	420	—	—	—	—	—	—
Putnam Berkeley	300	292	—	—	—	—	—	—	—
Harlequin	194	225	343	—	—	—	—	—	—
Rodale	198	220	245	—	—	—	—	—	—
Hungry Minds	—	—	—	—	—	200	—	—	—
Golden Books	255	171	172	—	—	—	—	—	—
Hearst Book Group	160	158	170	180	—	—	—	—	—
Disney Publishing	69	125	135	—	—	—	—	—	—
Barnes & Noble	85	120	150	—	—	—	—	—	—
Andrews & McMeel	92	100	87	—	85	—	—	—	—
IDG Books	60	98	121	165	—	—	—	—	—

SOURCE: *Subtext.*

NOTE: Data are not available for all publishers for all years. Fluctuations in revenues are due to a variety of factors, including currency exchange rates, mergers, and acquisitions. Some of the major acquisitions include (1) Bantam Doubleday Dell's of Random House, which acquired Golden Books; (2) HarperCollins' of the Hearst Book Group; (3) Pearson's of Putnam Berkeley; (4) Scholastic's of Grolier; (5) John Wiley's of IDG Books.

TABLE 3.9
Professional publisher total international revenues (millions of U.S. dollars)

	YEAR						
Publisher	1997	1998	1999	2000	2001	2002	2003
Thomson	3,954	4,346	3,959	4,865	5,175	5,248	5,425
Reed Elsevier	3,778	4,167	4,544	4,692	4,997	6,411	6,420
Wolters Kluwer	2,286	2,341	2,647	2,963	3,097	2,630	2,211
Harcourt	451	527	698	745	—	—	—
John Wiley	355	389	451	456	530	759	819
McGraw-Hill	451	429	429	443	448	485	470
BNA	220	230	250	250	260	263	267
Taylor & Francis						262	309
Simon & Schuster	200	190	—	—	—	—	—

SOURCE: *Subtext.*

NOTE: Fluctuations in revenues are due to a variety of factors, including currency exchange rates, mergers, and acquisitions.

Overall, the disparity between modest increases in revenues and flat or declining unit to-tals is unsettling. A review of data on average net dollars per unit between 1985 and 2004 (with projections through 2009) indicated clearly that many publishers did not follow a cost advantage strategy in the U.S. market. The majority raised prices in excess of changes (or

TABLE 3.10
Educational publisher international revenues (millions of U.S. dollars)

Publisher	YEAR						
	1997	1998	1999	2000	2001	2002	2003
Pearson	906	1,130	2,580	3,090	3,704	4,933	4,387
McGraw-Hill	1,320	1,390	1,310	1,550	2,322	2,275	2,286
Thomson	484	677	659	834	1,851	2,036	2,052
Harcourt	802	918	948	1,120	—	1,768	1,598
Houghton Mifflin	709	773	858	925	1,008	985	1,074
Scholastic	200	191	231	310	316	326	369
WRC Media	—	—	214	219	232	209	203
John Wiley	101	119	155	160	165	176	189
Simon & Schuster	1,360	1,200	—	—	—	—	—
Tribune	226	329	340	—	—	—	—
Primedia	160	331	318	—	—	—	—
Reed Elsevier	—	—	—	291	834	—	—
Torstar	89	116	135	104	—	—	—

SOURCE: *Subtext.*

NOTE: Fluctuations in revenues are due to a variety of factors, including currency exchange rates, mergers, and acquisitions.

projections) in the CPI. Average price of adult hardbounds grew from $5.89 in 1985 to a projected $13.90 in 2009 (+135.99 percent). Five of the other trade categories posted similar results for these same years: adult paperbound, up 162.84 percent; juvenile paperbound, up 158.06 percent; mass-market paperback, up 97.86 percent; religious hardbound, up 138.59 percent; and religious paperbound, up 165.22 percent. Only the increase of juvenile hardbound (+88.24 percent) was smaller than the CPI's 95.36 percent. See table 3.11 for details on the consumer-book market.

This same pattern (i.e., eschewing a cost advantage strategy) was also evident in the professional book segment (1985–2009: hardbound +133.96 percent; paperbound +113.30 percent). However, a cost advantage strategy was evident in the business (+77.84 percent) and legal book (+76.30 percent) categories. This strategy was adopted because these categories were hammered by the seductive electronic distribution opportunities offered by a number of major firms (e.g., Moody's, McGraw-Hill, Dow Jones, VNU) in marketing information, economic and financial data, etc. Ironically, a cost advantage strategy was not present in the medical (+148.56 percent) and eclectic technical, scientific, and other (+132.31 percent) book segment, although it is likely that these two categories will adopt a cost advantage strategy since they both face the specter of electronic distribution systems cutting deeply into print sales. See table 3.12 for details.

Educational publishing totals were quite high: elhi hardbound increased 348.09 percent; elhi paperbound, 446.57 percent; college hardbound, 596.87 percent; and college paperbound, 553.20 percent. See table 3.13 for details.

Detailed information on the CPI's 95.35 percent increase between 1985 and 2009 (as well as data on the GNP and changes in the U.S. population) are in table 3.14.

Ironically, despite sagging unit sales and lackluster export totals, U.S. book publishers released at least 1,820,608 new titles between 1980 and 2003 (because of statistical undercounting before 1997, it is likely the total was much larger). See table 3.15 for details on new title output and table 3.16 for export tallies.

TABLE 3.11
Net publisher revenues: consumer books, 1985–2009 (average dollars per unit)

Year	Adult hardbound	Paperbound	Juvenile hardbound	Paperbound	Mass-market paperback	Religious hardbound	Paperbound
1985	5.89	3.31	3.40	1.24	1.87	6.79	2.30
1986	6.23	3.51	3.47	1.34	1.88	7.06	2.43
1987	6.88	4.11	3.55	1.70	2.07	8.18	2.76
1988	7.43	4.52	3.64	1.96	2.13	9.04	3.05
1989	7.91	4.87	3.74	2.11	2.20	9.54	3.21
1990	8.40	5.19	3.92	2.24	2.35	9.79	3.27
1991	8.82	5.44	4.14	2.36	2.49	10.13	3.44
1992	9.29	5.73	4.31	2.41	2.55	10.50	3.51
1993	9.79	6.07	4.48	2.51	2.67	10.92	3.67
1994	10.47	6.20	4.49	2.70	2.68	11.06	3.74
1995	10.60	6.75	4.50	2.86	2.83	11.27	3.83
1996	10.85	7.10	4.39	3.18	2.96	11.41	3.89
1997	11.19	7.26	4.72	3.14	3.03	11.55	3.94
1998	9.30	6.00	4.75	3.22	3.70	11.73	4.01
1999	11.20	7.40	4.90	2.10	2.80	12.60	4.60
2000	11.40	7.80	5.10	2.20	2.90	13.10	4.80
2001	11.80	8.00	5.30	2.60	3.00	13.50	4.90
2002	12.50	8.20	5.30	2.60	3.00	13.60	4.90
2003	12.80	8.50	5.80	2.60	3.10	14.60	5.30
2004	13.00	8.60	5.90	2.70	3.20	14.90	5.50
2005	13.20	8.60	6.00	2.80	3.30	15.10	5.60
2006	13.3	8.60	6.10	2.90	3.40	15.30	5.70
2007	13.50	8.60	6.20	3.00	3.50	15.60	5.80
2008	13.70	8.70	6.30	3.10	3.60	15.90	6.00
2009	13.90	8.70	6.40	3.20	3.70	16.20	6.10

SOURCE: Book Industry Study Group, Book Industry Trends, various years.

NOTE: As of 1999, new data on net publisher revenues were obtained from highly reliable industry data sets. It was not possible to reevaluate the data for 1985–1998.

TABLE 3.12
Net publisher revenues: professional books, 1985–2009 (average dollars per unit)

Year	Hardbound	Paperbound	Business	Law	Medical	Technical, scientific, & other
1985	26.80	7.22	11.64	36.87	26.35	8.48
1986	28.09	7.20	11.52	36.80	27.28	8.87
1987	29.42	7.39	11.85	37.68	28.03	9.31
1988	31.25	7.64	12.71	38.58	29.93	9.76
1989	33.12	7.95	13.09	40.15	32.70	10.32
1990	34.53	8.31	13.64	42.11	34.18	10.61
1991	36.08	8.69	14.13	43.81	36.51	10.62
1992	37.68	9.07	14.17	45.12	38.44	11.23
1993	39.56	9.50	14.77	46.79	43.82	11.71
1994	41.57	9.94	14.66	49.39	41.66	12.55
1995	43.70	10.42	15.29	52.06	43.75	13.09
1996	45.56	10.81	15.96	56.29	46.62	13.43
1997	47.21	11.18	16.14	59.16	48.66	13.79
1998	48.80	11.52	15.93	62.44	51.34	14.38
1999	50.50	11.70	16.00	63.70	51.20	15.10
2000	52.20	12.00	16.90	65.50	53.30	15.60
2001	53.50	12.40	17.30	54.60	55.30	17.50
2002	54.60	13.10	17.80	55.60	55.60	17.90
2003	52.60	13.90	18.20	56.90	56.90	18.00
2004	53.90	14.50	18.60	58.20	58.20	18.30

TABLE 3.12
(*Continued*)

Year	Hardbound	Paperbound	Business	Law	Medical	Technical, scientific, & other
2005	55.40	14.80	19.10	59.70	59.50	18.60
2006	56.80	15.00	19.50	61.10	61.10	18.90
2007	58.30	15.30	19.90	62.40	62.60	19.20
2008	60.90	15.30	20.30	63.80	63.80	19.50
2009	62.70	15.40	20.70	65.00	65.50	19.70

SOURCE: Book Industry Study Group, Book Industry Trends, various years.

NOTE: As of 1999, new data on net publisher revenues were obtained from highly reliable industry data sets. It was not possible to reevaluate the data for 1985–1998. Revenues for business, law, and medical and scientific, technical, and other are for total revenues (hardbound and paperbound).

TABLE 3.13
Net publisher revenues: educational textbooks, 1985–2009 (average dollars per unit)

Year	Elhi hardbound	Paperbound	College hardbound	Paperbound
1985	9.15	4.08	15.35	5.94
1986	9.80	4.55	16.45	6.37
1987	11.15	5.44	16.87	6.54
1988	11.95	6.07	17.43	6.73
1989	12.40	6.62	18.09	7.08
1990	12.81	6.92	19.32	7.68
1991	13.25	7.12	19.98	8.05
1992	13.54	7.06	20.76	8.09
1993	13.93	7.33	21.69	8.42
1994	13.98	7.20	21.96	8.56
1995	14.16	7.40	22.45	8.83
1996	14.46	7.53	22.89	9.05
1997	14.69	7.64	23.81	9.42
1998	15.65	8.08	24.67	9.77
1999	35.60	18.10	73.96	29.30
2000	37.20	18.84	75.66	30.10
2001	36.80	19.48	78.31	30.60
2002	36.20	18.18	82.03	32.00
2003	35.30	19.20	84.32	32.80
2004	36.20	19.70	86.52	34.00
2005	37.10	20.20	88.78	34.90
2006	38.00	20.70	91.31	35.90
2007	39.00	21.20	93.80	36.80
2008	40.00	21.70	96.19	37.80
2009	41.00	22.30	106.97	38.80

SOURCE: Book Industry Study Group, Book Industry Trends, various years.

NOTE: As of 1999, new data on net publisher revenues were obtained from highly reliable industry data sets. It was not possible to reevaluate the data for 1985–1998.

THREAT OF SUBSTITUTES

Why was there a decline in unit sales? Individuals purchase books for different reasons. Consumers buy a trade book to be entertained, informed, or educated. Professional book publishers, on the other hand, rely on individuals seeking cutting-edge information about medical or scientific data, directory-type information, or updated information about business or legal issues (perhaps an analysis of a new ruling from the Financial Accounting Standards

TABLE 3.14

U.S. consumer price index, gross national product, and population, 1985–2009 (billions of dollars)

Year	CPI	Change from previous year (%)	GNP ($)	Change from previous year (%)	Population (thousands)	Change from previous year (%)
1985	107.6	3.6	4,180.7	7.13	238,466	0.90
1986	109.6	1.9	4,422.2	5.78	240,651	0.92
1987	113.6	3.6	4,692.3	6.11	242,804	0.89
1988	118.3	4.1	5,049.6	7.61	245,021	0.91
1989	124.0	4.8	5,489.1	8.70	247,342	0.95
1990	130.7	5.4	5,803.1	5.72	250,132	1.13
1991	136.2	4.2	5,995.9	3.32	253,493	1.34
1992	140.3	3.0	6,337.7	5.70	256,894	1.34
1993	144.5	3.0	6,657.4	5.04	260,255	1.31
1994	148.2	2.6	7,072.2	6.23	263,436	1.22
1995	152.4	2.8	7,397.7	4.60	266,557	1.18
1996	156.9	2.9	7,816.9	5.67	269,667	1.17
1997	160.5	2.3	8,304.3	6.24	272,912	1.20
1998	163.0	1.6	8,747.0	5.33	276,115	1.17
1999	166.6	2.2	9,268.4	5.96	279,295	1.15
2000	172.2	3.4	9,817.0	5.92	282,388	1.11
2001	177.0	2.8	10,100.8	2.89	285,321	1.04
2002	179.2	1.6	10,480.8	3.76	288,205	1.01
2003	184.0	2.3	10,987.9	4.84	291,049	0.99
2004	188.9	2.7	11,730.0*	6.75	—	—
2005	193.4	2.4	12,396.0*	5.68	—	—
2006	197.1	1.9	13,059.0*	5.35	—	—
2007	201.3	2.1	13,725.0*	5.10	—	—
2008	205.7	2.2	14,425.0*	5.10	—	—
2009	210.2	2.2	15,160.7*	5.10	—	—

SOURCE: Congressional Budget Office estimates for 2005–2009. Bowker Annual, various years. U.S. Department of Commerce, Bureau of the Census.

NOTE: Base year 1982–1984 = 100.

*Estimate.

TABLE 3.15

U.S. book title output

Year	New titles	Change (%)
1980	42,377	−6.21
1981	48,793	15.14
1982	46,935	−3.81
1983	53,380	13.73
1984	51,058	−4.35
1985	50,070	−1.94
1986	52,637	5.13
1987	56,027	6.44
1988	55,483	−0.97
1989	53,446	−3.67
1990	46,743	−12.54
1991	48,146	3.00
1992	49,276	2.35
1993	49,757	0.98
1994	51,863	4.23
1995	62,039	19.62
1996	68,175	9.89
1997	119,262*	—
1998	120,244	0.82

TABLE 3.15
(*Continued*)

Year	New titles	Change (%)
1999	119,357	−0.74
2000	122,108	2.30
2001	141,703	16.05
2002	147,120	3.82
2003	164,609	11.89
2004	195,000	18.46

SOURCE: Bowker Annual.

*In 1997 Bowker evaluated its methodology, discovering undercounting. While the total for 1997 reflected this change, Bowker did not recalculate tallies for previous years, producing a significant increase over 1996's total.

TABLE 3.16
U.S. book exports, number of book-publishing establishments, and number of employees, 1977–2002

Year	Exports (millions of dollars)	Number of book publishing establishments	Number of employees
1977	—	1,745	60,000
1982	—	2,130	67,000
1985	591.2	—	—
1987	—	2,298	70,000
1990	1,415.1	—	—
1992	1,636,799	2,644	80,000
1993	1,663,605	—	—
1994	1,703,174	—	—
1995	1,779,485	—	—
1996	1,775,638	—	—
1997	1,896,636	2,684	89,898
1998	1,841,821	—	—
1999	1,871,068	—	—
2000	1,876,958	—	—
2001	1,712,335	—	
2002	1,681,229	3,570	95,175
2003	1,693,574	—	
2004	1,740,519	—	

SOURCE: U.S. Department of Commerce, International Trade Administration.

Board or opinions on a recent U.S. Supreme Court decision). Students in public elementary or secondary schools are provided free textbooks by their school district (Newman et al. 2001); college students purchase books selected (i.e., adopted) by college professors.

Clearly, consumer-book publishing was whipsawed by the seductive array of media and entertainment options, ranging from satellite and cable television to iPods and the Internet. The end result was a substantive change in media usage for consumer books (i.e., the total number of hours per year every person older than 18 spends reading books. In 1984, a leap year, consumer-book usage stood at 80 hours (i.e., 13.11 minutes per day). By 1996 (the best year in recent history), that annual total increased to 123 hours (20.16 minutes per day).

TABLE 3.17
Media usage hours per person per year, 1984–1993

Format	1984	1985	1986	1987	1988	1989	1990	1991	1992	1993
Network-affiliated television stations	1,000	985	985	912	865	835	780	838	914	920
Independent TV stations	335	335	339	332	349	345	340	227	159	162
Total broadcast television	1,335	1,320	1,324	1,244	1,214	1,180	1,120	1,065	1,073	1,082
Basic cable & satellite TV	100	120	126	157	182	210	260	340	359	375
Premium cable & satellite TV	—	—	—	—	—	—	—	90	78	78
Total cable & satellite TV	100	120	126	157	182	210	260	430	437	453
Total TV	1,435	1,440	1,450	1,401	1,396	1,390	1,380	1,495	1,510	1,535
Broadcast & satellite radio	1,190	1,190	1,205	1,155	1,165	1,155	1,135	1,115	1,150	1,082
Recorded music	191	185	173	200	215	220	235	219	233	248
Consumer Internet	—	—	—	—	—	—	—	1	2	2
Daily newspapers	185	185	184	180	178	175	175	169	172	170
Consumer magazines	110	110	109	110	110	90	90	88	85	85
Consumer books	80	80	88	88	90	96	95	98	100	99
Home video	9	15	22	29	35	39	42	40	42	43
Box office	12	12	10	11	11	11	10	11	11	12
Interactive TV	—	—	—	—	—	—	—	—	—	—
Total	3,212	3,217	3,241	3,174	3,200	3,176	3,162	3,236	3,305	3,276

SOURCE: Veronis Suhler Stevenson, various years.

TABLE 3.18
Media usage hours per person per year, 1994–2003

Format	1994	1995	1996	1997	1998	1999	2000	2001	2002	2003
Network-affiliated television stations	919	865	811	752	710	710	799	767	721	704
Independent TV stations	172	179	177	174	171	157	67	67	66	65
Total broadcast television	1,091	1,044	988	926	881	867	866	833	787	769
Basic cable & satellite TV	388	447	487	521	571	615	633	692	760	809
Premium cable & satellite TV	81	89	88	101	99	106	136	151	158	167
Total cable & satellite TV	469	537	575	622	670	720	769	843	918	975
Total TV	1,560	1,580	1,563	1,548	1,551	1,588	1,635	1,676	1,705	1,745
Broadcast & satellite radio	1,102	970	975	941	911	939	943	955	990	1,002
Recorded music	294	288	292	264	275	281	258	229	220	184
Consumer Internet	3	5	8	26	39	64	107	139	158	176
Daily newspapers	169	166	192	186	186	183	180	177	175	171
Consumer magazines	84	113	125	136	134	134	135	127	125	121
Consumer books	102	101	123	116	118	119	109	106	109	108
Home video	45	49	34	49	51	48	51	56	65	70
Box office	12	12	12	12	13	13	12	13	14	13
Interactive TV	—	—	—	—	—	2	2	2	2	2
Total	3,401	3,284	3,324	3,278	3,278	3,371	3,492	3,540	3,606	3,663

SOURCE: Veronis Suhler Stevenson, various years.

By 2004 the total number of hours dropped to 107 (17.54 minutes per day); the projection for 2008 is 104 hours (17.05 minutes per day). Tables 3.17, 3.18, and 3.19 outline these trends and provides detailed information about the increase in total media usage in the United States between 1984 (3,212 hours) and 2008 (4,059 hours; +26.37 percent).

A substantive shift away from printed professional books (and indeed a similar shift away from both printed newspapers and printed magazines) in the United States toward the electronic delivery of media and entertainment content (via broadcast, cable, or satellite

TABLE 3.19
Media usage hours per person per year, 2004–2008

Format	2004	2005	2006	2007	2008
Network-affiliated television stations	717	721	726	731	738
Independent TV stations	65	64	64	63	62
Total broadcast television	782	785	790	794	800
Basic cable & satellite TV	834	861	882	903	934
Premium cable & satellite TV	176	181	186	190	197
Total cable & satellite TV	1,010	1,042	1,068	1,093	1,131
Total TV	1,792	1,826	1,858	1,887	1,931
Broadcast & satellite radio	1,035	1,040	1,070	1,080	1,120
Recorded music	180	176	174	170	167
Consumer Internet	189	200	213	225	236
Daily newspapers	169	168	165	165	164
Consumer magazines	118	116	113	111	110
Consumer books	107	106	106	105	104
Home video	78	85	94	103	110
Box office	13	13	13	13	14
Interactive TV	3	3	4	4	5
Total	3,757	3,809	3,890	3,949	4,059

SOURCE: Veronis Suhler Stevenson, various years.

television or radio; podcasting; the Internet; etc.) cut precariously into what had been a rather stable print market segment.

By the 1990s it became apparent, and painfully so to many, that a major change occurred in the college textbook market because of the used-book market (Pecorino 2004). For example, in 2001 we were told during numerous interviews with industry leaders that sell-through rates stood at about 90 percent in the first year a new text was released. By the second year, that total slipped drastically to between 30 and 45 percent (depending on the availability of used texts); and by the third and final year of the average text's life only a 10 percent sell-though was the norm. In 2006 this ratio had shifted sharply to a 90 percent sell-through rate in the first year and a 30 percent rate in the second year, compelling many publishers to use a two-year revision cycle since sales in the third year were, at best, remarkably small. So the emergence of a sophisticated used-book market jeopardized the college publisher's traditional three-year business model. Companies emerged as if by wizardry, buying used textbooks from college bookstores and students (and faculty members) and offering them to college bookstores eager to capitalize on a growing market for used texts. The fact that the profit margin for a used book (33 percent) exceeded that of a new text (25 percent) was an additional inducement for beleaguered college bookstore managers to stock used textbooks. The vast majority of college bookstores adopted a cost advantage strategy. Their goal for a course was to acquire at least half the total number of required texts as used books; some store managers actually tried to buy 75 percent used and 25 percent new. Of course, the proliferation of online sites selling used textbooks at deep discounts posed a challenge to traditional college bookstores, forcing the stores to adopt this robust 75 percent/25 percent cost advantage strategy.

We estimate that the used textbook market cost book publishers at least $2 billion in 2006, with steady increases projected for the next few years.

Compounding the problem was the development of sophistical electronic reserve (ERes) systems in college libraries, allowing faculty members to place on the library's computer system trade and textbook chapters, articles, and case studies for student use (and ultimately avoiding ordering textbooks). ERes enabled students to read and download these materials in the library, in a dorm room, etc. In addition, the widespread availability of high-quality copiers allowed students to copy course readings inexpensively. We were unable to develop any reliable models to generate estimated revenues lost to textbook publishers because of ERes or copier options.

One possible solution could be the adoption of a print-on-demand (POD) strategy. POD allows a publisher to utilize the Dell computer business model: that is, sell the product and then manufacture it (rather than producing a product on speculation, which has been the business model since Gutenberg). While unit manufacturing costs are higher with a POD book (versus the traditional lithographic process), POD's digital output is impressive (as is the binding). Concerns have been expressed, however, about (1) the possibility of someone gaining control illegally over the digital version of a book (and then crafting an effective book piracy strategy), and (2) the logistics of launching and maintaining POD operations (in retail stores, on college campuses, etc.). It is likely that these concerns will be addressed and that a national POD system could be created, assuming enough publishers agreed to allow their books to be under the control of outside vendors running POD operations.

However, used books were freely available in the adult consumer-book marketplace (Ghose, Smith, and Telang 2004) as well as in the religious and professional book category. For example, many of the online and auction services offered new and used copies of new consumer books; we know that used copies of the Harry Potter book published in the United States on July 16, 2005, were available online one to three days after the official publication date (and a review of various online bookselling sites revealed that a small number of used books were available on July 16). Our models indicate that the used-book market for consumer and religious books in 2006 hovered near the $1 billion mark, with additional increases (perhaps as much as 10 percent annually) projected for 2006 and the next few years.

The emergence of used books helped undermine the inherent appeal and vitality of the mass-market paperback in America. This was due to an odd combination of disparate albeit powerful market forces. First, adult trade books were generally discounted (often by 20–30 percent). Second, many book retailers (and especially the big superstore chains) rarely discounted paperbacks. Third, the average suggested retail price for a mass-market paperback in 2004 was $7.99, versus the average adult trade hardbound book's $25. So the price point for a hardbound book discounted 30 percent was $17.50 versus $7.99 for a paperback, a savings of $9.51. Fourth, the proliferation of used books (often selling at discounted rates well in excess of 50 percent) lowered the price of a more durable hardbound book to perhaps $12, a difference of only $4.01 between hardbound and paperback books. So a consumer could buy a discounted hardbound best seller now for $12 or wait perhaps 9 to 12 months for a $7.99 version. That is, of course, unless one wanted a copy of *The Da Vinci Code*, a bestselling book available only in hardbound two years after its publication date; the paperback version did become available when the motion picture was released in June 2006. While it is difficult to argue that the 1.7 percent decline in net revenues of mass-market paperbacks in 2004 was due solely to the impact of used books, it is clear that a portion of that decline was attributable to used-book sales since used books were also readily available in a number of different channels, including traditional bookstores and the Internet.

While a book is not a commodity, the tremendous array of media and entertainment formats, when coupled with the constantly spreading availability of used books, amplified the threat of substitutes for new books (Greco 2000a, 2000b).

BUYER POWER

In 2006 more than 23,000 retail establishments sold books in the United States (including Wal-Mart, supermarkets, convenience stores, and transportation terminals). Of that total, approximately 5,700 were traditional bookstores (i.e., their primary business was bookselling). Independent (nonchain) bookstores totaled about 2,700, although their total continued to drop in recent years (noticeably in the Christian bookstore segment), and the large chains accounted for about 3,000 stores.

Traditional bookstores account for 42.52 percent of all book sales in the United States. The remaining portion is purchased by libraries and individuals shopping for books in retail stores, including price clubs, large retail stores (e.g., Wal-Mart; Kmart), convenience stores, online, and bus-subway-airline newsstands.

However, the traditional bookstore market was dominated by Barnes & Noble (with 866 stores), Borders (1,242 stores), Books-A-Million, Family Christian Stores, Musicland, Hastings, and Tower. Of these companies, Barnes & Noble and Borders amassed tremendous buyer power after 1985 with the emergence of sophisticated superstores, averaging 170,000 unique book titles and offering coffee, cappuccino, bagels, comfortable furniture, attractive signage, lighting, and ambiance. If Barnes & Noble or Borders decided not to stock a publisher's new trade book or order only "ones" (i.e., order one copy for each store in the chain), or if Wal-Mart decided not to sell a book because of its content or cover artwork, the publisher's economic business model for that title was jeopardized.

Both Barnes & Noble and Borders sell books online (competing for market share with Amazon.com). For example, Barnes & Noble offers more than 1,000,000 new titles and 30,000,000 used and out-of-print books for what they describe as the "fast and free delivery" of books (i.e., free on orders of $25 or more).

Traditional bookstore revenues experienced 30.68 percent growth between 1997 and 2004. While the seven largest chains accounted for 53.88 percent of all book revenues, the two principal ones (Barnes & Noble and Borders) handled 47.52 percent of these transactions. Table 3.20 outlines total revenues, and table 3.21 lists market shares.

A substantive development was the decision of Barnes & Noble and Borders to become trade and professional book publishers. While both companies had long published attractive leather-bound versions of the classics (all out of copyright protection), by 2000 both decided to enter the new trade book business, effectively competing with the trade houses for authors, titles, and "real estate" (i.e., shelf and display space in the bookstores).

Clearly, by 2005 and 2006 the buyers had more power than the publishers, prompting several publishers to start selling books directly to consumers. It is too soon to evaluate the

TABLE 3.20
Largest U.S. bookstore chains, 1997–2004 (millions of dollars)

Chain	1997	1998	1999	2000	2001	2002	2003	2004
Barnes & Noble	2,796.8	3,000.0	3,006.0	3,552.0	3,681.0	3,681.0	3,917.0	4,221.0
Borders	2,260.0	2,590.4	2,595.0	3,271.2	3,387.3	3,413.2	3,486.0	3,699.0
Books-A-Million	324.8	347.9	347.9	418.6	442.9	442.9	438.2	460.2
Family Christian Stores	—	—	220.0	332.5	325.0	325.0	334.0	325.0
Musicland	—	—	—	157.0	162.0	162.0	149.0	136.0
Hastings	—	—	—	114.0	118.0	118.0	122.0	117.0
Tower	—	—	—	33.0	32.4	32.5	26.0	23.0
Crown Books	297.5	189.0	—	—	—	—	—	—
Total U.S. bookstore sales	12,755	13,390	14,540	15,375	15,743	16,226	16,809	16,668

SOURCES: *Subtext*, various years; U.S. Department of Commerce.

TABLE 3.21
Market share of largest U.S. bookstore chains, 1997–2004 (millions of dollars)

Chain	1997	1998	1999	2000	2001	2002	2003	2004
Barnes & Noble	21.93	22.40	20.67	23.10	23.38	22.69	23.30	25.32
Borders	17.72	19.35	17.85	21.28	21.52	21.04	20.74	22.19
Books-A-Million	2.55	2.60	2.39	2.72	2.81	2.73	2.61	2.76
Family Christian Stores	—	—	1.51	2.16	2.06	2.00	1.99	1.95
Musicland	—	—	—	1.02	1.03	1.00	0.89	0.82
Hastings	—	—	—	0.74	0.75	0.73	0.73	0.70
Tower	—	—	—	0.21	0.21	0.20	0.15	0.14
Crown Books	2.33	1.41	—	—	—	—	—	—
Total revenues of leading chains	5,679.1	6,127.3	6,168.9	7,878.3	8,148.6	8,174.6	8,472.2	8,981.2
Total market share of largest chains	44.52	45.76	42.43	51.24	51.76	50.38	50.40	53.88

SOURCES: *Subtext*, various years; U.S. Department of Commerce.

effectiveness of this strategy, although it seems difficult to believe that many big book publishers will be able to handle the vast array of consumer services and the inherently time-consuming pick-and-pack requirements of an effective direct-to-consumer business model.

SUPPLIER POWER

For several decades, the United States has had a plethora of excess printing plant capacity. So traditional supplier (i.e., manufacturing) power has been minimal, especially with the emergence of viable, high-quality, and inexpensive printing plants in India, the People's Republic of China, Singapore, Hong Kong, and elsewhere. A significant amount of offshore printing was evident as early as 1992, especially in the juvenile and religious book categories.

However, a variation of supplier power does exist, specifically the influence if not supremacy of agents in the consumer-book market. Agents control the supply of star talent, that is, authors able to write and sell blockbusters; and as Peter Drucker pointed out, that type of genius is in short supply. So if an editor wants to negotiate a multibook contract with a promising or established author, the editor is compelled to deal with an agent; and the price can be steep. For example, Stephen King was granted an advance of $5 million per book and 50 percent of the profits by Simon & Schuster; King's old contract with Penguin called for an individual book advance of $25 million. So this new arrangement offered King the possibility of larger total profits for each book.

While agents are active in the professional and educational fields, their real power is centered in the consumer niche; and it is highly unlikely that trade book editors will regain the upper hand in negotiations in the coming years.

BARRIERS TO ENTRY AND THREAT OF ENTRY

All it takes to launch a book-publishing firm is an idea, a computer, access to editorial-production personnel (who can be hired as freelance), a few authors, and a relatively small amount of working capital. Book publishing is protected by Article 1, Section 8 of the U.S. Constitution (covering copyrights, trademarks, and patents) and the First Amendment (providing First Amendment free speech protection). So there are no legal impediments, licenses, etc., needed to enter this business (providing any federal, state, or local municipal regulations regarding taxes, etc., are followed). Barriers to exit the business are also minimal, again assuming financial debts, etc., are addressed.

So the threat of entry into book publishing remains a real threat to the existing firms. In 1977 there were 1,745 publishing firms tracked by the U.S. Department of Commerce. By 2002 Commerce reported data on 3,570 companies (an increase of 104.58 percent). See table 3.16 for details. However, Bowker, which supplies ISBNs to all U.S. publishers, insisted there were more than 81,000 publishing companies in 2006. Commerce, on the other hand, counts a company only if it has a federal ID number, it has at least one paid employee, and book publishing is the primary business.

However, the overwhelming majority of these 81,000 firms are exceptionally small. We analyzed detailed statistical data from a complete survey of all 81,000-plus firms in 2005 and 2006 in the Bowker database; results revealed that some of these firms had no revenues in 2004 or 2005. The pronounced CRs outlined previously corroborated the Bowker survey results. For the most part, these companies pose a small threat to the established large firms with high CRs.

GENERIC STRATEGIES TO COUNTER THE FIVE FORCES

Different publishing firms followed different strategies, although there were some commonalities.

On the corporate level, almost all of the largest firms developed bigness strategies. Large U.S. publishing houses, along with a cluster of global media companies, acquired U.S. companies because of the country's factor endowments, such as skilled resources; its strong technological base; and a need to increase market share and revenues. So News Corporation added Collins to Harper & Row, Pearson PLC acquired Putnam for its Penguin operations, Bertelsmann AG added Bantam Doubleday Dell and later Random House, etc. On the business-unit level, ineffective, low-performing units were sold.

Some companies developed differentiation or positional advantages. On the functional or departmental level, differentiation strategic decisions to focus on specific niches (e.g., romance novels at Harlequin, religious titles at HarperCollins' Zondervan unit, or textbooks at McGraw-Hill) were made. Some houses developed cost leadership strategies (e.g., Harlequin's mass-market paperback strategy), which did not always prove successful (e.g., Harlequin sustained a financial setback in 2004 and again in 2005).

Almost all of the houses, at least the larger ones, purchased enterprise software to track editorial, production, and distribution-fulfillment activities and royalty calculations, etc. While costly, this decision proved to be exceptionally important to firms trying to maintain control over expenses and operations. There was an impressive emphasis on quality, innovation, and investment in this information technology sector.

This meant that large, impressive value-creation enterprises emerged, allowing these entities to create more overall value than competitors in its specific book niche or category.

GLOBAL ISSUES

In the book export sector, the major publishing firms in the trade, professional, and educational markets adopted a product differentiation strategy and minimized the importance of a cost leadership strategy. Their rational was simple. U.S. publishers released topflight books in English by major authors with a global appeal in all of the major categories: (1) consumer books, by John Grisham, Mary Higgins Clark, and Michael Crichton, etc.; (2) professional books, major works in business and legal affairs; and (3) educational books, college textbooks by Philip Kotler, Paul Samuelson, etc. Price was often not a consideration since these books and authors had an international reach and steady, impressive annual sales.

This strategy worked until the publishing world felt the backlash from the Asian currency contagion in 1997 and the impact of a strong dollar versus major currencies (Greco 2004). Hardbound books (an amalgamation of fiction and nonfiction titles) sustained deep declines in export sales revenues starting in 1997; by 2004 this market's revenues were still 20.57 percent below the 1996 total. A similar pattern was evident in the professional, technical, and scientific category, although the decline started later, dropping 22.70 percent from 1997 to 2004.

The mass-market paperback category's export sales pattern was uneven, growing in 1997 and 1998, declining between 1999 and 2002, and finally posting better tallies in 2003 and 2004. The only category to generate impressive growth figures was the religious book category, with a sterling 66.56 percent growth rate.

Total export revenues declined 0.86 percent between 1996 and 2004. Table 3.22 lists this data.

FUTURE ORGANIZATIONAL CHOICES

All things considered, the various organizational choices selected by the eight major book-publishing firms succeeded. This was, after all, a business generating more than $26 billion in net revenues on the sale of almost 2.3 billion units in 2004.

TABLE 3.22
U.S. book export revenues, 1996–2004 (millions of dollars)

Category	1996	1997	1998	1999	2000	2001	2002	2003	2004
Hardbound	184,583	146,475	141,677	129,737	136,801	132,381	110,390	114,055	146,608
Mass-market paperback	208,067	233,132	239,261	232,363	220,875	191,757	165,273	208,822	228,901
Religious	51,845	53,546	50,559	56,355	67,789	80,273	73,893	72,127	86,352
Professional, technical, & scientific	506,512	549,431	541,743	509,945	502,538	415,692	376,576	371,129	391,532
Textbooks	316,898	370,482	331,820	323,140	326,855	341,525	380,637	355,071	402,057
Total for all exports	1,755,638	1,896,636	1,841,821	1,871,068	1,876,958	1,712,335	1,681,229	1,693,574	1,740,519

SOURCE: U.S. Department of Commerce, International Trade Administration.

However, on the basis of our interviews and review of the substantive data, we believe the U.S. book-publishing industry will have to address the following organizational choices to remain competitive domestically and globally.

First, the U.S. book industry supply chain is inherently inefficient. Publishers ship books today and handle their returns tomorrow. In spite of the launch of BookScan by VNU (which monitors about 70 percent of U.S. book sales in certain categories), publishers lack knowledge about real-time sales and actual retail selling prices, especially since Wal-Mart and many religious bookstores do not participate in BookScan. The industry must spend the time and financial resources needed to create integrated supply and value chains; special attention should be paid to the following: (1) the production cycle (authors-agents and publishers); (2) the highly diverse universe of intermediaries (distributors, wholesalers, and jobbers; retailers and the vast channels of distribution); and (3) the constantly changing and evolving world of book buyers and consumers. The industry needs to reconfigure the value chain in response to global competition and pay more attention to currency conversion issues since both directly affect the export market.

Second, sophisticated analytical models are needed to provide better estimates of real-time book sales and actual retail selling prices in the domestic and global markets (Bass 1969; Hansmann and Kraakman 1992).

Third, reliable consumer behavior research is needed for budgetary, editorial, and marketing decisions. The general rule of thumb followed since 1639 (when the first printing press was operational in Colonial Massachusetts) is to use the first printing as the marketing tool, a procedure fraught with error and numbing book returns.

Fourth, some serious consideration must be given to merchandising issues, which proved to be a successful revenue stream in the motion picture industry.

Fifth, far too little attention has been paid to the relationship of a book company with its parent company (especially since a number of firms are foreign owned) regarding capital deepening, production efficiencies, foreign partnerships, and business relations with sister publishing firms through international cooperative arrangements.

Sixth, the industry has rarely undertaken macro and micro studies of key issues. We believe it is prudent for the entire industry to evaluate a number of substantive issues that have a direct impact on current and future strategies, including the following:

- the impact of specialization
- the lack of publishing house brand identity (with the exception of Golden Books, the Dummies series, Harlequins, and Disney books)
- the piracy of books, estimated to exceed $500 million annually (Arkenbout, Van Duk, and Van Wuck 2004; Davis 2004)
- the various Google initiatives (while still too new to evaluate, they could have an impact on backlist sales to libraries)
- the impact of offshore production and distribution operations
- major changes in the channels of distribution (Greco, Wharton, and Estelami, 2005; Greco et al. 2003)

- the real impact of book critics, television shows and personalities, and author tours (Basuroy, Chatterjee, and Ravid 2003; Sorensen 2004)
- elasticity of demand studies (Glass 2001; Gourville and Koehler 2004)

Seventh, serious attention must be paid to the current and potential impact of e-commerce and the electronic distribution of content (Dellarocas 2003; Dellarocas, Awad, and Zhang 2004; Kotha, Rajgopal, and Venkatachalam 2004; Kranton and Minehart 2001; Litan and Rivlin 2001; Nie et al. 2004; Palmer 2005).

Lastly, we believe that the economics of publishing are harsh and unforgiving but understandable (Greco 2005). We urge industry leaders to take a long-term perspective with appropriate goals, a viable and realistic entrepreneurial strategy based on a unique value proposition, and an understanding that, in the real world of commerce, everything matters.

Book publishing is, as De Vany and Walls (1996) pointed out, a complex, adaptive, and at times semichaotic industry constantly trying to handle complex cultural issues and commercial demands, no easy task even for students of Michael Porter.

Arkenbout, Erwin, Frans Van Duk, and Peter Van Wuck. 2004. Copyright in the Information Society: Scenarios and Strategies. *European Journal of Law and Economics* 17: 237–49.

Bass, Frank M. 1969. A New Product Growth Model for Consumer Durables. *Management Science* 15:215–27.

Basuroy, Suman, Subimal Chatterjee, and S. Abraham Ravid. 2003. "How Critical Are Critical Reviews? The Box Office Effects of Film Critics, Star Power, and Budgets." *Journal of Marketing* 67:103–17.

Book Industry Study Group. Book Industry Trends. New York: Book Industry Study Group. [Published annually.]

Bowker Annual Library and Book Trade Almanac. New York: Bowker. [Published annually.]

Congressional Budget Office. 2004. "Economic Forecasts." http://www.cbo.gov.

Davis, Lee. 2004. "Intellectual Property Rights, Strategy, and Policy." *Economic Innovation and New Technology* 13 (5): 399–415.

De Vany, Arthur, and W. David Walls. 1996. "Bose-Einstein Dynamics and Adaptive Contracting in the Motion Picture Industry." *Economic Journal* 106:1493–514.

Dellarocas, Chrysanthos. 2003. "The Digitization of Word of Mouth: Promise and Challenges of Online Feedback Mechanisms." *Management Science* 49 (10): 1407–24.

Dellarocas, Chrysanthos, Neeven Farag Awad, and Xiaoquan (Michael) Zhang. 2004. "Exploring the Value of Online Reviews to Organizations: Implications for Revenue Forecasting and Planning." Working paper, Massachusetts Institute of Technology.

Ghose, Anindya, Michael D. Smith, and Rahul Telang. 2004. "Internet Exchanges for Used Books: An Empirical Analysis for Welfare Implications." Working paper, Carnegie Mellon University.

Glass, Amy Jocelyn. 2001. "Price Discrimination and Quality Improvement." *Canadian Journal of Economics* 34 (2): 549–69.

Gourville, John T., and Jonathan J. Koehler. 2004. "Downsizing Price Increases: A Greater Sensitivity to Price than Quantity in Consumer Markets." Working paper, Harvard Business School Marketing Research Papers; No. 04-01.

Greco, Albert N. 1997. "The Market for Consumer Books in the U.S.: 1985–1995." *Publishing Research Quarterly* 13 (1): 3–40.

———. 2000a. "Market Concentration Levels in the U.S. Consumer Book Industry: 1995–1996." *Journal of Cultural Economics* 24 (4): 321–36.

———, ed. 2000b. *The Media and Entertainment Industries*. Boston: Allyn & Bacon.

———. 2001. "The Market for University Press Books in the United States: 1985–1999." *Learned Publishing* 14 (2): 97–105.

———. 2004. "The Changing Market for U.S. Book Exports and Imports." In Bowker Annual, 2004. Medford, NJ: Information Today, Inc.

———. 2005. *The Book Publishing Industry*. Mahwah, NJ: Erlbaum.

Greco, Albert N., Walter O'Connor, Sharon Smith, and Robert Wharton. 2003. "The Price of University Press Books, 1989–2000." *Journal of Scholarly Publishing* 35 (1): 4–39.

Greco, Albert N., Robert Wharton, and Hooman Estelami. 2005. "The Changing Market for University Press Books: 1997–2002." *Journal of Scholarly Publishing* 36 (4): 187–220.

Hansmann, Henry, and Reinier Kraakman. 1992. "Hands-Tying Contracts: Book Publishing, Venture Capital Financing, and Secured Debt." *Journal of Law, Economic, and Organization* 8 (3): 628–55.

Kotha, Suresh, Shivaram Rajgopal, and Mohan Venkatachalam. 2004. "The Role of Online Buying Experience as a Competitive Advantage: Evidence from Third-Party Ratings for E-Commerce Firms." *Journal of Business* 77 (2): S109–S133.

Kranton, Rachael E., and Deborah F. Minehart. 2001. "A Theory of Buyer-Seller Networks." *American Economic Review* 91 (3): 485–508.

Litan, Robert E., and Alice M. Rivlin. 2001. "Protecting the Economic Impact of the Internet." *American Economic Review* 91 (2): 313–17.

Newman, Susan, Donna Celano, Albert N. Greco, and Pamela Shue. 2001. *Access for All: Closing the Book Gap for Children in Early Education*. Newark, DE: International Reading Association.

Nie, Norman H., Alberto Simpser, Irene Stepanikova, and Lu Zheng. 2004. Ten Years After the Birth of the Internet, How Do Americans Use the Internet in Their Daily Lives? Report; Stanford University Center for the Quantitative Study of Society.

Palmer, Jonathan W. 2005. "Electronic Markets and Supply Chains: Emerging Models, Execution, and Performance Measurement." *Electronic Markets* 14 (4): 268–69.

Pecorino, Paul. 2004. "Rent Seeking: A Textbook Example." Working paper; University of Alabama, Economics, Finance, and Legal Studies.

Porter, Michael E. 1980. *Competitive Strategy: Techniques for Analyzing Industries and Competitors*. New York: Free Press.

———. 1991. "Towards a Dynamic Theory of Strategy." *Strategic Management Journal* 12:95–117.

Porter, Michael E., and Scott Stern. 2001. "Innovation: Location Matters." *MIT Sloan Management Review* 42 (4): 28–36.

Raff, Daniel M. G. 2000. "Superstores and the Evolution of Firm Capabilities in American Bookselling." *Strategic Management Journal* 21:1043–59.

Sorensen, Alan T. 2004. "Bestseller Lists and Product Variety: The Case of Book Sales." Working paper; Stanford University.

Subtext. Perspective on Book Publishing: Numbers, Issues, and Trends. Darien, CT: Open Book Publishing. [Published annually.]

Sugano, Joel Yutaka, and Toshio Kobayashi. 2002. *Amazon.com E Commerce Platform: Leveraging Competitiveness Through the Virtual Value Chain*. Osaka Economic Papers 52 (2): 228–58.

Szenberg, Michael, and Eric Youngkoo Lee. 1994–1995. "The Structure of the American Book Publishing Industry." *Journal of Cultural Economics* 18 (4): 313–22.

Thornton, Patricia H. 2004. *Markets from Culture: Institutional Logics and Organizational Decisions in Higher Education Publishing.* Stanford, CA: Stanford University Press.

U.S. Department of Commerce, Bureau of the Census. 2004. *2002 Economic Census: Information Industry Series Book Publishing 2002.* Washington, DC: GPO.

U.S. Department of Commerce, International Trade Administration. www.ita.doc.gov.

Veronis Suhler Stevenson. 2005. Communications Industry Forecast and Report, 2005–2009. New York: Veronis Suhler Stevenson.

Wharton, Robert, and Albert N. Greco. 2001. "Educational Publishing: Elhi and College Textbooks." Book Industry Trends, 2001. New York: Book Industry Study Group.

———. 2003a. "Trade Publishing: Adult, Juvenile, Mass Market, Book Clubs, and Mail Order." Book Industry Trends, 2003. New York: Book Industry Study Group.

———. 2003b. "U.S. Book Exports and Imports, 1997–2002." Book Industry Trends, 2003. New York: Book Industry Study Group.

———. 2004. "Small and Independent Book Publishing: An Analysis of Sales Data." Book Industry Trends, 2004. New York: Book Industry Study Group.

For the past six years, we have been carrying out an annual intensive analysis of the book publishing industry in the United States, under the auspices of the Book Industry Study Group (BISG). Within this analysis, we provide six years of historic data and forecasts five years into the future for the following:

- publisher net dollar sales (millions of dollars)
- domestic consumer expenditure (millions of dollars)
- publisher units (millions of books)
- publisher average dollars per unit

From these results, we obtain the following four metrics:

- percentage change from prior year of publisher net dollar sales
- percentage change from prior year of publisher units
- compound annual growth rate of publisher net dollar sales
- compound annual growth rate of publisher units

These metrics are calculated for the following:

- total trade
- adult trade, total
- adult trade, hardbound
- adult trade, paperbound
- juvenile trade, total
- juvenile trade, hardbound
- juvenile trade, paperbound
- mass market, paperback
- book clubs
- mail-order publications
- religious books
- professional books
- university press
- elementary and high school textbooks (elhi)
- college textbooks
- standardized tests
- subscription reference books

These results, along with reports by industry experts on the most important trends and events affecting the publishing industry, are published annually by BISG in Book Industry Trends.

Data Sources

Our determination of the four metrics for each of our 17 industry segments within the six-year historic period is very painstaking. This is particularly true for the last of the six years in our historic period, since the initial forecasts our analysis are based on must be completed before the year in question has ended. In these efforts, we make use of multiple industry-specific data sources as well as data on various macroeconomic forces that may affect the performance of the industry as a whole or some specific segment or segments within the industry.

Two of our major data sources are the U.S. Department of Commerce Census of Manufactures and the estimates of economic activity within the publishing industry provided by the American Association of Publishers (AAP). The U.S. Department of Commerce Census of Manufactures is carried out every five years in years ending in 2 and 7 with results from the publishing industry representing one segment of the report. AAP surveys the industry on a monthly basis and provides both monthly and annual reports on sales within various industry segments.

Along with the Department of Commerce and AAP data, we also use the following:

Publishing Industry–Specific Sources

American Booksellers Association (ABA) statistical overview of retail bookselling

Association of Research Libraries (ARL) statistics

ARL supplementary statistics

Bowker Annual of Library and Book Trade Almanac

communications industry report published by Veronis Suhler Stevenson

MPI Monthly Study of College Sales and Returns

NACS College Store Industry Financial Report

General Economic Publications

Annual Survey of Manufactures, prepared by the Department of Commerce, Bureau of the Census between five-year censuses.

Economic Indicators, prepared by the Council of Economic Advisors to the Joint Economic Committee of the U.S. Congress

PPI [producer price index] *Detailed Report*, produced by the U.S. Department of Labor

Social Indicators, prepared by the U.S. Office of Management and Budget

Statistical Abstract of the United States

In addition to these formal statistical data sources, interviews are conducted with Department of Commerce officials, publishing industry executives, and officers of professional organizations representing specific industry segments such as the Association of American University Presses (AAUP).

Methodology

In the forecasting of the four metrics, we use the following:

publisher net dollar sales (millions of dollars)

domestic consumer expenditure (millions of dollars)

publisher units (millions of books)

publisher average dollars per unit

We focus our attention on publisher net dollar sales, since it is the most readily available within the industry of our four measures of interest. Unit data would be optimal for forecasting purposes but is too difficult to obtain because of different unit definitions and bundling procedures within various segments within the industry.

In forecasting publisher net dollar sales for the 17 industry segments, we calculate real publisher net dollar sales in 1982 dollars. We calculate real dollars by deflating the actual dollar values by the accumulated change in the consumer price index (CPI) inflation rate up to the year in question, where the accumulated index for 1982 equals 1. The annual changes in CPI are obtained from the Congressional Budget Office. For our forecast over the five-year forecast period, we use annual real publisher net dollar sales from 1985 to the present year. We have two reasons for using real rather than actual dollar values in our forecast. First, it eliminates a major source of variability in the time series, i.e., the effects of inflation, and thus provides a more stable time series to apply our forecasting models to. Second, since real dollar sales correlate more accurately with unit sales than actual dollar sales, we obtain a set of forecast values that measure the real growth of each industry segment without the distorting effect of inflation, which can create the perception of positive growth in an environment of flat demand or even contraction.

ARIMA Models

After reviewing a number of possible statistical forecasting models, we decided that the autoregressive integrated moving average (ARIMA) class of models provided the most practical and applicable class of forecasting methods. ARIMA models are the most general and hence usually the most accurate models among the class of forecasting models known as time series models. The other major class of forecasting models is known as econometric or explanatory models. Time series models are distinguished from econometric models by their use of the values of the time series only (in our case the 20 values of real publisher net dollar sales) in generating forecasts. In contrast, econometric models use adjunct time series such as macroeconomic or demographic variables as part of the forecasting process. We chose ARIMA models for our application because of the accuracy we were able to achieve and because of the difficulties inherent in obtaining forecast data for potential explanatory variables, which would be needed for use in possible econometric models.

When forecasting time series data, two questions must be addressed:

1. Do the data exhibit a systematic pattern?
2. Can this pattern be exploited to make meaningful forecasts?

Let us assume that a particular time series is generated by a black box.

$$\text{Black box} \rightarrow \text{Observed time series} \qquad\qquad (A.1)$$

For econometric or explanatory models, we assume a particular model structure (e.g., linear, quadratic, exponential) and attempt to identify causal variables that explain the behavior of the time series, taking as a given the a priori model structure.

Econometric or Explanatory Methodology

1. Assume a particular model structure.
2. Specify the causal variables.
3. Estimate the coefficients of the model.
4. Examine the summary statistics and try other model specifications.
5. Choose the most desirable model specification (perhaps based on the root-mean-square error or the coefficient of determination).

In the ARIMA model methodology, we do not start with any explanatory variables but rather with the observed time series itself; what we attempt to determine is the black box that could have produced such a series from white noise, or purely random numbers, exhibiting the following characteristics:

1. There is no relationship between consecutively observed values.
2. Previous values do not help in predicting future values.

A white noise series exhibits no systematic pattern.

ARIMA Methodology

1. Start with the observed time series.
2. Pass the observed time series through a black box.
3. Examine the time series that results from passage through the black box.
4. If the black box is correctly specified, the residual series coming out of the black box is white noise.
5. If the residual series is not white noise, try another black box (i.e., model form).

The key difference between these two methodologies is that, unlike the situation with econometric models, for ARIMA models we do not assume an a priori model's structure but let the time series itself define the most appropriate model structure (which we have been describing as a black box). This is achieved by examining the autocorrelation structure among successive observations in the time series. A residual series of white noise for the model implies that no systematic variability remains. Thus our model has explained all of the systematic variability, or pattern, exhibited by the time series, which is the objective of developing a forecasting model.

When choosing the black box, or model, structure, we have only three basic types of models to examine; however, there are many variations within each of these three types. The three types of models are (1) autoregressive (AR) models, (2) moving average (MA) models, and (3) mixed autoregressive moving average (ARMA) models.

An AR model generates forecasts for future values of the time series using a linear combination of previous values of the time series. The equation for an AR model has the following form:

$$Y_t = A_0 + A_1 Y_{t-1} + A_2 Y_{t-2} + A_3 Y_{t-3} + \cdots + A_p Y_{t-p} + e_t, \tag{A.2}$$

where

Y_t = the time series value for period t

$A_0, A_1, A_2, \ldots, A_p$ = coefficients

$Y_{t-1}, Y_{t-2}, \ldots, Y_{t-p}$ = p lagged value of the time series (hence the name *autoregressive*)

e_t = error term for the forecast for period t (this is white noise if the model is correctly specified)

This autoregressive model would be denoted AR(p) indicating that it used p lagged variables.

An MA model is one that predicts Y_t as a function of the past forecast errors in predicting Y_t. Letting e_t represent the series of forecast errors, an MA model equation would take the following form:

$$Y_t = W_0 + W_1 e_{t-1} + W_2 e_{t-2} + W_3 e_{t-3} + \cdots + W_q e_{t-q} + e_t, \tag{A.3}$$

where

Y_t = the time series value for period t

$W_0, W_1, W_2, \ldots, W_q$ = coefficients

$e_{t-1}, e_{t-2}, \ldots, e_{t-q}$ = q previous values of the error term series

e_t = error term for the forecast for period t (this is white noise if the model is correctly specified)

This MA model would be denoted MA(q), indicating that it used q error series terms.

The third and final of the three classes of models that we need to examine is a combination of AR and MA models, an ARMA. The equation for this mixed model is the following:

$$Y_t = A_0 + A_1 Y_{t-1} + A_2 Y_{t-2} + A_3 Y_{t-3} + \cdots + A_p Y_{t-p}$$
$$+ W_1 e_{t-1} + W_2 e_{t-2} + W_3 e_{t-3} + \cdots + W_q e_{t-q} + e_t, \tag{A.4}$$

where the various terms in the equation are defined as in the equations for the AR and MA models. This model would be denoted ARMA(p, q), indicating that it used p lagged variables and q error series terms.

The three classes of models introduced thus far are applicable only to stationary time series. A *stationary* time series is one in which two consecutive values in the series depend on the time interval between them and *not* on time itself. Thus any series exhibiting a trend will not be stationary. To apply the forecasting methodology previously described to a nonstationary time series, we perform a differencing transformation on the time series of interest to obtain a related time series, which is stationary. *Differencing* refers to subtracting each observation from its previous observation in the data set:

$$Y_t' = Y_t - Y_{t-1},$$
(A.5)

where

Y_t' = the first difference of observation at time t

Y_t = time series observation at time t

Y_{t-1} = time series observation at time $t - 1$

This transformation, referred to as *first differencing* will generally produce a stationary time series if the original series exhibited a linear trend. Applying the class of forecasting model described above to the first differenced series will give us a forecast for Y_t', observation t in the differenced series. Since we know that $Y_t' = Y_t - Y_{t-1}$, then if we know Y_{t-1}, we can solve for Y_t, observation t for our original time series. Thus the ability to forecast the first differenced series also allows us to obtain forecasts for the series of interest. Sometimes, when the trend present in the data is more extreme than a linear trend (i.e., exponential or quadratic), a *second differencing* transformation may be required to achieve a stationary series. We obtain a second differenced series by differencing the first difference series. The differencing transformation could be carried on indefinitely, but it is rare to require more than a second order differencing to achieve stationarity.

When differencing is used to make a time series stationary, it is common to refer to the resulting model as an autoregressive integrated moving average or ARIMA(p, d, q) where *integrated* refers to the integrated, or differencing, term in the model and

p is the number of autoregressive terms

d is the number of differences

q is the number of error terms

Two questions still must be addressed before we can use an ARIMA model to forecast future values of a time series:

1. What model form should be used (i.e., which values of p, d, and q should be selected)?

2. How should the coefficients of the model be estimated from the data?

With regard to the estimation of the coefficients, or parameters, of an ARIMA model, a statistical estimation procedure called *maximum likelihood estimation* is most commonly used. This estimation procedure determines the set of model parameters that would make the

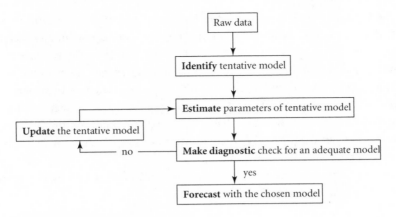

Jenkins Identification Process

set of observed values in our sample most probable if the model is correctly specified. The maximum likelihood procedure produces an unbiased minimum variance estimate of the model parameters and hence the statistically best estimates available from our sample data. Maximum likelihood estimation is carried out using a mathematically complex iterative procedure. This estimation procedure is available in most sophisticated statistical software.

Regarding correct specification of the model, this is carried out using the Box-Jenkins identification process, which is described above. The approach is an iterative one, in which we loop through the process many times before reaching a model we are comfortable with.

In the identification process we will use the autocorrelation and partial autocorrelation functions for time series to tentatively identify the optimal value of p, d, and q for our ARIMA model. The parameters for this model form will then be estimated using maximum likelihood estimation. We will ascertain whether the tentative model is correctly specified by once again using the autocorrelation and partial autocorrelation functions—this time applied to the residuals of our tentative model. We will use these functions as diagnostics to determine whether our tentative model is correctly specified. If the functions indicate that the residual series is white noise, the model is correctly specified and we can use the model to generate forecasts. If not, we must update our tentative model and return to the estimation phase of the process. The autocorrelation and partial autocorrelation functions for the residuals will provide guidance in this updating process.

Once we have determined our correctly specified ARIMA model, summary statistics for the model such as the standard error of the estimate from which a margin of error for our forecast can be obtained, the coefficient of determination and the mean absolute percentage error can be calculated. These summary statistics can be used to measure the accuracy of the ARIMA forecast.

Final Forecast

After we have forecast real publisher net dollar sales in 1982 dollars, using the appropriately specified ARIMA model, we then calculate the forecast of the actual values of publisher net dollar sales through the forecast period by reinflating the real values using our CPI calculations. We then review these initial forecast values and subjectively adjust the results based on macroeconomic projections for the forecast period and our expectations of possible blockbuster books coming out in a particular year (Harry Potter, *Da Vinci Code*). Finally, these numbers are reviewed by publishing industry experts such as industry executives and journalists who specialize in the book-publishing industry. Incorporating their inputs, we can then come up with our final set of forecasts for publisher net dollar sales.

We use trend analysis to forecast publisher average dollars per unit through the forecast period for all 17 of our categories. We then estimate units by dividing publisher net dollar sales by publisher average dollars per unit.

The following table presents a comparison of our 2004 forecast for 2004 publisher net dollar sales and the actual 2004 values.

Forecast versus Actual Publisher Net Dollar Sales for 2004

Category	2004 Actual	2004 Forecast	% Difference
Trade (total)	6,789.5	6,977.4	2.77
Adult trade (total)	5,020.3	4,868.4	−3.03
Hardbound	3,047.0	2,922.7	−4.08
Paperbound	1,973.3	1,945.7	−1.40
Juvenile trade (total)	1,769.2	2,109.0	19.2
Hardbound	868.7	1,127.9	29.8
Paperbound	900.5	981.1	8.96
Mass market	1,713.9	1,775.3	3.58
Book clubs (total)	1,033.9	1,120.2	8.35
Hardbound	815.7	892.8	9.54
Paperbound	218.2	227.4	4.22
Mail order	393.6	393.6	0.00
Religious (total)	1,946.3	1,781.8	−8.45
Hardbound	1,165.8	1,064.6	−8.68
Paperbound	780.5	717.2	−8.11
Professional (total)	5,312.1	5,215.4	−1.82
Hardbound	3,775.3	3,755.1	−0.53
Paperbound	1,536.8	1,460.3	−4.98
University press (total)	437.8	460.0	5.07
Hardbound	213.9	222.2	3.88
Paperbound	223.9	237.8	6.21
Elhi (total)	4,051.7	4,169.0	2.90
Hardbound	2,022.9	2,268.0	12.12
Paperbound	2,028.8	1,901.0	−6.30
College (total)	3,899.1	3,973.5	1.91
Hardbound	2,612.8	2,682.1	2.65
Paperbound	1,286.3	1,291.4	0.18
Standardized test	2,133.1	2,130.0	−0.15
Subscription reference	873.0	875.0	0.23
All books (incl. stand. test)	28,584.0	28,871.2	1.00

4 THE ECONOMICS OF PUBLISHING
AND THE IMPACT OF TECHNOLOGY
ON BOOK PUBLISHING

Why does a book have a suggested retail price (SRP) of $35? How does the publisher determine the print run (the number of printed copies of a book) or the book format (e.g., adult trade cloth, adult trade paperback, mass-market paperback) of a book? How does an editor determine the various costs associated with the production of a book (prepress, printing, binding, paper, etc.)?

THE ECONOMICS OF BOOK PRODUCTION:
LITHOGRAPHIC PRINTING

Lithography (often called litho, offset, photo-offset, or photolithography) is a planographic printing process using positive printing plates; the type, illustrations, or halftones on the plate are neither raised nor recessed (thus the term *planographic*). There are two types of lithographic printing presses: sheetfed presses that print onto individual sheets of fine paper and web presses that print onto large rolls of paper. Lithography is an exceptionally economical printing process capable of high-quality work at fast speeds; sheetfed presses can print between 1,000 and 15,000 sheets per hour (on both sides of a piece of 25′ × 38′ paper, known as *perfecting*); web presses can print upwards of 25,000 sheets per hour (also on both sides of the paper). The Offset Paperback printing plant in Pennsylvania can produce upwards of 1.1 million paperback books during a 24-hour shift. The vast majority of all books printed in the United States are done on litho presses, as are most newspapers and magazines.

The business of most litho printers is mass manufacturing. In large-scale manufacturing for book publishing, printing more units means achieving a lower cost per unit and, theoretically, a larger profit margin on the sale of the units. Everyone benefits from big runs: the printer, who makes more money the longer he or she can keep the presses running; the paper manufacturer, who sells more fine paper; the publisher, whose financial projections depend on keeping unit costs to a minimum; and the consumer, who pays less for the book than if its run had been smaller.

The long-run model makes perfect sense for publishers of Bibles, textbooks, trade books, and other kinds of books with a potentially large sale or distribution. Short-run books, on the other hand, have always been problematic for publishers. The costs of manufacturing a book begin to mount long before the press run commences; and if these costs cannot be spread over a sufficient number of units, individual copies become expensive to print.

Consequently, specialized professional or scholarly books pose a particular challenge. The high cost of developing content for a short-run title, including fees paid to authors, editors, artists, and so on, has to be added to the technical cost of producing the book, placing more upward pressure on the unit cost. The extra cost must be borne by the publisher or by a limited number of customers willing to pay a high cover price (Romano 2001).

In certain markets, where a best seller may generate sales of only a few thousand copies (e.g., professional or scholarly publishing), publishers' choices are stark indeed. Declining demand for a short-run title may force the publisher to take it quickly out of print, given the cost of printing a subsequent edition. This harsh economic framework prevents some publishers and editors from approving contracts for books written for only a select few (Cost 2003).

Cost factors dependent on run lengths often make short-run printing by conventional photo-offset lithographic methods difficult (and at times impossible) to justify. All printing processes have three main stages:

1. Prepress, in which the content is created and formatted for printing
2. Press, in which ink or toner is deposited on paper or another substrate
3. Postpress, in which the printed matter is cut, folded, and bound into a usable form

In offset lithography and other analog processes, prepress costs are high because this stage consists of many labor- and material-intensive steps, particularly if film is used to image the plates as opposed to direct imaging via the computer-to-plate process. Setting up the press for the run (the make-ready process) adds costly billable time and labor to the operation.

These fixed costs have to be amortized somehow, and in conventional printing the only practical way to do it is to divide them by as large a number of units as possible. This is why using conventional litho printing almost always dictates long runs.

Offset lithographic presses are paragons of cost-efficient production, guaranteeing the lowest unit cost but only at higher run lengths. It is generally uneconomical, for example, to run anything less than a few thousand impressions of a full-color job on a sheetfed offset press. Web presses, with their even greater manufacturing capacity, may not produce maximum per-unit cost savings until the run length reaches the hundred-thousand-plus-copies mark in certain kinds of work (Kotok and Lyman 1997).

Before digital printing, publishers who wanted to produce short-run books were forced to make disagreeable compromises. They resigned themselves to ordering more books than they needed or they generalized their content in hope of reaching a broader audience (Webster 2000). If they chose the former option, they took their chances on inefficient, waste-prone distribution methods that might ultimately require thousands of unsold copies to be written off and destroyed.

Admittedly, deliberate overproduction has been the only feasible way around the always perplexing unit-cost obstacle for many publishers. Even with the best of intentions, however, estimating conventional print runs is always something of a leap in the dark, forcing publishers to rely on editorial instinct, prior sales experience, and blind faith in a title's marketability. Moreover, because of the inherent variability of conventional print runs, there is no way to know exactly how many usable copies of a book will be delivered until the order is ready to ship. This is why every printing contract specifies a percentage of "overs" and "unders" that the customer agrees (in the contract with the printer) to anticipate in the final count (overs and unders are generally 10 percent more to 10 percent less, respectively, of the contract's specified print run). Spoilage on press and in the bindery have to be factored in as well.

All of this prods some publishers and editors to overestimate sales since absorbing the cost of unsold units is preferable to running out of copies of a book that is selling well (Fleming 1999). The increased unit cost of shorter-than-normal runs only magnifies the guesswork and stiffens the penalty for making a faulty judgment call. Because the link between unit cost and run length in conventional litho printing is inescapable, these methods simply are not flexible enough to make the production of small-run books worthwhile.

THE PROFIT AND LOSS STATEMENT

The profit and loss statement (P&L) outlines clearly the business model assumptions of the editor when reviewing the viability of a book proposal. Since the essential econometric suppositions differ for cloth and paperback versions of a title, or for certain types of books (notably college textbooks), a series of analyses follow that illustrate the complexity of publishing economics.

The basic business model assumptions for an adult trade paperback or an adult trade cloth (hardbound) book parallel those for mass-market paperbacks as well as cloth or paperback juvenile books (which include children's books and young adult books) and religious books.

The data in table 4.1 were based on a series of discussions with editors and publishing house executives and statistical analyses of the typical adult trade paperback book.

Adult Trade Paperback P&L

An adult trade paperback is a reprint of a cloth title the publishing house initially released 9–12 months ago. To be eligible for paperback release, sales of the cloth book would have been significant, making an adult trade paperback version a financially viable project.

The editor surveyed the book-publishing landscape and determined that (1) authors of competing paperback titles in this book's genre had average sales in the range of 35,000–40,000 units (sophisticated computer tracking systems provided reliable data on the sales of competing books); (2) the author of this specific book had a cloth-sales track record that justified a book contract and an initial print run of 50,000 copies; (3) the market for consumer trade paperbacks in the $20 range had been strong in the last year; and (4) members of the sales and marketing departments were confident the book's genre and content, the

TABLE 4.1

Sample P&L statement for adult trade paperbound book

BUSINESS MODEL ASSUMPTIONS

Print run:	50,000 copies
Gross sales:	49,000 copies [a]
Returns:	9,751 (19.9% return rate)
Net sales:	39,249 copies
Suggested retail price:	$19.95
Average discount:	47% (industry range is between 42% and 48%; publisher nets $10.57 per copy)
Unit PPB:	$79,000 ($1.58 at 50,000 copies)
Plant:	$10,000
Direct marketing:	$50,000 ($1 × the total number of printed copies)
Royalty advance:	$50,000 (royalty rate: 10% of suggested retail price)
Other publishing income:	
Subsidiary rights:	

	Gross	Author's percentage	Publisher's percentage
Reprint rights:	0	0	0
Book clubs:	$3,000	50%	50%
First serial:	$600	90%	10%
Second serial:	$3,000	30%	70%
Total:	$6,300	$2,804 (44.5%)	$3,496 (55.5%)

REVENUE AND EXPENSE ASSUMPTIONS

1. Gross sales:	$517,930	(49,000 copies × $10.57 each)
2. Returns:	$103,068	(9,751 copies × $10.57 each)
3. Net sales:	$414,862	(line 1 − line 2)
4. Plant:	$10,000	
5. PPB:	$79,000	
6. Royalty:	$78,301	(39,249 copies at $19.95/copy × 10%)
7. Total cost:	$167,301	(line 4 + line 5 + line 6)
8. Gross margin:	$247,561	(line 3 − line 7)
9. Other publishing income:	$3,496	
10. Inventory write-off:	$15,407	($1.58 × 9,751 returns)
11. Royalty write-off:	0	(difference between the advance and the earned royalty)
12. Gross margin:	$235,670	(line 8 + line 9 − line 10 − line 11)
13. Direct marketing:	$50,000	
14. Overhead:	$124,458	(standard 30% of net sales revenues)
15. Net profit:	$61,192	(line 12 − 13 − 14; 14.75% of net sales)

NOTE: All numbers were rounded off. Shipping and handling costs were excluded since some publishers provide free shipping; actual shipping and handling costs vary significantly due to numerous variables (e.g., geographical location, rush versus normal delivery schedules). PPB = paper, printing, and binding.

[a]Publishing house internal use and distribution of a title often averages 1,000 copies, hence the difference between the total print run and potential gross sales.

author's reputation, and the book's cover art meant they could sell enough copies in the major channels of distribution, specifically the large superstores (e.g., Barnes & Noble, Borders), the mass merchandisers (e.g., Wal-Mart, Kmart, Target), price clubs (e.g., Costco, Sam's Club), and other general retailers (e.g., supermarkets).

While the initial print run was 50,000 copies, the potential gross sale was 49,000; the difference due to the industry's practice of providing free copies of a title to employees, the author, key book buyers, etc.

A projected return rate of 19.9 percent was assumed (based on the national average return rate for adult trade paperback books). Net sales were assumed to be 39,249 units.

The editor surveyed the adult trade paperback field and determined that an SRP of $19.95 made this title competitive. Since books are sold at a discount (generally 42–48 percent), the editor assumed a 47 percent discount rate, generating a net of $10.57 per copy to the publisher.

Manufacturing costs were calculated. Printing, paper, and binding (PPB) costs totaled $79,000, for an average unit cost of $1.58. Plant (i.e., editorial expenditures) was $10,000 (based on an internal analysis of the house's cost structure).

Direct market costs reached $50,000 (i.e., $1.00 for every printed copy). The author received an advance of $50,000 and a royalty rate of 10 percent of the SRP.

Other publishing revenues were modest. No reprint rights were estimated; book-club sales were projected to be $3,000 (with a 50 percent split between the house and the author). First and second serial rights (in newspapers or magazines) were equally modest, with standard splits between author and house of 90 percent–10 percent (first rights) and 30 percent–70 percent (second rights). The projected rights total of $6,300 generated $2,804 (44.5 percent) for the author and $3,496 (55.5 percent) for the publishing firm.

Revenues and expenses were then calculated. Gross sales were estimated to reach $517,930 (49,000 copies at $10.57). A return rate of 19.9 percent meant 9,751 copies were returned (at $10.57 each), totaling $103,068. Net sales were $414,862 (i.e., gross sales minus returns equaled net sales). Plant and PPB expenses were known. The author earned a royalty of $78,301 (10 percent of $19.95 each for 39,249 copies). Plant, PPB, and royalty generated a total cost of $167,301. The gross margin was $247,561 (i.e., total net sales minus total costs).

Other publisher income was $3,496. Since 9,751 copies were returned and could not be resold or remaindered, the book had an inventory write-off of $15,407. There was no royalty write-off since the author earned back the advance.

This title had a total gross margin of $235,670 (i.e., gross margin plus other publisher income minus the inventory write-off minus the royalty write-off). Direct market costs were $50,000. The publishing house employed a standard (industry) overhead average of 30 percent of net sales revenues to cover corporate expenditures (e.g., salaries, rent, mortgage, interest expenses).

This title was projected to generate a net profit of $61,192 (i.e., gross margin minus direct marketing and overhead expenses), for 14.75 percent of net sales. While this amount was not overwhelming, the book helped cover overhead expenses and provided a nice revenue stream to total sales.

Adult Trade Hardcover P&L

Not all books are successful financially. Table 4.2 illustrates the problems associated with an adult trade cloth book with high expectations and an equally high return rate. Using the same methodology found in table 4.1, table 4.2 shows that this book posted a loss of $51,141. While some individuals might argue that the 30 percent overhead charge ($259,726) doomed this book to lose money, in reality an overhead charge must be allocated for every published book since the company's cost structure must be covered by all projects. In reality, the returns doomed this book.

TABLE 4.2
Sample P&L statement for adult trade hardbound (cloth) book

BUSINESS MODEL ASSUMPTIONS

Print run:	100,000 copies	
Gross sales:	99,000 copies[a]	
Returns:	33,600 copies	(34% return rate)
Net sales:	65,340 copies	
Suggested retail price:	$25.00	
Average discount:	47%	(publisher nets $13.25 per copy)
Unit PPB:	$300,000	($3.00 × 100,000 copies)
Plant:	$10,000	
Direct marketing:	$100,000	($1 × the total number of printed copies)
Royalty advance:	$125,000	(royalty rate: 10% of suggested retail price)
Other publishing income:		
Subsidiary rights:		

	Gross	Author's percentage	Publisher's percentage
Reprints:	$20,000	50%	50%
Book clubs:	$10,000	50%	50%
First serial:	$600	90%	10%
Second serial:	$3,000	30%	70%
Total:	$33,600	$16,400 (48.93%)	$17,160 (51.07%)

REVENUE AND EXPENSE ASSUMPTIONS

1. Gross sales:	$1,311,750	(99,000 copies × $13.25 each)
2. Returns:	$445,995	(33,660 copies × $13.25 each)
3. Net sales:	$865,755	(line 1 − line 2)
4. Plant:	$10,000	
5. PPB:	$300,000	
6. Royalty:	$163,350	(65,340 copies at $25/copy × 10%)
7. Total cost:	$473,350	(line 4 + line 5 + line 6)
8. Gross margin:	$392,405	(line 3 − line 7)
9. Other publishing income:	$17,160	
10. Inventory write-off:	$100,980	($3.00 × 33,660 returns)
11. Royalty write-off:	0	
12. Gross margin:	$308,585	(line 8 + line 9 − line 10 − line 11)
13. Direct marketing:	$100,000	
14. Overhead:	$259,726	(standard 30% of net sales revenues)
15. Net profit:	−$51,141[b]	(line 12 − 13 − 14)

NOTE: All numbers were rounded off. Shipping and handling costs were excluded since some publishers provide free shipping; actual shipping and handling costs vary significantly due to numerous variables (e.g., geographical location, rush versus normal delivery schedules). PPB = paper, printing, and binding.

[a] Publishing house internal use and distribution of a title often averages 1,000 copies, hence the difference between the total print run and potential gross sales.

[b] Despite net sales of 5,340 copies, this book lost money, adversely affected by the large number of returns.

PUBLISHING ECONOMICS: A CASE STUDY
OF U.S. ECONOMICS TEXTBOOKS

In 1996 the U.S. college textbook industry had net publisher revenues hovering near the $2.5 billion mark on net sales of 162.6 million units. By 2005 those totals reached more than $3.9 billion in net revenues while unit sales dropped sharply to the 67.1 million threshold (Book Industry Study Group [BISG] 2003, 2005). During those years, the suggested retail price of college textbooks skyrocketed, with some texts retailing for more than $150 by 2005.

TABLE 4.3

Net publisher revenues of U.S. top 15 textbook categories, 1999–2002 (thousands of dollars)

Textbook category	1999	2000	2001	2002
Business administration	440,875	253,383	376,189	390,211
General management	126,507	74,343	115,897	133,797
Marketing	75,904	47,397	70,474	71,879
General marketing	N/A	74,343	115,897	133,797
Finance	75,184	30,248	60,722	69,516
Business statistics	15,568	7,031	31,554	17,339
Introduction to business	42,294	35,507	20,898	21,359
Production & operations management	12,631	6,993	12,342	11,383
Other business administration	73,886	58,159	84,300	86,605
Mathematics (total)	411,685	369,981	414,373	476,650
English (total)	301,548	175,203	254,747	384,362
Psychology	222,113	141,232	200,092	263,963
Biology	220,854	118,000	230,869	322,164
Accounting	196,961	117,921	175,441	196,974
Computer science	143,973	148,202	141,493	123,893
History	129,129	95,239	128,429	155,131
Career education & occupational education	128,000	123,787	156,764	190,247
Economics	120,476	78,811	123,285	128,008
Chemistry	120,631	84,186	97,567	150,387
Sociology	108,792	89,540	111,468	128,526
Education	105,381	90,660	112,153	137,508
Communications	104,130	65,936	113,997	119,461
Spanish	100,620	41,400	84,619	94,377

SOURCE: Our estimates based on data from the Book Industry Study Group, Book Industry Trends (New York: Book Industry Study Group, 2003): 185–202.

NOTE: All numbers were rounded off and may not add up to 100%. Annual differences are attributable to annual differences between frontlist and backlist sales, the impact of the used textbook market, course packs, documents placed on reserve or electronic reserve, the incomplete submission of publisher data (especially for 2000), etc. Data for 1996, 1997, and 1998 were not available. Accounting texts are tracked separately from business administration books.

Why are college textbooks so expensive? Some individuals believe publishers and college bookstores were involved in an elaborate predatory pricing scheme to gouge helpless students, the ultimate consumers of the product. Publishers responded that editorial processes, production, marketing, and overhead costs escalated while the sale of used textbooks increased, undermining the economic vitality of textbook publishing.

College bookstore operators opined that publishers determined the suggested retail price for a text, and the bookstore merely complied with whatever price the publisher mandated. In reality, confusion obfuscates the question.

Because of space limitations, economics textbook prices will be the focus of this chapter because (1) economics is one of the top 15 academic disciplines in terms of textbook sales, (2) a significant percentage of U.S. students take one or two economics survey courses, and (3) highly reliable textbook price data for this discipline were available.

Table 4.3 outlines net publisher revenues for the top 15 textbook categories between 1999 and 2002; 2002 was the last year data were available in these categories. Our analyses and discussions indicated that the patterns evident with 2002 data were remarkably similar to the patterns evident in 2003–2006.

Table 4.4 outlines the significance of economics textbook percentage sales among the top 15 textbook categories between 1999 and 2002. In book publishing, gross dollar sales minus returns equals net publisher revenues; the same holds true for net units.

TABLE 4.4
Estimated market share of U.S. top 15 textbook categories, 1999–2002

Textbook category	MARKET SHARE			
	1999	2000	2001	2002
Mathematics (total)	10.2	12.4	10.6	10.5
Business administration (total)	10.5	9.3	9.9	8.8
General management	3.1	2.7	3.1	3.0
General marketing	1.9	2.7	3.1	3.0
Marketing	N/A	1.7	1.9	1.6
Finance	1.9	1.1	1.6	1.6
Business statistics	0.4	0.3	0.8	0.4
Introduction to business	1.0	1.3	0.6	0.5
Production & operations management	0.3	0.0	0.3	0.3
Other business administration	1.8	2.4	2.2	2.0
English (total)	7.5	6.5	6.3	7.7
Psychology	5.5	5.2	5.3	6.0
Accounting	4.9	4.3	4.6	4.4
Biology	5.5	4.3	6.1	7.3
Spanish	2.5	1.5	2.2	2.1
Computer science	3.8	5.4	3.7	2.8
Career education & occupational education	3.2	4.6	4.1	4.3
Economic	3.0	2.9	3.3	2.9
Chemistry	3.0	3.1	2.6	3.4
History	3.2	3.5	3.4	3.5
Sociology	3.0	3.3	2.9	2.9
Education	2.6	3.3	3.0	3.1
Communications	2.6	2.4	3.0	2.7

SOURCE: Our estimates based on data from the Book Industry Study Group, Book Industry Trends (New York: Book Industry Study Group, 2003): 185–202.

NOTE: All numbers were rounded off and may not add up to 100%. Annual differences are attributable to annual differences between frontlist and backlist sales, the impact of the used textbook market, course packs, documents placed on reserve or electronic reserve, the incomplete submission of publisher data (especially for 2000), etc. Data for 1996, 1997, and 1998 were not available. Accounting texts are tracked separately from business administration books.

What Is a College Textbook?

What is a college textbook? In reality, there are two distinct types of college textbooks. The first is the traditional book that synthesizes information, facts, theories, and knowledge in a specific academic field. Using economics as our model, a standard economics text contains detailed analyses of macroeconomic (e.g., national output and income, fiscal policy, business cycles) and microeconomic (e.g., supply and demand in individual markets, demand and utility, and consumer behavior) theories and applied practices. These books generally contain four-color illustrations and photographs, statistical tables, charts, review questions, a glossary, an index, etc.

The second type of textbook, as defined by college bookstore managers, is a work adopted as a primary or secondary reading in a college class. For example, a course on 19th-century U.S. literature might not have a formal textbook containing excerpts from important works of fiction, nonfiction, and poetry. Instead, an instructor might use a series of paperbacks, perhaps Melville's *Moby-Dick*, a biography of Emily Dickinson, and other original works and secondary sources. This type of text is technically classified as an adult trade book. Data on adult trade books were excluded from this analysis.

We used college textbook data sets generated by the BISG covering 1996–2005. BISG data are considered highly reliable. Their data sets are used by the U.S. Department of Commerce in *The Statistical Abstract of the United States*; investment bankers (Veronis Suhler Stevenson etc.); accounting firms (PricewaterhouseCoopers); consulting firms (Accenture, etc.); and a variety of publications (including the *New York Times*, the *Wall Street Journal*, Reuters, Bloomberg, Dow Jones, the Associated Press). BISG collects and releases data on net publisher revenues and net publisher units (i.e., gross unit sales minus returns equals net units).

The years 1996–2005 were selected because it was a period of basic economic growth and overall prosperity (although there was an economic downturn in 2001–2002 that lingered into late 2003). During those years, the Internet emerged as a viable medium and the used-textbook industry adopted the new Web sites to market their titles, events that had a profound impact on the college textbook market.

We also reviewed data from the U.S. Department of Commerce and the U.S. Department of Education. Between 2002 and 2005, we had a series of discussions with representatives from the following U.S. college textbook publishers about the state of textbook publishing (specifically net unit and net dollar sales on an annual and monthly basis): (1) Bedford Books, (2) Hacket Publishing, (3) Houghton Mifflin, (4) Jones & Bartlett Publishers, (5) Lynne Rienner Publishers, (6) McGraw-Hill, (7) Oxford University Press, (8) Pearson Education, (9) Thomson Learning, (10) W. H. Freeman / Worth Publishing Group, (11) W. W. Norton, and (12) John Wiley & Sons.

We also had a series of discussions with a representative from R. R. Bowker Company about textbook prices. Bowker issues all of the ISBNs in the United States; the company also publishes a series of major reference works (*Book in Print*, *Paperback Books in Print*, etc.) and maintains a database of more than 4.5 million books, videos, etc.

Review of the Literature

A firm enters a market to maximize its profits. However, consumers, as well as policy makers, often question the pricing policies of dominant firms (e.g., established textbook publishers).

Athey and Schmutzler discovered that "in markets where increasing dominance is expected, apparently anticompetitive behavior, such as predatory pricing, mergers, and acquisitions, might be of particular concern. However, in our model, firms gain market share through investments that may benefit consumers, such as cost reduction or quality improvements—issues raised in almost all of the textbook publisher interviews (Athey and Schmutzler 2001). Agarwal and Gort (2001) insisted that cost advantages accruing to first movers rested on the transfer of knowledge and skills as well as the growth of these new markets, a pattern evident with many textbooks.

Han, Kim, and Kim (2001) investigated switching costs (an obvious concern to college professors used to the organization and coverage of topics in a specific textbook). Thomas's research on market entry strategies emphasized the importance of price, advertising, or new products to limit or deter entry. New "entrants are more likely to be met with aggressive price response," conditions often observable in textbook publishing (Thomas 1999).

Nevo measured market power and prices in the ready-to-eat cereal industry, which "is characterized by high concentration, high price-cost margins, large advertising-to-sales ratios, and aggressive introduction of new products" (Nevo 2001), factors evident in the textbook market.

Success in the market often depends on creating effective branding campaigns. In college publishing, the author is the brand. Chaudhuri and Holbrook (2001) analyzed the impact of brand trust and brand performance. Their "results indicate that when the product and brand level variables are controlled for, brand trust and brand performance affect combine to determine purchase loyalty and attitudinal loyalty. Purchase loyalty, in turn, leads to greater market share, and attitudinal loyalty leads to a higher relative price for the brand," a situation readily evident in textbook publishing. Odin, Odin, and Valette-Florence (2001) developed a mathematical model to test strong and weak brand loyalty and the inevitable impact of inertia in the purchase decision process, a factor that might explain why many textbook adopters (i.e., faculty members) are reluctant to change books. Cabral (2000) evaluated a firm's perceived image and quality, factors that are pivotal in "brand stretching" (e.g., launching a junior college version of an existing four-year college textbook).

Fudenberg and Tirole (2000) analyzed "inducements" crafted to convince customers to switch brands; they believed that "long term contacts lead to little switching." Inducements exert a powerful influence over an instructor's commitment to a specific text because of its related ancillary products, which often include a teacher's edition, a student study guide, color overhead transparencies, a prerecorded videocassette, a presentation-software file, a computer disk containing test and quiz questions.

Extensive research has been published on behavioral marketing (including related economic and sociological issues). DiClemente and Hantula (2003) reviewed the applied behavioral literature regarding consumer choice, including a detailed analysis of the behavioral perspective model and the behavioral ecology of consumption. Smith and Hantula's (2003) experimental research offered "evidence of congruence between the effects of price and delay on consumer preferences, and support the contention that the price of goods may be interpretable as contributing to total delay time to primary reinforcement." Oliveira-Castro (2003) evaluated search behavior and responses to pricing issues among consumers in a supermarket.

Anderson and Simester (2000) argued that, contrary to prevailing economic literature showing that demand curves are downward and sloping, their data revealed that "increasing the price of an item from $44 to $49 may increase unit demand by up to thirty percent." Their research revealed that "$9 price endings lead to more favorable customer price perceptions and increased customer demand." Mullainathan and Thaler (2000) analyzed various behavioral economics issues, including what "happens in markets in which some of the agents display human limitations and complications" as well as "three important ways in which humans deviate from the standard economic models." Gifford evaluated the impact of "information overload," imperfect information available to consumers, and "conditions under which limited attention implies endogenous positive costs of information acquisition." Her research results indicated that "net information costs are positive if and only if there is a current information source that warrants updating of the information that it provides. . . . If this condition is met, then the optimal policy takes the form of one of two simple behavioral rules, 'stay with a winner' or 'put out the fires'" (Gifford 2001). Testing Basu's rational expectations equilibrium model ("an economic model of the phenomenon in which consumers are fully rational"), Ruffle and Shtudiner (2003) found "ample support for Basu's model. Convergence to the 99-cent equilibrium is faster and more widespread when firms are able to observe the previous pricing decisions of others."

Shipp (2000) evaluated conflicts between commercial and cultural forces in commercial academic publishing. Raff (2000) analyzed bookselling patterns between 1970 and 1995 and the importance of scale economies. Greco (2005) evaluated the economic structure of the publishing industry, including textbooks.

Will electronic books (e-books) replace costly printed textbooks? O'Brien et al. (2000) at Forrester Research predicted (as it turned out, incorrectly) that digital textbooks (e-texts) would develop into a $1.3 billion market by 2003 and account for 14 percent of the total U.S. textbook market. Blumenstyk reported that "McGraw-Hill, John Wiley & Sons, and Thomson, three of the largest textbook publishers in North America working with the University of Phoenix, will provide e-texts for all of its students, allowing it to become a 'book-less college'" (2001). Letts, analyzing MetaText, Blackboard, and netLibrary, insisted e-texts are still in "formative states at this point." However, he believed the electronic distribution of text was inevitable and would someday replace printed texts (2001). Young, evaluating the use of e-texts at the University of Virginia, discovered that, "unlike paper books, e-books sometimes crash and lines of poetry in the electronic versions are often broken because the screen is not wide enough" (2001). Kirkpatrick (2001) remarked, "The main advantage of electronic books appears to be that they gather no dust. Almost no one is buying."

The Basic College Textbook Business Model

For decades, college textbook publishers followed a simple business model that worked and generated steady (and growing) annual profits.

First, publish college textbooks in two formats: cloth and paperback. Cloth books generate the clear majority of all revenues, generally accounting for about two-thirds of all net revenues between 1996 and 2005. However, paperbacks held a slight advantage in the net unit category with a 55 percent market share between 1996 and 2002. Table 4.5 outlines this trend.

Second, survey the relevant academic textbook field, determine the potential market, and evaluate the strengths and weaknesses of the existing textbooks in this niche.

Third, hire an author (preferably an exceptionally well-known one) to prepare an effective (and all too often a hefty) textbook with all of the necessary elements: four-color illustrations and photographs, statistical tables, charts, illustrations, review questions at the end of each chapter, a glossary, and an index.

Fourth, provide examination copies (generally hundreds of copies; in the big textbook sectors, thousands of copies) to college professors, the potential adopters of the text. Fifth, send out a plethora of direct mail pieces and place advertisements in key journals. Sixth, send members of the college textbook editorial-marketing staffs to academic conferences

TABLE 4.5

U.S. book revenues and units: college textbook data, 1996–2002 (millions of dollars; millions of units)

Format	1996	1997	1998	1999	2000	2001	2002
Textbook revenues							
Cloth	1,650.9	1,795.4	1,936.8	2,093.2	2,163.8	2,341.4	2,631.3
Paperback	807.9	874.3	951.8	1,035.6	1,073.3	1,127.5	1266.9
Total	2,485.8	2,669.7	2,888.6	3,128.8	3,237.1	3,468.9	3,898.2
Cloth percentage of total revenues	67.5	67.2	67.0	66.9	66.8	67.5	67.6
Paperback percentage of total revenues	32.5	32.8	33.0	33.1	33.2	32.5	32.4
Grand total: U.S. books	20,107.0	20,940.5	22,302.4	23,758.6	24,587.2	24,564.0	26,068.2
Textbook units							
Cloth units	73.3	75.4	78.5	81.7	83.1	86.7	95.0
Paperback units	89.3	92.8	97.4	102.1	103.2	107.1	116.9
Total	162.6	168.2	175.9	183.8	186.3	193.8	211.9
Cloth percentage of total units	45.1	44.8	44.6	44.5	44.6	44.7	44.8
Paperback percentage of total units	54.9	55.2	55.4	55.6	55.4	55.3	55.2
Grand total: U.S. book units	2,368.9	2,324.9	2,402.3	2,504.9	2,493.2	2,411.3	2,488.3
Export revenue	204.8	220.0	238.0	257.8	266.6	285.5	320.7
Cloth	134.5	144.0	155.4	167.9	173.4	187.4	210.3
Paperback	70.3	76.0	82.6	89.9	93.2	98.1	110.4
Export units	13.1	13.9	14.6	15.1	15.5	16.2	17.6
Cloth	5.6	5.8	6.2	6.3	6.5	6.9	7.5
Paperback	7.5	8.1	8.4	8.8	9.0	9.3	10.1

SOURCE: Book Industry Study Group, Book Industry Trends (New York: Book Industry Study Group, 2003): 186–187, 192–193, 198–199.

NOTE: All numbers are rounded off and may not add up to 100%.

searching for new authors, staffing booths to sell existing texts, and conducting on-campus visits to see professors.

Seventh, develop supplemental content to reinforce the usefulness of the text to the instructor, including (1) a teacher's edition; (2) a student study guide; (3) an instructor's CD (containing chapter questions, midterm questions, final examination questions, and an electronic grade book); (4) black-and-white or color transparencies; (5) a presentation-software file; (6) and a prerecorded videocassette. The goal is to lock in adopters (i.e., faculty members) who would be reluctant to change textbooks since course lectures and presentations, overhead transparencies and presentation slides, and tests are pegged to a specific text.

Eighth, set an SRP to capture in the first year of publication all developmental, marketing, production, etc., costs and generate a profit. Ninth, minimize the impact of the used-text market by issuing a new edition every three years.

This model worked for decades, especially since publishers sold a product with inelastic demand. After all, publishers assumed that students had to buy the book to pass the course. Table 4.6 outlines these issues.

Analysis of the Traditional Three-Year Business Model

To determine textbook supply, demand, and costs, we conducted a series of interviews (between 2002 and 2005) with a cross section of major U.S. college textbook publishers. On

TABLE 4.6

College textbooks by U.S. channel of distribution, 1996–2002 (millions of dollars; millions of units)

Format & channel	1996	1997	1998	1999	2000	2001	2002
Cloth revenues							
General retailers	73.2	77.6	83.7	90.7	93.3	100.7	112.9
College bookstores	1155.7	1238.2	1335.7	1443.0	1493.1	1616.5	1817.7
Libraries & institutions	142.8	152.6	164.7	178.0	183.9	199.1	223.7
Schools	123.9	132.1	142.5	154.2	159.0	171.8	192.8
Direct to consumers	43.3	46.0	49.5	53.7	55.3	59.7	66.9
Other	4.54	4.9	5.3	5.7	5.9	6.3	7.0
Paperback revenues							
General retailers	34.8	37.7	41.0	44.6	46.3	48.6	54.7
College bookstores	603.7	653.3	711.4	773.9	802.1	842.7	946.8
Libraries & institutions	23.0	25.0	27.3	29.6	30.7	32.2	36.1
Schools	52.2	56.4	61.4	66.8	69.2	72.7	81.7
Direct to consumers	21.1	22.9	24.9	27.1	28.1	29.4	33.0
Other	2.8	3.0	3.2	3.5	3.7	3.9	4.4
Cloth units							
General retailers	3.6	3.7	3.8	4.0	4.0	4.2	4.5
College bookstores	51.1	52.6	54.7	57.0	57.9	60.5	66.4
Libraries & institutions	4.8	4.9	5.4	5.4	5.6	5.9	6.3
Schools	5.6	5.7	5.9	6.2	6.3	6.5	7.1
Direct to consumers	1.5	1.6	1.5	1.7	1.7	1.7	1.9
Other	1.1	1.1	1.0	1.2	1.1	1.1	1.2
Paperback units							
General retailers	3.9	4.0	4.3	4.5	4.5	4.7	5.2
College bookstores	67.0	69.3	73.1	76.5	77.2	80.2	87.5
Libraries & institutions	2.4	2.4	2.5	2.7	2.8	2.9	3.3
Schools	5.6	5.9	6.1	6.4	6.5	6.7	7.3
Direct to consumers	1.6	1.8	1.7	1.9	1.9	1.9	2.1
Other	1.3	1.3	1.3	1.4	1.4	1.4	1.5

SOURCE: Book Industry Study Group, Book Industry Trends (New York: Book Industry Study Group, 2003): 186–187, 192–193, 198–199.

NOTE: All numbers are rounded off and may not add up to 100%.

the basis of these discussions, information provided by publishers, and a review of industry statistical data sets, we made the following assumptions about the textbook in the model:

- In 2002 the total market for economics textbooks (of all types) in the United States was 2,400,300 net publisher units with net publisher revenues of $128,000,810.

- The strategic goal was to capture approximately 10 percent of the annual basic survey macroeconomic and microeconomic economics textbook market in the first year; the target was set at 200,000 net publisher units.

- This typical basic cloth economics college macroeconomic and microeconomic textbook will have standard features, approximately 600 pages (with illustrations, tables, color charts, etc.), and an SRP of $100.00 (lower than the average suggested price of $110.63).

- This text will be sold at an average 25 percent discount rate to a college bookstore.

- The publisher will have net revenues of $75 per copy.

- The estimated textbook's PPB manufacturing expenditures were $15.94 per copy (an industry average).

TABLE 4.7
Sample P&L statement: year 1

Print quantity:	275,000 copies (units)
Number of free copies:	4,000
Gross sales:	271,000
Returns:	66,340 (24.48% return rate)
Net sales:	204,660 (75.52% sell-through rate)
Suggested retail price:	$100.00 per unit
Average discount:	25%
Publisher net income:	$75.00 per unit
Royalty terms:	10%: at $7.50 per unit
Subsidiary and foreign rights:	
Reprints:	$0
Book club:	$0
Foreign rights:	$100,000
Misc.:	$0
Total:	$100,000
Author's share:	$50,000 (50%)
Publisher's share:	$50,000 (50%)
Unit PPB:	$15.94
Plant:	$75,000
(editorial costs and proofreading, etc.)	
Royalty advance:	$500,000
Direct marketing:	$400,000
Profit & loss analysis:	
Gross sales:	$20,325,000 (271,000 units at $75 each)
Returns:	$4,975,500 (66,340 units at $75 each)
Net sales:	$15,345,500 (204,660 units at $75 each)
PPB:	$4,383,500 (275,000 units at $15.94 each)
Plant:	$50,000
Earned royalty:	$1,534,950
Total cost:	$5,918,450
Gross margin A:	$9,427,050
Other publishing income:	$50,000
Inventory write-off:	$0
Royalty write-off:	$0
Gross margin B:	$9,477,050
Direct marketing:	$400,000
Overhead:	$4,604,850 (30% of net sales)
Net profit:	$4,472,200
Net profit as a percentage of net sales:	29.14%
Net profit per net copy:	$21.85

NOTE: PPB = paper, printing, and binding; gross margin A = net sales minus total costs; gross margin B = gross margin A plus other publishing income minus inventory write-off; net profit = gross margin B minus direct marketing and overhead.

- The book would be published in September 2003 with a revised second version available by September 2006 (a standard three-year revision cycle).

Table 4.7 outlines in detail these assumptions for the first year. Tables 4.8 and 4.9 provide data on sales for the second and third years.

How many copies will be sold in the first edition's three-year cycle? What will be the costs and other related expenses? What will be the book's profit margin? What will the book contribute to the publisher's overhead?

Publishers insisted in the interviews that a 100 percent sell-through rate was never possible in the college market because of the following reasons:

- Some students refused to buy a text.

- Others shared a book or made copies of chapters from the book.

TABLE 4.8
Sample P&L statement: year 2

Print quantity:	200,000 copies (units)
Number of free copies:	500
Inventory carry-over:	66,340
Gross sales:	265,840
Returns:	65,077 (24.48% return rate)
Net sales:	200,763 (75.52% sell-through rate)
Suggested retail price:	$100.00 per unit
Average discount:	25%
Publisher net income:	$75.00 per unit
Royalty terms:	10%: at $7.50 per unit
Subsidiary and foreign rights:	
Reprints:	$0
Book club:	$0
Foreign rights:	$0
Misc.:	$0
Total:	$0
Author's share:	$0
Publisher's share:	$0
Unit PPB:	$15.94
Plant:	$0
(editorial costs and proofreading, etc.)	
Royalty advance:	$0
Direct marketing:	$50,000
Profit & loss analysis:	
Gross sales:	$19,938,000 (265,840 units at $75 each)
Returns:	$4,880,775 (65,077 units at $75 each)
Net sales:	$15,057,225 (200,763 units at $75 each)
(gross sales minus returns equals net sales)	
PPB:	$3,188,000 (200,000 units at $15.94 each)
Plant:	$0
Earned royalty:	$1,505,723
Total cost:	$4,693,723
Gross margin A:	$10,363,502
Other publishing income:	$0
Inventory write-off:	$0
Royalty write-off:	$0
Gross margin B:	$10,363,502
Direct marketing:	$50,000
Overhead:	$4,517,168 (30% of net sales)
Net profit:	$5,896,334
Net profit as a percentage of net sales:	36.19%
Net profit per net copy:	$29.37

NOTE: PPB = paper, printing, and binding; gross margin A = net sales minus total costs; gross margin B = gross margin A plus other publishing income minus inventory write-off; net profit = gross margin B minus direct marketing and overhead.

- Some students purchased only used copies of a text.
- Some instructors relied exclusively on cases, course packs, or handouts rather than textbooks.
- Some professors placed copies of the text in the library reserve system.
- Some instructors relied on lecture notes, handouts, etc., and eschewed a textbook.

Using the standard annual industry averages found in Book Industry Trends (BISG 2005) for a gross, return, and net formula (i.e., 24.48 percent return rate and a 75.52 percent sell-through rate), the P&L indicated that total net sales revenues for years one, two, and three (as shown in tables 4.7, 4.8, and 4.9) should top $41,994,000 (559,920 copies at $75 each)

TABLE 4.9
Sample P&L statement: year 3

Print quantity:	140,000 copies (units)
Number of free copies:	500
Inventory carry-over:	65,077
Gross sales:	204,577
Returns:	50,080 (24.48% return rate)
Net sales:	154,497 (75.52% sell-through rate)
Suggested retail price:	$100.00 per unit
Average discount:	25%
Publisher net Income:	$75.00 per unit
Royalty terms:	10%: at $7.50 per unit
Subsidiary and foreign rights:	
Reprints:	$0
Book club:	$0
Foreign rights:	$100,000
Misc.:	$0
Total:	$100,000
Author's share:	$50,000 (50%)
Publisher's share:	$50,000 (50%)
Unit PPB:	$15.94
Plant:	$0
(editorial costs and proofreading, etc.)	
Royalty advance:	$0
Direct marketing:	$50,000
Profit & loss analysis:	
Gross sales:	$15,343,275 (204,577 units at $75 each)
Returns:	$3,756,000 (50,080 units at $75 each)
Net sales:	$11,587,275 (154,497 units at $75 each)
PPB:	$2,231,600 (140,000 units at $15.94 each)
Plant:	$0
Earned royalty:	$1,158,728
Total cost:	$3,390,328
Gross margin A:	$8,196,947
Other publishing income:	$0
Inventory write-off:	$798,275 (50,080 at $15.94 each)
Royalty write-off:	$0
Gross margin B:	$7,398,672
Direct marketing:	$50,000
Overhead:	$3,476,182 (30% of net sales)
Net profit:	$3,872,490
Net profit as a percentage of net sales:	33.42%
Net profit per net copy:	$25.07

NOTE: Net sales = gross sales minus returns. PPB = paper, printing, and binding; gross margin A = net sales minus total costs; gross margin B = gross margin A plus other publishing income minus inventory write-off; net profit = gross margin B minus direct marketing and overhead.

with an additional $50,000 in foreign rights. Total three-year costs for the book totaled $14,002,501, and they included printing, paper, and binding; plant (editorial expenses, proofreading costs, etc.); the author's earned royalty; inventory write-offs; direct marketing; and overhead. Overhead for years one, two, and three reached $12,868,200 and included general and administrative costs, including corporate office expenditures, rent or mortgage, insurance, warehouse and fulfillment expenditures (including freight costs), information technology costs, travel, catalogs and brochures, exhibit expenditures, and costs associated with processing and mailing free copies to instructors.

This model book generated a three-year net profit of $14,241,024 ($25.43 per net copy) on sales of 559,920 copies. The book's net profit as a percentage of net sales stood at 33.91 percent (all before taxes).

TABLE 4.10
Total college textbook returns, 1996–2002

Units & revenues	1996	1997	1998	1999	2000	2001	2002
Total college textbook units							
Return rate (%)	23.1	23.2	23.6	22.8	24.7	23.0	21.9
Sell-through rate (%)	76.9	76.8	76.4	77.2	75.3	77.0	78.1
Shipped units (millions)	211.4	219.0	230.2	238.0	247.4	251.7	271.3
Number of returned units (millions)	48.8	50.8	54.3	54.3	61.1	57.9	59.4
Net units (millions)	162.6	168.2	175.9	183.8	186.3	193.8	211.9
Total college textbook revenues (millions of dollars)							
Value of shipped textbooks	3,232.5	3,476.2	3,780.9	4,052.9	4,298.9	4,505.1	4,991.3
Value of returned textbooks	746.7	806.5	892.3	924.1	1,016.8	1,036.2	1,093.1
Net publisher revenues	2,485.8	2,669.7	2,888.6	3,128.8	3,237.1	3,468.9	3,898.2

SOURCE: Book Industry Study Group, Book Industry Trends (New York: Book Industry Study Group, 2003): 186–187.
NOTE: All numbers are rounded off and may not add up to 100%.

Tables 4.7, 4.8, and 4.9 (using the same methodology employed in the P&Ls in tables 4.1 and 4.2) outline the details of the sample P&L models for the first edition's three-year cycle.

Revised P&Ls: Uncertainty in the Marketplace

In spite of uneven annual sell-through net units, the system provided a steady stream of cash flow and profits for publishers until the late 1990s when other events undermined the basic business model.

First, the college textbook business averaged a 76 percent sell-through rate between 1996 and 2002. This meant that 386.6 million books worth $6.52 billion were returned to the publishers during those years. While many of these texts were resold, a sizable number were written off as a total financial loss. Table 4.10 outlines these trends. Second, companies were launched to buy used books and sell them to college bookstores. Sales personnel visited college bookstores to buy used textbooks. Other representatives called on college professors to buy new textbooks for cash; these representatives, using handheld computers containing databases of adoption cycles, new editions, etc., scanned the book's ISBN bar code into the computer to ascertain the price they should pay for the book. Other faculty members received e-mails or direct mail pieces inviting them to sell their textbooks.

College bookstores had an incentive to stock used textbooks. Aside from placating student and faculty members concerned about high prices, used books were profitable. According to the National Association of College Stores (NACS; 2003), the profit margin on the typical new textbook averaged 21.42 percent, versus an average of 33.65 percent for the typical used book. NACS estimated that the average college student spent $704 in the college bookstore in 2002–2003 (the last year reliable data were available). New textbooks accounted for 48.9 percent of all expenditures ($339.37), used books averaged 17.12 percent ($118.81), and course packs averaged 1.14 percent ($7.91). The remaining balance ($227.91) was spent on supplies, clothing, etc. NACS determined that the average new college textbook cost $72.83 in the fall of 2002 while the average used book cost $51.16, a difference of 42.36 percent (NACS 2003).

This meant that college students spent approximately $1.76 billion on used textbooks and $4.81 billion on new texts (for a total of $6.57 billion) in college bookstores. Our

TABLE 4.11
Estimated frontlist and backlist sales of economics textbooks, 1999–2002

Revenues & units	1999	2000	2001	2002
Net publisher revenues ($ millions)				
Frontlist	58,933,980	56,467,530	87,803,730	95,148,270
Backlist	23,400,090	22,343,580	35,480,970	32,859,540
Total	82,334,070	78,811,110	123,284,700	128,007,810
Net publisher units (millions)				
Frontlist	1,442,151	1,386,691	1,402,951	1,784,143
Backlist	572,589	548,667	553,199	616,157
Total	2,014,740	1,935,360	1,956,150	2,400,300

SOURCE: Our estimates based on data from the Book Industry Study Group, Book Industry Trends (New York: Book Industry Study Group, 2003): 185–202.

NOTE: All numbers were rounded off and may not add up to 100%. Annual differences are attributable to annual differences between frontlist and backlist sales, the impact of the used textbook market, course packs, documents placed on reserve or electronic reserve, the incomplete submission of publisher data (especially for 2000), etc. Data for 1996, 1997, and 1998 were not available.

econometric models indicated that the amount spent for used books from used-book bookstores or from Internet sites probably totaled at least another $200 million annually.

These facts prompted a sizable number of college bookstores to develop new textbook ordering ratios to accommodate the growing number of students who wanted inexpensive texts and to reach the store's desired profit margin.

Third, dynamic marketing Web sites were launched to sell new and used college textbooks directly to students. The end result was that the traditionally marginal used-textbook industry became far more organized, sophisticated, and successful. Fourth, with the introduction of library computer systems, an increasingly larger number of instructors placed book chapters on electronic reserve (i.e., e-reserve or ERes), allowing students to access, download, or print the text in the library, in dorm rooms, or at home, effectively negating the need for a text.

The end result was a shift in the marketplace. A used-book sale generates no income for publishers, authors, stockholders, etc. Backlist sales, long considered the cash cow of book publishing, sagged, hovering in the 20 percent range between 1999 and 2002. Table 4.11 outlines this trend. This meant textbook publishers became dependent on frontlist sales, a strategy that can work if there is little competition from the used-book market and sell-through rates remain high.

Industry averages of gross, return, and net statistics did not take into account the large number of books that remained in the warehouse and were never ordered. By 2006 the average college textbook had a real annual sell-through rate of only 90 percent for the first year, 45 percent for the second year, and at best 10 percent for the third year. If the annual target goal were 200,000 copies of our model text, actual three-year tallies would be 180,000, 90,000, and 20,000.

Tables 4.12, 4.13, and 4.14 contain a series of revised P&L models that we generated drawing on these revised sell-through rates.

An analysis of these three models revealed the following:

Net sales, $21,750,000 (off $20,244,000 from the results in tables 4.7, 4.8, and 4.9)

TABLE 4.12
Revised sample P&L statement: year 1

Print quantity:	275,000 copies (units)
Number of free copies:	4,000
Gross sales:	271,000
Returns:	20,000
Net sales:	180,000 (90% sell-through rate of projected net target)
Suggested retail price:	$100.00 per unit
Average discount:	25%
Publisher net income:	$75.00 per unit
Royalty terms:	10%: at $7.50 per unit
Subsidiary and foreign rights:	
Reprints:	$0
Book club:	$0
Foreign rights:	$100,000
Misc.:	$0
Total:	$100,000
Author's share:	$50,000 (50%)
Publisher's share:	$50,000 (50%)
Unit PPB:	$15.94
Plant:	$75,000
(editorial costs and proofreading, etc.)	
Royalty advance:	$500,000
Direct marketing:	$400,000
Profit & loss analysis:	
Gross sales:	$15,000,000 (200,000 units at $75 each)
Returns:	$1,500,000 (20,000 units at $75 each)
Net sales:	$13,500,000 (180,000 units at $75 each)
PPB:	$4,383,500 (275,000 units at $15.94 each)
Plant:	$50,000
Earned royalty:	$1,350,000
Total cost:	$5,783,500
Gross margin A:	$7,716,500
Other publishing income:	$50,000
Inventory write-off:	$0
Royalty write-off:	$0
Gross margin B:	$7,766,500
Direct marketing:	$400,000
Overhead:	$4,050,000 (30% of net sales)
Net profit:	$3,316,500
Net profit as a percentage of net sales:	24.57%
Net profit per net copy:	$18.43

NOTE: PPB = paper, printing, and binding; gross margin A = net sales minus total costs; gross margin B = gross margin A plus other publishing income minus inventory write-off; net profit = gross margin B minus direct marketing and overhead.

Author royalties, $2,175,000 (off $2,024,401)

Overhead revenue, $6,525,000 (off $6,343,200)

Net profits, $6,891,300 (off $7,349,724)

Net profit per net copy, $23.76 (off $1.67)

Net profit per net copy, 31.68 percent (versus 33.91 percent)

This tectonic shift cut deeply into net sales, net profits, and overhead contributions, compelling some publishers to price the book at a higher SRP to capture as much revenue in the first year; they knew full well that revenues would be decimated in the second year and barely visible in the third year.

TABLE 4.13
Revised sample P&L statement: year 2

Print quantity:	50,000 copies (units)
Number of free copies:	500
Inventory carry-over:	91,000
Gross sales:	140,500
Returns:	50,500
Net sales:	90,000 (90% sell-through rate of projected net target)
Suggested retail price:	$100.00 per unit
Average discount:	25%
Publisher net income:	$75.00 per unit
Royalty terms:	10%: at $7.50 per unit
Subsidiary and foreign rights:	
Reprints:	$0
Book club:	$0
Foreign rights:	$0
Misc.:	$0
Total:	$0
Author's share:	$0
Publisher's share:	$0
Unit PPB:	$15.94
Plant:	$0
Royalty advance:	$0
Direct marketing:	$50,000
Profit & loss analysis:	
Gross sales:	$10,537,500 (140,500 units at $75 each)
Returns:	$3,787,500 (50,500 units at $75 each)
Net sales:	$6,750,000 (90,000 units at $75 each)
PPB:	$797,000 (50,000 units at $15.94 each)
Plant:	$0
Earned royalty:	$675,000
Total cost:	$1,472,000
Gross margin A:	$5,278,000
Other publishing income:	$0
Inventory write-off:	$0
Royalty write-off:	$0
Gross margin B:	$5,278,000
Direct marketing:	$50,000
Overhead:	$2,025,000 (30% of net sales)
Net profit:	$3,203,000
Net profit as a percentage of net sales:	47.45%
Net profit per net copy:	$35.59

NOTE: PPB = paper, printing, and binding; gross margin A = net sales minus total costs; gross margin B = gross margin A plus other publishing income minus inventory write-off; net profit = gross margin B minus direct marketing and overhead.

As De Vany and Walls (1996) posited, book publishing is a complex, adaptive, semi-chaotic industry with Bose-Einstein distribution dynamics, dual-sided uncertainty, and Pareto power law characteristics. In essence, every new textbook in a specific academic field (e.g., the basic survey economics text) is a new product. This means every textbook is in a tournament, competing for sales and shelf space against every other textbook in its field. In addition, editors and publishers create a portfolio of texts (in economics, history, etc.) to generate the total required revenues since, in spite of the claims of editors and publishers, the unpredictable nature of consumer behavior allows no one to predict precisely actual sales. Consumers (e.g., students) make small individual choices not to buy the text, or to buy a used copy, or to share a copy with friends. These small decisions have a gigantic impact on sales in a specific academic category. "The crucial factor is just this: nobody

TABLE 4.14

Revised sample P&L statement: year 3

Print quantity:	0 copies (units)
Number of free copies:	500
Inventory carry-over:	50,500
Gross sales:	50,000
Returns:	30,000
Net sales:	20,000 (90% sell-through rate of projected net target)
Suggested retail price:	$100.00 per unit
Average discount:	25%
Publisher net income:	$75.00 per unit
Royalty terms	10%: at $7.50 per unit
Subsidiary and foreign rights:	
Reprints:	$0
Book club:	$0
Foreign rights:	$0
Misc.:	$0
Total:	$0
Author's share:	$0
Publisher's share:	$0
Unit PPB:	$15.94
Plant:	$0
Royalty advance:	$0
Direct marketing:	$50,000
Profit & loss analysis:	
Gross sales:	$3,750,000 (50,000 units at $75 each)
Returns:	$2,250,000 (30,000 units at $75 each)
Net sales:	$1,500,000 (20,000 units at $75 each)
PPB:	$0
Plant:	$0
Earned royalty:	$150,000
Total cost:	$150,000
Gross margin A:	$1,350,000
Other publishing income:	$0
Inventory write-off:	$478,000 (30,000 units at $15.94 each)
Royalty write-off:	$0
Gross margin B:	$871,800
Direct marketing:	$50,000
Overhead:	$450,000 (30% of net sales)
Net profit:	$371,800
Net Profit as a percentage of net sales:	24.79%
Net profit per net copy:	$18.59

NOTE: PPB = paper, printing, and binding; gross margin A = net sales minus total costs; gross margin B = gross margin A plus other publishing income minus inventory write-off; net profit = gross margin B minus direct marketing and overhead.

knows what makes a hit or when it will happen. When one starts to roll, everything must be geared to adapt successfully to the opportunities it presents. A hit is generated by the information cascade. A flop is an information cascade too" (De Vany and Walls 1996, 1493).

So editors and publishers publish a textbook, often with competing texts in the same subdiscipline, hoping to succeed. Publishing is a hit-driven business, and editors count on the few hits to cover the losses of the misses. While the sample economics textbook exhibited profits, clearly the ravages of the declining 90–45–10 sales profits undermines the current and long-term financial health of textbook publishing, reduces stockholder revenues, reduces taxes, etc.

The empirical data in the various P&Ls were compelling. These results triggered a series of questions. Just how effective and influential was the used-textbook market? How pervasive was the Internet used-book market? Was there a significant price differential between new and used economics textbooks on the Internet? Did the Internet push down the price of textbooks, as some theorists argued, since all of the available information about prices was accessible by all vendors and consumers?

SHOPBOT ANALYSIS

A study of the nine most popular basic two-semester economics books was initiated to determine answers to many of these questions. Confidential sources provided the names of the best-selling texts.

To determine prices, a shopbot (computerized shopping robot) generated up to 20 prices for every used book in the textbook segment. The effectiveness of shopbots as a marketing tool has been well documented. The published literature contains a number of substantive theories regarding the effectiveness of information on prices and the impact of the Internet on book prices.

Review of the Literature

The best starting point on the impact of information on consumers is in the financial and economic literature; and one of the principal theories is the efficient market hypothesis (sometimes called the random walk theory).

The efficient market hypothesis deals with how consumers respond to information. According to Malkiel and Fama, individual consumers take a random walk, gather and analyze information about a product (perhaps a stock price or a book), and then decide which product to purchase and which to exclude from their "market basket" (Malkiel 1996; Fama 1970, 384–417; Fama 1997, 1; Fama 1996, 415–28; Fama 1976, 1–83; Fama et al. 1969, 1–21; Fama and French 1992, 427–65). To Malkiel and Fama, the marketplace essentially operates in an efficient manner. *Efficient* refers to the fact that the market is informationally efficient; in essence, the current price of a product incorporates all known information affecting the selling price, and consumers operate in a rational manner, responding to changes in prices to perhaps make a purchase or sell a stock (Malkiel 1996, 1).

This efficient market theory has been the subject of rigorous analysis. Bills and Chang (1999) evaluated the impact of costs and production on prices. Curry (2001) investigated the impact of uncertainty on decision making and purchases.

Shiller, in a series of papers and a major book (2000), rejected the essential theses of the efficient market theory. He asked, "Must we rely on such evidence to make the case against market efficiency? Yes, there is no alternative to human judgment in understanding human behavior" (Shiller 1984, 497). He investigated the "volatility of mass behavior" and posited that "different groups (or groups at different times) have different tendencies—different in terms of conversation patterns as well as circumstances promoting information cascades—to transmit certain kinds of information and thereby place it in their collective memories" (Shiller 1995, 185). In "Human Behavior and the Efficiency of the Financial System" (a review of behavioral theory in finance), Shiller argued, "It is critically important for research to maintain an appropriate perspective about human behavior and an awareness of its complexity. When one does produce a model, in whatever tradition, one should do so with a sense of the limits of the model, the reasonableness of its approximations, and the sensibility of its proposed applications" (Shiller 1998, 27; 2003, 83).

Thaler also investigated behavioral issues related to financial matters. Thaler rejected the efficient market theory since, "even if asset prices were set only by rational investors in the aggregate, knowing what individual investors are doing might still be of interest" (Thaler 1999, 12). His analysis of behavioral finance and human behavior compelled Thaler to insist that economists must include the impact of consumer behavior in any calculus, even though "behavioral models are harder than traditional models. Building models of rational, unemotional agents is easier than building models of quasi-rational emotional humans" (Thaler 2000, 140).

Brynjolfsson and Smith developed the frictionless commerce theory at Massachusetts Institute of Technology (MIT) in a series of major economics papers. "Our research empirically analyzes the characteristics of the Internet as a channel for two categories of homogeneous products—books and CDs" (Brynjolfsson and Smith 2000a, 563). They argued that "Shopbot data has unique strengths for analyzing consumer behavior" since the cost of acquiring information is essentially zero in their frictionless environment as consumers jump from one Internet selling site to another one looking for the best price (Brynjolfsson and Smith 2000b, 2).

Clay, Krishnan, and Wolff developed the same-price theory at Carnegie-Mellon University. They posited that "low-cost information on price—specifically the rise of comparison shopping agents [shopbots]—will lead all Internet retailers to charge the same price for mass-produced physical goods" (Clay, Krishnan, and Wolff 2001, 521). Their ideas regarding the impact of the constant flow of information on prices is a pivotal concept in Internet retailing theory, and it directly challenges the frictionless commerce theory of Brynjolfsson and Smith (Clay et al. 2002).

The Shopbot Study

Publishers determine the SRP for books, but under existing federal law a vendor is free to charge any price for a book. We conducted a detailed shopbot analysis of book prices on August 14, 2005.

In the study, shipping and handling costs were calculated and included in the total price of a book unless the Internet site offered free shipping regardless of the size of the order; the delivery time for these books averaged three to seven days. All of the books listed in table 4.15 were available from the Internet site. No sales tax was calculated since some states do not charge a sales tax and some Internet sites are not obligated to charge a sales tax if they lack a physical presence in the buyer's state. Average prices were calculated for new and used books, as were average used-book savings. It was impossible to determine the condition of any used book, so it was assumed each book was in a usable and acceptable condition.

The nine top-selling two-semester basic economics textbooks were analyzed. All of the titles were available at used prices, ranging from a high of 54.85 percent of the SRP (for a savings of $52.35 on the Baumol-Blinder book) down to a more modest 84.59 percent (a savings of $19.70 on the McConnell-Brue title). Table 4.15 lists these prices and savings.

TABLE 4.15

New and used prices for economics textbooks, August 2005, two-semester course textbooks;
hardbound (cloth) books

Author	Suggested retail price	Average shopbot price: used	Average shopbot price: used: S&H	Average shopbot price: used and S&H	Average shopbot price: used and S&H % of new	Average used-book savings
Baumol & Blinder (16)						
July 2004	$115.95	$59.86	$3.74	$63.60	54.85	$52.35
Boyes & Melvin (16)						
February 2004	$125.56	$80.64	$3.81	$84.45	67.26	$41.11
Case & Fair (8)						
December 2003	$120.00	$80.44	$2.13	$82.57	68.81	$37.43
Frank & Bernanke (14)						
January 2004	$127.80	$79.26	$3.29	$82.55	64.59	$45.25
McConnell & Brue (12)						
January 2004	$127.80	$104.41	$3.69	$108.10	84.59	$19.70
Mankiw (4)						
January 2004	$118.95	$84.09	$4.50	$88.59	74.48	$30.36
Samuelson & Nordhaus (7)						
October 2004	$132.10	$106.53	$2.83	$109.36	82.79	$22.74
Schiller (12)						
February 2004	$94.80	$74.64	$3.09	$77.73	81.99	$17.07
Stiglitz & Walsh (14)						
January 2002	$119.30	$81.55	$3.60	$85.15	71.37	$34.15

SOURCE: http://www.bestbuys.com, August 14, 2005. The number in parentheses following the author name is the number of shopbot sites selling used copies of the textbook. Each textbook was considered the best-selling textbook in its category based on confidential information provided by major college textbook publishers and other reliable sources in the college textbook industry. While international (i.e., foreign) versions of a textbook generally sold at lower used prices (and often at significantly lower prices) than U.S. prices, only data on used U.S. versions were used in this study.

Summary of Shopbot Analysis

First, while all of the model P&Ls revealed profits, publishers must set SRPs at a high enough level to recover costs and earn a profit to cover developmental costs for other projects, to pay taxes, etc.

Second, the impact of the used-book market casts a dark cloud over the economic viability of textbook publishing. Most industry experts insisted that decreased new-book sales are anticipated in the next few years; and even modest declines in unit sales will erode profitability and the ability of publishers to invest in new projects. Additional P&Ls were calculated to ascertain the impact of decreased new-book sales. For example, if the text analyzed in the P&L statement in table 4.7 had a sell-through rate of 70 percent (instead of 75.52 percent), net profit as a percentage of net sales fell to 23.73 percent; a 65 percent sell-through triggered a 19.78 percent net profit; and a 60 percent sell-through generated a 15.18 percent net profit. If the industry experts are correct that more students will purchase used textbooks, the financial stability in the textbook business will be undermined. However, any substantive upward change in the sunk cost categories (PPB, plant, etc., areas where publishers have exceptionally limited flexibility) could destabilize profitability faster than shifts in the new-to-used book ratio.

Third, shopbots allow consumers and vendors to check book prices with the click of a computer mouse, resulting in a highly competitive marketplace and viable competitors to college bookstores. Yet the shopbot pricing data for used economics textbooks indicated clearly that the efficient market hypothesis was not operational because of widely divergent used-book prices. So if the Internet is supposed to flatten prices, and if the efficient market hypothesis has validity, why was there such a wide gap in all of these prices?

Fama addressed the issue of long-term anomalies, which he viewed as chance results and an overreaction to information (Fama 1970; Fama et al. 1969). So are differences in used-textbook prices merely the chance byproduct of anomalies? The influence and reach of shopbots is rather new; and additional longitudinal research is needed to ascertain why there were significant gaps in the total used and new prices. Clearly, the Internet has yet to flatten prices, at least for economics textbooks. The bottom line is that the Internet provides consumers with the opportunity to buy used textbooks.

Fourth, according to the National Center for Education Statistics (*The Statistical Abstract of the United States 2001*), the number of college students will grow 5.73 percent between 2003 and 2007, hardly an uplifting sign of future growth in the college textbook marketplace.

Fifth, during fall 2003, spring and fall 2004, and spring 2005 semesters, criticism directed toward textbook publishers and their prices appeared in the *New York Times* in a highly visible article by Tamara Lewin (October 21, 2003, pp. A1, A18), an editorial (October 25, 2003, p. A18), and letters to the editor. The editorial addressed the issue of prices and remarked that "publishers are driving up textbook costs wherever they can, often with the help of colleges and professors. For example, bookstores now sell bundled academic products that include a main textbook and as many as five supplements—including study guides and CD-ROMs—that are rarely sold separately." The *New York Times* offered some sobering thoughts. "Now that the cat is out of the bag, book publishers will have to moderate their prices . . . [and ensure] that students have access to used-book services on campus."

Book publishers responded by blaming college bookstores for marking up the price of textbooks while arguing that publishers might start selling textbooks directly to students.

Finally, college textbook publishers face the daunting challenge of producing reliable and useful books for students and professors; and textbooks are expensive, perhaps far too expensive for many students. Yet publishers have sizable sunk costs, paying for editorial process, production, marketing, etc., expenses before a single copy is sold. Their sell-through rates are unsettling; the life span of the typical book is no more than three years. The used-book market is undermining sales and profits as well as royalty payments for authors; and publishers have a fiduciary responsibility to their stockholders to maximize profits, which has become exceedingly difficult since the late 1990s.

In essence, the tested business model has broken down, and publishers have been hard-pressed to develop a new one in the current business environment. Will digital textbooks, the electronic distribution of content, or a print-on-demand textbook provide publishers with a realistic strategy to stem the tide of used books while providing students with reasonably priced books? Or will a "Napsterization" take place, undermining the fiscal integrity and intellectual property rights of publishers and authors?

Clearly, many textbook publishers are resorting to the one strategy they know best: raise prices, prompting additional complaints and compelling even more students to rely on used books. The life of this vicious circle will be, as Hobbes might say, "nasty, brutish, and short."

THE ECONOMICS OF PRINT ON DEMAND

One of the most compelling descriptions of the future of book publishing did not material-ize in the pages of *Publishers Weekly*, the *New York Times*, or the *Journal of Scholarly Pub-lishing*. It appeared, of all places, in a news story in *MacAddict* ("Publish Your First Novel"), a monthly magazine for die-hard devotees of Apple computers. In its April 2002 issue, *MacAddict* told the enlightening story of Christopher Paolini, an 18-year-old who wrote, edited, designed, and published *Eragon*, a 316-page book using his Mac, some off-the-shelf software, and the services of the digital print-on-demand (POD) division Lightning Source. *Eragon* was the first book in a trilogy planned by the young author. Paolini and his family viewed the book as a personal venture, one that would not be of interest to the large New York City–based trade publishers. At first, they were correct.

Lightning Source, based in LaVergne, Tennessee, is no more a traditional book publisher than Paolini is a traditional author. For one thing, the company's sole responsibility to this first-time author was to print and bind just enough copies of *Eragon* to support sales through Amazon.com on an order-by-order basis. Lightning Source did not have to type-set, format, or paginate the manuscript; digitize the cover images; or perform file con-versions for the final output. As a digitally enabled self-publisher, Paolini did all of his own prep work on his desktop computer, including the procedures that once could be per-formed only by trained professionals operating costly, highly specialized equipment. Light-ning Source did not even have to make the traditional book publisher's guess about how many copies to run for inventory. Thanks to the capabilities of its all-digital IBM InfoPrint and InfoColor presses, Lightning Source does not need to worry about conventional run-length minimums, the strictures they place on distribution and marketing, or for that mat-ter, traditional inventory issues. Whenever someone orders Paolini's book, Lightning Source simply prints a copy and delivers it to Amazon.com, which then sells the book to the customer.

Paolini's self-publishing experiment caught the eye of an author and his son, and the au-thor recommended the book to an editor at Random House; it is highly unlikely that a book by a teenager, without an agent, could ever have interested anyone at a large trade house. The fact that the book existed and readers liked it sparked the interest at Random House. In December 2002, Paolini signed a contract with Random House (through its Alfred A. Knopf Books for Young Readers imprint). Random House acquired world rights for *Eragon* and the remaining two books in Paolini's trilogy (terms of the financial arrangement were not released). Sales via Lightning Source were terminated, and the final sell-through rate for the self-published book was never revealed (Subtext 2002). However, once Random House published the book and supported it in the marketplace, sales were impressive, topping 950,000 copies as of March 2005.

Until the 1990s, producing books in short, strictly order-driven press runs was technically possible but commercially suicidal. A decade ago, unless one was speaking of exotic collectors' volumes with dizzyingly high cover prices or library reprints, there was no economically justifiable method of manufacturing books except by the thousands on conventional lithographic presses.

By 2003, however, this book manufacturing technology had made special-order small runs marketable and profitable. The production process known as digital POD enabled small-press publishers, university presses, nonprofit organizations, businesses, and of course, the legions of self-publishing authors like Christopher Paolini to tell their own versions of the *Eragon* story. Even mainstream publishers (e.g., Random House, Time Warner Books) are beginning to realize POD's potential for backlist titles and other kinds of books that do not fit into the industry's mass-market approach to manufacturing and distribution.

Review of the Literature

POD is so new that only a few authors have addressed it in published scholarly articles. We reviewed all the major scholarly journal abstracting services, including ProQuest, EconLit, the International Bibliography on the Social Sciences, the General BusinessFile ASAP, the Wilson Business Abstracts, the *International Encyclopedia of the Social and Behavioral Sciences*, the widely used Research Papers in Economics Web site (including Economic Papers, WoPEc, and BIBEC), and the Oxford Scholarship Online service.

We found only four articles in English (through Communications Abstracts and EBSCO) of interest. While these articles were useful, the highly technical nature of POD compelled us to rely on a few scholarly papers as well as a plethora of professional articles and books addressing the diverse POD and graphic arts issues related to this new technology.

Levack described the POD program at MIT's university press. The press provides portable document format (PDF) files to its POD printer, which turns out copies within 48 hours. Ellen W. Faran, press director, remarked, "We sought partnerships, technical solutions, and a business model that would enable us to succeed, and we waited to launch until all these components were in place" (2002). The MIT POD series contained 247 publications in a variety of academic areas, including architecture, the humanities, biology, medicine, and political science. "Eventually, the MIT Press hopes to make available any book whose sales have fallen below the point at which it is economically feasible to keep it in print via traditional avenues."

Davis and Solla (2003) analyzed the efforts of the American Chemical Society to monitor the electronic downloads of its journals via format (PDF versus hypertext markup language [HTML]). Their research "suggests that individuals are using the system like a networked photocopier for the purposes of creating print-on-demand copies of articles."

Euromoney Institutional Investor PLC (1999) reported, through its publication *Managing Intellectual Property*, about the efforts of a POD printer in the United Kingdom to reissue "books that have gone out of print" and to work with authors to keep their books in print.

Tzouvaras and Hess (2001), writing in a Swiss scholarly journal, analyzed costs, setup efforts, storage requirements, and revenues available to POD publishers. They maintained that "the creation of books with different levels of complexity and quality becomes viable with digital technology . . . we expect for the future that the economic advantages of POD will grow."

Digital POD Technology

Digital POD is a blanket term for an emerging market niche encompassing advanced production technologies, new print-run economic models, and evolving marketing strategies. POD will not replace conventional book manufacturing, at least not in the next few years, and it is not cost effective for every form of book publishing. Its core concepts (which include digital reproduction, short runs of one or two copies, and demand-based output) can be ambiguous and are subject to conflicting interpretations, even among experts. Despite its digital underpinnings, POD is not immune to competition from the Internet, which is currently draining billions in revenue annually from the industries that deposit data, words, and images onto paper.

Nevertheless, POD will have an impact on the transformation of publishing into an enterprise that theoretically denies no one with a manuscript the chance to see his or her work packaged between the covers of a "real" book. Authors are not the only beneficiaries. No longer must university press publishers inevitably risk costly mistakes about how many books to print in an initial run or when to authorize a reprint. With digital POD, they can keep inventories comfortably small and let the pace of actual, not forecast, sales be their guide.

In essence, they can match demand (an order) with supply (a newly printed book). When more copies are requested, they can be printed in a few minutes on a high-speed, all-digital production line with a start button at one end and a receptacle for bound, trimmed, and carton-ready books at the other.

Publishers, Printers, Short Runs, and POD

Not all digital printing systems are this fully integrated, but every digital printing system has capabilities that are well matched to changes in demand for printed scholarly information of all kinds (Mann Ronand Druckmaschin 2001). When the first digitally controlled output devices (e.g., the Siemens ND2 black-and-white laser printer) appeared in the mid- to late 1970s, most components of the publishing community did not notice this development, although Compaine's comments (1978) did generate interest in many segments of the publishing community at that time. However, what publishers could not fail to realize in the ensuing years was that while they were being called upon to publish larger volumes of information, the volumes comprised smaller but more numerous press runs (Kippan 2001). This trend to the individualization of content required directors and editors to rethink the business of printing and manufacturing. The stage was set for digital printing's irresistible entry into markets once dominated by the technology and the economics of photo-offset lithography (much as offset challenged traditional letterpress printing in the 1970s).

Digital printing might not eclipse offset lithography in the same way that offset replaced letterpress, but it has ended offset's reign as the lone option for the manufacture of books. Book printers who invested in digital print systems produced half of their volume on them by 2002 (Roth 2002); by 2005 that ratio is expected to reach 60 percent in favor of digital. The emerging POD market reached $21 billion in sales in 2000, and it was projected to reach $52 billion by 2005 with an impressive 20 percent compound annual growth rate between 2000 and 2005 (eclipsing the low-single-digit growth percentages foreseen for most other non-POD print markets; Hamilton 2002).

Digital systems better enable publishers to cope with a corollary to the exploding demand for information in small batches and to produce it in correspondingly small amounts of time. Publishers are used to rush book printing work, but where *rush* once meant a matter of days, it now can mean a matter of hours, a veritable while-you-wait paradigm that litho presses, with their costly time-consuming make-ready requirements, may not be flexible enough to satisfy. By 2005, according to one estimate, 40 percent of all print jobs were requested for delivery on the same day (the figure was less than 2 percent in 1995). Print buyers think the average time to produce a digital job is about half that of a conventional job (three to four days versus eight days), a perception that will continue to drive work away from offset into the quicker-turnaround digital camp.

Photo-offset lithography, with its predisposition for large runs and substantial product inventories, has been compared to a warehouse trying to coexist with digital print's convenience-store character in a market where shrinking product life cycles strongly favor convenience stores. The norms and the numbers are shifting, mostly to offset's disadvantage, when it comes to short-run printing.

A print run of 2,000 is a tall order for most of today's digital operations. Yet there is a striking opportunity for many presses to leverage the technology's unique advantages in the manufacture of their important books as unit costs decline and productivity increases.

Digital printing companies and manufacturers of digital printing equipment predict impressive growth for books produced in this way. Xerox Corporation, maker of the DocuTech production printer (the most widely used high-capacity digital output device), correctly forecast that digital book production would account for as much as 30 percent of all book printing volume by 2003. Others go even further, declaring that book printing is well on the way to becoming the first major graphic arts market to produce better than half its volume digitally by 2015 at the latest. Yet whatever its ultimate share, digital on-demand book printing seems certain to become a multibillion-dollar segment of the overall market for books.

However, in our discussions with a number of publishing leaders we heard some concern about using POD for frontlist books. As one publisher told us, "We would not consider publishing a frontlist book as POD. If the market were that small [for a specific title], why publish it." We were told, however, that backlist titles were better suited for POD since small POD print runs could match orders economically.

Yet another publisher felt POD offered incredible opportunities for both frontlist and backlist titles. It will take some time before any analysis of long-term patterns regarding frontlist POD versus backlist POD can occur.

Print on Demand

Digital POD promises benefits that directly address the challenges of packaging and distributing information for targeted audiences with highly specialized requirements. It is now possible for publishers to provide short-run books, "instant" books, and digital content storage as alternatives or possibly as replacements for the products and services to which they have been limited by conventional production technologies.

Among all publishing houses, large and small, the need for a new approach to print production is urgent. Not only are the costs of publishing (printing, paper, and binding) rising every year but the amount of material being published is increasing dramatically.

Additionally, progress in certain fields (especially in professional and scholarly publishing) intensifies demand for new editions. Since it can take anywhere from 9 to 18 months to publish and print books using traditional offset lithographic methods, many publishing companies are hard put to keep up with their market's appetite for the latest information.

Seasonality is another concern. Orders swell at certain times of the year but decline at others, cutting deep troughs into financial performance. Even at peaks in the cycle, many publishers must play an educated guessing game when it comes to forecasting demand for specific titles. These uncertainties tend to increase dependence on conventional production economics and its built-in assumptions of unsold product, inventory cost, waste, returns, and write-offs.

POD points to a way out of these compromises and constraints for many university press directors. The fastest and most flexible of all production methods, POD can compress to an unprecedented minimum the time between the completion of a book by its author and its purchase by a college bookstore, a library, or a reader. Digitally equipped publishers can use the technology to produce revisions and updates while the information is still as fresh as the scholarship that generated it. When there is always something new to publish, seasonal swings disappear. The market for new books can be tested with first printings in small, presold quantities but without the extravagant per-unit costs of small runs produced conventionally on photo-lithographic presses.

This means that a publisher's long-term thinking does not have to be dominated by long-run printing. Volume no longer reigns supreme as a criterion for decision making, and this represents a breakthrough that could have been triggered only by the major advances in POD publishing technology. Books now can be published because people want them and not because publishers feel they must accept the calculated risk of releasing them. As one print industry journalist recently observed, "The whole face of publishing is changing as companies that once would publish three books a year, choking on 1,000-book minimum runs, can now publish 30 books a year, reprinting the ones that succeed, and not losing their shirts on the ones that don't" (Yosefi 2000).

However, digital POD does not work equally well for all kinds of book publishing. In some categories, publishers clearly are better off sticking with the traditional photolithographic production and distribution methods that have served them well for many years. For others, POD gives them a means of overcoming the restraints that traditional methods impose both on their budgets and on their marketing decisions.

As the story of Paolini's *Eragon* demonstrates, one of the immediate benefits of a digital POD workflow is the reduction of some of a publisher's up-front investment risk by minimizing some (but not eliminating all) preparatory costs. For example, armed with Microsoft Word, QuarkXPress, Adobe Acrobat, and other powerful publishing tools, today's digital content creators are also digital content managers who can produce print-ready digital files. Bound galleys for proofing can be quickly and inexpensively produced on the same digital output devices that will be used to produce finished books in quantity. Internet portals to publishing houses and printers streamline image correction procedures and other prepress tasks, further reining in many production overhead costs.

With a print-ready file in hand, a publisher is free to do more than just estimate a run length and commit the book to the harsh uncertainties of the traditional distribution channels. The publisher may opt to fulfill orders by printing batches of presold copies strictly as orders are received, forestalling later worries about unsold inventory. This way, relatively little money would be gambled in printing books that fail to find audiences. The publisher could also consider licensing electronic master files for reprinting, possibly in bookstore or retail chains with in-store digital printing equipment able to print "instant" books with customized features for readers. This means that, even if a publisher decides to remove a book from production, it remains a viable product, not out of print but merely reposing in a state of digital suspended animation until market conditions favor another on-demand press run (Roth 2002).

Offset Paperback Manufacturers (OPM) of Dallas, Pennsylvania, one of the pioneers of digital POD for books, understands how the technology has reshaped the business of book manufacturing. At OPM, which prints hundreds of millions of books each year using a variety of production methods, 40 percent of the volume in 2001–2002 was for publishers ordering runs of 250 to 500 books at a time (Roth 2002). Digital POD has made orders of this kind economically feasible. Grasping that reality and capitalizing on it begins with defining its concepts and clarifying its terminology.

Defining Digital Print-on-Demand

Analog printing systems use changing physical elements (e.g., light, electrical impulses, chemical concentrations) to represent words and pictures. Digital printing systems reconstruct them from the 1s and 0s of binary data. All digital printers convert digital input into a visual image applied directly to the final surface of what is being printed (Fleming 1999). This basic description of digital printing can be expanded to denote the various kinds of printing machines that output from a computer database (Oak 2002).

Unfortunately, these terms are complex and not always uniformly used, including the word *directly*. Some people distinguish between digital printing systems that image directly and those that do not. *Directly*, to someone making this distinction, means that no durable image carrier (i.e., the traditional photolithographic printing plate) is created. Another point of view holds that computer-to-plate (CTP) presses using durable image carriers exposed directly from stored data are digital printing systems in their own right, plate or no plate.

As a result, the broad definition of digital printing systems spans a range of equipment, from networked color copiers to CTP-equipped lithographic presses in commercial printing plants. What all of these machines have in common is that they do away with the intermediary steps that separate content creation from content production in conventional work flows (Lampartner 2002).

In practical terms, this means that digital systems eliminate costly film and film-based operations from the imaging process, in essence no more stripping, dot etching, or plate burning in vacuum frames. These analog steps have no place in the digital creation of words and images.

Digital POD systems may be either fixed imaging (in which the content of the image does not change from impression to impression) or variable imaging (in which some or all of the printed matter can be different on every page). In both, the source of the content is a digital file that images a plate mounted on a photo-offset press or drives an internal imaging device that transfers the content straight to paper (Roth 2002).

Printing authorities continue to debate whether offset presses with on-board digital plate imaging capability are true digital presses, given that all modern printing systems are digital to some degree (Rutherford 2002). Publishers should focus instead on the business advantages of digital printing, regardless of platform. Because all digital systems, including offset presses with integrated CTP, dispense with the film masters of conventional printing, they all eliminate significant production time and cost. By streamlining the flow of content from creation to output and placing control of the process in the hands of a few people, they compress the production cycle to a point where the notion of short-run, on-demand printing becomes economically feasible.

The cost effectiveness, speed, and convenience of digital printing have made it possible to produce books, frequently updated documents containing time-sensitive materials and information (notably in the sciences), and similar items not only in small quantities (a press run of one) but in once unheard-of minimums of time. On-demand printing, defined as the ability to print current or variable data at the time or place of need, has created new kinds of print markets, a new breed of print buyers at certain types of presses, and a new category of print service providers (Webster 2000).

In a fundamental departure from the rules of conventional printing, on-demand printing assumes that the customer's requirements, not the printer's capabilities, will dictate run lengths, turnaround times, and delivery logistics. Publishers, editors, and production departments no longer have to buy more copies (units) than they need because of the printer's unit-cost structure. Reserving press time weeks in advance becomes unnecessary when digital files can be output on high-speed digital equipment at a moment's notice. Thanks to an Internet transmission technique known as "distribute and print," digital POD enables manufacturing books at any remote site capable of receiving and outputting the file. In this way, product can be printed where it is to be consumed instead of delivered from where it was printed.

Some technical clarifications are needed. As separate processes, *on-demand* printing and *digital* printing can mean different things. *On-demand* printing should be viewed as a subset of *digital* printing. The reason is that, while on-demand work is always digital, not all digital printing is on demand (Webster 2000). For example, although digital printing equipment might be used to print billing statements for a publisher, the print run would not qualify as on demand since the end users of the product (the recipients of the bills) did not order them. Nor can all short-run or quick-turnaround jobs automatically be described as on-demand work, even if digitally printed. The definition of *digital POD* must always be market-demand focused rather than production focused, emphasizing customer requirements over simple job specifications (Koenig & Bauer Group 2001).

Another helpful way to think about digital POD is to see it as a form of just-in-time (JIT) manufacturing. Instead of ordering entire inventories of printed books all at once, a publisher can request delivery in small batches as needed until the equivalent of a single large run has been delivered, but without a large-scale storage requirement either on the printer's end or the publisher's. Since content can be updated between batches, the JIT approach is especially beneficial for books and other time-sensitive publications that could become obsolete before a large inventory is exhausted (Lampartner 2002).

This can be done only on digital printing equipment; and it should be done only if digital printing is the most cost-efficient means of getting the work produced. Understanding the run-length economics of photo-offset printing as well as digital POD is a critical issue if the technology is to be used for profit as well as for convenience.

The Economics of Digital Print-on-Demand

At first glance, the unit-cost characteristics of digital POD appear even less flexible. Today in the typical digital press run, unit cost does not change, regardless of the number of copies produced. The up-front, fixed costs of offset lithography have no counterpart in digital printing; so there are no such costs to spread across units. Therefore, the first digital impression costs the same as the 10th, the 100th, or the 1,000th. In fact, by the time 1,000 or so units have been printed, the digital machine may already have exited its so-called sweet spot, the limited run-length range wherein it can print more economically than offset. Beyond the sweet spot's upper limit, the per-unit cost of offset will be notably lower, and it will continue to fall for as long as the offset press continues to run.

Unfortunately, digital POD is usually more expensive than conventional printing. The cost of digital printing has basically ruled out its adoption for certain types of books in the trade publishing segment; these presses have little incentive to give up tried-and-true production economies based on traditional methods. However, since a significant number of publishing firms rely on limited runs, digital POD could be the key to productivity improvements, inventory reductions, diminished product obsolescence, and other benefits that outweigh the higher price (Kippan 2001).

One of the added attractions is that digital POD creates new revenue streams from products and services that were impractical if not impossible to deliver with conventional printing. Most short-run digital work, perhaps as much as 85 percent, represents business that did not exist previously. In implementing digital POD, book publishers will not simply shift their manufacturing from one mode to another. The traditional and emerging technologies will coexist, with the latter supplementing the former as it creates its own product categories and market opportunities.

Sometimes the coexistence will prompt publishers to let digital printing pick up where offset leaves off as demand for a given title changes. A book with a strong sales potential could be printed conventionally for its initial run and then switched to POD as the pace of sales slows, a procedure adopted by many textbook, professional, and scholarly establishments. As publishers grow more comfortable with small runs, they will get better at balancing JIT print runs for initial distribution with the low-volume and one-off routines of digital POD (Kippan 2001). A book produced in this way can remain on the market as long as there are readers who want the information, not just until its first wave of sales is behind it.

However, the question of how to make digital POD's rigid run-length economics work for book publishing still needs an answer. If there is so much waste from unsold copies in conventional litho publishing (i.e., returns or copies in the warehouse), one might ask why more book printing has not migrated to the sell one–print one model made possible by digital technologies. There are probably two reasons: (1) the costs associated with switching to POD are substantial and possibly beyond the budget of some small presses, and (2) decades of experience have taught some publishers how to contain their expenses and keep them from threatening profit margins. The reality is that digital printing, with its higher per-unit cost, often fails to give some publishers much leeway in achieving further savings.

Making an absolute per-page cost comparison between digital printing and offset lithography is exceptionally difficult, if not impossible, because so many different kinds of work can be compared. Press manufacturers and industry analysts offer conflicting formulas; and in any case, the cost of digital pages will decline as the technology evolves (Walker 1999).

Partisans of digital POD insist that its value should be measured in terms other than unit cost, given its ability to do so many things that conventional printing cannot. In the everyday world of book publishing, however, the strength of this argument bears an inverse relationship to the size of the run. Assume, for example, that an offset press operating at high speed can print an adult trade paperback book for about $1.50 (depending on the print-run length). The same book printed digitally on demand in 2006 carried a unit manufacturing cost of between $4.80 and $8.00 (excluding savings on warehousing and shipping), regardless of quantity. Since the publisher must subtract the unit cost from its share of the cover price (perhaps 40 percent or less, after deducting the bookseller's, the distributor's, and the author's fees) to derive its margin of profit, digital printing is hard to justify for run lengths typical of most books sold through retail bookstores.

However, POD becomes more attractive when off-the-shelf sales are bypassed by printing books after orders are received (i.e., using the Dell computer sales-to-manufacture-business model), thus eliminating the risk of tying up capital in unsold inventory. In this situation, the money spent on producing the book is not the speculative investment that it would be in conventional production since the book already has been sold; so a return on investment is guaranteed. Publishers also profit from being able to produce and sell reprints in quantities too small for conventional printing; modest reissues of out-of-print works often represent another previously unavailable revenue opportunity. Even in retail bookstore sales, short runs of digitally produced books can turn an acceptable profit if returns are low and cover prices adequately reflect the higher per-unit cost.

The cost-competitiveness of digital POD will improve, leading ultimately to a reduction in unit costs. Although its up-front costs are higher, offset lithography retains its long-run edge partly because its incremental costs (i.e., paper and ink) are lower than those of digital printing (as well as a distinctive qualitative advantage in terms of color work, illustrations, etc.). However, as the prices of toner, substrates, and machinery for digital systems decline, the technology will push the upper limits of its sweet spot into run-length ranges that were once the sole preserve of the analog processes (Kotok and Lyman 1997). Digital presses also are considerably less expensive to purchase, house, and operate on an hourly basis (and generally free from the numerous state and federal environmental protection agency guidelines regarding emissions, silver recovery processes, etc.) than the sheetfed and web presses that have dominated book manufacturing.

In many ways, digital POD is already so competitive with offset for black-and-white book printing that some predict the conventional litho process, if used at all for monochrome book work, eventually will be limited to long runs with ultrahigh quality requirements for halftone photo images (Oak 2002). For example, a monochrome printer, the Scitex VersaMark 90/500, is capable of imaging pages for less than a 10th of 1¢ each; so a 300-page book could be printed on this machine for approximately $1.95. Books in color remain too costly to produce digitally, but digital color presses are expected to soon improve to where their cost per page will dip below 10¢, a price point at which they will begin to rival offset equipment for full-color book work (Kippan 2001).

For certain kinds of publishing, there is no alternative to digital POD; either the job is printed this way, or it is not printed at all. When the centralized business services division of one university adopted the technology for printing customized course materials, it was able to produce books in runs as small as 15 copies for about $25 each. The director of the center estimated that a traditional publisher or university press would have charged $40 to $60 per copy, that is, if one could have been found; no provider was willing to take on work in quantities this limited (Harper 2000).

Because of digital POD, the days of inhospitality toward short-run books and their publishers are over. Monochrome digital printing installations now routinely produce batches of 25 to 3,000 books, with an average run length of about 1,000 copies (Hamilton 2002). For start-up commercial publishing houses and other small operations, runs of just a few hundred have become a way of business life. The economics of digital POD is having a leveling effect on the industry as a whole, inasmuch as a publishing giant and a small literary press are on the same footing when each goes to the printer with a digital file and a 500-copy print order (Alexander 1998).

THE ECONOMICS OF SELF-PUBLISHING

If an author cannot get his or her book published, is it possible this individual might consider self-publishing? What are the economics of self-publishing?

As for the first question, various companies were launched successfully to provide venues for self-publishing, and countless thousands of self-published books appeared starting in the late 1990s. So this has become a viable option for a significant number of individuals.

However, it is likely that many of these books found distribution in traditional channels (e.g., bookstores) and untraditional channels (e.g., barber shops, beauty salons, hobby stores, health stores). It is equally likely that a significant number of these books languished in warehouses and on the shelves of the authors. Unfortunately, hard data on unit sales are not available for self-published books. The success stories are well known; the failures are not.

The second question can be answered. In reality, self-publishing, up to a certain point, is remarkably easy. An author prepares the manuscript on a computer, and he or she can buy all of the relevant services or products in the self-publishing process, including hiring an editor to edit the manuscript; purchasing software, perhaps Adobe; and contracting out the printing and binding processes. The real obstacles for fledgling self-publishers arise in distribution and marketing, chiefly because first timers have little idea how expensive and tricky these steps can be. For example, distribution through conventional bookselling channels incurs heavy fees; and a new ISBN must be purchased every time a work is reissued with changes, even minor typographic ones.

An Analysis of the Economics of Self-Publishing

Assume the following:

1. An author created a 362-page black-and-white book as a Microsoft Word document.

2. The author imported the Word document into PageMaker, formatted it and used royalty-free art for the color cover, and saved it as a PDF file, a now-standard procedure for publishing work flows.

How much would it cost to have 500 adult trade paperback copies (with standard trade paperback trim dimensions and standard paper) printed and bound?

We discussed the economics of litho and POD printing and binding with an experienced printing industry expert in New York and generated the following manufacturing quotes (which excluded all prepress costs):

- A commercial printer with traditional litho equipment would charge $10 per unit for a $5,000 total cost

- A quick printer with digital capability would charge $6 per unit and an additional $1.50 per unit for binding for a $3,750.00 total cost

- A general-purpose digital printer would charge $5 per unit for a $2,500.00 total cost

- A digital printer specializing in books would charge $3.75 per unit for a $1,875.00 total cost

However, this self-published title will compete in the marketplace with books printed on litho presses for as little as $1.50 per unit.

We generated a second set of printing quotes. We assumed this 362-page trade paperback would be printed on 50 lb. paper in a litho run of 5,000 copies, far beyond digital's cost-competitive sweet spot. The estimate was $2.16 per unit, for a total cost of $10,800.00.

The self-publisher faced other "costs," including determining discount rates, creating relationships with online and traditional booksellers, shipping and fulfillment costs, and promotional expenditures. There are often other costs: sometimes the heat of the POD equipment's electrophotographic print engines curl paper stocks and produce wavy pages in some copies, making them unsuitable for sale, and the printer's $46 setup charge for each job must be added to the cost of going back on press with repeated small runs.

While not rocket science, self-publishing is time consuming and potentially expensive, especially for individuals enamored with the mystique of books but unfamiliar with the harsh realities of the retail bookselling environment. However, since some authors in the non-best-selling book categories found it difficult to get a press to publish their book, is it possible that this digitally facilitated self-publishing strategy might grow in popularity, especially among authors seeking control over all copyrighted material and possibly libraries with special relationships to their audiences? Only time will tell if there is a seismic shift toward self-publishing by these constituencies.

As for the real or perceived value of a self-published book, beauty and truth are in the eyes of the beholder.

THE FUTURE OF PRINTED BOOKS VERSUS THE ELECTRONIC DISTRIBUTION OF CONTENT

With the availability of POD options, should a profit or nonprofit publishing operation consider printing a book using only POD? Should an editor consider issuing content exclusively via an electronic distribution format (e.g., e-books, through a download from a computer database, or from a computer disk)?

On the basis of detailed discussions with a number of commercial publishing editors and publishers as well as university press directors, chief financial officers, and other press officials (as well as talks with graphic arts personnel and observations of POD processes), we think it is possible that some publishing organizations publishing certain kinds of books might find a POD-only strategy exceptionally appealing. A small- or medium-size press active in specialized niches, perhaps poetry or literature, with limited annual sales might be able to print 5 poetry books, each with a POD run of 100 copies rather than 1 book with a litho run of 500 copies. While unit costs will be higher for POD (perhaps 30 percent higher than a short litho run), if sales exceed the initial POD run, additional copies can be produced on an as-needed basis, keeping a title in print for decades. So POD offers many publishers financial flexibility in terms of production expenses as well as costs associated with warehousing, etc.

Other positive features of POD for many editors and publishers include launching a test marketing campaign for a new title or an out-of-print book with a minimal financial outlay, getting a title into the marketplace faster, eliminating faulty sales estimates, reducing production schedules, extending the life of profitable backlist books, minimizing write-offs of unsold books in the warehouse and costly returns, and ultimately, improving cash flow. An oft-forgotten advantage to a POD book is the positive response of an author whose book remained in print. The designation "OP" (out of print) is anathema to most authors who spend one to two years researching and writing a book.

The second question—whether to issue content exclusively electronically—is rather complex since it touches on a raw nerve: the very future of the printed book.

The e-book reader is, in reality, a handheld consumer electronic device. Current models are expensive. In 2006 the basic black-and-white screen version retails for between $200 and $300 and the color screen model is a bit pricey, hovering between $500 and $600. Since the average consumer spends less than $100 annually for consumer books, it is highly unlikely e-book reading devices will emerge as strong competitors to books (litho or POD) since there are very few e-book readers in use (estimates in 2006 vary between 30,000 and 50,000, excluding Palm Pilot or personal data assistant–type devices). There are obvious concerns about any business model based on downloading content from a computer's hard drive to a disk or buying the content on a disk. First, reading long documents on a screen has not emerged as a pleasant experience for the majority of people despite more than 3,000 books being available on the Internet free of charge. Even Bill Gates admitted he prints out any document longer than seven pages.

Second, downloading and printing a 362-page book will cost perhaps $1.81 in paper (at $2.50 for a ream of 500 pages) and approximately $18.10 in black toner costs (assuming 500 high-quality copies per cartridge and $25.00 per cartridge). So an initial outlay of $19.91 saves a reader $10.04 if the suggested retail price of a 362-page paperback book is $29.95 and significantly more if the book is available only in cloth. The reader still has to cope with 362 unbound pages; if the consumer relies on a binder to keep the pages together, another cash outlay of perhaps $9.95 for the binder is needed, reducing the savings to only 9¢ for a paperback book.

Third, while computers and the Internet revolutionized both U.S. society and the academic community, there is scant evidence that reading printed books will be replaced by reading book content on a computer screen or a handheld reader. In fact, the sale of e-book readers has been unimpressive, and downloads onto these readers has not been a source of any significant revenues for publishers (total industry estimated 2006 revenues: between $12 million and $14 million), even those with superb editorial content.

The printed book will endure, even in the college textbook market (and probably until 2020) as long as e-book readers retain their limited battery life spans and awkward screens and the cost of the e-book readers exceeds annual U.S. expenditures for consumer books.

Summary of Print versus Electronic Distribution

POD offers presses an opportunity to publish titles (including frontlist titles and not just reprints of backlist books) that otherwise might not be published strictly because of financial constraints. The ability to accept frontlist books and use POD to minimize sunk costs and increase the reach of presses and authors is an appealing opportunity.

Clearly, POD is not a perfect answer for every press and its frontlist, but it is a viable technological answer for a cluster of for-profit and nonprofit presses publishing certain types of books.

One is reminded, however, of the thoughtful comments of the noted economist Hal Varian (Shapiro and Varian 1999) about traditional business models and the impact of new technologies. "Every day brought forth new technological advances to which the old business models seemed no longer to apply. Yet, somehow, the basic laws of economics asserted themselves. Those who mastered these laws survived in the new environment. Those who did not failed. . . . The thesis of this [Shapiro and Varian's] book is that durable economic principles can guide you in today's frenetic business environment. Technology changes. Economic laws do not."

After a careful analysis of the various existing printing and electronic distribution opportunities and detailed (and remarkably candid) discussions with a cross section of publishing executives, we conclude that at the current time litho is (and is likely to remain) the best available solution for the majority of presses eager to publish both frontlist and backlist books and authors eager to see their ideas, theories, or research disseminated among the entire universe of readers.

Agarwal, Rajshree, and Michael Gort. 2001. "First-Mover Advantage and the Speed of Competitive Entry, 1887–1996." *Journal of Law and Economics* 44, no. 1 (April): 161–77.

Alexander, George A. 1998. "Books on Demand at Lighting Print: POD Goes Head-to-Head with Offset." *The Seybold Report on Publishing Systems* 28, no. 7 (December 14): 3–5.

Anderson, Eric, and Duncan Simester. 2000. "The Role of Price Endings: Why Stores May Sell More at $49 than at $44." Paper available from the Social Science Research Network Electronic Library (May): 1–27. http://papers.ssrn.com/sol3/papers.cfm?abstract_id=232542.

Anon. 2002. "Alfred A. Knopf Books for Young Readers." *Subtext* (December 16): 8.

Athey, Susan, and Schmutzler, Armin. 2001. "Investment and Market Dominance." *RAND Journal of Economics* 32, no. 1 (Spring): 1–26.

Bills, Mark, and Youngsing Chang. 1999. "Understanding How Price Responds to Costs and Production." National Bureau of Economic Research paper no. W7311 (August): 1–13.

Blumenstyk, Goldie. 2001. "Publishers Promote E-textbooks, but Many Students and Professors Are Skeptical." *Chronicle of Higher Education*, May 18, A35.

Book Industry Study Group. Book Industry Trends. New York: Book Industry Study Group. [Published annually.]

Brynjolfsson, Erik, and Michael D. Smith. 2000a. "Frictionless Commerce? A Comparison of Internet and Conventional Retailers." *Management Science* 46, no. 4 (April): 563–85.

———. 2000b. "The Great Equalizer? Consumer Choice Behavior at Internet Shopbots." 2000b. Working Paper MIT Sloan School of Management (July): 1–63.

Cabral, Luis M. B. 2000. "Stretching Firm and Brand Reputation." *RAND Journal of Economics* 31, no. 4 (Winter): 658–73.

Carlton, Dennis W., and Judith A. Chevalier. 2001. "Free Riding and Sales Strategies for the Internet." *Journal of Industrial Economics* 49, no. 4 (December): 441–61.

Chaudhuri, Arjun, and Morris B. Holbrook. 2001. "The Chain of Effects from Brand Trust and Brand Affect to Brand Performance: The Role of Brand Loyalty." *Journal of Marketing* 65 (April): 81–93.

Clay, Karen, Ramayya Krishnan, and Eric Wolff. 2001. "Prices and Price Dispersion on the Web: Evidence from the Online Book Industry." *Journal of Industrial Economics* 49, no. 4 (December): 521–39.

Clay, Karen, Ramayya Krishnan, Eric Wolff, and Danny Fernandes. 2002. "Does A Seller's Ecommerce Reputation Matter? Evidence from Ebay Auctions." *Journal of Industrial Economics*, 50, no. 3 (September): 351–67.

Compaine, Benjamin M. 1978. *The Book Industry in Transition*. White Plains, NY: Knowledge Industry Publications, 190–91.

Cost, Frank. 2003. *The Pocket Guide to Digital Printing*. Albany, NY: Delmar Publishers, 80.

Curry, Philip A. 2001. "Decision Making under Uncertainty and the Evolution of Interdependent Preferences." *Journal of Economic Theory* 98 (2): 357–69.

Davis, Philip M., and Leah R. Solla. 2003. "An IP-Level Analysis of Usage Statistics for Electronic Journals in Chemistry: Making Inferences about User Behavior." *Journal of the American Society for Information Science and Technology* 54 (11): 1062–68.

De Vany, Arthur, and W. David Walls. 1996. "Bose-Einstein Dynamics and Adaptive Contracting in The Motion Picture Industry." *Economic Journal* 106 (November): 1493–514.

DiClemente, Diane F., and Donald A. Hantula. 2003. "Applied Behavioral Economics and Consumer Choice." *Journal of Economic Psychology* 24, no. 5 (October): 589–602.

Euromoney Institutional Investor PLC. 1999–2000. Books Revolution Takes Off. *Managing Intellectual Property* 95 (December 1999–January 2000): 12.

Fama, Eugene F. 1970. Efficient Capital Markets: A Review of Theory and Empirical Work. *Journal of Finance* 25:384–417.

———. 1976. *Foundations of Finance*. New York: Basic Books.

———. 1996. "Discounting under Uncertainty." *Journal of Business* 69:415–28.

———. 1997. "Market Efficiency, Long-Term Returns, and Behavioral Finance." Working paper Graduate School of Business, University of Chicago (June).

Fama, Eugene F., and Kenneth R. French. 1992. "The Cross-Section of Expected Stock Returns." *Journal of Finance* 47:427–65.

Fama, Eugene F., Lawrence Fisher, Michael Jensen, and Richard Roll. 1969. "The Adjustment of Stock Prices to New Information." *International Economic Review* 19:1–21.

Fleming, Mark. 1999. "Printing on Demand in Color." *Digital Output* (January): 41.

Fudenberg, Drew, and Tirole, Jean. 2000. "Customer Poaching and Brand Switching." *RAND Journal of Economics* 31, no. 4 (Winter).

Gifford, Sharon. 2001. "Endogenous Information Costs." Paper available at the Social Science Research Network Electronic Library (February 24, 2001). http://papers.ssrn.com/sol3/papers.cfm?abstract_id=262183.

Greco, Albert N. 2005. *The Book Publishing Industry*. Mahwah, NJ: Erlbaum.

Hamilton, Jim. 2002. "Trends in Color on Demand Printing." *Digital Output* (February): 28–30.

Han, Jin. K., Kim, Namwoon, and Kim, Hong-Bumm. 2001. "Entry Barriers: A Dull-, One,- or Two-Edged Sword for Incumbents? Unraveling the Paradox from a Contingency Perspective." *Journal of Marketing* 65 (January): 1–14.

Harper, Eliot. 2000. DPC White Paper No. 3: Digital Printing Issues: Economics, Markets, Technology, and the Digital Future. Digital Printing Council of the Printing Industries of America (May): 5.

Kippan, Helmut, ed. 2001. *Handbook of Print Media*. Berlin: Springer-Verlag, 946.

Kirkpatrick, David D. 2001. Forecasts of an E-Book Era Were, It Seems, Premature. *New York Times*, August 28, A1, A18.

Koenig & Bauer Group. 2001. "Digital Printing 2000: Technology, Markets, and Scenarios." KBA Report No. 16 (January): 2.

Kotok, Alan, and Ralph Lyman. 1997. *Print Communications and the Electronic Media Challenge.* Plainview, NY: Kotok and Lyman: 17.

Lampartner, William C. 2002. Digital Printing Technology Developments and Market Growth Lags Earlier Forecasts. *GATF World/2002: GATF Technology Forecast* (January-February): 77.

Letts, Mike. 2001. "MetaText: Building a New Kind of Textbook." *Seybold Report Analyzing Publishing Trends* 1, no. 7 (July): 4–16.

Levack, Kinley. 2003. Pressing the POD Issue: The MIT Classics Series. *EContent* 26, no. 7 (July): 9.

Malkiel, Burton. 1996. *A Random Walk Down Wall Street.* New York: Norton.

Mann Ronand Druckmaschin AG. 2001. "What's Digital Here?" *Expressis Verbis* (March): 12.

Mullainathan, Sendhil, and Richard H. Thaler. 2000. "Behavioral Economics." Paper available at the Social Science Research Network Electronic Library (October): 1–31. http://papers.ssrn.com/sol3/papers.cfm?abstract_id=245733.

National Association of College Stores. 2003. Available at http://www.nacs.org; June 1, 2003.

National Center for Education Statistics. 2003. Available at http://nces.ed.gov/pubs2002/proj2012/table_10.asp; June 13, 2003.

Nevo, Ariv. 2001. "Measuring Market Power in the Ready-to-Eat Cereal Industry." *Econometrica* 69, no. 2 (March): 307–42.

Oak, Leslie, ed. 2002. *Print 2020/ From Pulp to Pixels.* Rochester, NY: Rochester Institute of Technology, 24.

O'Brien, Daniel P., John Bernoff, Meredith Gerson, Eric Monson, and Jennifer Parr. 2000. Tech Strategy Report. Forrester Research (December): 1–65.

Odin, Yorick, Nathalie Odin, and Pierre Valette-Florence. 2001. "Conceptual and Operational Aspects of Brand Loyalty: An Empirical Investigation." *Journal of Business Research* 53:75–84.

Oliveira-Castro, Jorge M. 2003. "Effects of Base Price upon Search Behavior of Consumers in a Supermarket: An Operant Analysis." *Journal of Economic Psychology* 24, no. 5 (October): 637–52.

"Publish Your First Novel: Your Mac Makes It Possible." 2002. *MacAddict* (April): 15.

Raff, Daniel M. G. 2000. "Superstores and the Evolution of Firm Capabilities in American Bookselling." *Strategic Management Review* 21:1043–59.

Romano, Frank. 2001. *Digital Basics 3.0.* Cohoes, NY: Mohawk Paper Mills: 14.

Roth, Jill. 2002. "Digital Printing: Emerging Markets." *American Printer* (March): 29.

Ruffle, Bradley J., and Ze'ev Shtudiner. 2003. "99: Are Retailers Best Responding to Rational Consumers? Experimental Evidence." Paper available at the Social Science Research Network Electronic Library (July 2003): 1–33. http://papers.ssrn.com/sol3/papers.cfm?abstract_id=331466.

Rutherford, Brett. 2002. "Print-on-Demand Here to Stay for Region's Successful Printers." *Printing News* (April 15): 24.

Shapiro, Carl, and Hal Varian. 1999. *Information Rules: A Strategic Guide to the Network Economy*. Cambridge: Harvard Business School Press: 1–2.

Shiller, Robert J. 1984. Stock Prices and Social Dynamics. Yale University Cowles discussion paper 616:457–510.

———. 1995. Conversation, Information, and Herd Behavior. *Rhetoric and Human Behavior* 85 (2): 181–85.

———. 1998. "Human Behavior and the Efficiency of the Financial System." Yale University Cowles discussion paper, 1–34.

———. 2000. *Irrational Exuberance*. Princeton, NJ: Princeton University Press.

———. 2003. "From Efficient Market Theory to Behavioral Finance." *Journal of Economic Perspectives* 17, no. 1 (Winter): 83–104.

Shipp, John. 2000. "Commercial Scholarly Publishing: The Devil Incarnate or Divine Savior?" *History of Economic Review* 32 (Summer): 37–45.

Smith, Carter L., and Donald A. Hantula. 2003. "Pricing Effects on Foraging in a Simulated Internet Shopping Mall." *Journal of Economic Psychology* 24, no. 5 (October): 653–74.

Thaler, Richard H. 1999. "The End of Behavioral Finance." *Financial Analysts Journal* 55, no. 6 (November–December): 12–17.

———. 2000. "From Homo Economicus to Homo Sapiens." *Journal of Economic Perspectives* 14, no. 1 (Winter): 133–41.

Thomas, Louis A. 1999. "Incumbent Firms' Response to Entry: Price, Advertising, and New Product Introduction." *International Journal of Industrial Organization* 17: 527–55.

Tzouvaras, Antonios, and Thomas Hess. 2001. "Keyword: Print-on-Demand." *International Journal of Media Management* 3 (1): 39–41.

U.S. Department of Commerce, Bureau of the Census. 2001. *The Statistical Abstract of the United States 2001*. Washington, DC: Government Printing Office.

Walker, Jill Cohen. 1999. "Gutenberg's 'Gotcha'? Gee-Whiz Digital Technology Returns Book Printing to Its Short-Run Roots." *Print on Demand* (September): 14.

Webster, Edward. 2000. *Print Unchained: Fifty Years of Digital Printing, 1950–2000 and Beyond: A Saga of Invention and Enterprise*. West Dover, VT: DRA of Vermont, xiii.

Yosefi, Hanan. 2000. "The Convergence of Graphic Arts and Digital Print." *DocuWorld* (Fall): 46.

Young, Jeffrey R. 2001. "A University That Reveres Tradition Experiments with E-Books." *Chronicle of Higher Education*, May 18, 2001, A39.

II PEOPLE IN BOOK PUBLISHING

CHANGING DEMOGRAPHICS, PRODUCERS, AND CONSUMERS IN BOOK PUBLISHING

When *Books: The Culture and Commerce of Publishing*, the first comprehensive and substantive review of the book-publishing industry, was published in 1982, the country was already experiencing major demographic changes (Council of Economic Advisors 1998). For example, at the start of the 20th century, almost 85 percent of the immigrant population was from Europe and less than 2 percent was from Latin America and Asia combined. By 1980 European immigration to the United States had declined and immigrants came largely from Latin America and Asia. With the release of the 1990 census data a decade later, journalists and others began to routinely refer to the "browning of America," as it was noted that one of every four Americans no longer hailed from Europe. Since then, these demographic changes have intensified.

According to the last decennial census, minorities now make up roughly one-third of the nation's population (Cohn and Fears 2001, A1). Now, almost one of every three Americans is of non-European origin. In the 2000 census, non-Hispanic whites accounted for 69.1 percent of the total U.S. population (or 194,552,774 people). Of the 30.9 percent who were minorities, Hispanics and Latinos accounted for 12.5 percent (or 35,305,818) of the total U.S. population[1]; blacks constituted 12.3 percent (or 34,658,190); Asians were 3.6 percent (or 10,242,998); American Indians, Alaska natives, and native Hawaiian and other Pacific Islanders were 1 percent (or 2,874,791); and those of some other race were 5.5 percent (or 15,359,073). Persons who had chosen two or more races accounted for 2.4 percent of the total population (or 6,826,228 people).[2] This changing face of the United States has been due in large part to immigration and "a healthy birth rate" (*New York Times* op-ed, April 2, 2001, p. A14).

With regard to immigration, between 1990 and 2000 the foreign-born population increased 44 percent and comprised 28.4 million, or 10 percent, of the total U.S. population. In 2003 more than one in five students had at least one foreign-born parent.[3] Half the foreign-born population (or 51 percent) was from Latin America and more than a quarter was from Asia (U.S. Bureau of the Census 2002b, 1), with Mexico accounting for the largest share (one-quarter) of the foreign born and more than half of those who came from Latin America (U.S. Bureau of the Census 2002c, 1; Schmidley 2001).

Both foreign-born and U.S.-born Hispanics and Latinos have grown dramatically during the past two decades. Between 1980 and 1990, Latinos grew more than seven times faster than the population of the nation as a whole, increasing by half, while the white (non-Hispanic) population increased by only 6 percent (U.S. Bureau of the Census 1991, table 1; U.S. Bureau of the Census 1993, 2). In the next decade, the Hispanic population increased 58 percent. Between 2003 and 2004, one of every two people added to the nation's population was Hispanic.[4] Consequently, not only are Latinos a substantial part of the U.S. population, but they account for half its population growth.

The most recent census estimates on the Hispanic population show this population to be 41.3 million as of July 1, 2004, or 14 percent of the nation's total population. However, this estimate does not include the 3.9 million residents of Puerto Rico, who are also U.S. citizens and would raise the total to 45.2 million.[5] This would make the U.S. population of Latinos larger than the population of Spain and the second-largest Spanish-origin population in the hemisphere, after Mexico (Thomas 2005, 73–76). In 1999 the United States was already acknowledged as the "fifth largest Spanish-speaking nation in the world" (Kiser 1999). In essence, in terms of population growth, the major census story of the last 20 years has been the growth of the Hispanic and Latino population. The Asian population has also grown dramatically, but their numbers are smaller. Between 1990 and 2000, the Asian population grew by 48 percent, or 3.3 million (Okura and Su 2003, 61). The Asian population is strikingly diverse, with the Chinese, Filipino, Indian, Vietnamese, Korean, and Japanese subgroups constituting the largest ones within this category. In 2000 the majority (53 percent) were foreign born (Okura and Su 2003, 63).[6]

Other major U.S. demographic changes include the aging of baby boomers, a decline in the proportion of Protestants (Smith and Kim 2004), increased use of a second language, and the growth of a more diverse population of young people. Here again Hispanics figure significantly. On average, Hispanics have larger families and a higher proportion of children younger than five (11 percent) than any other racial or ethnic group.[7]

Hispanics also have a fairly high level of mother-language retention. In today's U.S. households, 10 percent of residents age five or older speak Spanish at home. Of the 30 million Hispanics who speak Spanish at home, more than half report they speak English "very well." This suggests a strong bilingual market. Not surprisingly, the proportion of women to men has remained relatively constant, with women making up 50.9 percent (or 143,368,343) of the total population in 2000 and men accounting for 49.1 percent (or 138,053,563; U.S. Bureau of the Census 2002a, table DP-1). Having examined the major demographic shifts in the country, let us now turn to the demographics of the people who produce books and those who consume books.

PRODUCTION

Are the changes in the racial and ethnic composition of the country reflected on the production side? To what degree are the producers of books reflective of the gender and racial and ethnic mix of the country today? Also, to what degree are minorities and women evenly or proportionately distributed across occupation and income categories within publishing?

Data from the Department of Labor's Current Population Survey indicate that, of those employed in "publishing, except newspapers and software," 86.8 percent are white and 13.2 percent are minorities. However, this category also includes other businesses in addition to book publishing, for example, publishers of magazines, train schedules, and mailing list compilers. The Equal Employment Opportunity Commission (EEOC) has data for 2002 that are specific to book publishing. The data show that 18.2 percent of those employed in the book-publishing industry were minorities and 81.8 percent were white (49.5 percent were white women and 32.3 percent were white men).[8] What is clear is that, whatever data source you use, minorities are underrepresented in the industry relative to their proportion in the population, which you will recall is 30.9 percent.

However, white women have increased their numbers since Coser, Kadushin, and Powell (1982) made their study and, according to the EEOC data, now outnumber men. But what does the picture look like when we examine what women and minorities do and what they receive for what they do?

Data on changes in salaries and employment in the book-publishing industry are hard to assess in part because of the government's change in industry classification between 1990 and 2000. However, *Publishers Weekly* does conduct yearly salary surveys of those in the publishing industry. Their most recent survey shows, as might be expected, that those in management positions (this includes presidents, chief executive officers, owners and directors, and vice presidents) have the highest median salaries.[9] Management positions have also had the largest increases in salary in the period measured ("Salary Survey" 2004, 34). This reflects the tendency in the current economy for those at the top to have greater income and wealth gains relative to those in lower occupational rungs. Interestingly, sales and marketing positions averaged higher incomes than those on the editorial side.

As figures 5.1 and 5.2 show, proportionately, whites tend to be more represented in higher-paying, decision-making categories, while minorities are proportionately more represented in the operative and laborer categories. For example, if we examine those employed as officials and managers, we find that proportionately twice as many whites as minorities are found in this category (13.7 percent of whites versus 6 percent of minorities). Similarly, in the professional category, the respective figures are 16.3 percent versus 9.5 percent. Whites are also more represented in sales, 10.8 percent versus 7.3 percent of minorities, while in the clerical area, the reverse is the case, with 19.4 percent of minorities in this area compared with 16.6 percent of whites. The technical area has a more equal representation of each group (4.1 percent of whites and 3.4 percent of minorities).

As figure 5.2 shows, with the exception of craft work, minorities are more represented in the blue-collar occupational categories compared with whites; 20.1 percent of minorities are laborers in contrast to 8.6 percent of whites, and 20.2 percent of minorities are in the operative occupational category compared with 12.8 percent of whites. There are similar proportions of both groups in the service area.

We obtain a slightly different picture when we examine 2002 data from the EEOC by gender and racial or ethnic group. While women make up 60.6 percent of all book-publishing employment, white men fill the highest positions in disproportionate numbers. White men are proportionately more employed as officers and managers—25.1 percent.

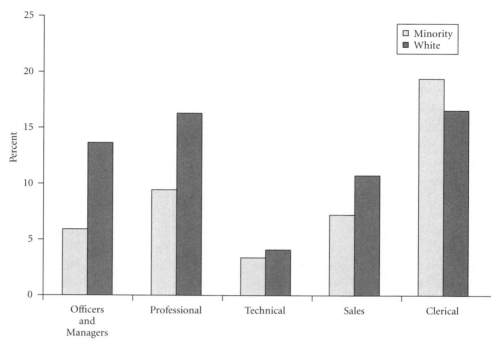

Figure 5.1   Representation of whites and minorities in higher-paying, decision-making occupational categories.

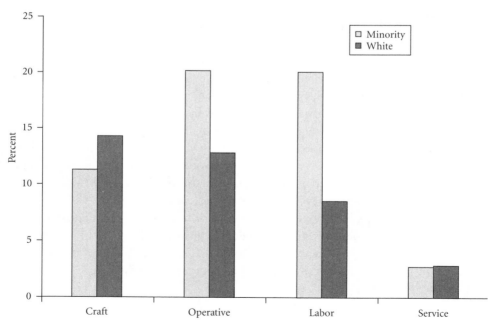

Figure 5.2   Representation of whites and minorities in operative and labor occupational categories.

This is compared with 17.1 percent of white women in this category and less than 15 percent of any male or female minority group.[10] This suggests that in book publishing a glass ceiling may exist for women (Falk and Grizard 2003) and a concrete ceiling for other minorities. The Annenberg Center at the University of Pennsylvania has been documenting the number of women in executive positions and on boards of directors of the nation's largest companies in the areas of publishing, printing, telecommunications, entertainment, and advertising. They found that the "percentage of women cracking into executive offices of top communications companies is stagnant" (p. 3). They constitute no more than 15 percent of top executive positions and are an even smaller proportion of their boards. No company has a majority of women on its board or in these positions (Falk and Grizard 2003).

In the professional category, which would include much of the editorial staffs, the picture is quite different and somewhat unexpected, with 36 percent of Asian American men and women working in the professional category compared with white women (25.2 percent) and white men (25.0 percent). Hispanics, blacks, and Native Americans all have fewer than 15 percent of the professional occupations, with only minor differentiation by gender. Asian American men are more represented (14.4 percent) in technical jobs than men and women in all other groups, including white men, who had the second highest representation (5.2 percent) in these occupations.

Women in each of the groups continue to be more employed in the clerical area than men: 37.7 percent of black women are in this area, as are 29.5 percent of Hispanic women and 27.8 percent of white women. A higher proportion of white men (11.7 percent) and women (9.6 percent) are in sales compared with other groups. (All other racial and ethnic groups of men and women were below the proportion of 7.8 percent black women in sales.) In the blue-collar occupations, group differences reflect the larger picture, with the proportion of each minority group employed as operatives or laborers in the double-digit range, while white and Asian American women and men register in the single digits. Few reported they were employed in the service sector.

This analysis of between- and within-group differences shows some interesting and surprising results. However, it should be borne in mind that white men and women constitute 81.8 percent of those employed in book publishing and that the absolute numbers in the case of the minority groups are not large. While blacks constitute a slightly higher proportion of those employed in book publishing (8.4 percent)—compared with Hispanics (6.2 percent), Asian Americans (3.3 percent), and American Indians (0.3 percent)—the between-group differences noted are small relative to the overall picture, in which minorities are not only generally concentrated in the lower-paying jobs but also constitute only 18.2 percent of the total. Yet, according to census figures, minorities constitute close to a third of the country's population. In essence, despite the interesting wrinkles in this picture, employment in the industry falls far short of reflecting the country's current population. To summarize the major findings, we find that, (1) relative to white men, smaller proportions of white women and minorities are officials in the top income category, i.e., officials and managers; (2) conversely, larger proportions of minorities are in lower-income occupational categories, i.e., laborers and operatives; (3) higher proportions of Asian men and women are found in professional jobs than any other group; and (4) in all groups, women continue to outnumber men in the clerical area.

CONSUMPTION

When *Books: The Culture and Commerce of Publishing* was published, there were already intimations that people were reading less than they had in the past. A more recent report from the National Endowment for the Arts ([NEA] 2004) indicates that people are reading less literary fiction.[11] It found that the proportion of adults who read literature—defined as novels, short stories, plays, and poetry—for pleasure was down from more than half of the population in 1982 to less than half in 2002 (56.9 percent in 1982 to 46.7 percent in 2002). Furthermore, in the last 10 years, the percentage of the U.S. adult population reading any books (literary or not) declined by 7 percent, and the rate of decline continued to accelerate during this period.[12] The decline was across the board, with whites, African Americans, Hispanics, men and women, and all educational levels declining substantially. The conclusion of the NEA report was that "reading is at risk."

However, Carla Hayden, executive director of the Enoch Pratt Free Library in Baltimore and also the immediate past president of the American Library Association, argues that "reading less literature is not necessarily an indicator that people are not reading." For example, they could be reading other nonliterary works. She also noted that public library use is at an all-time high, with 1.5 billion visits in 2004, up from nearly 1.2 billion visits in 2003. Moreover, as the NEA study itself points out, despite these declines, literary reading is still an important activity in the United States. According to the NEA report, "The proportion of people reading literature is higher than participation in most cultural, sports, and leisure activities. In fact . . . only TV watching, movie going and exercising attract significantly more people than reading literary works" (NEA 2004, 5).

However, the decline in *literary* reading is clearly a shift from how most envision the American public, i.e., as a literate reading community. And according to the chair of the NEA, Dana Gioia, this decline has serious implications, for literary readers tend to be active citizens who are more likely than nonliterary readers to perform volunteer and charity work, visit museums, and attend performing arts and sporting events. So a decline in such readers means a decline in U.S. civic health (NEA 2004, xii). Furthermore, a decline in readership may also indicate a greater split between engaged citizens and passive consumers of electronic media and, also, a shrinking of the country's common ground. In short, despite the increase in the number of new titles produced each year, literary fiction is down and there are concerns about the impact of this on our civic culture. However, some question whether reading less literary fiction means that people are reading less in general.

Are People Buying More or Fewer Books?

Given that the proportion of adults who read literature is down, are people also buying fewer books? We know that the number of new titles published increases each year, having jumped an estimated 19 percent between 2002 and 2003 (Bandler and Trachtenberg 2004). To some extent, this depends on your time frame and on what you count as a book.

According to the Book Industry Study Group ([BISG] 2003, 23), from 2001 to 2002, people bought about the same number of books in each of these two years (1.6 billion). But if we exclude e-books and audio books purchased for those age 14 and older, then the number of print books bought appears to have gone up during these two years. On the other hand, if we take a longer view, this increase is only because there was a 4 percent decrease in the numbers of print books purchased in 1998. Since then, purchases have been increasing 1 percent per year. Consequently, there has been an increase in purchases over four years' time but static growth over the five-year period (BISG 2003, 24).[13]

Who Buys Books?

If reading is down, who are the people still buying books? What are the socioeconomic characteristics of the main book buyers? The general expectation is that the main buyers of books would be those with greater education. While college grads and those who had completed some postgraduate studies do buy more books, relative to their proportion in the total population, in general, books are most likely to be purchased by households headed by someone with just a high school education.[14] This is true regardless of the type of book purchased. In fact, in 2002, while 26.8 percent of the U.S. population (25 and older) were high school graduates, 54 percent of *all* books purchased were bought by households headed by someone with just a high school education. This was compared with the 25 percent and 13 percent that had been purchased by households headed by college grads and those who had completed some postgraduate work, respectively.[15] Moreover, from 1997 to 2002 the purchase of books by those who had done postgraduate work declined.[16] An important but not fully researched question is whether these more highly educated groups have been replacing book reading and purchasing with shorter printed material, e.g., magazines, or with other more electronic formats, such as the Internet.

With regard to the occupations of book buyers, as might be expected, those in the professional and managerial professions purchased the most books. While those in management, professional, and related occupations represented 33.65 percent of the employed civilian population age 16 and older (QT-P27 Occupation by Sex, Based on 2000 U.S. Census data), this occupational grouping accounted for 35 percent of all books purchased in 2002. (They also purchased more books for teens and children.) Although those in this group purchased slightly more books relative to their proportion in the population, they also reduced their purchase of books from 1997 to 2002. As in the case of those with postgraduate work, this again raises the question of what, if anything, has replaced this activity.

As might be expected, those with more free time on their hands, for example, retired or unemployed, were the second-largest group of book purchasers, accounting for 25 percent of all books sold in 2002. The remaining occupational categories, i.e., laborers, craft and skilled workers, and sales and clerical had similar shares of 10–15 percent. The purchase of adult books followed a similar pattern, although unskilled laborers had a smaller share of purchases, 5 percent, and craft and skilled workers had a larger share, 14 percent.

How old are the main book buyers? Focusing just on books for adults (age 18 and older), we see that, generally, the older the customer, the higher the proportion of books purchased. Indeed, more than half of all adult books were bought by customers who were 50 or older—yet they constituted only 14.8 percent of the population.[17] The largest proportion of adult books was purchased by customers who were 55–64 years of age (22 percent), followed by those who were 65 and older (18 percent). These figures are in stark contrast to the 6 percent of all units purchased by those ages 25–29, 8 percent of those ages 30–34, and 7 percent of those ages 35–39. Moreover, from 1997 to 2002, those ages 35–49 cut back on their adult book purchases,[18] while those ages 55–64 increased their purchases substantially (from 13 percent in 1997 to 22 percent of all books purchased in 2002). The NEA report also found that over the past 20 years it is the young adults (ages 18–34) who have declined from the group most likely to read literature to the group least likely to do so.[19] Have younger people dropped the habit, hobby, or enjoyment of reading? Or, is it just that older people have more time and money to spend on books?

Are those who buy books better off than those who do not? Disposable income apparently also plays a role in whether people purchase books, but only in the case of adult books. Although households earning $75,000 or more constituted 22.5 percent of all households, they purchased 33 percent of all adult books. Those at the next highest income level, $60,000–$74,000, also purchased slightly more than their proportion in the population, 12 percent of all books, yet they accounted for 10.4 percent of all families in 2000. In contrast, those at the lowest income level (less than $30,000) purchased 25 percent of all units but constituted 35 percent of all households. The middle income level ($30,000–$59,000) also purchased 29 percent of all adult books, or slightly less than their 32 percent share of households. However, when we look at all books purchased (including teen and children's books), it is the lower-middle income group (those with annual incomes of $30,000–$59,000) that purchased the greatest share of books (37 percent) and the lowest income group ($30,000) that was the second-largest purchaser of all books (25 percent).

The picture that emerges from these data shows that who the average book buyer is varies, depending on the type of book purchased, i.e., adult or children's books. Looking at all books purchased, the typical book buyer is a head of household with a high school diploma. However, those in professional and managerial positions purchase more books than other occupational groups, followed by those who are retired or unemployed. It does appear that the more money households have, the more they purchase adult books. But it is the group with household incomes between $30,000 and $59,000 that purchases the most books overall. Despite the interest in the younger demographics of many marketing people, it is those who are older who buy proportionately more books. Yet this picture is very much being altered by rapid social and technological change.

There has been an increase in the use of electronic media at the same time that book reading has declined. In particular, children are, and have been, growing up in households where Internet use, video games, and portable digital devices are becoming increasingly common. Indeed, a 1999 study "showed that the average American child lives in a household with 2.9 televisions, 1.8 VCRs, 3.1 radios, 2.1 CD players, 1.4 video game players, and 1 computer."[20] However, according to the NEA (2004) study, it is not clear that electronic media are mainly responsible for the decline in literary book reading. Nonliterary readers do watch more TV (3.1 hours/day) compared with literary readers (2.7 hours/day). But watching too much TV (4 hours or more per day) or watching no TV are both related to the probability that someone would read 12 or more books a year. Moreover, "frequent readers watch only slightly less TV per day than infrequent readers" (NEA 2004, 15). Sometimes watching TV may lead viewers to read more, as when authors discussing their books on television stimulate interest in reading their books. Whether the relationships noted here will change with the advent of greater technological alternatives to books, e.g., iPods and games, remains to be seen.

Race, Ethnicity, Gender, and Other Variables Influencing Consumption

What impact have the demographic changes noted previously had on book consumption? Latinos are rapidly increasing in the United States, both absolutely and relatively. Other data also show that as consumers of the media their influence is being strongly felt. For example, while most national broadcast networks were losing viewers, the Spanish-language network Univision has recorded large audience increases over the last nine years (Univision 2002, 14). In addition, Spanish radio stations are also major attractions. Latinos, as a whole, have been found to attend movies at a higher rate than any other group, and according to Nielsen Media Research (2000), Latino households watch an average of four hours more television per week than non-Latino households do.[21] But what about Latinos as purchasers and readers of books? What about the other racial and ethnic groups' reading habits and what about the role of women in each group? How do other variables influence book buying, e.g., age, household structure, family size, and geographical area of residence?

According to the NEA (2004, 11) study, within each racial and ethnic group "women have much higher literary reading rates than men." (The literary reading rate refers to the percentage of the group that read literature during 2002.) Among the different racial and ethnic groups, the ranking from highest literary reading rates to lowest is as follows: female white Americans (61 percent), female African Americans (43 percent), male white Americans (41 percent), female Hispanic Americans (34 percent), male African Americans (30 percent), and male Hispanic Americans (18 percent). These results reflect the gender difference found in other studies—with white and black women reading more than all other men. The exception here is Hispanic women, who read less fiction than white men. According to Tepper (2000) this gender difference is influenced by childhood socialization and notions of gender-appropriate leisure activities.

Age figures differently in each group. Among white Americans, literary reading "is fairly evenly distributed by age," while among African Americans, literary reading is more common among the younger age group, or those 25–44 (NEA 2004, 11). Among Hispanic Americans it is those who are ages 25–34 or 55–64 who have the highest rates. Reading rates are related to education and family income; as these increase, reading rates also increase. However, "differences in literary reading between the higher and lower income groups are larger for Hispanic Americans and African Americans than for white Americans" (NEA 2004, 12). Also, while the literary reading rates of all groups declined between 1982 and 2002, that of Hispanic Americans was not only the lowest of all groups in 2002 it also declined the most (from 36 percent to 26 percent). Moreover, while the gap between African Americans and white Americans declined slightly from 1982 to 2002, the gap between Hispanic Americans and white Americans increased. However, in reviewing these results, it is important to bear two points in mind. One is that what was measured were "literary reading rates," not newspaper, technical, or nonfiction reading (NEA 2004, 11ff). Second, the shifts in the Hispanic American population are likely related to changing demographics, i.e., the increased presence of unskilled immigrants and the addition of new births in this group. Because of the absolute increase in total numbers the actual numbers of Hispanics reading literature increased by nearly 3 million—despite the decline in literary reading rate (NEA 2004, 24). We can expect this growth to continue as Hispanics and Latinos continue to improve their educational attainment.

As might be expected, the larger the household, the more books purchased. This is especially true for teen and children's books. But relative to their representation in the population, households with two members are the heaviest buyers of books for adults.

Where are the main buyers of books located? Interestingly, and somewhat contrary to the expectations of some that the Yankee Eastern intellectual establishment would, far and away, buy the most books, it is the residents in the Pacific region that buy the most books (18 percent), followed by those in the northeastern Central and south Atlantic regions (17 percent each), and in the mid-Atlantic area (14 percent). New England accounted for only 4 percent of all books purchased in 2002 (BISG 2003, 77). When taking into account population size,[22] the Pacific and Mountain regions are the heaviest buyers of adult books per capita, with the Pacific region being the heaviest buyer since 1997 and the Mountain region since 2000. In addition, households in the northeastern United States cut back on adult book buying in 2002. Nevertheless, despite these regional differences, city size continues to be even more important. "Large metropolitan areas, such as New York City and Los Angeles, represent nearly one-third of annual book purchases intended for adults" (BISG 2003, 79). In general, the greater the size of the city, the greater the percentage of books purchased. This has been the case since 1997, although "some growth was noted in the mid-sized and small cities/suburbs over the past couple of years" in adult books,[23] and there has been some decline in the heavy purchaser index in cities of 2.5 million or more since 2001 (BISG 2003, 80).

How Much Do People Pay for Books?

Individuals may be reading less, but the aggregate number of books bought in 2001 was the same as in 2002. Because of population growth, this represents a decline in per capita purchases. Given this, are they paying less for books? Yes and no. Although people bought about the same number of books in 2001 and 2002, they paid slightly more in 2002 ($13.2 billion compared with $13 billion in 2001 [BISG 2003, 23]). In addition, although the average price per print book has been declining, the price of some books has been increasing. For example, consumers have been paying more for trade, hardcover, and audio books, but mass-market books have declined in price. This has stabilized the price of books as a whole (BISG 2003, 58).

It is of interest, and may come as a surprise to academics, who routinely order books that cost $25 and up, that the majority (53 percent) of all books purchased in 2002 cost less than $10.00. Indeed, 73 percent of all books purchased were less than $15.00, while those books costing more than $25.00 accounted for only 8 percent of all books purchased.[24] The sale of mass-market paperbacks very likely accounts for these figures and for the fact that three-quarters of all books sold cost less than $15.00 (BISG 2003, 56).

Why Do People Buy Books?

What prompts a person to purchase a book? To some extent, this depends on the type of book being purchased. The BISG's panel study, which consists of 16,000 households reporting monthly, found that there were many ad hoc reasons for purchasing a book, but cover art and book reviews were cited most often as primary reasons for purchasing adult books.[25] Price, display, and recommendations from someone they knew followed closely, while ads and endorsements were third in significance.

In contrast, when purchasing teen books, the panel found that a recommendation from people they knew was the primary reason; this was followed closely by cover art. Display, price, and reviews were next in line, with ads and endorsements cited less frequently. Interestingly, recommendations by a media personality, the best-seller list, and hearing the author in person did not influence purchases of either teen or adult books. Nor did the fact that books were movie- or TV-based.[26]

With regard to children's books,[27] where impulse buying often plays a much larger role, customers noted that the store display was a key driver in choosing the book. Advertisements, recommendation, the "recipient asking for them," newspaper flyers or inserts, and the Internet were (in order of significance) the next set of factors that influenced children's books purchases. However, there were also other variables, of which they were less immediately aware, that also influenced their decision to buy a children's book. These included, in order of significance, the following: the perceived educational development value of the book, whether the recipient liked the type of book, its price, and special offers. Also noted, but to a lesser degree, was whether the book would add to a collection, e.g., the Harry Potter series; had a specific character, e.g., Dora the Explorer; or had been asked for by the recipient.

Are book purchases premeditated or spur of the moment? This differs according to the type of book purchased. Adult books are as likely to be planned as impulse purchases, teen books are mainly planned, and children's books are purchased on impulse. Teen and children's books are more likely to be purchased as gifts for others, while adult books are purchased for oneself (BISG 2003, 31).

What Types of Books Do People Buy?

The NEA (2004) report found significant declines in the reading of literary works, i.e., novels, short stories, plays, and poetry. As our society has moved toward more technical careers, gadgetry, and communication modes, are people buying less literature and more nonfiction works? This does not appear to be the case. Popular fiction is still, by far, the most common type of book bought, with the majority (57.3 percent) of all books purchased for adults being in this category. The next largest categories are nonfiction religious (8.9 percent), cooking and crafts (8.4 percent), and general nonfiction (7.6 percent), each of which accounts for less than 10 percent of all purchases. The remaining 18 percent is accounted for by purchases in the areas of psychology and recovery, technical, science, and education; art, literature, and poetry; children's reference; travel and regional; and all other. In addition, while the popular fiction area has been growing consistently since 1997, all of the other areas have either declined or fluctuated during this period. Some of these areas, such as travel and psychology and recovery, may have been affected by the expansion of Internet sites, which now provide services or information that were once found in published books.

Where Do People Buy Books?

Given the remarkable technological changes our society has undergone, how are books generally purchased, via Internet, mail, or in person? Remarkably, despite the tremendous growth in Internet use, as of 2002 the great majority of all books were still purchased in person. Indeed, 85 percent of teen books, 72 percent of children's books, and 67 percent of adult books were purchased this way. Purchases by mail were the second-most-often-used method for purchasing, with faxing used for 9 percent of children's books. Although the Internet was still a distant third in 2002—accounting for less than 10 percent of all books purchased—this means of purchasing books has been increasing since 1997, while in-person and by-mail purchases decreased during the same period. This is an area that is expected to change dramatically in the future, but it may affect the purchase of particular types of books more than others. For example, since impulse buying plays a large role in the sale of children's books, it may affect this area less than adult or technical books, where planned purchases are more common.

Would people read or purchase more books if they were more easily available? Where do most people buy books today? Books are sold today in a wide variety of places, e.g., large supermarkets, discount stores, and department stores like Wal-Mart. However, bookstores are still the main places that customers go to buy books. In 2002, 37 percent of all books were purchased in traditional bookstores. While the large chain bookstores, such as Barnes & Noble and Borders, captured 22 percent of all sales, the small chains or independent bookstores accounted for another 15.4 percent. Interestingly, book clubs were the second-largest outlet for the sale of books, accounting for 19.2 percent of all sales in 2002. The Internet was third, with 8.1 percent, followed by wholesalers and price clubs, such as Costco and Sam's Club, with 6.8 percent of all book purchases. Mass merchandisers, e.g., Wal-Mart (5.9 percent), used-book stores (5.0 percent), and food and drug stores (3.1 percent) were other important sites for book buys. These shares have remained relatively constant since 1999, although there have also been year-to-year shifts in each category.[28] From 1997 to 2002, the Internet, used-book stores, and small chain and independent bookstores contributed to an increase in the purchase of adult books.

Customers also use different channels to buy different types of books. In particular, people tend to go to bookstores to buy teen and adult books (59 percent of teen books and 38 percent of adult books were purchased in bookstores in 2002). In contrast, book clubs, fairs, and malls are where more (32 percent) children's books are purchased. Mass merchandisers are the third-most popular place to purchase children's and teen books. People also tend to buy children's books in discount and variety stores (7 percent) and in food and drug stores (7 percent). Discount and variety stores are also where 13 percent of teen books are purchased. Used-book stores, toy stores, and all other stores account for the remainder of purchases. In terms of adult books, bookstores, book clubs, fairs, and malls are the major places were books were purchased in 2002. The Internet and wholesale and price clubs also accounted for a larger share of adult purchases (8 percent and 7 percent, respectively) compared with the purchase of children's books.

Given the demographic changes and the picture that emerges of the consumers and the producers in the book world, what do those we contacted in the industry tell us about the culture and commerce of publishing today? We turn to the next chapter for their insights.

1. The terms Hispanic and Latino are used interchangeably here. Hispanics can be of any race. Although we speak of Hispanics or Latinos as one group, the Latino pot is made up of a variety of national origin groups. Moreover, there are substantial socioeconomic differences among these Hispanic national origin groups. These socioeconomic differences between Hispanic national origin groups are the result of different migration histories. For example, the Cuban community's demographic profile was skewed upward as a result of the early Castro migration in the 1960s.

2. The total U.S. population in the 2000 census was 281,421,906. A note on the percentages: The total population is equal to the number of respondents. The total for all race categories alone or in combination with one or more other races is equal to the number of responses and therefore its sum is more than the total population. The proportion of Hispanics and Latinos in the population is based on responses to the Hispanic item in the census and not to the race question. (U.S. Census Bureau 2002a).

3. Based on figures from the Current Population Survey, 2003. www.census.gov/population/www.socdemo/school.html, June 1, 2005.

4. Cited in http://www.census.gov/Press-Release/www/releases/archives/population/005164.html.

5. Data from http://www.census.gov/Press-Release/www/releases/archives/population/005164.html and http://www.census.gov/Press-Release/www/releases/archives/population/003153.html.

6. For additional data on the Asian population in the United States, see Barnes and Bennett (2002).

7. For additional, comparative data on children by racial or ethnic group, see http://www.census.gov/Press-Release/www/releases/archives/population/005164.html.

8. These data come from EEO-1 reports filed in 2002. See www.eeoc.gov/stats/jobpat/2002/sic4/2731.html.

9. This study was based on a sample of 563 respondents to a survey sent to 10,000 *PW Newsline* subscribers. The majority (62 percent) of the sample, with an average age of 39, was in trade publishing. Women constituted 66 percent of the sample, and 48 percent of all respondents were in sales and marketing, 25 percent in editorial, and 13 percent in management. Since this survey was conducted online it netted a younger sample than previous years', with 41 percent of the 2003 survey's sample younger than 35 in contrast to 21 percent the previous year. The survey did not collect data on race and ethnicity.

10. Hispanic women are the least proportionately represented in this group, with only 4.7 percent officers or managers. They are preceded by black women (7.4 percent), Hispanic men (7.8 percent), Native American women (8.1 percent), Asian women (11.4 percent), Asian men (14.6 percent), and Native American men (14.7 percent).

11. The NEA (2004) report was based on a sample of 17,135 adults, age 18 and older. Weighting was used to ensure that results matched characteristics of the total U.S. adult population. This descriptive survey of national trends in adult literary reading was

conducted by the U.S. Bureau of the Census, which also did similar surveys in 1982 and 1992. Respondents were interviewed mainly by telephone in August 2002 about their arts participation in the prior 12 months. The response rate was 70 percent.

12. In 2002, 57 percent of Americans age 18 older reported they had read a book outside of work and school. This is compared to 67 percent of Canadians age 15 or older who had read a book in 1998 (NEA 2004, 7). In comparison with Europe as a whole (comprising 15 countries), the United States had a higher proportion of literary readers, 57 percent versus 45 percent. However, the U.S. rate was lower than that of the United Kingdom (63 percent), Finland (66 percent), and Sweden (72 percent).

13. BISG examined an extensive number of data sources to determine publishers' net revenues and units purchased. Summary data in this report were based on a 4 1/2 month analysis of all significant and relevant data sets. The data were then reviewed by industry experts (from each book category) to verify their accuracy for 1998–2003. Data for 2002 was also compared to U.S. Department of Commerce data, and estimates came within 0.44 percent of the government data.

14. An additional 12.1 percent have completed grades 9 through 12 but have no diploma. In the United States those with bachelor's degrees represent 15.5 percent of the U.S. population age 25 and older; master's degrees, 5.9 percent; professional degrees, 2 percent; and doctoral degrees, 1 percent (www.census.gov).

15. Those with less than a high school education accounted for the remaining 8 percent.

16. This is as measured by the heavy purchaser index, which is the ratio of the distribution of books to the distribution of household population.

17. Population data source was http://factfinder.census.gov/home/en/atanotes/expsflu.htm.

18. Though an interesting and curious reversal of this trend is to be found in the modest share lift in books purchased by the age group younger than 30.

19. Interestingly, the group age 65 and older was even less likely to read literature than the young adult group.

20. Cited in NEA (2004, xii).

21. In 1999 Univision became not just the number one Spanish-language network but also the fifth-most-watched network in the country. This put it ahead of Time Warner's WB and Viacom's UPN as well as cable channels like HBO and ESPN. In 1997 Univision reached an average of 1.4 million households during prime time (Pollack 1998; Watrous 1999).

22. Measured by the heavy purchaser index.

23. Though more teen books are purchased in cities of 1 million–2 million (BISG 2003, 55).

24. This excludes used-book store, remainder, and book-club purchases.

25. This panel study is perhaps the best and largest data source available, but it does underrepresent African Americans and Latinos.

26. This was, however, more important in the purchase of teen books compared with adult books.

27. Children's books are defined here as books for those age 14 and younger.

28. For example, the share of the large chain bookstores was affected during this period by the closings of Crown Books and Lauriat/Encore.

REFERENCES

Bandler, James, and Jeffrey A. Trachtenberg. 2004. "So Much to Read, So Few Readers." *Wall Street Journal*, November 22. www.Wsj.com.

Barnes, Jessica S., and Claudette E. Bennett. 2002. "The Asian Population: 2000," Census 2000 Brief, U.S. Department of Commerce, Economics and Statistics Administration, U.S. Census Bureau, issued February 2002.

Book Industry Study Group (BISG). 2003. *2002 Consumer Research Study on Book Purchasing*, 22–80. New York: Book Industry Study Group.

Cohn, D'Vera, and Darryl Fears. 2001. "Multiracial Growth Seen in Census." *Washington Post*, March 13, p. A1.

Coser, Lewis A., Charles Kadushin, and Walter W. Powell. 1982. *Books: The Culture and Commerce of Publishing*. New York: Basic Books.

Council of Economic Advisors. 1998. *Changing America: Indicators of Social and Economic Well-Being by Race and Hispanic Origin*. Washington, DC: U.S. Government Printing Office.

Falk, Erika, and Erin Grizard. 2003. *The Glass Ceiling Persists: The 3rd Annual APPC Report on Women Leaders in Communication Companies*. The Annenberg Public Policy Center of the University of Pennsylvania.

Kiser, Karin. 1999. "Selling to the Spanish-Language Market in the U.S." *Publishers Weekly* 246 (37): 35.

National Endowment for the Arts. 2004. *Reading at Risk: A Survey of Literary Reading in America*. Research Division Report 46. June.

Nielsen Media Research. 2000. *2000 Report on Television, the First Fifty Years*. New York: Nielsen Media.

Okura, Mindy, and Jill Su. 2003. "The Asian American Market for Publishers in the United States," *Publishing Research Quarterly* 19 (3): 60–68.

Pollack, Andrew. 1998. "The Fight for Hispanic Viewers: Univision's Success Story Attracts New Competition." *New York Times*, January 19, Business Section, pp. 1, 6.

"Salary Survey for the Publishing Industry." 2004. *Publishers Weekly*, July.

Schmidley, A. Dianne. 2001. U.S. Census Bureau, Current Population Reports, Series p23-206. "Profile of the Foreign-Born Population in the United States: 2000." Washington, DC: U.S. Government Printing Office.

Smith, Tom W., and Seokho Kim. 2004. "The Vanishing Protestant Majority." NORC/University of Chicago, GSS Social Change Report no. 49, July.

Tepper, Steven J. 2000. "Fiction Reading in America: Explaining the Gender Gap." *Poetics* 27:25–75.

Thomas, Edward A. 2005. *The World Almanac and Book of Facts for Booksellers*. New York: World Almanac Books.

U.S. Department of Commerce, Bureau of the Census. 1991. "Census Bureau Releases 1990 Census Counts on Hispanic Population Groups," table 1. Press release, June 12, 1991. Washington, DC: U.S. Bureau of the Census.

U.S. Department of Commerce, Bureau of the Census. 1993. *We, the American . . . Hispanics.* Ethnic and Hispanic Statistics Branch, Population Division. Washington, DC: U.S. Government Printing Office, November.

U.S. Bureau of the Census. 2002a. "U.S. Summary: 2000." Washington, DC: U.S. Department of Commerce, Economics and Statistics Administration. July.

U.S. Bureau of the Census. 2002b. "Coming from the Americas: A Profile of the Nation's Foreign-Born Population from Latin America (2000 Update)." Washington, DC: Economics and Statistics Administration. January. http:/www.census.gov/population/www/socdemo/foreign.html.

U.S. Bureau of the Census. 2002c. "Hispanic Heritage Month (2002)." CBOS-FF:15 9/3/2002 Hispanic Heritage Month 2002: 9/15–10/15/2002. Washington, DC. Press release. factfinder.census.gov/servlet/BasicFactsServlet.

Univision. 2002. *Annual Report 2001.* Los Angeles: Univision Communications.

Watrous, Peter. 1999. "A Country Now Ready to Listen." *New York Times*, June 27, pp. 25, 27.

6 PEOPLE IN BOOK PUBLISHING:
"I'M GLAD I'M NOT AN AUTHOR. . . ."

Given the major demographic changes described in the previous chapter, how has the book-publishing world changed since Coser, Kadushin, and Powell (1982) did their landmark, now classic, study *Books: The Culture and Commerce of Publishing* in the late 1970s? What is different today, what is the same?

To gather reliable data, 11 questionnaires were developed for people in the following positions: top management, editorial, sales, marketing, production, warehouse-fulfillment, financial, information technology, publicity, legal and rights (subsidiary rights and foreign rights), and human resources. We conducted both an e-mail survey and targeted interviews that were intended to highlight unique, emerging trends and issues that deserved special attention. The in-person interviews were conducted using the same questionnaire outlines as the e-mail questionnaires, and they focused on selected leaders in the industry and other individuals involved in areas of particular interest to us, e.g., administrators in training programs, bloggers, literary agents, and those in minority publishing. Our samples consisted of 33 e-mail respondents and 24 in-person interviews, making for a total of 57 respondents. Although we cannot make generalizations about the publishing industry as a whole, the responses provide interesting insights into the nature of the culture and commerce of publishing today.[1]

DIFFERENCES BETWEEN THE TWO SAMPLES

First, let us review the differences between the two samples. Our e-mail survey had similar proportions of men (48 percent) and women (52 percent) and was 88 percent white. Thus our sample had a higher proportion of white respondents than the 82 percent noted in the EEOC (2002) data for book publishing as a whole; it also had a lower proportion of women, which was 61 percent in the EEOC (2002) data. The majority of respondents were ages 30–39 (33 percent) and 50–59 (39 percent), with about 15 percent ages 20–29. The majority (75 percent) had received educational training beyond the bachelor's degree, with the plurality (39 percent) having master's degrees. PhDs accounted for 18 percent, and another 18 percent had some graduate education. Occupationally, they were concentrated in the upper echelons, 60.6 percent being managers and officials. Editorial staff constituted 24.2 percent, sales representatives 6.1 percent, and other occupations the remaining 9.1 percent.

As might be expected in a purposive sample, those whom we interviewed differed substantially. The majority (70.8 percent) consisted of women, only 50 percent of the sample was white, and they were more evenly distributed across age groupings. There were similar proportions in all age groups, except for the two oldest groups, which had 33.3 percent in the 50–59 age group and 25 percent in the 60 and older age group. Educationally, the purposive sample had lower educational attainment. The majority (54 percent) had only bachelor's degrees, 25 percent a master's, and 17 percent a PhD. Occupationally, they were slightly less concentrated in the upper tiers, with 58.3 percent managers and officials, 16.7 percent editorial staff, 8.3 percent consultants, and 16.7 percent in other occupations, e.g., literary agents.

Despite the differences between both samples, both are clearly skewed toward top management. Hence their views reflect those with a higher vantage point. Also, both samples come from somewhat privileged backgrounds, with 63.6 percent of the e-mailed sample reporting that their fathers had been professionals and 50 percent of those personally interviewed indicating the same. Another 33.3 percent and 37.5 percent of the respective samples indicated that their mothers had also had professional occupations. Similar proportions (9.1 percent and 8.3 percent, respectively) reported that their fathers had been businessmen. These results conform somewhat to what Coser, Kadushin, and Powell (1982) found in their study[2] and to the general impression that publishing tends to attract the highly educated, privileged children of professional parents.[3]

THE MORE THINGS CHANGE . . .

Based on the responses in our samples, publishing continues to be an accidental profession (Coser, Kadushin, and Powell 1982, 99, 160, 165) with more than 58 percent of each group indicating that they had never aspired to work in publishing. Even among those who said they had always aspired to work in publishing, a number indicated that they had first come to the profession because they were either lovers of books or aspiring writers themselves. As in the past, many also admitted that they were helped along their way into the profession. The majority (in each group) did have a mentor who assisted them in reaching their current position.[4] Some had more than one mentor and, reflecting the gender changes in the profession, there were as many female as male mentors. This is a contrast from earlier times, where most mentors were men because men predominated. Mentors were in a variety of positions, but usually in decision-making roles, such as president, publisher, manager, or chief editor.

There has been little change in other areas. One is in the emphasis on what was referred to in Coser, Kadushin, and Powell (1982, chapter 1ff) as big books, today known as blockbusters. Circles of influence, patrons, and the role of agents as gatekeepers also continue, but there are now questions about how many minorities are to be found within such circles and about the relationship between agents and writers of color (Coser, Kadushin, and Powell 1982, 76, 306). For example, in textbook publishing, which has the best profit margins in the business, agents were seen to be very powerful in terms of recommending or submitting résumés—yet there appeared to be few minorities in this area.

Media Platforms

The trend toward media packages noted in Coser, Kadushin, and Powell's *Books* (1982, 30, 218–19, 221, 267–68, 317) continues, but now this is a consideration for all books, not just certain books. There are concerns over consolidation, and the tension implicit in their subtitle, *The Culture and Commerce of Publishing*, continues, with the issue being, what is more important: making money or making quality contributions to the culture?

Indeed, the role that media plays in book publishing appears to have intensified. Today, it appears that media platforms have become increasingly important. A number of our respondents indicated that a media platform or program was now part of what publishers expected authors to bring to the table (along with their book manuscript). A media platform is a way of reaching many people, whether via the Internet or connections to book buyers or as media personalities or newspaper columnists. This was seen as very important in determining whether to publish a book. One respondent went so far as to say, "There's almost no nonfiction book sold that doesn't have a media outlet," and that this was becoming true for fiction books as well. Another noted that this was part of the criteria that they used to determine whether to work with an author as an agent, i.e., how well connected the author was to the media. Yet another respondent, in evaluating what variables influenced the decision to publish, volunteered, "How marketable the author was." While in the past the emphasis—or at least what was articulated—was on the search to find great writers, today, an editorial consultant said, companies are looking for "marketable writers." As successful writer Alisa Valdes-Rodriguez remarked, "Writers that are surviving are concerning themselves with marketing as much as writing" (cited in Ayala 2005). However, what is curious about this emphasis on the media and markets is that—in contrast to many other businesses—very little consumer research is done. As the respondents who stated this noted, book publishing is an industry steeped in tradition, which means that people often go with their gut and their gut often feeds on others' projections in the media, e.g., the cult of celebrity lifestyles, current events, and spin doctors.

Sales versus Quality and the Changing Role of the Editor

This, of course, raises the question of whether the possibility of potential sales is replacing book quality as the main criterion for determining whether a book is to be published—an issue raised in Coser, Kadushin, and Powell's *Books* (1982, 140) and, more recently, in the *New York Times* profile of Random House's CEO, Peter Olson (Hirschberg 2003). This same tension was also manifested in response to our questions concerning editorial decisions on which books to publish and how to handle them, e.g., how much money to put behind each book for marketing. In the Coser, Kadushin, and Powell (1982, 141, 145ff) work, there were suggestions of tension between the editorial and the sales and marketing staff in meetings where such decisions were made. Some of our respondents echoed this and indicated that today this may manifest itself as more of a power struggle between departments, with the power of the editorial staff being diminished. One of our respondents said the editor may "have the power to say no but not the power to say yes." The person with the money, often the publisher, has this power. It was also noted by another respondent that, "today, editors have to be both marketing experts and PR people. . . . The focus is on product ideas and less on cultural necessity and quality." Bottom line, the emphasis is on "what will sell."[5]

Another respondent, who was an author, blogger, and book lover, bemoaned the disappearance of the editor's job as editor, adding that (as a reader) it was a disappointment to see an unedited book. Others have been writing about this issue for some time. For example, Thomas Whiteside wrote in 1981 that "critics, together with several authors and agents, argue that consolidation only occurred at the expense of literary diversity, worked to *reduce* author advances, and discouraged the best and brightest from participating in the creative game" (cited in Anand, Barnett, and Carpenter 2004, 12). Others opposed to consolidation maintain that book publishing was never "a particularly profitable business or a notably efficient one, but it was a business in which publishers and editors could feel sustained not only by their love [of] books but also by their sense of professional independence" (Anand, Barnett, and Carpenter 2004, 12). However, the sense of many today is that "most books from the major publishing houses these days, are edited haphazardly, if at all" (Jacob Weisberg 1991, cited in Anand, Barnett, and Carpenter 2004, 12).

Despite the acknowledged tensions between sales and editorial interests, few (less than 10 percent in each group) saw the mission of their organization as purely commercial—most saw the mission as cultural or a combination of cultural and commercial interests. The same balance or tension between qualitative and quantitative perspectives was also found when respondents were asked how they measured success at their company, with many respondents noting *both* financial and qualitative measures of success. "Financial" criteria or "best sellers" was the measure of success of 41 percent of the e-mailed responses and 43 percent of those interviewed. The majority (57.5 percent) of the responses in the e-mail group pointed to the "quality" of the books produced or the "number of awards" their books had received, while those personally interviewed also noted these but added "whether they had been successful in distributing their product" and "how well the public received the book."

Despite the balance portrayed in the responses about the mission of their organization, the influence of financial considerations was an important theme throughout the interviews. As one agent put it, when speaking about the power of the sales and marketing force, "Now, it is a product, not just a book." The intent, the agent continued, is not to produce good books but to replicate the monetary success that other publishers have had. Indeed, when some respondents were asked to rank what criteria they would use in deciding what to publish, both samples agreed that "the commercial prospects of the book" ranked above all other considerations. There was also general agreement between the two groups on the ranking and importance of "the book's potential profitability in the first year" (ranked 6th of 23) and "the long-term profitability" (11th)—although these were both ranked below other considerations.[6] Agreement between the two groups in this monetary area was striking, as the groups differed on other criteria. For example, although both thought that "the reputation of an author among general readers" was important, the e-mail group ranked this 7th and those personally interviewed ranked it 1st.

The emphasis on "sales" was also seen as very much affected by the competition books now have from other forms of entertainment and leisure, TV, film, iPods, videos, the net, etc. As one respondent put it, "books now compete with everything." Contributing to the concern over sales and competition from other sectors was the sense that there was not enough media attention paid to books in general. Respondents noted that the number of book reviews in different outlets was being cut back, newspaper pages on books had also been curtailed, there was little on the radio about books and, finally, as one long-time manager in a large publishing firm bluntly put it, "When was the last time you saw an actor in a movie reading a book?"

The concern with the financial side was also evident in the university press area. One respondent, who was an author and had had many years as an editorial board member at a number of university presses, noted how much academic publishing had changed in the last 20 years in this regard and described the situation at one well-known university press:

> The focus had been on quality (prizes and the courses in which the books were used). Now there is greater emphasis on how much money [a book] makes, how widely it can be marketed . . . even at university presses, it is difficult to get a book published without a wide market. It used to be assumed that the book did not have to make money, now you have to pay your own way.

As part of this greater interest in "the market," this respondent noted that manuscripts were now being sent to reviewers teaching large courses at state universities and community colleges to determine whether there was a market for the book. In the past, the focus had been on the quality of the manuscript. Another head of a university press was told when he was hired that it was a nonprofit organization, but his university also held the press responsible for producing a substantial proportion of the funds needed to run the press. Coming from the private sector, he quickly also realized that money had to be made so as to reinvest in the company.[7]

Coser, Kadushin, and Powell (1982, 140ff) found a similar, though perhaps more muted and emerging concern with the sales side. They found, for example, that it was the younger editors who were more concerned with sales, "In the past, trade and college editors were more likely to go 'to the mat' over a worthy book with little sales potential. In today's publishing market, both college and trade editors reported that they can no longer afford the luxury of books with limited appeal" (pp. 140–41). They also found considerable difference among types of house in the degree the marketing or sales group was involved in publishing decisions (p. 141). They cited the following proportions that did *not* rely on sales or marketing: 40 percent of trade, 10 percent of college, and 25 percent of scholarly. Finally, they noted that in both large and small houses they were more likely to use marketing and sales departments—if other companies owned them (Coser, Kadushin, and Powell 1982, 145).

MAJOR CONCERNS: CONSOLIDATION, DECLINES IN READING

Ken Auletta (1997, 54) described how when acquisition frenzy for book houses began in the 1970s, large communications companies began to be driven by the idea of creating media synergy and buying a publishing company seemed to be a good way to "become more vertically integrated."[8] But subsequently publishing companies began to be looked at simply for the money they made. The more traditional single-digit profits of the book-publishing business did not look so good—especially when they were compared with other companies in the content business. He also noted at that time that "most outlets were dominated by the chains, most orders placed not in shops but in a chain or discount store's central office, where buying is concentrated within a relatively small group." Thus Barnes & Noble then had 35 central buyers who worked out of their corporate headquarters; they ordered books for each store and also decided on the number of books for each store.[9] He also noted that 25 percent of all books were already sold through chains and that accounted for about 40 percent of adult hardcover or trade books. In other words, bookstores were no longer selling the majority of all books; rather the majority was sold through discount stores, such as Wal-Mart and Kmart, price clubs, and drugstores. In addition, he pointed out that airport stores, supermarkets, and coffee shops accounted for a disproportionate percentage of best-seller turnover. Finally, he predicted that what was big would get bigger and that they would also get smaller as these big conglomerates would trim (i.e., fire) their staff.

When we asked some of our respondents in 2005 what concerns they had about the publishing industry, consolidation was at the top of the list. (This was mentioned by 21 respondents—percentages were not calculated, as this was not asked of all respondents.) So along with the issue of finances and markets driving which books are published was the concern over the impact that consolidation had on small presses, the reading public, publishing personnel, and what is published. As one respondent commented in relation to the latter, the trade area was seen as so market driven that publishers published dumbed-down books, with the cult of celebrity and anti-intellectualism reigning. Book publishing was seen as reflecting the TV diet of reality shows, in which street smarts will get you further than school smarts. And yet, as the National Endowment for the Arts ([NEA] 2004) study underscored, people still need to read, as this is correlated with their contributions to civic culture, to say nothing of the need that people have to grow and know more. Yet, according to one respondent, publishers don't want to take the chance of publishing a book that they fear has no market. It is all self-reinforcing and the result is dumbed-down books. A related concern on the retail side was that "fewer buyers were making greater decisions for more people." Another respondent, discussing consolidation, said one major impact was that "there were more good people on the street" as the result of layoffs and that it used to be that when a good person was on the street, people attributed this to personality differences. This was no longer the assumption made.

Another effect of consolidation noted was the shift in company objectives. As one respondent at a large publishing house said, "Profit is what our parent company wants to see." Another, president of one small independent publishing company—who had been a sales rep within a large multinational company for 10 years before establishing his company and so spoke from experience—put it this way, "In a large corporation, sales forces are evalu-ated on the *number* of books they sell, not the *quality* of the books sold." Speaking in a more positive vein about the results of consolidation, a high-level executive in a large corporation made a similar statement but saw advantages to consolidation. He said, "Despite consoli-dation, more books are coming to the market." However, a third respondent was highly critical and said that "business growth was being dictated by Wall St. [and that] companies sold stock so they could make more money to acquire another company. They will also sell a perfectly fine division, so they can buy something else. For example, if GM decides people can read a book in the car, they'll buy a publishing company."

Coser, Kadushin, and Powell (1982, 8) had also noted that "publishing executives now worry a great deal about how Wall St. evaluates their operations." They also made mention of the Hollywoodization of literature and that "Wall St. control will mean that Money, Pure Money, becomes the boss." Their book was published just as we entered the 1980s and mergers and acquisition mania in media businesses was taking off and foreign publishers were opening U.S. offices or taking over U.S. companies. They speculated that this would mean absentee ownership, but they did not yet envision the sale of U.S. firms to interna-tional conglomerates based in other countries. They were also unclear about the full impact of concentration. For they saw, as people still see today, that a greater number of books were published per year despite the concentration. In essence, they saw, as many do today, that despite the "urge to merge," there were still a large number of small houses. They also noted greater diversity in the books published and overproduction of books, which has also con-tinued today. Finally, they noted that there were cycles in publishing (Coser, Kadushin, and Powell 1982, 29ff). In essence, the major trends they noted of media packages, the lessen-ing power of editors, the focus on big books leading to less contact between editors and writers, continues today, making it appear that the more things change, the more they stay the same.

With regard to small, independent presses, there was also concern expressed. As one avowed cynic responded, "When large corporations acquire a small press, they either want to change it or close it." The end result is that the alternative views that smaller presses may bring to publishing are lost as the corporation seeks to garner profits for its shareholders. Another head of a small university press said that, after having squeezed all the dollars out of dimes they could, the future—or the choice—for many small presses was one of priva-tization (being acquired by a corporate firm) or shutting down. The downside to connect-ing to a larger unit was that other bureaucratic layers would be added. In addition, it was an-ticipated that the content would be "lightened up." This respondent also feared that another perspective (foreign to the original mission) would be introduced that would no longer re-flect the press's audience and might even be seen as "off the wall" by its former readers. This scenario was seen as particularly possible in those companies where women's studies, eth-nic studies, or local-interest areas predominated.

Another of our respondents who described the unlevel playing field his company faced profiled the dilemma of the small press in this context. He said they had to compete with large companies that sell large quantities to the larger outlets (e.g., Barnes & Noble, Bor-ders) and that can give discounts of up to 60 percent on their books. Large companies can also pay co-op dollars to have their books well displayed—all of which increases their sales and outreach. Small presses, like his, could not afford to pay co-op dollars or give large discounts, nor could they sell large numbers of books, for each of their books have small runs of 1–2000. Therefore it is difficult for them to get their books into the larger stores. They have to be very creative and persuasive and spend quite a bit of time convincing buyers to carry their books. All this, with fewer staff.

Some companies have devised survival modes to compete within this current context of consolidation. For example, they do one layout, one print run in four colors, and change the language or text for each country in which they publish, or they publish one novel at the same time in four different countries in Spanish or in another non-English language. In this way, they keep costs down, share costs of production with other companies, and increase sales. Others use the money they make as middlemen in distribution to fund the production of their own books.

The establishment of large bookstore chains has had a major impact on small, independent shops (Anand, Barnett, and Carpenter 2004, 2). Because Puerto Rico is a strong market, particularly for Spanish-language books, we interviewed persons in publishing there. (Kiser [1998, 58] gives numbers for sales of Spanish-language books in Puerto Rico: the island accounts for around 50 percent of Simon & Schuster's sales [varying from title to title], roughly 23 percent of Llewellyn's, and approximately 25 percent of Doubleday Dell's.) One of our respondents noted the impact that the establishment of a large bookstore in Puerto Rico had on the local book business and Puerto Rican culture. Not only did the superstore put two other local bookstores—which had both included a large selection of Puerto Rican books—out of commission, but it also relegated Puerto Rican books to a local-interest area in the store. This section came to have fewer and fewer books *by* and *on* Puerto Ricans—even though the store was in Puerto Rico.

"Declining readership" was another major concern noted by our respondents. As noted in the previous chapter, this is an issue that has also recently received much public attention (see NEA 2004; Bandler and Trachtenberg 2004).[10] But at least two respondents said they were not convinced that there was declining readership but rather that reading requirements had changed—with some readers wanting a more interactive format—and other respondents said that some people who liked to read were just not interested in what was being published. (For example, anecdotal evidence shows urban or graphic novels are having an impact on the younger generation, particularly those who are not major readers.) It has also been noted that library usage is up, indicating that more people are reading (Dawkins 2005).

OTHER CONCERNS

Being "hit or blockbuster driven" was the third major concern expressed, and "competition from other media" was fourth among our respondents. Book publishing's concern with "profits and losses" as well as the belief that there were "too many books being published" made up the remainder of the main concerns noted. It is worth noting that the concern of "too many books being published" was offered independently by our respondents, i.e., it was not on our checklist. But one respondent did not feel that this was an area of concern. As he saw it, people create books for reasons other than to make money, e.g., for artistic expression or to compile family histories, so the "proliferation of content" was not really problematic to the business of publishing. Another respondent, however, argued that with so many books being published, it was hard for any one book to get any attention. One respondent involved in publishing for more than 40 years said there were so many books coming out now that even those concerned with national issues risked losing their three minutes in such a crowded field. She said that everything now moved faster, which led to quick sound bites on books, shorter opinion pieces, more ebbs, and the sense that authors and those involved in publishing had to change and reposition themselves often. The earlier clarity of who does what in publishing was blurring. She summed it up when she said, "I'm glad I'm not an author."

Do Agents and Networks Determine whether a Book Is Published?

As was the case in *Books*, referrals through networks were important, and there seemed to be general agreement that in the trade area few published books had come over the transom and that agents were critical. Indeed, one respondent at a very large publishing house said that agents had become very powerful because they performed an important weeding out function and gave a brand to the product. This person added that the odds of having a book come in over the transom and get published at their company were 180,000:1; Anand, Barnett, and Carpenter (2004, 2) state the odds as 15,000:1. More than 23 years ago, Coser, Kadushin, and Powell (1982, 133ff) stated that the chances were 10:1 for a recommended manuscript and 1000:1 for one that was unsolicited. There were, however, some interesting differences, depending on location and the firm's size. In small presses based outside New York, the role of agents was negligible or nonexistent for both university and trade books. Rather, influentials in academia, government, or the media played important roles.

Advantages and Disadvantages of Corporate and Independent Structures

As did Coser, Kadushin, and Powell, we saw a similar vagueness with regard to how manuscripts were acquired, but today there appears to be defensiveness on the part of some, who allude to the existence of "procedures" (sometimes spelled out in Web sites). The advantages and disadvantages of being with a large corporate firm versus a small, independent press were similar then and now (Coser, Kadushin, and Powell 1982, 179, 181). The advantages of being associated with a larger corporate structure involved corporate financial backing (i.e., availability of capital), corporate services and technical expertise (e.g., financial and accounting expertise and services), access to global markets, some greater financial security, personal benefits (e.g., better salaries, health benefits, retirement plans, greater corporate mobility), and expanded job opportunities. The disadvantages included the sense that the parent corporation was too concerned with the bottom line and were not producing books in the traditional fashion. The advantages of being small and independent involved the greater freedom that small firms have traditionally had, and the disadvantages were lack of money, financial security, and clout in the current publishing context.

What Are Major Changes since *Books*?

While former academic status and Ivy League credentials appeared to influence whether a book was published, our samples did not consider either "the existence of an academic patron for the author" or "an Ivy League academic base for the author" as critical or very important in deciding whether to publish a book. Actually, they ranked these last in what to consider when deciding whether to publish a manuscript. Self-publishing, briefly noted in *Books* (Coser, Kadushin, and Powell 1982, 259), is increasingly seen as an option, especially for minority or new writers, who garner free advertising this way, and who, if moderately successful with a self-published book, may be picked up subsequently by a larger press, or who may sell their rights to the self-published book to a larger press. Numerous stories are told of minority authors (and others) who used unconventional methods to promote their books—often because they felt their books were not being promoted by the companies that published them. Some of these stories surfaced in our interviews: (1) A man gave talks at schools on his book and gave students coupons to go buy the book. He sold 10,000 copies in six months. (2) A woman, with a pleasant manner and speaking style ("she makes people feel comfortable"), sold 1,000 copies in one month while speaking at schools. Some bookstores, especially minority bookstores, will stock many self-published books—because they sell. However, distribution remains a key issue for those who self-publish, and so the question remains as to whether this is still a viable alternative publishing mode. The growth of the Internet has assisted these efforts. The World Wide Web was not yet a fixture when *Books* was published.

Minorities

As Coser, Kadushin, and Powell reported, the industry employed few minorities (1982, 113). This "monoethnic publishing world" has continued (Reid 1997), and this has been noted in a number of journalistic articles (e.g., Brown 1995). Indeed, in 1996, employment data collected by the EEOC showed that the industry had "fallen behind national and metropolitan employment averages" for minority employment. As one observer noted recently, "it is rare to spot more than one black guest at an industry cocktail party" (Edwards 2004, 36), and in our own interviews we noted few visible people of color in company offices. Most of our respondents acknowledged that minority representation was "still a problem." One respondent involved with recruitment said that today you will find "blacks and Asians at junior levels, but fewer at senior levels." A key industry leader, with a broad view of people employed in the industry, commented that there was "less pressure for diversity because [trade publishers] did not perceive the need to hire minority people to do trade." Another noted that there was a great deal of "lip service" given to diversity at the higher levels, but when it came to hiring such candidates, fault was found with them and the often-heard refrain was that "they don't meet the specs" of the position. Sometimes the specs of the position were such that it would be nearly impossible to find a minority candidate—as when universities advertise for positions in Irish American studies. But even when qualified candidates were found, fault was found with them, we were told. The analogy of publishing houses being "silos" with "different publishers doing different things" was used by a number of our respondents; there was also agreement that people tended to be hired from inside and companies went outside only when it was absolutely called for. Some progress has been made, e.g., in the human resources area, sales, customer service, and technology, but there was "large room for improvement," said one white respondent involved in placing diversity candidates.

One CEO noted that they tried "to have programs include minorities or be about minorities" but also said that they "did not know" why this was still a problem. So why so few minorities? An article in 1996 noted that the explanations from "publishing executives have not changed much." They include the low starting salaries, which discourage talented minority applicants from seeking starting jobs as lowly assistant editors and publicists (Carvajal 1996a). As one respondent put it, many talented minorities have gone to the dot-com world or moved to Wall Street. Also acknowledged by some is the closed nature of book publishing. As the German-born CEO exec of Henry Holt & Company stated, "The system of assistant editors is a self-recruiting system for the cultural establishment of this county. . . . You can only get a job if your parents subsidize you or pay your rent." There are also few white working-class kids working as editorial assistants (Arnold 1998).

Would improving the pay scale make a difference? Perhaps. But one minority respondent alluded to a lack of genuine interest in publishing houses in hiring more minorities, saying, "There's always that . . . we'd love to have them but can't find them." There are also indications of difficulties even after minorities take entry-level jobs. Of those who successfully enter a career of book publishing and make the necessary sacrifices, once they get the job "they do not have the networking power that for instance, gay men and lesbians have" (cited in Arnold 1998). David Unger, director of the publishing certificate program started at CCNY to bring diversity to publishing, also noted that "it was hard to place interns because the business is so clubby. . . . The children of editors and writers get most of the internships" (cited in Arnold 1998). Calvin Reid, an African American editor at *Publishers Weekly*, said that word of mouth is so important in getting into publishing that "it's not so much that the door is not open, it's also that minorities don't even consider knocking" (cited in Coleman 1997). Publishing in the United Kingdom is also a "white, middle class ghetto" (Edwards 2004), even in London, where the publishing industry is based and 30 percent minority. The director of a minority-recruiting agency there said, "Your automatic thought is that there is no point trying to get into publishing unless you went to Cambridge or know the right people" (Edwards 2004). However, the publishing programs that have been started at some universities and companies do appear to make a difference as a number of our minority respondents got their start in publishing through such programs.

Consequences of Minority Absence

The absence of minorities in publishing has a number of consequences. For one, it makes it difficult for minorities to publish, for they do not have access to persons who can greenlight book projects. Also, critics contend that, because of the predominance of whites in this area, when a work by a person of color reaches an agent or editor, their works are often misread and they are pressured to conform to stereotypes in their writing. There is also a lack of understanding of, lack of sensitivity to, or fear of minority communities that makes marketing or the production of minority books problematic. One story that illustrates this concerns a black author who fired a white publicist after the publicist asked to be escorted to the bathroom because she was afraid to visit it by herself at an all-black event. There are so few black publicists that "often authors hire free lancers who are comfortable running a marketing campaign aimed at a black audience." The now-very-successful Terry McMillan was asked to rewrite her first book so the characters would be more "believable," i.e., less educated and more working class. It was difficult for her editors to envision a professional black woman as a lead character (Carvajal 1996a). There is also a "scarcity of Hispanic employees in exec publishing positions in editing, marketing and sales" (Carvajal 1996b). Hispanics have also related stories of pressure to conform to stereotypes that the literary community has about Latino groups.[11] Despite the recent surge of interest in Hispanic literature, some Latino writers say "they are uneasy about the attention to their background and worry that Eastern publishers expect them to write books that conform to stereotypes about particular groups of immigrants" Carvajal (1996b). Mainstream publishing houses are also unfamiliar with the way to build interest in Hispanic and black literature.

Coser, Kadushin, and Powell's (1982) chapter "Women in Book Publishing" referred to women's situation as "a qualified success story." Very few of our respondents mentioned access or involvement issues with regard to women. One female respondent specifically noted that originally diversity had been an issue for women, but that this was no longer the case. However, Falk and Grizard (2003) studying women in large communications companies found that the glass ceiling persists, particularly with regard to access and influence at the highest levels, i.e., women on corporate boards and in leadership positions.

Cultural and Experiential Sensitivities

For many white Americans the O.J. verdict brought home the dramatic differences in perspectives and experiences that many whites and blacks have in this country. Many blacks were not surprised at the verdict or the differences in views, because they have known this all along (P. Holt 1997). Reflecting these different worlds, one of our black respondents, when ranking the methods that were most effective in selling books, made a separate list for African American publications. This included in rank order: word of mouth; the Web; in-store events; black-oriented radio, especially morning shows; networks of black community events; Black Expo; and street vendors, especially in New York City, who tend to reflect current black tastes. Although black literature speaks to this often-found difference in perspective and experiences, the literature is not limited in appeal to black readers, as the success of many black authors in mainstream markets has demonstrated. Consequently, some interest has developed for black books, but critics argue that some publishers are "trying to cash in on the growing African American market" but don't know what they are doing. Some of the works being produced are offensive to many blacks. For example, titles like *Baby You're So Fine, I'd Drink a Tub of Your Bathwater* (Hyperion) and *Pimps, Whores and Welfare Brats* are being bought by whites, perhaps further contributing to stereotypic depictions of blacks. Moreover, while black book sales may grow, black publishing staff does not (Jacques 1996).

One minority respondent, who works with minority books, had a series of original ideas on how to deal with the decline in reading. She suggested that if publishers wanted more minorities to read books (and, she added, if they wanted to produce better books), they should look at what minorities were doing with, e.g., music and films. It was not necessary to appeal to the lowest common denominator. Why not, for example, have a hip-hop version of Dr. Faustus? More trial and error is needed to see what works, but from this person's perspective, most houses were not very serious about trying more than once. This same respondent also felt that it was important to "hook them while they're young. Put a book in their hands," referring to all children, not just minority children. Developing the habit of reading should be introduced early as pleasure, for soon enough, children come to see reading as associated with homework, school, and other demands that are often less associated with fun. Focusing on children this way would also counter the exclusivity that she felt many minorities associated with books but not with movies and music, which she said really "seek to seduce you." She felt this exclusivity and the association of books with upper, white, leisure classes was mirrored in the larger society as a whole. A reflection of this could be seen in, for example, the books that were carried by large chain pharmacies in high-income areas compared with low-income areas, which tended to carry more magazines. Finally, she argued that books should not have "the usual suspects" but should introduce new characters that did not fold into people's expectations (read, stereotypes).

Access

The lack of minorities in publishing also raises the access question. One of our white respondents, when asked whether an author's connection to a circle of scientists, scholars, or writers increased chances of being published, noted,[12] "It's who you know who knows you know." And added, "Who *who* is depends on the particular area." Many minorities do not belong or have access to the privileged circles that influence book publishing. These circles were seen to be extremely important in *Books* and continue to be seen so but in different ways today. However, as one respondent pointed out, "Minorities and agents live in segregated worlds." For example, the question this person heard most often from Latino writers was, "How do I find an agent?" The question this person heard most often from agents was, "How do I find Latino writers?"

We found that, when our respondents ranked the variables that influence whether a book should be published, "the existence of an important, non-academic patron for the author" was seen as critical by those involved with minority publishing, but was seen as less important for those involved with nonminority works. This may illustrate the still marginal status of minority works within publishing. This despite the relative success and popularity among all groups of major best-selling authors, such as Toni Morrison, Oscar Hijuelos, Walter Mosley, and Amy Tan.

We also found that, when conducting this ranking, minority respondents generally had one set of criteria for books with minority content and another for books without. For example, minority respondents stated that "the relevance of content to minorities" was critical for them, but "not very important" for others. One respondent first ranked the variables in terms of what would be published in general and then ranked all the variables in terms of what would determine the publishing of a book in the African American market.

Dual Standards?

Another respondent spoke about the discrepancies between how minorities were handled in publishing compared with nonminorities. She noted that minority publishing was seen as a smaller market and added, "If the minority was on Oprah, or, if the minority writer had a book popular with a mass audience, this could be seen as a plus" by the publishing industry. Otherwise, the book written by the minority about a minority would be seen as being within a "minority niche and this was negative." It was this white's view that minority writers writing about minorities had a harder time getting published because publishers feared they wouldn't recover their costs. When asked whether people of color *writing about whites* would have a less difficult time, she answered, "We're not there yet." (This was despite her personal interest and efforts in seeing more of this occur.)

The view that there are dualities such as these within publishing are striking because as one white respondent noted there is a sense among whites in the industry that people of color can "publish with ease." Yet one respondent who had had numerous professional conversations with younger scholars of color reported that these scholars feel there are incredible obstacles to getting published. They feel that there is a "hyper-vigilance" with regard to their work, that their manuscripts are reviewed by more people, the standards are more demanding, and that marketing considerations were more closely surveyed than if they were white. In essence, and for example, they feel that they must prove that they can attract a mass audience plus black readers.

Other Issues

Other issues were raised in relation to minorities and publishing. For example, the expansion of the ethnic studies field has created a market for such books, but it is still seen as a narrow market tied to undergraduate courses. There is also a lot of publishing *about* minorities but not necessarily *by* minorities. Indeed, a number of respondents indicated that minorities find it difficult to publish their first book and there is not an established network of senior scholars of color to assist them. Although authors of color are sometimes seen as a new voice, only a few will get in — often the superstars. In relation to this, one respondent commented that Colin Powell might well receive a huge advance for his book, which means other authors will get less. This person raised the following questions: (1) Will these large advances be justified in terms of sales? (2) Shouldn't the money go to other works and authors who really need the money?

Another respondent noted that women still have difficulty getting into circles of influence — as most senior authors are still men. Women of color have even greater difficulty and there is not a sufficiently large mass of female senior scholars of color for a tipping phenomenon to occur in terms of felt influence and referral circles for books. Thus more senior authors of color were needed for circles to form and have a tipping-point influence.

At this point, only "star minoritiarians," e.g., Cornell West, Skip Gates, may have access to some circles.

But there are circles and there are circles. Moreover, circles do not always function in the same way. As one Latino respondent noted, "Circles help but are not very important for Latino books." Another said, "Circles help with word of mouth"; a third noted that circles are important but not as much as in the mainstream U.S. market.

Another issue raised by a white respondent was "who's going to read these 'minority' books?" Can these books really break through those written by white people writing on race, who according to one respondent, still have a better shot at being published and being marketed? The example given to illustrate this was of a recent book by a white author, which focused on his discovery of racial injustice in the area of the south that he studied. This, the respondent argued, was seen to be of greater general interest than a black person writing on the same theme. The respondent said, "Despite the fact that many whites have published on this, we have yet to hear this from blacks in the mainstream publishing [trade] world. It is different in the academic market where people of color have written on this."

The establishment of imprints oriented specifically to African American, Latino, or Asian American books has been one way to deal with these issues, but they also introduce other issues and paradoxes. According to one respondent, they can take advantage of the market that is there, but it also allows "the big publishers not to deal with it," i.e., they don't have to incorporate these works into more mainstream publishing venues. On the other hand, if authors or agents do not want to go to one of these imprints, e.g., Amistad, then they will not easily find their market and many people who want to read their books will not easily find them.

Why have these separate imprints come about? One respondent stated that segmentation occurs because people have different tastes, but that this is also reinforced by publishers who feel they have a mandate to serve these communities. The existence of these imprints has also improved the supply of such books and better identified marketing niches. Personal stories of successful grassroots marketing campaigns have influenced their creation. For example, Terry McMillan's story of carrying around her books in the trunk of her car, so people could buy and read them, and distributing them in beauty shops and barbershops, showed many that there was a market in the black community for books.

Latino and Spanish Books

Given the major demographic changes in the United States detailed in the previous chapter with regard to the rapid growth of the Latino and Hispanic populations, what did those in the industry tell us about what is happening (or not happening) with regard to publishing books for Latinos? What are the problems? Before addressing that, we remark that the Hispanic market is complicated, for it includes books written and read in Spanish, written and read in English, and translations of both. These four types of books can be written or produced in the United States, Latin America, the Caribbean, or Spain or coproduced in any of these areas. The settings of the characters or the reference points in the books can also be in any of these areas. Second, there are books geared to a generic Hispanic or Latino American audience and others that are specifically oriented toward (or that reflect) the Mexican community, the Puerto Rican community, the Cuban community, etc.[13] Persons working in this area often specialize in one area, for example, in Spanish-language books or in English-language books oriented toward Latinos in the United States. Because of the large growth of the Hispanic population, especially in school systems,[14] there is also growing concern that books used in the school system do not include or reflect Latinos. Publishing personnel constitute yet another group involved in the Hispanic market, i.e., those producing textbooks or children's books that are more inclusive. Add to this fiction and nonfiction divisions, and the complexity of the field is apparent. The following references to Hispanic and Latino books will reflect these circumstances.

At the 2005 Book Expo America, a number of panels were specifically dedicated to disseminating information on books in the Hispanic market and ways of reaching the U.S. Latino communities, and the repeated refrain that there are not enough books in Spanish was heard.[15] Perhaps because of the complexity of the field, perhaps because of unfamiliarity with the Hispanic and Latino group or with the books in this area, a number of our respondents felt that there was a certain "cluelessness" in the publishing world with regard to Latino books. As one respondent stated, there was a sense that "we have to do something" but not much clarity on what should be done. This respondent continued, "They don't know whether to approach us in Spanish or English." Another respondent sensed a "lack of support" and that they—especially upper management—did not quite know what to do with the product.

We also heard from those we spoke with, who handle Latino books, that "limited time and effort was spent on Latino books because publishers think they will never do that well." And with regard to books that did not do that well, they raised questions, such as, "Was it pushed? In the right places?" Authors echo this, citing the lack of support. One respondent also noted that there were few book buyers with knowledge or sensitivity in this area, especially in the larger chains. With regard to Hispanic and Latino books, a curious contrast surfaced. On the one hand, those we spoke with in this area were passionate about the need to develop broadly and deeply (*fomentar*) Latin American culture and literature in the United States. On the other hand, almost all of those *not* involved in this area barely mentioned Hispanics or Latinos in any way. One—a high-level executive in one of the largest publishing entities—when asked about books with racial or ethnic (read, minority) content, nonchalantly referred to them as "just another constituency." The general sense that we took away from these interviews with regard to both Spanish- and English-language publishing was that—as one respondent put it—the "Spanish market is struggling to make its way into the mainstream."

Distribution also surfaced as a major issue in this field. As Kiser (1999, 38ff) observes, "Knowing what the market is demanding is only half the battle in Spanish-language publishing. The other half is reaching the consumer." She further noted that there were "not enough Latino bookstores and that mainstream stores don't adequately service the market." Our respondents in this area believed this applied to both English- and Spanish-language Latino books—with one respondent saying that one of their main goals was to develop different forms of distribution so Latino books would be available where Latinos lived. This, they noted, would also help demonstrate to the publishing world that there was a Latino market. As was the case with the black reading public, mainstream publishers had to see the success of the Terry McMillans in publishing and marketing before being convinced that blacks do read. Another of our respondents noted that the channels for distribution were not clear yet and that there was a need to connect international companies producing books in Spanish with U.S. distributors and sales forces. But no price regulation for Spanish-language books and the possibility of high return rates were also seen to affect development in this area. Respondents indicated that people tend to limit what they buy from other countries because they do not want the expense of shipping books back. Time lags on overseas shipments were also noted as problematic, particularly if other events had been organized for marketing or adoption purposes in the United States. (This problem was also noted with regard to the production of books overseas, e.g., in China.)

Distributing Latino children's books in Spanish- or English-language independent book stores and small chain stores was seen as "important because they are in neighborhoods of people [we] want to reach." As one respondent involved in this field for a long time noted, "They do not have the personnel in large chains to help Latinos," and, "They don't speak the Spanish language." This it was noted made it more difficult for Latinos to buy their books. Respondents also pointed to the limited selection of Spanish-language books in major bookstore aisles. Kiser (1998, 54) had noted this was a problem in 1998, saying that "Spanish only titles still have a long way to go before finding their way in large numbers into chains such as Borders and Barnes & Noble."[16] Our respondents saw this as a continuing problem. One respondent referred to how Barnes & Noble worked with publishing companies (via co-op dollars and purchases of large numbers of books with hefty discounts) to influence which books become best sellers. They said, "The industry doesn't think outside the box. Just Barnes & Noble. They decide the best seller." The current structure of distribution favoring the big guns was seen as hampering the expansion of Hispanic and Latino books.

However, according to the Barnes & Noble Web site, best sellers account for only 3 percent of their sales. In addition, they state that they seek to work with small presses, reporting that "more than 50,000 small publishers and university presses are a growing percentage our business."[17] They did not note the percentage that small publishers constitute nor were Hispanic and Latino books specifically mentioned.

Other problems noted were the minimal press coverage of Spanish-language books, the general lack of promotion of books in Spanish, and the difficulties experienced in getting Spanish-language books reviewed. Spanish-language books are often published outside the United States, but these companies do not send galleys to the United States; therefore galleys can't be sent to reviewers—and many reviewers work only from galleys—and reviews come out about the same time as the books. Other issues raised had to do with finding and hiring highly qualified staff, i.e., not just people who were bilingual, but those who were extremely proficient in both English and Spanish and familiar with the nuances of different cultures and settings. Errors in translated editions were noted.

Ayala (2005), Kiser (2000), and Ospina (2003) cite improvements in the Hispanic and Latino publishing area. Book clubs, the Web, virtual bookstores, more aggressive grassroots marketing, and the development of imprints targeting Hispanic and Latino books, for example, are slowly changing the field. Also "more and more U.S. publishers" announced that they will be developing Spanish editions for their best-selling English-language titles and that major Spanish-language works will be produced in English (Ospina 2004). Ospina (2003) also notes some changes with regard to Barnes & Noble's and Borders' distribution of Spanish-language books, e.g., titles being more accessible in a store or on their Web site and Borders opening up a new store in Pico Rivera, California (more than 80 percent Hispanic), that has bilingual signs and staff and a Spanish-language section at the front of the store. But many challenges remain, e.g., book prices, piracy (illegal international editions), scheduling and rights conflicts over publications, little media coverage, and insufficient dialogue among publishers, agents, and distributors.

In essence, the Spanish-language market has been acknowledged but is far from being exploited, and challenges remain. Distribution of Spanish-language books is fragmented, and reaching buyers is a challenge because, although the size of the Spanish-speaking population is large, readers are dispersed. Moreover, the media that cover such books is often local to each city. There are too few sources that review books, including the Spanish-language media network. Determining what buyers want requires experienced personnel, and there are not many of those (Kiser 2004a). Moreover, past reductions in bilingual education programs and a slow economy also hurt. There have been library budget cuts, and some Spanish-language imprints and stores have closed (Kiser 2004b), Lastly, getting advertising and culturally and linguistically competent translators is still difficult (K. Holt 2004).

But on the plus side, more U.S. publishers are putting out Spanish-language titles and more wholesalers are partnering with international and domestic distributors and with book clubs. Barnes & Noble and Borders also have greater numbers of Spanish-language titles and sections now. But most important is a growing recognition that Hispanic and Latino literature has great growth potential because of the projected increase in these populations. Some demonstrated successes have occurred in this area. For example, Sandra Cisneros's Spanish-language version of her book *Caramelo* demonstrates how successful Spanish-language publishing can be, especially if it is also published with an English-language version (Ospina 2003). Religious publishers have also discovered that there are large and committed evangelical Hispanic denominations who are thirsty for religious books (e.g., bilingual Bibles, seminary-oriented titles), youth-oriented books, and home-schooling materials in Spanish for themselves and their children (Laitman-McAnally and Crosby 2001). Finally, the growth and success of Hispanic and Latino children's books and books targeted to young adults (e.g., *The Dirty Girls Social Club*) suggest positive future trends, which are supported by the demographics of the group outlined in the previous chapter.

1. After the initial construction of the questionnaires, pretests were sent out to 19 individuals in all of the categories listed, with the exception of warehouse, and legal and rights. We received 10 usable questionnaires from the pretest group. We reviewed the results and made modifications in the questionnaires.

Drawing on the methodology employed by Coser, Kadushin, and Powell (1982), we developed a list of representative publishers in the following five categories: (a) commercial scholarly monograph publishers; (b) major, large trade publishers; (c) slightly smaller trade publishers; (d) college textbook publishers; and (e) university presses. A complete census of all employees at the representative firms was prepared, based on information in *The Literary Marketplace*. We developed a list of e-mail addresses of 821 individuals working in the U.S. book-publishing industry. All employees in specific categories (e.g., editorial, marketing) received an e-mail saying we were working on a book and outlining our research. Each was asked to go to our Web site to complete and submit the questionnaire and then fill out a brief form. We offered a $10.00 Starbucks gift certificate to the first 100 submitting a questionnaire. We sent out two rounds of e-mails, and we received a total of 33 usable questionnaires for a response rate of 4.41 percent. After receiving the completed questionnaires, we conducted our targeted interviews. Given the demographic changes reviewed in the previous chapter, we made a special effort to incorporate minority actors in publishing, especially those involved with Latino or Spanish-language publishing. We conducted a total of 24 such interviews, making for a total of 57 respondents.

A second major e-mail survey was initiated in November and December 2004. Working with the Book Industry Study Group, we sent a questionnaire via e-mail to approximately 88,000 U.S. book-publishing firms. In essence, every publisher who had purchased an ISBN received a detailed questionnaire. The response rate for this survey was similar to the first. Since this survey did not include personal or demographic information, its results are not reviewed in this chapter.

2. Coser, Kadushin, and Powell (1982, 105–106ff) found that more than one-third of the editors they spoke with had gotten Ivy League or top-school degrees; this was even more the case for women in publishing. In our samples, a higher proportion had attended public schools, but those with lower educational attainments, e.g., bachelor's degrees, had gone to private, ivy schools. Coser, Kadushin, and Powell also described the class background of editors and of the white males as high, with only one-quarter coming from blue-collar backgrounds. Editors who had fathers who were professionals constituted 40 percent of all editors.

3. There were, however, higher proportions of fathers who had been laborers or service workers among those personally interviewed (21.8 percent) and higher proportions of mothers who had been clerical workers (15.2 percent) among the e-mail sample.

4. Of the e-mail survey 39 percent—and of those personally interviewed 29 percent—indicated they did *not* have mentors, but some of these had other forms of assistance, e.g., "contacts that helped them along the way."

5. This phrase and other phrases in quotes refer to respondents' comments unless otherwise specified.

6. Other considerations that were ranked high by both groups were (in ranked order) the following: the prestige of the author in his or her profession; the timeliness of the subject matter of the book; the previous track record of an author in publishing; how well the manuscript read; and the potential for a review in the major media. There was general agreement between the two groups on all of the above—except the issue of timeliness, with those personally interviewed ranking this slightly lower than the e-mail group.

7. Only one university press in our sample reported little financial pressure. This was a press that produced a limited number of titles, which were often of a regional literature. The press also had comprehensive funding from its university, was part of a consortium that handled many of the operations (e.g., distribution and sales), rarely used four-color, was responsible to the head librarian, had an advisory board made up of local business people and community leaders, and relied on POD publishing in many cases.

8. Coser, Kadushin, and Powell (1982) also noted that corporate executives liked to see media mergers as natural marriages that cross-fertilize. But they noted that these mergers were also business strategies in which an acquiring firm reduces its dependency in an uncertain business environment and, "by horizontally and vertically integrating related interests, gains economies of scale . . . large size has competitive advantages for advertising, inventory control and distribution. . . . However, in the process of consolidation, many employees are dismissed, title output is cut back, and writers are left wondering about the status of their books" (pp. 28–29).

9. Local stores could order on their own but this had to come from their own budgets.

10. *PW Daily* reported that in 2004 the number of new titles was up 14 percent (or "a whopping" 195,000) from the previous year and that this was driven by midsize and small publishers, POD, and vanity presses. In contrast, the number of new titles released by the largest trade houses rose 5.4 percent, the largest increase since 2001 but still relatively small. (www.pwdaily.com, May 24, 2005).

11. See Lopez (2005) for accounts of Latino writers who say they "want their writing to be noticed before their surnames." They want to be writers who are Latinos, instead of Latino writers.

12. These circles and the role of "informal brokers" were noted as particularly important in determining publication in the Coser, Kadushin, and Powell (1982, 73) book. They stated most emphatically, "In fact, if the reader who is unfamiliar with publishing takes but one message away from this book, it should be that formal channels of manuscript submission are the very last resort of would-be authors. To get a book published, recommendation through an informal circle or network is close to being an absolute necessity." They also noted that flow within circles and exchange was based on "sociability and affection" (p. 82).

13. See Kiser (1998, 16ff) for a discussion on how publishers dealing with Spanish-language books learn "the cultural makeup of a region" so they can be "more successful in selecting books for publication and in learning how best to sell them."

14. According to census data, Hispanic students constituted 18 percent of all elementary and high school students in 2003. Another 16 percent were black, and 4 percent were

Asian (www.census.gov/population /www/socdemo/school.html, June 1, 2005, Release on New School Enrollment).

15. Brown (1995) has also noted that there were not enough books, despite increased publishing, about and for African Americans.

16. Kiser (1998, 54) explained that "because of the chains' focus on fast turnover and low returns, they tend to purchase only the Spanish titles they know they can sell, namely, fiction, reference and works by well-known Latin American authors. As a result, semi-specialized titles in such categories as business, politics, history and even self-help are less likely to be picked up."

17. Barnes & Noble is huge. Again, in 2005 their Web site reported that they sell almost 445 million books per year and had $4.1 billion in sales for the year (www.barnesandnobleinc.com, March 20, 2005).

REFERENCES

Anand, Bharat N., Kyle Barnett, and Elizabeth Carpenter. 2004. "'Random House' Case Study." Harvard Business School. Boston, MA: President and Fellows of Harvard College.

Arnold, Martin. 1998. "It's the Cachet, Not the Money." *New York Times*, May 21, late edition, East Coast.

Auletta, Ken. 1997. "The Impossible Business." *New Yorker*, October 6, "Publishing World" section, pp. 50–63.

Ayala, Nancy. 2005. "Selling More than Words." May 1, VNU eMedia. www.marketingymedios.com.

Bandler, James, and Jeffrey A. Trachtenberg. 2004. "So Much to Read, So Few Readers." *Wall Street Journal*, November 22.

Brown, Carolyn M. 1995. "Writing a New Chapter in Book Publishing." *Black Enterprise* 25, no. 7 (February 1): 108. http://www.findarticles.com/p/articles/mi_m1365/is_n7_v25/ai_16552987.

Carvajal, Doreen. 1996a. "Authors Press for Change in Minority Hiring." *New York Times*, June 24, late edition, East Coast.

———. 1996b. "Of Hispanic Literature and Not so Equal Opportunities." *New York Times*, May 4, late edition, East Coast.

Coleman, Dandy. 1997. "Intern Program Introduces Minorities to the Industry." *Boston Globe*, October 19, city edition.

Coser, Lewis A., Charles Kadushin, and Walter W. Powell. 1982. *Books: The Culture and Commerce of Publishing*. New York: Basic Books.

Dawkins, Wayne. 2005. "Is Anybody Out There." *Black Issues Book Review*, May–June, p. 10.

Edwards, Catherine. 2004. "Do the Write Thing." *People Management* 10, no. 12 (June 17): 36.

EEOC. 2002. "2002 EEO-1 Aggregate Report for Book Publishing." U.S. Equal Employment Opportunity Commission. http://www.eeoc.gov/stats/jobpat/2002/sic4/2731.html.

Falk, Erika, and Erin Grizard. 2003. "The Glass Ceiling Persists: The 3rd Annual APPC Report on Women Leaders in Communication Companies." The Annenberg Public Policy Center of the University of Pennsylvania.

Hirschberg, Lynn. 2003. "Nothing Random." *New York Times Magazine*, July 20.

Holt, Karen. 2004. "Planeta's English Debut." *Criticas*, September 1. http://www.criticasmagazine.com/article/CA451387.html.

Holt, Patricia. 1997. "Behind Book Industry Transformation." *San Francisco Chronicle*, April 6, p. 2.

Jacques, Geoffrey. 1996. "Black Book Sales Grow, but Not Black Publishing Staff." *Publishers Weekly* 243, no. 50 (December 9): 38.

Kiser, Karin N. 1998. "Cracking the U.S. Market with Spanish-Language Titles." *Publishers Weekly* 245, no. 37 (September 14): 53–58.

———. 1999. "Selling to the Spanish-Language Market in the U.S." *Publishers Weekly* 246, no. 37 (September 13): 35.

———. 2000. "Spanish-Language Publishing in the U.S. Nears Critical Mass." *Publishers Weekly* 247, no. 38 (September 18): 47.

———. 2004a. "The Search for Distribution." *Criticas*, March–April, Reed Business Information.

———. 2004b. "The State of the Market." *Library Journal*, September 1, Reed Business Information.

Laitman-McAnally, Lillian, and Cindy Crosby. 2001. "Exploit Draws Bilingual Crowd." *Publishers Weekly* 248, no. 25 (June 18): 18.

Lopez, Adriana. 2005. "The L-Factor." *Publishers Weekly* 252, no. 8 (February 21).

National Endowment for the Arts. 2004. *Reading At Risk: A Survey of Literary Reading in America*. Research Division Report no. 46. June.

Ospina, Carmen. 2003. "If You Build It, Will They Come?" *Publishers Weekly* 250, no. 34 (August 25): 18.

———. 2004. "Bilingual Boom at BEA." *Publishers Weekly* 251, no. 25 (June 21): 33.

Reid, Calvin. 1997. "Where Are the Minorities?" *Publishers Weekly* 244, no. 31 (July): 16.

III CHALLENGES CONFRONTING THE BOOK-PUBLISHING INDUSTRY IN THE 21ST CENTURY

THE MAJOR CHALLENGES CONFRONTING

BOOK PUBLISHERS AND AUTHORS

EXPANDING THE MARKET FOR BOOKS

To expand the U.S. market for books, publishers, editors, and sales and marketing executives must come to grips with a Herculean problem. Book reading is on a downward spiral (and some might argue on a precipitous decline), and the short-term outlook (as well as the long-term outlook) is regrettably not sanguine.

The Decline in Reading

In 2004 the National Endowment for the Arts (NEA) released a landmark study of the state of literary reading in the United States in 1982, 1992, and 2002. *Literary reading* referred specifically to reading works of fiction and poetry, and the results were disheartening. While U.S. population increased 22.6 percent between 1982 and 2002, the percentage of adults (older than 18) reading literary works declined 17.9 percent. A review of major demographic indexes revealed the depth of this decline. Reading by males dropped 23.4 percent, while females posted a smaller decline (12.5 percent), again revealing the bald fact that women of all ages read more books than males of all ages. If ethnicity is taken into consideration, white Americans posted a 14.5 percent decline, African Americans were down 12.3 percent, and Hispanic Americans sustained a 27.2 percent drop. Table 7.1 outlines these trends.

Education remained an incredibly significant barometer of reading, with those having college degrees and postgraduate degrees accounting for the largest percentages, even though they also posted declines (college grads, -27.43 percent; graduate school grads, -18.76 percent). Americans between the ages of 45 and 54 were the strongest literary readers between 1982 and 2002; yet even they sustained a 6.0 percent decline in reading. Similar strong reading trends were recorded by individuals in age groups 35–44, 55–64, 65–74, and, remarkably, 75 and older. Unfortunately, these age cohorts sustained declines between 1982 and 2002: (1) 55–64, -7.4 percent; (2) 35–44, -21.94 percent; (3) 65–74, -4.03 percent; and (4) 75 and older, -10.27 percent.

TABLE 7.1
Decline in literary reading, 1982–2002

Demographic	1982	1992	2002
U.S. population 18 years or older (in millions)	168.0	185.8	205.9
U.S. adult population reading literature	56.9	54.0	46.7
Number of literary readers (in millions)	96	100	96
U.S. adult population reading any book	—	60.9	56.6
U.S. adult population reading literature	—	54.0	46.7
Literary reading by gender: men	49.1	47.4	37.6
Literary reading by gender: women	63.0	60.3	55.1
Literary reading by race/ethnicity: white	59.8	58.0	51.4
Literary reading by race/ethnicity: African American	42.3	45.6	37.1
Literary reading by race/ethnicity: Hispanic	36.4	34.0	26.5
Literary reading by race/ethnicity: other	50.2	42.7	43.7

SOURCE: National Endowment for the Arts (2004).

NOTE: Numbers are percentages unless otherwise noted.

TABLE 7.2
Literary reading by demographic groups, 1982–2002 (percent)

Demographic	1982	1992	2002
Education			
Grade school	21.2	17.3	14.0
Some high school	38.8	34.5	23.3
High school graduate	54.2	49.0	37.7
Some college	72.9	65.0	52.9
College graduate-graduate school	82.1	74.6	66.7
Age			
18–24	59.8	53.3	42.8
25–34	62.1	54.6	47.7
35–44	59.7	58.9	46.6
45–54	54.9	56.9	51.6
55–64	52.8	52.9	48.9
65–74	47.2	50.8	45.3
75 and older	40.9	40.4	36.7
All ages	56.9	54.0	46.7

SOURCE: National Endowment for the Arts (2004).

Table 7.2 outlines these developments. Similar patterns were evident when ethnicity, age, education, and income were evaluated by NEA in a one-year period, ending August 2002 (see table 7.3 for details).

While San Francisco, Boston, Philadelphia, Chicago, and Washington, D.C., have long been considered exceptionally important book-reading centers, and while New York remains the center of U.S. book publishing (at least to people living and working in New York City), the Western region accounted for the largest cluster (51.2 percent) of readers (older than 18) in 2002. The Mountain states (which include Arizona, Colorado, Idaho, Montana, Nevada, New Mexico, Utah, and Wyoming) paced the entire nation with a 53.4 percent reading rate, easily outdistancing the Pacific region's 50.4 percent (Alaska, California, Hawaii, Oregon, and Washington).

The northeastern section lagged with a 49.7 percent rate. New England stood at an even 50.0 percent tally (Connecticut, Maine, Massachusetts, New Hampshire, Rhode Island,

TABLE 7.3

Literary reading by race, ethnicity, education, and family income for the
12-month period ending August 2002 (percent)

Demographic	Hispanic Americans	African Americans	White Americans
Overall literature reading rate	26.5	37.1	51.3
Gender			
Males	18.4	29.8	41.4
Females	34.1	42.9	60.7
Age			
18–24	21.6	34.8	48.6
25–34	31.9	43.8	51.7
35–44	24.5	43.7	51.3
45–54	28.7	36.9	56.8
55–64	32.2	32.8	53.1
65–74	14.3	27.0	50.5
75 and older	17.7	16.7	40.3
Education			
Grade school	11.7	6.5	19.2
Some high school	19.9	22.2	14.0
High school graduate	28.7	29.3	40.4
Some college	34.0	45.8	55.6
College graduate	52.2	58.6	66.1
Graduate school	57.0	58.9	76.1
Family income			
$9,999 or less	19.5	26.9	38.6
$10,000–$19,999	26.8	33.5	41.6
$20,000–$29,000	21.9	33.4	42.4
$30,000–$39,000	25.4	38.4	48.9
$40,000–$49,000	23.4	45.7	50.3
$50,000–$74,999	37.1	45.6	54.9
$75,000 or more	39.6	51.8	62.8
Income not reported	22.7	30.2	44.5

SOURCE: National Endowment for the Arts (2004).

and Vermont). The mid-Atlantic's 49.7 percent included New Jersey, New York, and Pennsylvania.

While the Midwest's 46.7 percent was interesting, the totals generated by the northwestern Central states (49.9 percent; Iowa, Kansas, Minnesota, Missouri, Nebraska, North Dakota, and South Dakota) surpassed the literary stronghold of the mid-Atlantic states. The remaining states in the northeastern Central sector (Illinois, Indiana, Michigan, Ohio, and Wisconsin) stood at 45.5 percent.

The southern states (42.1 percent) comprised the fourth region. The south Atlantic cluster (Delaware, District of Columbia, Florida, Georgia, Maryland, North Carolina, South Carolina, Virginia, and West Virginia) exceeded the region's rate with a 43.3 percent result. The remaining sections included the southwestern Central's 40.9 percent (Arkansas, Louisiana, Oklahoma, and Texas) and the southeastern Central's 40.9 percent (Alabama, Kentucky, Mississippi, and Tennessee). Table 7.4 lists these trends.

Table 7.5 outlines reading trends among various occupations. As might be expected, the managerial, professional, and support cohorts posted the highest reading level (58.8 percent). Sales personnel were a distant second (with a 40.5 percent rate), barely eclipsing

TABLE 7.4
Literary reading rates by region, 2002: Americans age 18 and older (percent)

Region	Subregion	States
West, 51.2	Mountain, 53.4	Arizona, Colorado, Idaho, Montana, Nevada, New Mexico, Utah, Wyoming
	Pacific, 50.4	Alaska, California, Hawaii, Oregon, Washington
Northeast, 49.7	New England, 50.0	Connecticut, Maine, Massachusetts, New Hampshire, Rhode Island, Vermont
	Mid-Atlantic, 49.7	New Jersey, New York, Pennsylvania
Midwest, 46.7	Northwestern Central, 49.9	Iowa, Kansas, Minnesota, Missouri, Nebraska, North Dakota, South Dakota
	Northeastern Central, 45.5	Illinois, Indiana, Michigan, Ohio, Wisconsin
South, 42.1	South Atlantic, 43.3	Delaware, District of Columbia, Florida, Georgia, Maryland, North Carolina, South Carolina, Virginia, West Virginia
	Southwestern Central, 40.9	Arkansas, Louisiana, Oklahoma, Texas
	Southeastern Central, 40.9	Alabama, Kentucky, Mississippi, Tennessee

SOURCE: National Endowment for the Arts (2004).

TABLE 7.5
Literary reading by occupation, 2002 (percent)

Occupation	Reading literature
Managerial, professional, and support	58.8
Sales	40.5
Service	39.9
Production, craft, repair, and operators	27.7

SOURCE: National Endowment for the Arts (2004).

TABLE 7.6
Average number of hours per day adults watch television, 2002

Category	Hours
All adults	2.9
Did not read literature	3.1
Read literature	2.7
Light book readers: 1–5 books annually	2.8
Moderate book readers: 6–11 books annually	2.6
Frequent book readers: 12–49 books annually	2.4
Avid book readers: 50 or more books annually	2.6

SOURCE: National Endowment for the Arts (2004).

the service cohort's 39.9 percent. Individuals classified as production, craft, repair, and operators posted a 27.7 percent rate.

How are Americans spending their leisure hours? The NEA data paralleled the statistical reports released by Veronis Suhler Stevenson. NEA revealed that the average adult spent 2.9 hours per day watching television. Readers of all types (ranging from light readers to avid readers) watched fewer hours of television; but the actual difference between individuals "who did not read literature" (186 minutes per day) and those who "read literature" (162 minutes) was only 24 minutes per day, hardly a significant difference. See table 7.6 for details.

TABLE 7.7

Demographic characteristics of U.S. adults who read novels, short stories, or plays in the 12 months ending August 2002 (percent)

Demographic	Reading novels or short stories	Reading poetry	Reading plays
Overall reading rate	45.1	12.1	3.6
Gender			
Males	36.1	7.8	3.0
Females	53.4	16.0	4.1
Ethnicity and race			
Hispanic Americans	24.8	6.7	3.1
White Americans	50.0	13.1	3.8
African Americans	34.7	11.8	2.8
Other	42.3	9.8	3.1
Age			
18–24	40.7	13.9	5.9
25–34	45.8	10.9	3.5
35–44	45.1	10.9	3.4
45–54	50.2	14.2	3.7
55–64	47.9	12.4	2.5
65–74	43.8	11.9	2.5
75 and older	35.4	9.4	3.2
Education			
Grade school	13.4	2.5	1.1
Some high school	22.7	5.1	1.5
High school graduate	36.5	6.8	1.6
Some college	51.1	14.3	3.9
College graduate	60.7	18.0	6.4
Graduate school	72.3	26.1	8.2
Family income			
$9,999 or less	29.6	10.0	3.4
$10,000–$19,999	36.2	10.4	3.1
$20,000–$29,999	36.2	9.2	2.5
$30,000–$39,999	42.5	11.0	2.8
$40,000–$49,000	46.4	12.7	4.1
$50,000–$74,999	50.7	12.9	3.8
$75,000 or more	59.4	16.0	4.9
Income not reported	38.0	9.5	2.8
Region			
West	49.5	15.4	4.8
Northeast	48.3	11.9	3.9
Midwest	45.5	10.8	2.8
South	40.5	10.8	3.2

SOURCE: National Endowment for the Arts (2004).

When the NEA analyzed the reading of novels or short stories, poetry, or plays, a revealing profile emerged. Females were the most avid readers of these literary formats, as were white Americans. The 45–54 and 55–64 age cohorts remained the strongest readers, although the 25–34 group posted results higher than the 55–64 group. As indicated in other parts of the study, education, income, and regional patterns remained important indicators. Tables 7.7 and 7.8 list these trends.

TABLE 7.8
Literary reading by age cohorts, 1982 and 2002 (percent)

Cohort	1982	2002
18–24 in 1982; 28–44 in 2002	59.8	46.6
25–34 in 1982; 45–54 in 2002	62.1	51.6
35–44 in 1982; 55–64 in 2002	59.7	48.9
45–54 in 1982; 65–74 in 2002	54.9	45.3
55–64 in 1982; 75 and older in 2002	52.8	36.7

SOURCE: National Endowment for the Arts (2004).

Sales Data for 2004

If the reading patterns were not demoralizing enough, the book-sales trends in recent years have been unsettling.

Between 2003 and 2004, the Book Industry Study Group (BISG) reported, net unit sales dropped by 44 million units. Detailed BISG data can be found in earlier portions of this book (see the various tables in chapter 3).

A review of BookScan's data for 2004 was quite revealing. According to BookScan (2005), which tracks approximately 70 percent of all U.S. book sales, 79 percent of all new books sold in the United States in 2004 sold fewer than 99 copies, with 16.91 percent of all books selling between 100 and 999 copies. This meant that 95.91 percent of all books sold in the United States that year sold fewer than 1,000 copies. An analysis of sales in the entire marketplace was equally disconcerting: 5.58 percent of all sales were in the 1,000–4,999 units range; 1.92 percent, 5,000–49,999; 0.06 percent, 50,000–99,999; 0.03 percent, 100,000–249,999; 0.01 percent, 250,000–499,999; 0.002 percent, 500,000–999,999; and 0.001 percent, 1,000,000 or more.

The data for the other major book categories paralleled the trends for all books. In 2004, 86.06 percent of all adult trade fiction books sold fewer than 999 copies; 95.09 percent of all adult trade nonfiction sold fewer than 999 copies; 87.6 percent of all children's trade books sold fewer than 999 copies; 84.58 percent of all hardcover books were under the 1,000 threshold; and 87.76 percent of all adult trade hardcover nonfiction books sold fewer than 1,000 units.

Clearly, the vast majority of all new book sales were under the 1,000 mark. This meant, quite bluntly, that book editors and publishers either did not select titles consumers wanted or book sales and marketing personnel were unable to position their books effectively in the channels of distribution or the prices were too high. Whatever the reason, something drastic occurred: sales of these newly published books were putrid.

The Market for Used Books

While new book sales languished, the revenues generated by the sale of used books skyrocketed. According to research released by BISG, between 2003 and 2004 there was an 11 percent increase in the sales of used books (units +11.0 percent, revenues +11.1 percent); and the bulk of all sales were online (+34.2 percent in units; +33.3 percent in revenues). Table 7.9 outlines these developments.

TABLE 7.9
Sales data for used books

Units & revenues	2003	2004	Percentage change 2003–2004
Units (millions)			
Online	30.6	41.1	34.2
Bookstores	50.2	50.6	0.8
Other locations	19.3	19.5	0.9
Total	100.2	111.2	11.0
Revenues ($ millions)			
Online	457	609	33.3
Bookstores	1498	1567	4.6
Other locations	45	46	1.5
Total	2,001	2,223	11.1

SOURCE: Book Industry Study Group, various years.

TABLE 7.10
Sales data for new and used books, 2004: individual purchases

Category	MEAN OF INDIVIDUAL PURCHASES		MEDIAN OF INDIVIDUAL PURCHASES	
	New	Used	New	Used
Units				
Students	9.4	5.7	6.0	4.0
Nonstudents	10.1	4.7	6.0	2.2
Amount spent ($)				
Students	295	134	200	50
Nonstudents	142	32	90	10

SOURCE: Book Industry Study Group, various years.

TABLE 7.11
Reasons for not purchasing any used books (percent)

Reason	Students	Nonstudents
Prefer to purchase/own new books	33	43
Have not found any interesting used books	19	29
The title I was looking for was only available new	33	28
Price of used book was too high	18	18
Condition of used book was unacceptable	5	15
Shipping costs were too high for used books	10	7
Other	10	7

SOURCE: Book Industry Study Group, various years.
NOTE: Individuals were allowed to give one or more responses. Percentages may not add up to 100%.

While there was a veritable flood of newspaper accounts highlighting the plight of college students and the rapidly increasing price of college textbooks, the BISG data confirmed the trend that students were buying more used books. In 2004 used books accounted for 31.24 percent of total expenditures, and it is likely this trend will accelerate. Tables 7.10 and 7.11 outline these trends with information concerning why used books were not purchased by students. As for the amount spent for used books, students clearly were at the vanguard,

TABLE 7.12
Highest price willing to pay for a used book in very good condition (dollars)

New (range)	Student used	Nonstudent used
1–10	4.70	3.90
11–14	7.10	5.60
15–19	9.50	7.20
20–24	12.40	9.10
25–29	14.60	10.50
30–49	23.30	15.80
50–99	44.40	28.80
100–149	64.00	43.00

SOURCE: Book Industry Study Group, various years.

TABLE 7.13
Would recommend purchasing a used book to a friend (percent)

Reason	Student	Nonstudent
I would recommend considering a used book	74.9	73.0
Neither recommend for or against	16.5	21.0
I would not recommend considering a used book	8.6	6.0

SOURCE: Book Industry Study Group, various years.

willing to spend upwards of $50 for used textbooks (see table 7.12). As for consumer satisfaction, students overwhelmingly (74.9 percent) recommended that friends purchase a used book. See table 7.13 for data on this trend.

Irrational Exuberance

Is it possible that famed author William Goldman was correct about both the motion picture industry and the book-publishing industry when he said, "Nobody knows anything"? Is it possible that key book-publishing industry executives have paid little or no attention to substantive statistical indicators? A review of sales data sets seemed to indicate a lack of awareness of the wants and needs of the consumer book market.

In 2004, 195,000 new hardcover and paperback books were published in the United States (averaging slightly more than 22.2 new books every hour of the day, every day of the week. The prognosis for 2006 is for about 210,000 new titles.

Between 2003 and 2004, net publisher revenues increased 1.74 percent while net publisher units declined 1.87 percent. In 2004 trade books (e.g., adult trade, juvenile trade, and mass-market paperbacks) comprised the largest segment of the U.S. book-publishing industry, accounting for $8.503 billion of net publisher revenues (32.15 percent of all books), 1.48 billion net publisher units (64.49 percent), and $14.89 billion in domestic consumer expenditures (37.98 percent). These books were purchased with discretionary dollars. Trade books experienced a razor-thin 0.74 percent increase in net revenues, a 3.1 percent decline in net units, and a slender 0.72 percent increase in domestic consumer expenditures. So unit sales declined; and revenues increased because of increases in suggested retail book prices, not because consumers purchased more books.

While some publishers and editors (and very few of them in reality) can predict extraordinary sales for certain authors and genres (witness the dramatic sales tallies of the Harry Potter books in 2005 and the financial losses reported by Scholastic, U.S. publisher of the Potter books), most new books fail financially in the marketplace. In reality, 7 out of every 10 new frontlist books fail to earn any profits for publishers, a pattern hauntingly similar to newly released motion pictures.

Consumer book publishers hope and pray that backlist books, generally accounting for 80 percent of a firm's profits, along with a scattered number of hits (blockbusters by John Grisham, Mary Higgins Clark, Dan Brown, etc.) will provide enough cash to generate a modest profit at the end of the year. University press directors rely on their backlist titles to generate about 50 percent of annual revenues. Yet an outdated system of contracts with retailers (i.e., the existing book return system) is a financial burden for all publishers, sapping commercial firms and university presses of needed cash to support new books and authors. By 2002 the used-book market emerged as a potent threat to publishers, undermining both frontlist and backlist sales.

The industry never accepted the notion that carefully crafted marketing research programs might assist a beleaguered industry trying to publish important books and pay its bills. Just what do consumers want? Most publishers and editors that we interviewed, along with individuals from the national book chains, insisted they know what consumers want. If they do, why are returns out of control and annual sales increases hovering near the 2 percent mark?

Publishers were also slow in addressing the backward integration of the major book retailers selling proprietary books in their own bookstores. They were also at best rather sluggish in figuring out how to use the Internet and the electronic distribution of content as viable distribution formats.

Far too many of the major trade publishers never came to grips with skyrocketing author advances and sagging sales. University presses, or at least a number of them, continued to publish too many books that libraries would not buy and scholars avoided.

There was massive clutter in the marketplace, with books competing against television, cable and satellite television, iPods, the Internet, etc. While publishers and editors produced a significant number of good (and sometimes great books), the weakest part of their value chain was in distribution of books and the fulfillment of orders.

The book-publishing business, despite philosophical arguments from academia, *is* a business; and too many publishers, editors, authors, agents, etc., never figured out whether it was (1) a cultural *and* commercial endeavor or (2) a commercial *and* cultural enterprise. In reality, it is both, a double helix so intertwined that one cannot exist without the other. So much for assuming that marketing myopia was a thing of the past.

So industry creatives felt threatened by the bean counters, alleging that the barbarians were at the gates, undermining the cultural mission of publishing. At the same time, the managers tried to understand how so many shallow and underperforming books were released. No one was happy.

The entire industry never figured out how to get more people interested in and read-ing books. Oprah did; everyone else did not. They also failed to respond to critics, mainly academics, who castigated the rise of large publishing conglomerates as inherently anti-intellectual, monopolistic enterprises adversely affecting the marketplace of ideas and lead-ing to a homogenization of taste and culture in this nation.

In essence, far too few publishers and editors came to grips with the following:

- Irrational exuberance gripped the industry starting in the 1980s, prodding editors to increase title output, a phenomenon that escalated in a dramatic fashion in the late 1990s.

- The law of supply and demand cannot be rescinded, even though some editors and university press directors made a valiant attempt to rescind this pivotal law, and the supply of frontlist and backlist books exceeded their demand, triggering a Her-culean flood of returns and low profit margins.

- There was a substantive shift in the entire value chain, a fact that too many industry leaders either did not see or comprehend.

While the industry should be praised for selling almost $40 billion worth of books in 2004, doubts exist about the ability of this industry to grapple with flat or declining unit sales in the coming years (read Wall Street analysts' reports on book publishing and book retailing and see what they think about this industry's future).

This is especially upsetting since the vast majority of all Americans can read; they just have not found enough time and enough interesting books, a veritable blight on the cul-tural, intellectual, and economic landscape of this nation. This industry must spend the time and resources to develop an effective nationwide marketing study. After all, the pur-pose of a business is to satisfy the wants and needs of consumers; and so far, one could cer-tainly debate whether publishers have achieved this goal in light of the stark declines re-ported by the NEA.

THE IMPACT OF TECHNOLOGY AND THE INTERNET ON COPYRIGHT PROTECTION AND BOOK SALES

Technology, the Internet, and Intellectual Property Protection

Copyright protection, often called intellectual property rights (IPR) protection, is a pivotal component of Article 1, Section 8 of the U.S. Constitution that protects copyrights, patents, and trademarks.

> The Congress shall have power . . . to promote the Progress of Science and the useful Arts by securing for limited Times to Authors and Inventors the exclusive Right to their respec-tive Writings and Drawings.

As outlined by Teeter and Loving (2001), the substantive components of this constitu-tional clause are as follows:

- The Constitution provides a financial incentive for creativity.

- An original work of creativity (embodied in a tangible form) is protected for a "limited time," which the Congress has deemed to be the life of the author-creator plus 70 years.

- This time period was upheld in a pivotal U.S. Supreme Court decision; so copyright protection is both a protection of the creator's rights and a restriction placed on the publication of this material.

Teeter and Loving (2001) listed the types of works that can have copyright protection. They include the following:

fiction and nonfiction literary works

musical and dramatic works

motion pictures

audiovisual works

The Register of Copyrights, housed in the Library of Congress, administers the copyright registration and deposit requirements.

In the last 200 years, there have been a plethora of major lawsuits involving real or alleged copyright infringements; however, overall copyright protection has been maintained by the courts. However, with the introduction and acceptance of the Internet and the digitization of content, the legal landscape became cloudy.

Davis (2004) addressed many of these concerns, pointing out that the original scope of IPR has been extended to cover such diverse areas as biotechnology, computer software, and Internet business procedures. These substantive issues were the focal point of some major scholarly works, including studies by Shapiro and Varian (1999); Landes and Posner (1987); Mazzoleni and Nelson (1998); and Mowrey et al. (2001).

Arkenbout, van Duk, and van Wuck (2004) addressed digital rights management (DRM) issues, evaluating the impact of piracy, public policy issues, and the possibility of what they called "customized copyright" procedures allowing for "different levels of protection and degrees of public enforcement of rights and guarantees."

Attempts by a variety of online companies to digitize content and make it available online via the Internet or electronic transmission affected newspapers and magazines, resulting in sagging revenues and declines in circulation. By 2005 and 2006, the book industry faced the specter of companies placing books covered by copyright protection, as well as those not, online, perhaps available for free or a fee.

This metamorphosis has had, and will continue to have, a profound impact on the basic business model of book publishers as well as the rights of author-creators. Since this is an ongoing metamorphosis of the industry, in essence a story without an ending, and since it is likely that litigation will occur over this complex situation, it is impossible to say precisely what will happen.

One can argue, however, that it is highly unlikely that copyright protection will be struck down by any state or federal court since copyright protection is viewed as an important, well-entrenched legal right, and a right that will be defended strenuously by the publishing community. Yet the specter of existing technological developments and the impact of technologies not yet invented means that publishing will change because the marketplace will change. How publishers, authors, and the rest of the book-publishing community respond (or perhaps fail to respond) to these developments will have a dramatic impact on the very existence of publishing and reading in the coming decades.

Technology, the Internet, and Book Sales

It has been said that the Internet changed everything; that retail stores must create Internet sites to compete successfully in what has been called the "new economy." While not all observers of the retail world will agree with this belief, a position espoused by Underhill (1999), the Internet unquestionably affected consumers and retailers, especially consumers buying books.

Brynjolfsson and Smith (2000a), in a pivotal paper, addressed the issue of "frictionless commerce":

> We find that prices on the internet are 9–16 percent lower than prices in conventional outlets, depending on whether taxes, shipping, and shopping costs are included in the price. Additionally, we find that internet retailers' price adjustments over time are up to 100 times smaller than conventional retailers' price adjustments—presumably reflecting lower menu costs in internet channels.

Smith, Bailey, and Brynjolfsson (1999) studied factors leading to dispersion in Internet prices. "We review evidence that internet markets are more efficient than conventional markets with respect to price levels, menu costs, and price elasticity." Brynjolfsson, Hu, and Smith (2003) analyzed the economic impact of increased product variety made available through electronic markets, and found that "increased competition significantly enhance[d] consumer surplus, for instance, by leading to lower average selling prices." Additional research by Zettelmeyer, Morton, and Silva-Risso (2005) confirmed these findings. "There is convincing evidence that the internet has lowered the prices paid by some consumers in established industries. . . . We saw that the Internet lowers prices for two distinct reasons. First, the internet helps consumers learn the invoice price of [automobile] dealers. Second, the referral process of online buying services, a novel institution made possible by the internet, also helps consumers obtain lower prices." Clay and Strauss (2002) insisted that future growth of the Internet would "be limited by two factors—technical barriers and issues of trust and risk."

Substantial research has been undertaken to investigate the impact of the Internet on new- and used-book sales. Smith (2002) analyzed shopbots, which he posited "will radically reduce consumer search costs, reduce retailer opportunities to differentiate their products, and as a result will drive retailer margins toward zero." As for books, Smith argued that "in dollar terms Amazon.com holds a $1.72 (5 percent) price advantage of 'generic' retailers and a $1.30 (3 percent) price advantage over their two closest rivals, Barnes and Noble and Borders." Brynjolfsson, Hu, and Smith (2003) estimated the value of increased product variety at various Internet bookselling sites. Montgomery et al. (2003) calibrated "the model to price and response time data collected at online bookstores over a six-month period. Using prior expectations about price and response time we show how Shopbots can substantially increase consumer utility by searching more intelligently and selectively presenting offers." Iyer and Pazgal (2003) also investigated the impact of shopbots on market competition and prices, and they claimed shopbots allowed "consumers to costlessly search many online retailers and buy at the lowest price."

Pope and Kannan (2003) evaluated business models on the Web (e.g., free browsing, a charge for a printed copy) and sought to ascertain if these models would lead to a cannibalization of print. Would downloadable or printable book content become a substitute for printed books? Would publisher revenues decrease if a book were sold as a PDF file? Pope and Kannan offered a sample of 9,500 individuals the possibility of purchasing a book as a printed book or as a PDF file (at various price points). Did this lead to cannibalization? They used scientific and technical books to sample individuals in the scientific and technical community, and they argued that cannibalization could be stopped if the price of the PDF file were "close to print book price." Ghose, Smith, and Telang (2005) also investigated cannibalization by studying used-book sales on Amazon.com. Their research indicated that "only 16 percent of used book sales at Amazon.com cannibalize new book purchases. The remaining 84 percent of used book sales apparently would not have occurred at Amazon's new book prices."

Other significant research on book selling on the Internet was conducted by Smith and Brynjolfsson (2001); Clay, Krishnan, and Wolff (2001); Clay et al. (2002); and Fischer (2002).

While these research studies enhanced our understanding of the role technology has on consumer purchases, especially on consumer purchases of books, Internet bookselling is merely 10 years old; far more data must be analyzed, covering a substantially longer period of time, to ascertain with any clarity the ultimate impact of technology on book sales.

Yet this fact is known. The game changed in the summer of 1995 when Jeff Bezos opened Amazon.com; we just do not know whether the game changed for better or worse.

REFERENCES

Arkenbout, Erwin, Frans van Duk, and Peter van Wuck. 2004. "Copyright in the Information Society: Scenarios and Strategy." *European Journal of Law and Economics* 17:237–49.

BookScan. 2005. *2004 Overview*. Working paper, September 22.

Brynjolfsson, Erik, Yu Hu, and Michael D. Smith. 2003. "Consumer Surplus in the Digital Economy: Estimating the Value of Increased Product Variety at Online Booksellers." *Management Science* 49 (11): 1580–97.

Brynjolfsson, Erik, and Michael D. Smith. 2000a. "Frictionless Commerce? A Comparison of Internet and Conventional Retailers." *Management Science* 46 (4): 563–85.

Clay, Karen B., Ramayya Krishnan, and Eric Wolff. 2001. *Journal of Industrial Economics* 49 (4): 521–39.

Clay, Karen B., Ramayya Krishnan, Eric Wolff, and Danny Fernandes. 2002. "Retail Strategies on the Web: Price and Non-price Competition in the Online Book Industry." Working paper, Carnegie-Mellon University, 1–31.

Clay, Karen B., and Robert P. Strauss. 2002. "Institutional Barriers to Electronic Commerce: An Historical Perspective." *New Institutionalism in Strategic Management* 19: 245–71.

Davis, Lee. 2004. "Intellectual Property Rights, Strategy and Policy." *Economic Innovation and New Technology* 13 (5): 399–415.

Fischer, William A. 2002. "Stephen King and the Publishing Industry's Worst Nightmare." *Business Strategy Review* 13 (2): 1–10.

Ghose, Anindya, Michael D. Smith, and Rahul Telang. 2005. "Are Internet Used Product Markets Cannibalizing New Product Sales? An Analysis of Internet Markets for Books." Working paper, Carnegie-Mellon University and Stern School, New York University, SSRN 584401.

Iyer, Ganesh, and Amit Pazgal. 2003. "Internet Shopping Agents: Virtual Co-Location and Competition." *Marketing Science* 22 (1): 85–106.

Landes, W. M., and R. A. Posner. 1987. "Trademark Law: An Economic Perspective." *Journal of Law and Economics* 30:265–309.

Mazzoleni, R., and R. R. Nelson. 1998. "Economic Theories about the Benefits and Costs of Patents." *Journal of Economic Issues* 32 (4): 1031–52.

Montgomery, Alan L., Kartik Hosanagar, Ramayya Krishnan, and Karen B. Clay. 2003. "Designing a Better Shopbot." Working paper, Carnegie-Mellon University, 1–31.

Mowrey, D. C., R. R. Nelson, B. N. Sampat, and A. A. Ziedonis. 2001. "The Growth of Patenting and Licensing by U.S. Universities: An Assessment of the Bayh-Dole Act of 1980." *Research Policy* 30 (1): 99–119.

National Endowment for the Arts. 2004. *Reading at Risk: A Survey of Literary Reading in America*. Research Division Report 46.

Pope, Barbara Kline, and P. K. Kannan. 2003. "Will They Pay? Measuring Consumer Demand and Price Preferences for Electronic Delivery of Books." Working paper, National Academy Press, 1–34.

Shapiro, C., and Hal R. Varian. 1999. *Information Rules*. Boston: Harvard Business School Press.

Smith, Michael D. 2002. "The Impact of Shopbots on Electronic Markets." *Journal of The Academy of Marketing Science* 30 (4): 442–50.

Smith, Michael D., Joseph Bailey, and Erik Brynjolfsson. 2000. "Understanding Digital Markets: Review and Assessment." In *Understanding the Digital Economy*, ed. Erik Brynjolfsson and Brian Kahin. Cambridge: MIT Press.

Smith, Michael D., and Erik Brynjolfsson. 2001. "Consumer Decision-Making at an Internet Shopbot: Brand Still Matters." *Journal of Industrial Economics* 49 (4): 541–58.

Teeter, Dwight L., Jr., and Bill Loving. 2001. *Law of Mass Communications: Freedom and Control of Print and Broadcast Media*, 10th edition. New York: Foundation Press.

Underhill, Paco. 1999. *Why We Buy: The Science of Shopping*. New York: Simon & Schuster.

Zettelmeyer, Florian, Fiona Scott Morton, and Jorge Silva-Risso. 2005. "How the Internet Lowers Prices: Evidence from Matched Survey and Auto Transaction Data." Working paper, National Bureau of Economic Research 11515, pp. 1–32.

SELECTED BIBLIOGRAPHY

Aaker, David A. "Measuring Brand Equity across Products and Markets." *California Management Review* 38, no. 2 (1996): 102–20.

Abel, Richard, and Lyman W. Newlin. *Scholarly Publishing: Books, Journals, Publishers, and Libraries in the Twentieth Century*. New York: Wiley, 2002.

Agarwal, Rajshree, and Gort, Michael. "First-Mover Advantage and the Speed of Competitive Entry, 1887–1996." *Journal of Law and Economics* 44, no. 1 (April 2001): 161–77.

Aguirregabiria, Victor. "The Dynamic Markups and Inventories in Retailing Firms." *Review of Economic Studies* 66, no. 2 (April 1999): 275–308.

Alba, J., J. Lynch, B. Weitz, C. Janiszewski, R. Lutz, A. Sawyer, and S. Wood. "Interactive Home Shopping: Consumer, Retailer, and Manufacturer Incentives to Participate in Electronic Marketplaces." *Journal of Marketing* 61 (1997): 38–53.

Albarran, Alan, and Angel Arrese, eds. *Time and Media Markets*. Mahwah, NJ: Erlbaum, 2002.

Alexander, Alison, James Owers, Rod Carveth, C. Ann Hollifield, and Albert N. Greco, eds. *Media Economics: Theory and Practice*. 3rd edition. Mahwah, NJ: Erlbaum, 2004.

Alexander, George A. "Books on Demand at Lighting Print: POD Goes Head-to-Head with Offset." *Seybold Report on Publishing Systems* 28, no. 7 (December 14, 1998): 3–5.

"Alfred A. Knopf Books for Young Readers." *Subtext*, December 16, 2002.

Anand, Bharat N., Kyle Barnett, and Elizabeth Carpenter. "'Random House,' Case Study." Harvard Business School. Boston, MA: President and Fellows of Harvard College, 2004.

Anderson, Eric, and Duncan Simester. "The Role of Price Endings: Why Stores May Sell More at $49 than at $44." Paper available from the Social Science Research Network Electronic Library, May 2000. http://papers.ssrn.com/sol13/papers.cfm?abstract_id=232542.

Anglada, L., and N. Comellas. "What's Fair? Pricing Models in the Electronic Era." *Library Management* 23, no. 4 (April 2002): 227–33.

Arbatskaya, Maria. "Can Low Price Guarantees Deter Entry?" *International Journal of Industrial Organization* 19, no. 9 (November 2001): 1387–406.

Arkenbout, Erwin, Frans van Duk, and Peter van Wuck. Copyright in the Information Society: Scenarios and Strategies. *European Journal of Law and Economics* 17 (2004): 237–49.

Arnold, Martin. 1998. "It's the Cachet, Not the Money." *New York Times*, May 21, late edition, East Coast.

Association of American University Presses. The Association of American University Presses Directory, 2002–2003. New York, 2003.

Athey, Susan, and Armin Schmutzler. "Investment and Market Dominance." *RAND Journal of Economics* 32, no. 1 (Spring 2001): 1–26.

Athill, Diana. *Stet: An Editor's Life*. New York: Grove, 2001.

Attorney General's Commission on Pornography. *Final Report*. Washington, DC: GPO, 1986.

Auletta, Ken. "The Impossible Business." *New Yorker*, October 6, 1997. "Publishing World" section, pp. 50–63.

Ayala, Nancy. "Selling More than Words." May 1, 2005. VNU eMedia. www.marketingymedios.com.

Bagdikian, Ben H. *The Media Monopoly*. 6th edition. Boston: Beacon Press, 2000.

Bailey, Herbert S., Jr. "The Future of University Press Publishing." *Journal of Scholarly Publishing* 19 (1988): 63–69.

Baker, Nicholas. *The Oxford University Press and the Spread of Learning, 1478–1978*. Oxford: Clarendon Press, 1978.

Baker, Nicholson. *Double Fold: Libraries and the Assault on Paper*. New York: Random House, 2001.

Bakos, Yannis. "Reducing Buyer Search Costs: Implications for Electronic Marketplaces." *Management Science* 43, 12 (1997): 1676–92.

Bandler, James, and Jeffrey A. Trachtenberg. 2004. "So Much to Read, So Few Readers." *Wall Street Journal*, November 22. www.Wsj.com.

Banerjee, Anindya, and Bill Russell. "Industry Structure and the Dynamics of Price Adjustment." *Applied Economics* 33, 15 (2002): 1889–901.

Banner, James M., Jr. "Preserving the Integrity of Peer Review." *Journal of Scholarly Publishing* 19, no. 2 (January 1988): 109–15.

———. "Guidelines for Peer Review of Sponsored Book Manuscripts." *Journal of Scholarly Publishing* 20, no. 2 (January 1989): 116–22.

Barnes, Jessica S., and Claudette E. Bennett. "The Asian Population: 2000," Census 2000 Brief. U.S. Dept. of Commerce, Economics and Statistics Administration, U.S. Census Bureau, issued February 2002.

Barschall, H. H. "Electronic Versions of Printed Journals." *Serials Review* 18, nos. 1–2 (1992): 49–51.

Barzun, Jacques. *On Writing, Editing, and Publishing*. Chicago, IL: University of Chicago Press, 1986.

Bass, Frank M. "A New Product Growth Model for Consumer Durables." *Management Science* 15 (1969): 215–27.

Bass, Thomas A. *The Predictors: How a Band of Maverick Physicists Used Chaos Theory to Trade Their Way to a Fortune on Wall Street*. New York: Henry Holt, 1999.

Basuroy, Suman, Subimal Chatterjee, and S. Abraham Ravid. "How Critical Are Critical Reviews? The Box Office Effects of Film Critics, Star Power, and Budgets." *Journal of Marketing* 67 (2003): 103–17.

Baye, Michael R., and John Morgan. "Information Gatekeepers on the Internet and the Competitiveness of Homogeneous Product Markets." *American Economic Review* 91, no. 3 (June 2001): 454–74.

Bayus, Barry L., and William P. Putsis Jr. "Product Proliferation: An Empirical Analysis of Product Line Determination and Market Outcomes." *Marketing Science* 18, no. 2 (1999): 137–53.

Beahm, George, ed. *War of Words: The Censorship Debate.* Kansas City, MO: Andrews & McMeel, 1993.

Becker, Gary. "A Note on Restaurant Pricing and Other Examples of Social Influence on Price." *Journal of Political Economy* 99 (1991): 1109, 1114, 1115.

Becker, William C. "The Crisis—One Year Later." *Journal of Scholarly Publishing* 4 (1973): 291–302.

Bell, Bill, ed. *Where Is Book History?* Toronto: University of Toronto Press, 2002.

Bell, Hazel. *Indexers and Indexes in Fact and Fiction.* Toronto: University of Toronto Press, 2002.

Bell, J. G. "The Proper Domain of Scholarly Publishing." *Journal of Scholarly Publishing* 2 (1970): 15.

Benjamin, Curtis G. *U.S. Books Abroad: Neglected Ambassadors.* Washington, DC: The Library of Congress, 1984.

Bennett, Scott. "The Boat that Must Stay Afloat: Academic Libraries in Hard Times." *Journal of Scholarly Publishing* 23, no. 3 (April 1992): 131–37.

Benninga, Simon. *Financial Modeling.* Cambridge, MA: MIT Press, 1997.

Berg, A. Scott. *Max Perkins: Editor of Genius.* New York: Pocket Books, 1979.

Berthon, P., L. F. Pitt, and R. T. Watson. "The World Wide Web as an Advertising Medium: Toward an Understanding of Conversion Efficiency." *Journal of Advertising Research* 36, no. 1 (January–February 1996): 43–54.

Bettman, James R., Mary Frances Luce, and John W. Payne. "Constructive Consumer Choice Processes." *Journal of Consumer Research* 35 (December 1998): 187–217.

Bide, Mark. "Adding Value in Electronic Publishing: Taking the Reader's Perspective." *Business Information Review* 19, no. 1 (March 2002): 55–60.

Bills, Mark, and Youngsing Chang. "Understanding How Price Responds to Costs and Production." National Bureau of Economic Research paper no. W7311, August 1999.

Birkets, Sven. "Perseus Unbound." *Journal of Scholarly Publishing* 24, no. 3 (April 1993): 151–56.

———. *The Gutenberg Elegies: The Fate of Reading in an Electronic Age.* Boston: Faber & Faber, 1994.

Biswas, Tapan. *Decision-Making under Uncertainty.* London: Macmillan, 1997.

Black, M. H. *Cambridge University Press, 1584–1984.* Cambridge, UK: Cambridge University Press, 1984.

Bloom, Alan. *The Closing of the American Mind: How Higher Education Has Failed Democracy and Impoverished the Souls of Today's Students.* New York: Simon & Schuster, 1987.

Blumenstyk, Goldie. "Publishers Promote E-textbooks, But Many Students and Professors Are Skeptical." *Chronicle of Higher Education*, May 18, 2001, A35.

Boldrin, Michel, and David Levine. "The Case Against Intellectual Property." The *American Economic Review* 92, no. 2 (May 2002): 209–12.

Bonn, Thomas L. *Undercover: An Illustrated History of American Mass Market Paperbacks*. New York: Penguin, 1982.

———. "Victor Weybright as Gatekeeper." *Book Research Quarterly* 3 (Fall 1987): 60–83.

———. *Heavy Traffic and High Culture: New American Library as Literary Gatekeeper in the Paperback Revolution*. Carbondale: Southern Illinois University Press, 1989.

———. "Uneasy Lie the Heads: New American Library in Transition." *Book Research Quarterly* 5 (Fall 1989): 3–24.

———. "Literary Power Brokers Come of Age." *Media Studies Journal* 6 (Summer 1992): 63–72.

———. "Henry Holt A-Spinning in His Grave: Agenting, Yesterday, and Today." *Publishing Research Quarterly* 10 (Spring 1994): 55–65.

Book Industry Study Group (BISG). *2002 Consumer Research Study on Book Purchasing*, pp. 22–80. New York: Book Industry Study Group, 2003.

Book Industry Study Group. Consumer Research Study on Book Purchasing. New York: Book Industry Study Group, 1992–2002. [Published annually.]

Book Industry Study Group. Book Industry Trends. New York: Book Industry Study Group, 1991–2005. [Published annually.]

Borkowski, Susan C., and Mary Jeanne Welsh. "Ethical Practice in the Accounting Publishing Process: Contrasting Opinions of Authors and Editors." *Journal of Business Ethics* 25 (May 1, 2000), 15–31.

Bouchoux, Deborah E. *Protecting Your Company's Intellectual Property: A Practical Guide to Trademarks, Copyrights, Patents, and Trade Secrets*. New York: AMACOM, 2001.

Bowker Annual Library and Book Trade Almanac. New Providence, NJ: Bowker, 1961–2005. [Published annually.]

Bowles, Gloria. "'Feminist Scholarship' and 'Women's Studies': Implications for University Presses." *Journal of Scholarly Publishing* 19, no. 3 (April 1988): 163–68.

Brand, Stewart. *The Media Lab: Inventing the Future at M.I.T*. New York: Penguin Books, 1988.

Bratland, Rose Marie, and William S. Lofquist. "Economic Outlook for the U.S. Printing and Publishing Industry." *Publishing Research Quarterly* 11 (Summer 1995): 29–35.

Brenner, Reuwen. *The Force of Finance*. New York: Texere, 2002.

Brosius, Matt. "The OECD as Publisher." *Journal of Scholarly Publishing* 22, no. 1 (October 1990): 44–50.

Brown, Carolyn M. "Writing a New Chapter in Book Publishing." *Black Enterprise* 25, no. 7 (February 1): 108. http://www.findarticles.com/p/articles/mi_m1365/is_n7_v25/ai_16552987.

Brown, John. "University Press Publishing." *Journal of Scholarly Publishing* 1 (1970): 133.

Brynjolfsson, Erik, and Michael Smith. "Frictionless Commerce? A Comparison of Internet and Conventional Retailers." *Management Science* 46, no. 4 (April 2000a): 563–85.

Brynjolfsson, Erik, and Michael D. Smith. "The Great Equalizer? Consumer Choice Behavior At Internet Shopbots." Working Paper MIT Sloan School of Management, July 2000b, 1–63.

Brynjolfsson, Erik, Yu Hu, and Michael D. Smith. "Consumer Surplus in the Digital Economy: Estimating the Value of Increased Product Variety at Online Booksellers." *Management Science* 49, no. 11 (2003): 1580–97.

Burchfield, Robert. "The Oxford English Dictionary and the State of the Language." *Journal of Scholarly Publishing* 19, no. 3 (April 1988): 169–78.

Burlingame, Roger. *Of Making Many Books: A Hundred Years of Reading, Writing, and Publishing.* University Park: Pennsylvania State University Press, 1997.

Burress, Lee. *The Battle of the Books: Library Censorship in the Public Schools, 1950–1985.* Metuchen, NJ: Scarecrow, 1988.

Cabral, Luis M. B. "Stretching Firm and Brand Reputation." *RAND Journal of Economics* 31, no. 4 (Winter 2000): 658–73.

Campbell, Margaret. "Perceptions of Price Unfairness: Antecedents and Consequences." *Journal of Marketing Research* 36, no. 2 (1999): 187–99.

Campbell, Robert. "Document Delivery and the Journal Publisher." *Journal of Scholarly Publishing* 23, no. 4 (July 1992): 213–22.

Caplette, Michele. "Women in Publishing: A Study of Careers in Organizations." PhD dissertation, SUNY at Stony Brook, 1981.

Carlin, W., A. Glyn, and J. Van Reenen. "Export Market Performance of OECD Countries: An Empirical Examination of the Role of Cost Competitiveness." *Economic Journal* 111, no. 468 (January 2001): 128–62.

Carlton, D., and Judith A. Chevalier. "Free Riding and Sales Strategies for the Internet." *Journal of Industrial Economics* 49 (2001): 441–62.

Carmon, Ziv, and Dan Ariely. "Focusing on the Foregone: Why Value Can Appear So Different to Buyers and Sellers." *Journal of Consumer Research* 27 (December 2000): 360–70.

Caro, Robert A. "Sanctum Sanctorum for Writers." *New York Times*, May 19, 1995.

Carrigan, Dennis P. "Publish or Perish: The Troubled State of Scholarly Communication." *Journal of Scholarly Publishing* 22, no. 3 (April 1991): 131–42.

———. "Research Libraries' Evolving Response to the 'Serials Crisis.'" *Journal of Scholarly Publishing* 23, no. 3 (April 1992): 138–51.

———. "The Emerging National Periodicals System in the United States." *Journal of Scholarly Publishing* 25, no. 2 (January 1994): 93–102.

Carvajal, Doreen. "Authors Press for Change in Minority Hiring." *New York Times*, June 24, 1996a, late edition, East Coast.

———. "Of Hispanic Literature and Not so Equal Opportunities." *New York Times*, May 4, 1996b, late edition, East Coast.

Ceglowski, Janet. "Has the Border Narrowed?" *North American Journal of Economics and Finance* 11, no. 1 (August 2000): 61–75.

Cerf, Bennett. *At Random: The Reminiscences of Bennett Cerf.* New York: Random House, 1977.

Champlin, Dell, and Janet Knoedler. "Operating in the Public Interest or in Pursuit of Private Profits? News in the Age of Media Consolidation." *Journal of Economic Issues* 36, no. 2 (June 2002): 459–68.

Chandler, Alfred D. *Strategy and Structure: Chapters in the History of Industrial Enterprise.* Cambridge, MA: MIT Press, 1962.

———. *The Visible Hand: The Managerial Revolution in American Business.* Cambridge, MA: Harvard University Press, 1977.

Chaudhuri, Arjun, and Morris B. Holbrook. "The Chain of Effects from Brand Trust and Brand Affect to Brand Performance: The Role of Brand Loyalty." *Journal of Marketing* 65 (April 2001): 81–93.

Chen, Yuxin, and K. Sudhir. "When Shopbots Meet Emails: Implications for Price Competitions on the Internet." Yale School of Management. Working Paper Series MK Marketing no. 10.

Cheney, O. H. *Economic Survey of the Book Industry, 1930–1931.* New York: Bowker, 1960.

Chevalier, Judith A., and Austan Goolsbee. "Measuring Prices and Price Competition Online: Amazon and Barnes and Noble." Yale International Center for Finance. Working Paper no. 02-23, June 2002.

Chevalier, Judith A., and Dina Mayzlin. "The Effect of Word of Mouth on Sales: Online Book Reviews." Yale School of Management: working paper series ES & MK economics and marketing; ES no. 28 & MK no. 15; pp. 1–34, 2003.

The Chicago Manual of Style, 15th edition. Chicago: University of Chicago Press, 2003.

Chintagunta, Pradeep K. "Investigating Category Pricing Behavior at a Retail Chain." *Journal of Marketing Research* 39 (May 2002): 141–54.

Clay, Karen B., and Robert P. Strauss. "Institutional Barriers to Electronic Commerce: An Historical Perspective." *New Institutionalism in Strategic Management* 19:245–71.

Clay, Karen, Ramayya Krishnan, and Eric Wolff. "Prices and Price Dispersion on the Web: Evidence from the Online Book Industry." *Journal of Industrial Economics* 49, no. 4 (December 2001): 521–39.

Clay, Karen, Ramayya Krishnan, Eric Wolff, and Danny Fernandes. "Does A Seller's Ecommerce Reputation Matter? Evidence from Ebay Auctions." *Journal of Industrial Economics*, 50, no. 3 (September 2002): 351–67.

Clerides, Sofronis K. "Pricing, Product Selection, and Consumer Choice in a Durable Good Market: The Book Publishing Industry." PhD dissertation, Yale University, 1998.

Clurman, Richard M. *To the End of Time: The Seduction and Conquest of a Media Empire.* New York: Simon & Schuster, 1992.

Cohn, D'Vera, and Darryl Fears. "Multiracial Growth Seen in Census." *Washington Post*, March 13, 2001.

Cole, John Y., ed. *Responsibilities of the American Book Community.* Washington, DC: Library of Congress/Center for the Book, 1981.

———, ed. *Books in Our Future: Perspectives and Proposals.* Washington, DC: Library of Congress/Center for the Book, 1987.

Cole, John Y., and Thomas G. Sticht, eds. *The Textbook in American Society.* Washington, DC: Center for the Book at the Library of Congress, 1981.

Coleman, Dandy. "Intern Program Introduces Minorities to the Industry." *Boston Globe*, October 19, 1997, city edition.

Commins, Dorothy, ed. *What Is an Editor? Saxe Commins at Work*. Chicago: University of Chicago Press, 1978.

Compaine, Benjamin M. *The Book Industry in Transition*. White Plains, NY: Knowledge Industry Publications, 1978.

———. "The Expanding Base of Media Competition." *Journal of Communication* 35 (Summer 1985): 81–96.

Compaine, Benjamin M., and Douglas Gomery. *Who Owns the Media?* Mahwah, NJ: Erlbaum, 2000.

Conaway, James. *America's Library: The Story of the Library of Congress, 1800–2000*. New Haven, CT: Yale University Press, 2000.

Congressional Budget Office. Economic Forecasts. http://www.cbo.gov, 2004.

Connors, Linda E., Sara Lynn Henry, and Jonathan W. Reader. "From Art to Corporation: Harry N. Abrams, Inc., and the Cultural Effects of Merger." *Book Research Quarterly* 1 (Winter 1985–1986): 28–59.

Conway, J. North. *American Literacy: Fifty Books that Define Our Culture and Ourselves*. New York: William Morrow, 1993.

Copyright Revision Act of 1976. Chicago, IL: Commerce Clearance House, 1976.

Coser, Lewis A. "Professional Authors and Publishing Houses." *Book Research Quarterly* 3 (Summer 1987): 11–14.

Coser, Lewis A., Charles Kadushin, and Walter W. Powell. *Books: The Culture and Commerce of Publishing*. New York: Basic Books, 1982.

Coser, Lewis A., Charles Kadushin, and Walter W. Powell. *Books: The Culture and Commerce of Publishing*. Chicago: University of Chicago Press, 1985.

Cost, Frank. *The Pocket Guide to Digital Printing*. Albany, NY: Delmar Publishers, 2003.

Cotterill, Ronald W., William P. Putsis, and Ravi Dhar. "Assessing the Competitive Interaction between Private Labels and National Brands." *Journal of Business* 73, no. 1 (2000): 109–38.

Council of Economic Advisors. "Changing America: Indicators of Social and Economic Well-Being by Race and Hispanic Origin." Washington, DC: U.S. Government Printing Office, 1998.

Coyte, Peter C., and David L. Ryan. "Subscribe, Cancel, or Renew: The Econometrics of Reading by Subscription." *Canadian Journal of Economics* 24, no. 1 (February 1991): 101–23.

Crainer, Stuart, and Art Kleiner. "Who Wrote These Books?" *Across the Board*, November–December 1998, 22–28.

Crane, Gregory. "'Hypermedia' and Scholarly Publishing." *Journal of Scholarly Publishing* 21, no. 3 (April 1990): 131–56.

Crews, Kenneth D. *Copyright, Fair Use, and the Challenge for Universities: Promoting the Progress of Higher Education*. Chicago: University of Chicago Press, 1993.

Crider, Allen Billy, ed. *Mass Market Publishing in America*. Boston: G. K. Hall, 1982.

———. *Undercover: An Illustrated History of American Mass Market Paperbacks*. New York: Penguin, 1982.

Cronin, Blaise. The University Press. *Library Journal*, March 15, 2002, 60.

Cross River Publishing Consultants. "Book Industry Returns: An Analysis of the Problem; A Focus on Smaller Publishers; and Opportunities for Improvement." Publishers Marketing Association white paper, May 25, 2000.

Cummings, L. L., and Peter J. Frost. *Publishing in the Organizational Sciences*. Homewood, IL: Richard D. Irwin, 1985.

Curry, Philip A. "Decision Making Under Uncertainty and the Evolution of Independent Preferences." *Journal of Economic Theory* 98, no. 2 (June 2001): 357–69.

Curtis, Richard. *Beyond the Best Seller: A Literary Agent Takes You Inside the Book Business*. New York: New American Library, 1989.

Danesi, Marcel, ed. *Encyclopedic Dictionary of Semiotics, Media, and Communication*. Toronto: University of Toronto Press, 2000.

Darnton, Robert. *The Kiss of Lamourette: Reflections in Cultural History*. New York: W. W. Norton, 1990.

———. "Sex for Thought." *New York Review of Books*, December 22, 1994, 65–74.

———. *The Forbidden Best-Sellers of Pre-Revolutionary France*. New York: Norton, 1995.

Daum, Meghan. "Life on the Loaf: Two Weeks at the Bread Loaf Writer's Conference." *New York Times Book Review*, June 11, 1995.

Davidson, Cathy N. *Revolution and the Word: The Rise of the Novel in America*. Oxford: Oxford University Press, 1986.

———, ed. *Reading in America: Literature and Social History*. Baltimore, MD: Johns Hopkins University Press, 1989.

Davis, Kenneth C. *Two-Bit Culture: The Paperbacking of America*. Boston, MA: Houghton Mifflin, 1984.

Davis, Lee. "Intellectual Property Rights, Strategy, and Policy." *Economic Innovation and New Technology* 13, no. 5 (2004): 399–415.

Davis, Philip M., and Leah R. Solla. "An IP-Level Analysis of Usage Statistics for Electronic Journals in Chemistry: Making Inferences about User Behavior." *Journal of the American Society for Information Science and Technology* 54, no. 11 (2003): 1062–68.

Dawkins, Wayne. "Is Anybody Out There?" *Black Issues Book Review*, May–June 2005, p. 10.

Day for Women's Equality. Minneapolis, MN: Organizing Against Pornography, 1988.

de Grazia, Edward. *Girls Lean Back Everywhere: The Law of Obscenity and the Assault on Genius*. New York: Random House, 1992.

De Groote, Sandra, and Josephine L. Dorsch. "Measuring Use Patterns of Online Journals and Database at the University of Chicago." *Journal of the Medical Library Association* 91, no. 2 (2003): 231–40.

De Vany, Arthur, and David Walls. "Bose-Einstein Dynamics and Adaptive Contracting in the Motion Picture Industry." *Economic Journal* 106, no. 439 (November 1996): 1493–514.

———. "Uncertainty in the Movie Industry: Does Star Power Reduce the Terror of the Box Office?" *Journal of Cultural Economics* 23, no. 4 (November 1999): 285–318.

DelFattore, Joan. *What Johnny Shouldn't Read: Textbook Censorship in America*. New Haven: Yale University Press, 1992.

Dellarocas, Chrysanthos. "The Digitization of Word of Mouth: Promise and Challenges of Online Feedback Mechanisms." *Management Science* 49, no. 10 (2003): 1407–24.

Dellarocas, Chrysanthos, Neeven Farag Awad, and Xiaoquan (Michael) Zhang. "Exploring the Value of Online Reviews to Organizations: Implications for Revenue Forecasting and Planning." Working paper, Massachusetts Institute of Technology, 2004.

Demac, Donna A. *Liberty Denied: The Current Rise of Censorship in America.* New Brunswick, NJ: Rutgers University Press, 1990.

Derricourt, Robin. *An Author's Guide to Scholarly Publishing.* Princeton, NJ: Princeton University Press, 1996.

Desai, Kalpesh Kaushik, and Suman Basuroy. "Interactive Influence of Genre Familiarity, Star Power, and Critics' Reviews in the Cultural Goods Industry: The Case of Motion Pictures." *Psychology and Marketing* 22, no. 3 (March 2005): 203–23.

Dessauer, John P. "Coming Full Circle at Macmillan: A Publishing Merger in Economic Perspective." *Book Research Quarterly* 1 (Winter 1985–1986): 60–72.

———. "Cultural Pluralism and the Book World." *Book Research Quarterly* 2 (Fall 1986): 3–6.

———. "U.S. Retail Book Sales by Subject: A First Estimate." *Book Research Quarterly* 2 (Winter 1986–1987): 15–17.

———. "The Case for Reader Research." *Publishing Research Quarterly* 10 (Fall 1994): 4–8.

Dewan, Rajiv, Bing Jing, and Abraham Seidmann. "Product Customization and Price Competition on the Internet." University of Rochester, William E. Simon Graduate School of Business Administration. Computer and Information Systems Working Paper no. CIS 01-03, July 2001.

Dhar, Sanjay, and Stephen J. Hoch. "Why Store Brand Penetration Varies by Retailer." *Marketing Science* 16, no. 3 (1997): 208–27.

DiClemente, Diane F., and Donald A. Hantula. "Applied Behavioral Economics and Consumer Choice." *Journal of Economic Psychology* 24, no. 5 (October 2003): 589–602.

Dizard, Wilson P., Jr. *The Coming Information Age: An Overview of Technology, Economics, and Politics.* White Plains, NY: Longman, 1982.

———. *Old Media New Media: Mass Communications in the Information Age.* 3rd edition. New York: Longman, 2000.

Donthu, Naveen, and Adrina Garcia. "The Internet Shopper." *Journal of Advertising* 39, no. 5 (1999): 52–58.

Dowling, William C. "Saving Scholarly Publishing in the Age of Oprah: The Glastonbury Project." *Journal of Scholarly Publishing* 28, no. 3 (1997): 8.

Downs, Robert B. *Books that Changed the World.* New York: Macmillan, 1970.

Downs, Robert B., and Ralph E. McCoy. *The First Freedom Today: Critical Issues Relating to Censorship and to Intellectual Freedom.* Chicago: American Library Association, 1984.

Drucker, Peter. *Management: Tasks, Responsibilities, Practices.* New York: Harper & Row, 1974.

Dworkin, Andrea. *Pornography: Men Possessing Women.* New York: Putnam, 1981.

Dworkin, Andrea, and Catharine A. MacKinnon. 1988. *Pornography and Civil Rights: A New Day.* Minneapolis, MN: Organizing of Pornography.

Edelman, Hendrik. "Copyright and the Library of the Future." *Book Research Quarterly* 2 (Fall 1986): 51–61.

Edelman, Murray J. *The Politics of Misinformation.* Cambridge: Cambridge University Press, 2001.

Edgar, William B. "Toward a Theory of Collection Development: An Activities and Attributes Approach." *Library Collections* 27, no. 4 (2003): 393–423.

Edwards, Catherine. "Do the Write Thing." *People Management* 10, no. 12 (June 17, 2004): 36.

EEOC. "2002 EEO-1 Aggregate Report for Book Publishing." Washington, DC: U.S. Equal Employment Opportunity Commission, 2002. www.eeoc.gov/stats.

Eisenberg, Daniel. "The Electronic Journal." *Journal of Scholarly Publishing* 29, no. 1 (October 1988): 49–58.

———. "Problems of the Paperless Book." *Journal of Scholarly Publishing* 21 (October 1989): 11–26.

———. "Processing Electronic Manuscripts on the PC." *Journal of Scholarly Publishing* 22 (January 1991): 93–108.

Eisenstein, Elizabeth L. The *Printing Press as an Agent of Change,* 2 vols. New York: Cambridge University Press, 1979.

Epstein, Jason. "The Decline and Rise of Publishing." *New York Review of Books,* 1 March 1990, 8–12.

———. *Book Business: Publishing Past, Present, and Future.* New York: Norton, 2001.

Ervin, John., Jr. "The Dimensions of Regional Publishing." *Journal of Scholarly Publishing* 20, no. 3 (April 1989): 178–91.

———. "An Approach to Self-Appraisal by University Presses." *Journal of Scholarly Publishing* 21, no. 3 (April 1990): 157–70.

Euromoney Institutional Investor PLC. 1999–2000. Books Revolution Takes Off. *Managing Intellectual Property* 95 (December 1999–January 2000): 12.

Evans, Philip, and Thomas S. Wurster. *Blown to Bits: How the New Economics of Information Transforms Strategy.* Boston: Harvard Business School Press, 2000.

Ezell, Margaret J. M. *Social Authorship and the Advent of Print: The Editor's Advice to Writers.* Baltimore, MD: Johns Hopkins University Press, 2000.

Falk, Erika, and Erin Grizard. *The Glass Ceiling Persists: The 3rd Annual APPC Report on Women Leaders in Communication Companies.* The Annenberg Public Policy Center of the University of Pennsylvania, 2003.

Fama, Eugene F. "Efficient Capital Markets: A Review of Theory and Empirical Work." *Journal of Finance* 25 (1970): 384–417.

———. *Foundations of Finance.* New York: Basic Books, 1976.

———. "Discounting under Uncertainty." *Journal of Business* 69 (1996): 415–28.

———. "Market Efficiency, Long-Term Returns, and Behavioral Finance." Working paper Graduate School of Business, University of Chicago, June 1997.

Fama, Eugene F., Lawrence Fisher, Michael Jensen, and Richard Roll. "The Adjustment of Stock Prices to New Information." *International Economic Review* 19 (1969): 1–21.

Fama, Eugene F., and Kenneth R. French. "The Cross-Section of Expected Stock Returns." *Journal of Finance* 47 (1992): 427–65.

Felber, Lynette. "The Book Review: Scholarly and Editorial Responsibility." *Journal of Scholarly Publishing* 33, no. 3 (April 2002): 166–72.

Fischel, Daniel L. "Planning for Book Reprints." *Journal of Scholarly Publishing* 19, no. 4 (July 1988): 195–201.

Fischer, W. A. "Stephen King and the Publishing Industry's Worst Nightmare." *Business Strategy Review* 13, no. 2 (June 2002): 1–10.

Fish, Stanley. *There's No Such Thing as Free Speech: And It's a Good Thing, Too.* New York: Oxford University Press, 1993.

Flacks, Lewis. "The Evolution of Copyright." *Book Research Quarterly* 2 (Summer 1986): 14–24.

Fleming, Mark. "Printing on Demand in Color." *Digital Output* January 1999, 41.

Follett, Robert J. R. *The Financial Side of Book Publishing.* Oak Park, IL: Alpine Guild, 1988.

Fournier, Susan. "Consumers and Their Brands: Developing Relationship Theory in Consumer Research." *Journal of Consumer Research* 24, no. 4 (1997): 343–73.

Francois, Patrick, and Tanguy van Ypersele. "On the Protection of Cultural Goods." *Journal of International Economics* 56, no. 2 (March 2002): 359–69.

Frank, Robert H., and Philip J. Cook. *The Winner-Take-All Society: How the Few at the Top Get So Much More than the Rest of Us.* New York: Penguin, 1996.

Franklin, Ursula M. "Does Scholarly Publishing Promote Scholarship or Scholars?" *Journal of Scholarly Publishing* 24 (1993): 248–52.

Fraser, Lindsey. *The North American Children's Book Market: A Report for the Sir Stanley Unwin Foundation.* London: Book House, 1989.

Friedland, Martin L. *The University of Toronto.* Toronto: University of Toronto Press, 2002.

Fruge, August. *A Skeptic among Scholars: August Fruge on University Publishing.* Berkeley: University of California Press, 1993.

Fudenberg, Drew, and Jean Tirole. "Customer Poaching and Brand Switching." *RAND Journal of Economics* 31, no. 4 (Winter 2000): 634–57.

Gabor, Andre, and C. W. J. Granger. "Price as an Indicator of Quality: Report on an Enquiry." *Economica* 33 (February 1966): 43–70.

Gammell, Irene, and Elizabeth Epperly, eds. *L. M. Montgomery and Canadian Culture.* Toronto: University of Toronto Press, 1999.

Garber, Marjorie. "Maximum Exposure." *New York Times*, September 4, 1993.

Gates, Henry Louis, Jr., Anthony P. Griffin, Donald E. Lively, Robert C. Post, William B. Rubenstein, and Nadine Strossen. *Speaking of Race, Speaking of Sex: Hate Speech, Civil Rights and Civil Liberties.* New York: New York University Press, 1994.

Geiser, Elizabeth A., Arnold Dolin, and Gladys S. Topkis, eds. *The Business of Book Publishing.* Boulder, CO: Westview Press, 1985.

Germano, William. *Getting It Published: A Guide for Scholars and Anyone Else Serious about Serious Books.* Chicago: University of Chicago Press, 2001.

———. "Surviving the Review Process." *Journal of Scholarly Publishihg* 33, no. 1 (October 2001): 53–69.

Gershon, Richard A. *The Transnational Media Corporation: Global Messages and Free Market Competition.* Mahwah, NJ: Erlbaum, 1997.

———. "The Transnational Media Corporation: Environmental Scanning and Strategy Formation." *Journal of Media Economics* 13, no. 2 (2000): 81–101.

Getz, Malcolm. "Electronic Publishing: An Economic View." *Serials Review* 18, no. 1–2 (1992): 25–31.

Ghose, Anindya, Michael D. Smith, and Rahul Telang. "Internet Exchanges for Used Books: An Empirical Analysis for Welfare Implications." Working paper, Carnegie Mellon University, 2004.

———. "Are Internet Used Product Markets Cannibalizing New Product Sales? An Analysis of Internet Markets for Books." Working paper, Carnegie-Mellon University and Stern School, New York University; SSRN # 584401, 2005.

Gifford, Sharon. "Endogenous Information Costs." Paper available at the Social Science Research Network Electronic Library (February 24, 2001). http://papers.ssrn.com/sol13/papers.cfm?abstract_id=262183.

Giles, Michael W. "From Gutenberg to Gigabytes: Scholarly Communication in the Age of Cyberspace." *Journal of Politics* 58, no. 3 (1996): 613–26.

Gillerot, Dominique, and Marc Minton. "Development of the Internet, Market Structure, and Commercial Practices: The Case of the Publishing Sector." *Communications and Strategies* 38 (2nd quarter 2000): 221–39.

Ginsburg, Jane C. "What to Know before Reissuing Old Titles as E-Books." *Communications of the ACM* 44, no. 9 (September 2001): 25–27.

Givler, Peter. "University Press Publishing in the United States." In *Scholarly Publishing: Books, Journals, Publishers, and Libraries in the Twentieth Century*, eds. Richard E. Abel and Lyman W. Newlin. New York: Wiley, 2002.

Gladwell, Malcolm. *The Tipping Point: How Little Things Can Make a Big Difference*. Little Brown, New York, 2002.

Glass, Amy Jocelyn. "Price Discrimination and Quality Improvement." *Canadian Journal of Economics* 34, no. 2 (May 2001): 549–69.

Gleason, Paul. "Publishers' and Librarians' Views on Copyright and Photocopying." *Journal of Scholarly Publishing* 29, no. 1 (October 1988): 13–22.

Goldberg, Vicki. "Madonna's Book: Sex, and Not Like a Virgin." *New York Times*, October 25, 1992.

Goldman, William. "The Screenwriter." In *The Movie Business Book*, ed. Jason E. Squire. New York: Simon & Schuster, 1992.

Goolsbee, Austan. "In a World without Borders: The Impact of Taxes on Internet Commerce." *Quarterly Journal of Economics* 115 (May 2000): 561–76.

Gourville, John T., and Jonathan J. Koehler. "Downsizing Price Increases: A Greater Sensitivity to Price than Quantity in Consumer Markets." Working paper, Harvard Business School Marketing Research Papers; No. 04-01, 2004.

Grabois, Andrew. "U.S. Book Production Tops 150,000 in 2002: Trade Publishing Down, University Presses Up." R. R. Bowker news release, p. 2, 2003.

Grafton, Sue, ed. *Writing Mysteries: A Handbook by the Mystery Writers of America*. Cincinnati, OH: Writer's Digest Books, 1992.

Graham, Andrew. "The Assessment: Economics of the Internet." *Oxford Review of Economic Policy* 17, no. 2 (2001): 145–58.

Graham, Gordon, and Richard Abel, eds. *The Book in the United States Today*. New Brunswick, NJ: Transaction Publishers, 1996.

Grannis, Chandler B., ed. *What Happens in Book Publishing*. New York: Columbia University Press, 1952.

Graubard, Stephen R., and Paul LeClerc, eds. *Books, Bricks, and Bytes*. New Brunswick, NJ: Transaction Publishers, 1998.

Greco, Albert N. "University Presses and the Trade Book Market: Managing in Turbulent Times." *Book Research Quarterly* 3 (Winter 1987–1988): 34–53.

———. *Business Journalism*. New York: New York University Press, 1988.

———. "Mergers and Acquisitions in Publishing, 1984–1988: Some Public Policy Issues." *Book Research Quarterly* 5 (Fall 1989): 25–44.

———. "Teaching Publishing in the United States." *Book Research Quarterly* 6 (Spring 1990): 12–19.

———. *Advertising Management and the Business Publishing Industry*. New York: New York University Press, 1991.

———. "U.S. Book Returns, 1984–1989." *Publishing Research Quarterly* 8 (Fall 1992): 46–61.

———. "Publishing Economics: Mergers and Acquisitions within the Publishing Industry 1980–1989." In *Media Economics: Theory and Practice*, ed. Alison Alexander, James Owers, and Rodney Carveth. Hillsdale, NJ: Erlbaum, 1993.

———. "Teaching Publishing: A Global Perspective." In *Encyclopedia of Library and Information Science*, ed. Allen Kent. New York: Marcel Dekker, 1993.

———. "Mergers and Acquisitions in the U.S. Book Publishing Industry: 1960–1989." In *International Book Publishing: An Encyclopedia*, ed. Philip G. Altbach and Edith S. Hoshino. New York: Garland Publishing, 1995.

———. "The First Amendment, Freedom of the Press, and the Issue of 'Harm': A Conundrum for Publishers." *Publishing Research Quarterly* 11 (Winter 1995–1996): 39–57.

———. "Shaping the Future: Mergers, Acquisitions, and the U.S. Publishing, Communications, and Mass Media Industries, 1990–1995." *Publishing Research Quarterly* 12 (Fall 1996): 5–15.

———. "The Market for Consumer Books in the U.S.: 1985–1995." *Publishing Research Quarterly* 13 (Spring 1997): 3–40.

———. "Domestic Consumer Expenditures for Consumer Books: 1984–1994." *Publishing Research Quarterly* 14 (Fall 1998): 12–28.

———. "The Impact of Horizontal Mergers and Acquisitions on Corporate Concentration in the U.S. Book Publishing Industry, 1989–1994." *Journal of Media Economics* 12, no. 3 (Fall 1999): 165–80.

———. "U.S. Book Exports and Imports: 1998." In Bowker Annual 1999, ed. Dave Bogart. New Providence, NJ: Bowker, 1999.

———. "Market Concentration Levels in the U.S. Consumer Book Industry: 1995–1996." *Journal of Cultural Economics* 24, no. 4 (November 2000): 321–36.

———. "International Book Title Output: 1990–1999." In Bowker Annual 2000, ed. Dave Bogart, New Providence, NJ: Bowker, 2000, pp. 528–31.

————, ed. *The Media and Entertainment Industries*. Boston: Allyn & Bacon, 2000.

————. "U.S. Book Exports and Imports: 1999." In Bowker Annual 2000, ed. Dave Bogart. New Providence, NJ: Bowker, 2000.

————. "The General Reader Market for University Press Books in the United States, 1990–1999, with Projections for the Years 2000 through 2004." *Journal of Scholarly Publishing* 32, no. 2 (January 2001): 61–85.

————. "The Market for University Press Books in the United States: 1985–1999." *Learned Publishing* 14, no. 2 (April 2001b): 97–105.

————. "The Changing Market for U.S. Book Exports and Imports." In Bowker Annual 2004, ed. Dave Bogart. Medford, NJ: Information Today, 2004.

————. "The Economics of Books and Magazines." In *Media Economics: Theory and Practice*, 3rd edition, eds. Alison Alexander, James Owers, Rod Carveth, C. Ann Hollifield, and Albert N. Greco. Mahwah, NJ: Erlbaum, 2004.

————. *The Book Publishing Industry*. Mahwah, NJ: Erlbaum, 2005.

Greco, Albert N., Susan B. Neuman, Donna Celano, and Pamela Shue. *Access for All: Closing the Book Gap for Children in Early Education*. Newark, DE: International Reading Association, 2001.

Greco, Albert N., Walter O'Connor, Sharon Smith, and Robert Wharton. "The Price Of University Press Books, 1989–2000." *Journal of Scholarly Publishing* 35, no. 1 (2003): 4–39.

Greco, Albert N., Robert Wharton, and Hooman Estelami. "The Changing Market for University Press Books: 1997–2002." *Journal of Scholarly Publishing* 36, no. 4 (2005): 187–220.

Greenhouse, Linda. "Supreme Court Upholds Government's Ambiguously Written Child Pornography Law." *New York Times*, November 30, 1994.

Griffin, Keith. *Studies in Globalization and Economic Transitions*. London: Macmillan, 1996.

Gross, Gerald. *Editors on Editing*. New York: Grove Press, 1993.

Grossman, John. "Researching the Fourteenth Edition of *The Chicago Manual of Style*." *Journal of Scholarly Publishing* 25 (October 1993): 63–64.

Gu, Wulong, and Gary Sawchuk. "Canada's Growing Market Integration with the U.S.—With a Focus on Trade." *North American Journal of Economics and Finance* 12, no. 3 (November 2001): 283–300.

Hacken, Richard. "The Current State of European Studies in North America and Scholarly Publishing in Western Europe." *Journal of Academic Librarianship* 24 (1998): 201–7.

Hackett, Alice Payne, and James Henry Burke. *80 Years of Best Sellers, 1895–1975*. New York: Bowker, 1975.

Haight, Anne Lyon, and Chandler B. Grannis. *Banned Books, 387 B.C. to 1978 A.D.*, 4th edition. New York: Bowker, 1978.

Hall, Max. *Harvard University Press: A History*. Cambridge, MA: Harvard University Press, 1986.

Hamilton, Jim. "Trends in Color on Demand Printing." *Digital Output*, February 2002.

Han, Jin. K., Namwoon Kim, and Hong-Bumm Kim. "Entry Barriers: A Dull-, One,- or

Two-Edged Sword for Incumbents? Unraveling the Paradox from a Contingency Perspective." *Journal of Marketing* 65 (January 2001): 1–14.

Hancer, Kevin. *The Paperback Price Guide: First Edition.* New York: Harmony House, 1980.

Hansmann, Henry, and Reinier Kraakman. "Hands-Tying Contracts: Book Publishing, Venture Capital Financing, and Secured Debt." *Journal of Law, Economic, and Organization* 8, no. 3 (1992): 628–55.

Harnum, Bill. "The Characteristics of the Ideal Acquisition Editor." *Journal of Scholarly Publishing* 32, no. 4 (July 2001): 182–88.

Harper, Eliot. "DPC White Paper No. 3: Digital Printing Issues: Economics, Markets, Technology, and the Digital Future." Digital Printing Council of the Printing Industries of America, May 2000.

Hart, James D. *The Popular Book: A History of America's Literary Taste.* New York: Oxford University Press, 1950.

Harvey, William B., Herbert S. Bailey Jr., William C. Becker, and John B. Putnam. "The Impending Crisis in University Publishing." *Journal of Scholarly Publishing* 3 (1972): 195–97.

Hayes, Robert H., and William J. Abernathy, "Managing Our Way to Economic Decline." *Harvard Business Review* 58 (July–August 1980): 67–77.

Helgerson, Linda W. *CD-ROM: Facilitating Electronic Publishing.* New York: Van Nostrand Reinhold, 1992.

Henard, David H., and David M. Szymanski. "Why Some New Products Are More Successful than Others." *Journal of Marketing Research* 38 (August 2001): 362–75.

Hench, John B. "Toward a History of the Book in America." *Publishing Research Quarterly* 10 (Fall 1994): 9–21.

Henderson, Bill. *The Art of Literary Publishing: Editors on Their Craft.* Wainscott, NY: Pushcart Press, 1980.

———. *Rotten Reviews.* Wainscott, NY: Pushcart Press, 1986.

Henriques, Irene, and Perry Sadorsky. "Export-Led Growth or Growth-Driven Exports? The Canadian Case." *Canadian Journal of Economics* 29, no. 3 (August 1996): 540–55.

Henry, Robert W. *Comstockery in America: Patterns of Censorship and Control.* Boston, MA: Beacon Press, 1960.

Hentoff, Nat. *The First Freedom: The Tumultuous History of Free Speech in America.* New York: Delacorte Press, 1980.

"High-Priced College Textbooks." *New York Times,* October 25, 2003.

Hinckley, Karen, and Barbara Hinckley. *American Best Sellers: A Reader's Guide to Popular Fiction.* Bloomington: Indiana University Press, 1989.

Hirschberg, Lynn. "Nothing Random." *New York Times Magazine,* July 20, 2003.

Hoberg, George. "Canada and North American Integration." *Canadian Public Policy* 26, no. 2 (August 2000): S35–S50.

Hoch, S., B. Kim, A. Montgomery, and P. Rossi. "Determinants of Store-level Price Elasticity." *Journal of Marketing Research* 32 (1995): 17–29.

Hoffman, Donna, and Tom P. Novak. "Marketing in Hypermedia Computer-Mediated Environments." *Journal of Marketing* 60, no. 3 (1996): 50–68.

Hoffman, Frank. *Intellectual Freedom and Censorship: An Annotated Bibliography*. Metuchen, NJ: Scarecrow Press, 1989.

Hofstadter, Richard. *Anti-Intellectualism in American Life*. New York: Random House, 1966.

Holt, Karen. "Planeta's English Debut." *Criticas*, September 1, 2004. http://www .criticasmagazine.com /article /CA451387.html.

Holt, Patricia. "Behind Book Industry Transformation." *San Francisco Chronicle*, April 6, 1997.

Horowitz, Irving Louis. *Communicating Ideas: The Crisis of Publishing in a Post-Industrial Society*. New Brunswick, NJ: Transaction Publishers, 1992.

Horowitz, Irving Louis, and Mary Curtis. "The Impact of Technology on Scholarly Publishing." *Journal of Scholarly Publishing* 13 (April 1982): 211–28.

Howsam, Leslie. *Kegan Paul—A Victorian Imprint*. Toronto: University of Toronto Press, 1999.

Huenefeld, John. *The Huenefeld Guide to Book Publishing*. Rev. 5th edition. Bedford, MA: Mills & Sanderson, 1993.

Hurley, Robert F. "Putting People Back into Organizational Learning." *Journal of Business and Industrial Marketing* 17, no. 4 (2002): 270 – 81.

Hutchinson, Ann M. *Editing Women*. Toronto: University of Toronto Press, 1998.

Hutton, Frankie. *The Early Black Press in America, 1827 to 1860*. Westport, CT: Greenwood, 1992.

"In the Mail: Open Season." *New Yorker*, November 7, 1994, p. 20.

Iyer, Ganesh, and Amit Pazgal. "Internet Shopping Agents: Virtual Co-Location and Competition." *Marketing Science* 22, no. 1 (2003): 85 – 106.

Jacques, Geoffrey. "Black Book Sales Grow, but Not Black Publishing Staff." *Publishers Weekly* 243, no. 50 (December 9, 1996): 38.

Janssen, Maarten C. W., and Rob van der Noll, "Electronic Commerce and Retail Channel Substitution." Tinbergen Institute Discussion Paper, TI 2002-042/1.

Jeanneret, Marsh. "The Origins of Scholarly Publishing." *Journal of Scholarly Publishing* 29, no. 4 (July 1989): 197–202.

———. *God and Mammon: Universities as Publishers*. Urbana and Chicago: University of Illinois Press, 1990.

Jenish, D'arcy. "A Vintage Season for Readers." *Macleans* 23 (September 1996): 48 – 49.

Jenkinson, Edward B. *Censor in the Classroom*. Carbondale: Southern Illinois University Press, 1979.

Jones, Candace. "Creative Industries (Book)." *Administrative Science Quarterly* 46, no. 3 (September 2001): 567–71.

Josey, E. J., and Kenneth D. Shearer. *Politics and the Support of Libraries*. New York: Neal-Schuman, 1990.

Joyce, Donald Franklin. *Gatekeepers of Black Culture: Black-Owned Book Publishing in the United States, 1817–1981*. Westport, CT: Greenwood Press, 1983.

———. "Changing Book Publishing Objectives of Secular Black Book Publishers, 1900 – 1986." *Book Research Quarterly* 2 (Fall 1986): 42–50.

Kadiyali, Vrinda, Naufel J. Vilcassin, and Predepp Chintagunta. "Empirical Analysis of

Competitive Product Line Decisions: Lead, Follow, or Move Together." *Journal of Business* 69, no. 4 (1999): 459–87.

Kahin, Brian, and Hal R. Varian., eds. *Internet Publishing and Beyond: The Economics of Digital Information and Intellectual Property*. Cambridge, MA: MIT Press, 2000.

Kaiserlian, Penelope. "Kate Turabian's *Manual*: A Best-Seller for Fifty Years." *Journal of Scholarly Publishing* 19, no. 3 (April 1988): 136–43.

Kanter, Rosabeth Moss. *When Giants Learn to Dance: Mastering the Challenges of Strategy, Management, and Careers in the 1990s*. New York: Simon & Schuster, 1989.

Kashani, Kamran. "Beware the Pitfalls of Global Marketing." *Harvard Business Review* 67 (September–October 1989): 91, 92–98.

Katz, Leanne. "Censors' Helpers." *New York Times*, September 4, 1993.

Katzen, May. "A National Information Network." *Journal of Scholarly Publishing* 19, no. 4 (July 1988): 210–16.

Kazin, Alfred, Dan Lacy, and Ernest L. Boyer. *The State of the Book World, 1980: Three Talks Sponsored by the Center for the Book in the Library of Congress*. Washington, DC: Library of Congress, 1981.

Keller, Morton, and Phyllis Keller. *Making Harvard Modern: The Rise of America's University*. Oxford: Clarendon, 2001.

Kerr, Chester. "A National Enquiry into the Production and Dissemination of Scholarly Knowledge." *Journal of Scholarly Publishing* 7 (October 1975): 7.

———. "One More Time: American University Presses Revisited." *Journal of Scholarly Publishing* 18 (1987): 214.

Kim, Sang Yong, and Richard Staelin. "Manufacturer Allowances and Retailer Pass-Through Rates in a Competitive Environment." *Marketing Science* 18, no. 1 (1999): 59–76.

King, Donald W., Carol Tenopir, and Carol Hansen Montgomery. "Patterns of Journal Use by Faculty at Three Diverse Universities." *D-Lib Magazine* 9, no. 10 (2003): 1.

Kingston, Paul William, and Jonathan R. Cole. *The Wages of Writing: Per Word, Per Piece, or Perhaps*. New York: Columbia University Press, 1986.

Kippan, Helmut, ed. *Handbook of Print Media*. Berlin: Springer-Verlag, 2001.

Kirkpatrick, David D. "Forecasts of an E-Book Era Were, It Seems, Premature." *New York Times*, August 28, 2001.

———. "An 'Enemies List,' but No Enemies Exist." *New York Times*, September 2, 2002.

Kirsch, Jonathan. *Kirsch's Handbook of Publishing Law: For Authors, Publishers, Editors, and Agents*. Los Angeles: Acrobat Books, 1995.

Kiser, Karin N. "Cracking the U.S. Market with Spanish-Language Titles." *Publishers Weekly* 245, no. 37 (1998).

———. "Selling to the Spanish-Language Market in the U.S." *Publishers Weekly* 246, no. 37 (1999).

———. "Spanish-Language Publishing in the U.S. Nears Critical Mass." *Publishers Weekly* 247, no. 38 (2000).

———. "The Search for Distribution." *Criticas*, March–April 2004a, Reed Business Information.

————. "The State of the Market." *Library Journal*, September 1, 2004b, Reed Business Information.

Kister, Ken. "Encyclopedists Head for Cyberspace." *Library Journal*, November 15, 1998, S3–S6.

Klein, Benjamin, Andres V. Lerner, and Kevin Murphy. "The Economics of Copyright 'Fair Use' in a Networked World." *American Economic Review* 92, no. 2 (May 2002): 205–8.

Klemin, Diana. *The Art of Art for Children's Books.* New York: Clarkson Potter, 1966.

Knauer, Joyce. "Scholarly Books in General Bookstores." *Journal of Scholarly Publishing* 19, no. 2 (January 1988): 79–85.

Knopf, Alfred A. *Some Random Recollections.* New York: The Typophiles, 1949.

————. *Publishing Then and Now, 1912–1964.* New York: New York Public Library, 1964.

Kobrak, Fred, and Beth Luey, eds. *The Structure of International Publishing in the 1990s.* New Brunswick, NJ: Transaction, 1992.

Koenig & Bauer Group. "Digital Printing 2000: Technology, Markets and Scenarios." *KBA Report* no. 16, January 2001.

Korda, Michael. *Making the List: A Cultural History of the American Bestseller, 1900–1999.* New York: Barnes & Noble Books, 2001.

Koschat, Martin A., and William P. Putsis Jr. "Who Wants You When You're Old and Poor: Exploring the Economics of Media Pricing." *Journal of Media Economics* 13, no. 4 (2000): 215–32.

Kotha, Suresh, Shivaram Rajgopal, and Mohan Venkatachalam. "The Role of Online Buying Experience as a Competitive Advantage: Evidence from Third-Party Ratings for E-Commerce Firms." *Journal of Business* 77, no. 2 (2004): S109–S133.

Kotler, Philip. "From Sales Obsession to Marketing Effectiveness." *Harvard Business Review* 55 (November–December 1977): 67–75.

————. *Marketing Management.* 10th edition. Upper Saddle River, NJ: Prentice-Hall, 2000.

Kotok, Alan, and Ralph Lyman. *Print Communications and the Electronic Media Challenge.* Plainview, NY: Kotok & Lyman, 1997.

Kozak, Ellen. M. *Every Writer's Guide to Copyright and Publishing Law.* 2nd edition. New York: Henry Holt, 1997.

Kranton, Rachael E., and Deborah F. Minehart. "A Theory of Buyer-Seller Networks." The *American Economic Review* 91, no. 3 (June 2001): 485–508.

Kremer, John. *Book Marketing Made Easier.* Fairfield, IA: Jay Frederick Editions, 1986.

Kwak, Hyokjin, Richard J. Fox, and George M. Zinkhan. "What Products Can Be Successful Promoted and Sold Via the Internet?" *Journal of Advertising Research* 42, no. 1 (January–February 2002): 23–38.

Kyereme, Stephen S. "Determinants of United States' Trade Balance With Australia." *Applied Economics* 34, no. 10 (2001): 1241–50.

Laband, David N. "Measuring the Relative Impact of Economics Book Publishers." *Journal of Economic Literature* 28, no. 2 (June 1990): 655–60.

Laband, David, and John Hudson. "The Pricing of Economics Books." *Journals of Economic Education* 34, no. 4 (2003): 360.

Labunski, Richard. "The Evolution of Libel Laws: Complexity and Inconsistency." *Book Research Quarterly* 5 (Spring 1989): 59–95.

Lacy, Stephen, and Walter E. Niebauer Jr. "Developing and Using Theory for Media Economics." *Journal of Media Economics* 8, no. 2 (1995): 3–13.

Lafollette, Marcel C. *Stealing into Print: Fraud, Plagiarism, and Misconduct in Scientific Publishing.* Berkeley: University of California Press, 1992.

Laitman-McAnally, Lillian, and Cindy Crosby. "Exploit Draws Bilingual Crowd." *Publishers Weekly* 248, no. 25 (June 18, 2001): 18.

Lal, Rajiv, and Miklos Sarvary. "When and How is the Internet Likely to Decrease Price Competition?" *Management Science* 45 (1999): 485–503.

Lal, Rajiy, and J. Miguel Villas Boras. "Price Promotions and Trade Deals with Multiproduct Retailers." *Management Science* 44 (1998): 935–49.

Lampartner, William C. "Digital Printing Technology Developments and Market Growth Lags Earlier Forecasts." *GATF World/2002 GATF Technology Forecast*, January–February 2002.

Lancaster, K. "The Economics of Product Variety: A Survey." *Marketing Science* 9 (Summer 1990): 189–206.

Landes, W. M., and R. A. Posner. "Trademark Law: An Economic Perspective." *Journal of Law and Economics* 30 (1987): 265–309.

Landow, George P. *Hypertext: The Convergence of Contemporary Critical Theory and Technology.* Baltimore, MD: Johns Hopkins University Press, 1992.

Lanham, Richard D. *The Electronic Word: Democracy, Technology, and the Arts.* Chicago: University of Chicago Press, 1993.

Lanning, Meryl. "Working with Freelancers—and Enjoying It." *Journal of Scholarly Publishing* 24, no. 1 (October 1992): 52–56.

Lariviere, Martin A., and V. Padmanabhan. "Slotting Allowances and New Product Introduction." *Marketing Sciences* 16, no. 2 (1997): 112–28.

Layton, Allan P., and Daniel Smith. "A Further Note on the Three Phases of the US Business Cycle." *Applied Economics* 32, no. 9 (1999): 1133–43.

Lee, H. G. "Do Electronic Marketplaces Lower the Price of Goods?" *Communications of the ACM* 41 (1997): 73–80.

Lee, Marshall. *Bookmaking: The Illustrated Guide to Design/Production/Editing.* New York: Bowker, 1979.

Leong, E. K. F., X. Huang, and P. J. Stanners. "Comparing the Effectiveness of the Website with Traditional Media." *Journal of Advertising Research* 38, no. 5 (September–October 1998): 44–51.

Leslie, Larry Z. "Manuscript Review: A View From Below." *Journal of Scholarly Publishing* 29, no. 2 (January 1989): 123–28.

———. "Peering Over the Editor's Shoulder." *Journal of Scholarly Publishing* 23, no. 3 (April 1992): 185–93.

Letts, Mike. "MetaText: Building a New Kind of Textbook." *Seybold Report Analyzing Publishing Trends* 1, no. 7 (July 2001): 4–16.

Levack, Kinley. "Pressing the POD Issue: The MIT Classics Series." *EContent* 26, no. 7 (July 2003): 9.

Levant, Daniel J. "Marketing in the Crunch." *Journal of Scholarly Publishing* 4 (1973): 302.

Levin, Martin P. "The Publishing Executive of the 1990s." *Journal of Scholarly Publishing* 21, no. 1 (October 1989): 41–44.

Levitt, Theodore. "Marketing Myopia." *Harvard Business Review* 53 (September–October 1975): 26–37.

Levy, Leonard W. *Emergence of a Free Speech*. New York: Oxford University Press, 1985.

Lewin, Tamara. "Furor on Exhibit at Law School Splits Feminists." *New York Times*, November 13, 1992.

———. "Students Find $100 Textbooks Cost $50, Purchased Overseas." *New York Times*, October 21, 2003.

Lewis, Anthony. "The First Amendment, Under Fire from the Left." *New York Times Magazine*, March 13, 1994.

Lewis, Freeman. *A Brief History of Pocket Books*. New York: Pocket Books, 1967.

Li, Tiger, and Roger J. Calantone. "The Impact of Market Knowledge Competence on New Product Advantage: Conceptualization and Empirical Examination." *Journal of Marketing* 62, no. 4 (1998): 13–29.

Lichter, S. Robert, Stanley Rothman, and Linda S. Lichter. *The Media Elite: America's New Powerbrokers*. Bethesda, MD: Adler & Adler, 1988.

Lieberman, Al, with Patricia Esgate. *The Entertainment Marketing Revolution*. Upper Saddle River, NJ: Financial Times Prentice Hall, 2002.

Linnemann, Ludger. "The Price Index Effect, Entry, and Endogenous Markups in a Macroeconomic Model of Monopolistic Competition." *Journal of Macroeconomics* 23, no. 3 (Summer 2001): 441–58.

Lipscombe, Trevor. "The Greatest Story Ever Sold: The Pitfalls of Publishing." *Journal of Scholarly Publishing* 31, no. 4 (April 2000): 179–88.

Litan, Robert E., and Alice M. Rivlin. "Projecting the Economic Impact of the Internet." *American Economic Review* 91, no. 2 (May 2001): 313–17.

———. *Beyond the Dot.coms: The Economic Promise of the Internet*. Washington, DC: Brookings Institution Press, 2001.

Liu, Ziming. "Trends in Transforming Scholarly Communication and Their Implications." *Information Processing and Management* 39, no. 6 (2003): 889.

Long, Elizabeth. *The American Dream and the Popular Novel*. Boston: Routledge & Kegan Paul, 1985.

———. "The Cultural Meaning of Concentration in Publishing." *Book Research Quarterly* 1 (Winter 1985–1986): 3–27.

———. "The Book as Mass Commodity: The Audience Perspective." *Book Research Quarterly* 3 (Spring 1987): 9–30.

Long, Robert Emmet, ed. *Censorship*. New York: H. W. Wilson, 1990.

Lopez, Adriana. "The L-Factor." *Publishers Weekly* 252, no. 8 (2005).

Lowenstein, George F. "Out of Control: Visceral Influences on Behavior." *Organizational Behavior and Human Decision Processes* 3 (March 1996): 272–92.

Lowenstein, Roger. *When Genius Failed: The Rise and Fall of Long-Term Capital Management*. New York: Random House, 2000.

Lucas, Henry C., Jr. *Strategies for Electronic Commerce and the Internet*. Cambridge, MA: MIT Press, 2002.

Luey, Beth. "University Press Trade Books in the Review Media." *Journal of Scholarly Publishing* 25, no. 2 (January 1994): 84–92.

Lyall, Sarah. "Are These Books, or What? CD-ROM and the Literary Industry." *New York Times Book Review*, August 14, 1994.

Lynch, Clifford A. "Scholarly Communication in the Networked Environment: Reconsidering Economics and Organizational Missions." *Serials Review* 20, no. 3 (1994): 23–30.

Machlup, Fritz, and Kenneth Leeson. *Information through the Printed Word.* Vol. 1, *Book Publishing.* New York: Praeger, 1978.

MacKinnon, Catharine A. "Pornography, Civil Rights, and Speech." *Harvard Civil Rights–Civil Liberties Law Review* 20 (1985): 1–70.

———. *Feminism Unmodified.* Cambridge, MA: Harvard University Press, 1987.

———. *Only Words.* Cambridge, MA: Harvard University Press, 1993.

Maggio, Rosalie. *The Nonsexist Word Finder: A Dictionary of Gender-Free Usage.* Boston: Beacon Press, 1989.

Maguire, James H. "Publishing on a Rawhide Shoestring." *Journal of Scholarly Publishing* 22, no. 2 (January 1991): 78–82.

Malkiel, Burton G. *A Random Walk Down Wall Street.* New York: Norton, 1996.

———. "The Market Can Police Itself." *Wall Street Journal*, June 28, 2002.

Manguel, Alberto. *A History of Reading.* New York: Penguin Books, 1997.

Mann, Ronand Druckmaschin AG. "What's Digital Here?" *Expressis Verbis*, March 2001.

Max, D. T. "The End of the Book?" *Atlantic Monthly*, September 1994.

Mazzoleni, R., and R. R. Nelson. "Economic Theories about the Benefits and Costs of Patents." *Journal of Economic Issues* 32, no. 4 (1998): 1031–52.

McChesney, Robert W. *Rich Media, Poor Democracy: Communication Politics in Dubious Times.* Urbana: University of Illinois Press, 1999.

McCormack, Thomas. *The Fiction Editor: The Novel, and the Novelist.* New York: St. Martin's Press, 1988.

McLuhan, Marshall. *The Gutenberg Galaxy.* Toronto: University of Toronto Press, 1962.

McLuhan, Marshall, and Quentin Fiore. *The Medium Is the Message.* New York: Bantam Books, 1967.

McLuhan, Marshall, and Eric McLuhan. *The New Science.* Toronto: University of Toronto Press, 1992.

McQuivey, James L., and Megan K. McQuivey. "Is It a Small Publishing World After All: Media Monopolization and the Children's Book Market." *Journal of Media Economics* 11, no. 4 (1998): 35–48.

Mejias, Roberto J., and Jose G. Vargas-Hernandez. "Emerging Mexican and Canadian Strategic Trade Alliances under NAFTA." *Journal of Global Marketing* 14, no. 4 (2001): 89–117.

Meltzer, Françoise. *Hot Property: The Stakes and Claims of Literary Originality.* Chicago: University of Chicago Press, 1994.

Meredith, Lindsay, and Dennis Maki. "Product Cannibalization and the Role of Prices." *Applied Economics* 33, no. 14 (2000): 1785–93.

Meyer, Richard W. "The Library in Scholarly Communication." *Social Science Quarterly* 77, no. 1 (1996): 210–17.

Meyer, Sheldon. "Publishing Trade Books." *Journal of Scholarly Publishing* 9 (1978): 70.

Miles, Jack. "Intellectual Freedom and the University Press." *Journal of Scholarly Publishing* 15, no. 4 (July 1984): 291–99.

Miller, Arthur R., and Michael H. Davis. *Intellectual Property: Patents, Trademarks, and Copyright.* St. Paul, MN: West Wadsworth, 2000.

Miller-Francisco, Emily. "Managing Electronic Resources in a Time of Shrinking Budgets." *Library Collections* 27, no. 4 (2003): 507–12.

Milliot, Jim. "Publishers' Profits Lagged in 2000." *Publishers Weekly,* September 10, 2001.

———. "Lower Operating Margins Prevailed in 2001." *Publishers Weekly,* September 2, 2002.

Minor, Ryan. "What Determines Business Fixed Investment? Evidence from the Canadian Economy." *Applied Economic Letters* 9, no. 8 (July 2002): 497–500.

Mizzaro, Stefano. "Quality Control in Scholarly Publishing: A New Proposal." *Journal of The American Society for Information Science and Technology* 54, no. 11 (2003): 989.

The MLA Ad Hoc Committee on the Future of Scholarly Publishing. The Future of Scholarly Publishing. *Profession,* 2002.

Mlawer, Teresa. "Selling Spanish-Language Books in the United States." *Publishing Research Quarterly* 10 (Winter 1994–1995): 50–53.

Mokia, Rosemary Nturnnyuy. "Publishers, United States Foreign Policy, and the Third World." *Publishing Research Quarterly* 11 (Summer 1995): 36–51.

Montgomery, Alan L., Kartik Hosanagar, Ramayya Krishnan, and Karen B. Clay. "Designing a Better Shopbot." Working paper, Carnegie-Mellon University, 2003, 1–31.

Moon, Eric, ed. *Book Selection and Censorship in the Sixties.* New York: Bowker, 1969.

Moore, Terrence W. "Believe It or Not, Academic Books Are a Bargain." *Journal of Scholarly Publishing* 24 (1993): 161–65.

Morton, Herbert C. "A New Book on New Words." *Journal of Scholarly Publishing* 22, no. 2 (January 1991): 122–27.

———. *The Story of Webster's Third: Philip Gove's Controversial Dictionary and Its Critics.* New York: Cambridge University Press, 1994.

Motavalli, John. *Bamboozled at the Revolution: How Big Media Lost Billions in the Battle for the Internet.* New York: Viking, 2002.

Mott, Frank L. *Golden Multitudes: The Story of Best Sellers in the United States.* New York: Bowker, 1947.

Mowrey, D. C., R. R. Nelson, B. N. Sampat, and A. A. Ziedonis. "The Growth of Patenting and Licensing by U.S. Universities: An Assessment of Bayn-Dole Act of 1980." *Research Policy* 30, no. 1 (2001): 99–119.

Moylan, Michele, and Lane Stiles, eds. *Reading Books: Essays on the Material Text and Literature in America.* Amherst: University of Massachusetts Press, 1996.

Mullainathan, Sendhil, and Richard H. Thaler. "Behavioral Economics." Paper available at the Social Science Research Network Electronic Library, October 2000. http://papers.ssrn.com/sol13/papers.cfm?abstract_id=245733.

Muray, Heather. *Come, Bright Improvement! The Literary Societies of Nineteenth-Century Ontario.* Toronto: University of Toronto Press, 2002.

Myers, B. R. *A Reader's Manifesto.* Hoboken, NJ: Melville House, 2002.

National Association of College Stores. http://www.nacs.org, June 1, 2003.

The National Bureau of Economic Research. http://www.nber.org, 2005.

National Center for Education Statistics. http://nces.ed.gov/pubs2002/proj2012/table_10 .asp, June 13, 2003.

National Coalition Against Censorship. *Meese Commission Exposed*. New York: NCAC, 1986.

National Endowment for the Arts. *Reading at Risk: A Survey of Literary Reading in America*, Research Division Report no. 46, 2004.

Nauman, Matt. "Matching the Librarian and the Book." *Journal of Scholarly Publishing* 29, no. 4 (July 1989): 233–37.

Negroponte, Nicholas. *Being Digital*. New York: Knopf, 1995.

Neil, S. D. *Dilemmas in the Study of Information: Exploring the Boundaries of Information Science*. Westport, CT: Greenwood Press, 1992.

Nevo, Ariv. "Measuring Market Power in the Ready-to-Eat Cereal Industry." *Econometrica* 69, no. 2 (March 2001): 307–42.

Newman, Susan, Donna Celano, Albert N. Greco, and Pamela Shue. *Access for All: Closing the Book Gap for Children in Early Education*. Newark, DE: International Reading Association, 2001.

Nie, Norman H, Alberto Simpser, Irene Stepanikova, and Lu Zheng. "Ten Years after the Birth of the Internet, How Do Americans Use the Internet in Their Daily Lives?" Report, Stanford University Center for the Quantitative Study of Society, 2004.

Nielsen BookScan. Working paper, September 25, 2005.

NPD Group. *Consumer Research Study on Book Purchasing*. New York: Book Industry Study Group, 1991–2002. [Published annually.]

Oak, Leslie, ed. *Print 2020: From Pulp to Pixels*. Rochester, NY: Rochester Institute of Technology, 2002.

O'Brien, Daniel P., John Bernoff, Meredith Gerson, Eric Monson, and Jennifer Parr. "Tech Strategy Report." Forrester Research, December 2000.

O'Brien, Geoffrey. *Hardboiled America: The Lurid Years of Paperbacks*. New York: Van Nostrand Reinhold, 1981.

O'Connor, Maeve. *Editing Scientific Books and Journals*. Kent, UK: Pitman Medical, 1978.

———. *How to Copyedit Scientific Books*. Philadelphia: ISI Press, 1986.

Oda, Stephanie, and Glenn Sanislo. *The Subtext Perspective on Book Publishing: Numbers, Issues and Trends*. Darien, CT: Open Book Publishing, 2000–2005. [Published annually.]

Odin, Yorick, Nathalie Odin, and Pierre Valette-Florence. "Conceptual and Operational Aspects of Brand Loyalty: An Empirical Investigation." *Journal of Business Research* 53 (2001): 75–84.

Off, Lisa, ed. *Censorship: Opposing Viewpoints*. San Diego, CA: Greenhaven Press, 1990.

Okerson, Ann. "Publishing through the Network: The 1990s Debutante." *Journal of Scholarly Publishing* 23, no. 4 (April 1992): 170–77.

Okura, Mindy, and Jill Su. "The Asian American Market for Publishers in the United States." *Publishing Research Quarterly* 19, no. 3 (2003): 60–68.

Olivei, Giovanni P. "Exchange Rates and the Prices of Manufacturing Products Imported into the United States." *New England Journal of Economics*, first quarter 2002, 3–18.

Oliveira-Castro, Jorge M. "Effects of Base Price upon Search Behavior of Consumers in a Supermarket: An Operant Analysis." *Journal of Economic Psychology* 24, no. 5 (October 2003): 637–52.

Olmert, Michael. *The Smithsonian Book of Books*. Washington, DC: Smithsonian Institution Press, 1992.

One Book/Five Ways: The Publishing Procedures of Five University Presses. Chicago: University of Chicago Press, 1994.

Organization for Economic Co-operation and Development. *OECD Economic Surveys: Canada*. Paris: Organization for Economic Co-operation and Development, 2001.

Ormerod, Paul. *Butterfly Economics*. New York: Pantheon, 1998.

Ospina, Carmen. "If You Build It, Will They Come?" *Publishers Weekly* 250, no. 34 (2003).

———. "Bilingual Boom at BEA." *Publishers Weekly* 251, no. 25 (2004).

Owen, John MacKenzie. "The New Dissemination of Knowledge: Digital Libraries and Institutional Roles in Scholarly Publishing." *Journal of Economic Methodology* 9, no. 3 (2002): 275.

Packard, Ashley. "Copyright or Copy Wrong: An Analysis of University Claims to Faculty Work." *Communication and Law Policy* 7 (Summer 2002): 275–316.

Palmer, Jonathan W. "Electronic Markets and Supply Chains: Emerging Models, Execution, and Performance Measurement." *Electronic Markets* 14, no. 4 (2005): 268–69.

Parsons, Paul. "The Editorial Committee: Controller of the Imprint." *Journal of Scholarly Publishing* 20, no. 4 (July 1989): 238–44.

———. *Getting Publishing: The Acquisition Process at University Presses*. Knoxville: University of Tennessee Press, 1989.

———. "The Evolving Publishing Agendas of University Presses." *Journal of Scholarly Publishing* 23, no. 1 (October 1991): 45–50.

Pascarelli, Anne M. "Coping Strategies for Libraries Facing the Serials Crisis." *Serials Review* 16, no. 1 (1990): 75–80.

Pasco, Allan H. "Basic Advice for Novice Authors." *Journal of Scholarly Publishing* 23, no. 2 (January 1992): 95–105.

Pavliscak, Pamela, Seamus Ross, and Charles Henry. "Information Technology in Humanities Scholarship: Achievements, Prospects, and Challenges—The United States Focus." American Council of Learned Societies, Occasional Paper 37, 1–2, 1997.

Pecorino, Paul. "Rent Seeking: A Textbook Example." Working paper, University of Alabama, Economics, Finance, and Legal Studies, 2004.

Pedersen, Martin. "They Censor, I Select." *Publishers Weekly*, January 10, 1994.

Perkins, Maxwell E. *Editor to Author*. Ed. John Hall Wheelock. New York: Scribner's, 1950.

Perrin, Noel. *Bowdler's Legacy: A History of Expurgated Books in England and America*. Vol. 1. Hanover, NH: University Press of New England, 1969.

Peterson, Clarence. *The Bantam Story: Thirty Years of Paperback Publishing*. New York: Bantam, 1975.

Picard, Robert. *Media Economics: Concepts and Issues*. Newbury Park, CA: Sage, 1989.

———. "The Rise and Fall of Communication Empires." *Journal of Media Economics*, 9, no. 4 (1996): 23–40.

————. *The Economics and Financing of Media Companies*. New York: Fordham University Press, 2002.

————, ed. *Media Firms*. Mahwah, NJ: Erlbaum, 2002.

Piternick, Anne B. "Author Problems in a Collaborative Research Project." *Journal of Scholarly Publishing* 25, no. 1 (October 1993): 21–37.

Plant, Arnold. "The Economic Aspects of Copyright in Books." *Economica* 1, no. 2 (May 1934): 167–95.

Plotorask, Alexander I., and Paul J. Lerner. *Essentials of Intellectual Property*. New York: Wiley, 2002.

Pollack, Andrew. 1998. "The Fight for Hispanic Viewers: Univision's Success Story Attracts New Competition." *New York Times*, January 19, Business Section, pp. 1, 6.

Pool, Ithiel de Sola. "The Culture of Electronic Print." *Daedalus* 111 (Fall 1982): 17–32.

————. *Technologies of Freedom*. Boston: Harvard University Press, 1983.

Pope, Barbara Kline, and P. K. Kannan. "Will They Pay? Measuring Consumer Demand and Price Preference for Electronic Delivery of Books." Working paper, National Academy Press, 2003.

Porter, Michael. "How Competitive Forces Shape Strategy." *Harvard Business Review* 57 (March–April 1979): 137.

————. *Competitive Strategy: Techniques for Analyzing Industries and Competitors*. New York: Free Press, 1980.

————. "Towards a Dynamic Theory of Strategy." *Strategic Management Journal* 12 (1991): 95–117.

Porter, Michael E., and Scott Stern. "Innovation: Location Matters." *MIT Sloan Management Review* 42, no. 4 (2001): 28–36.

Posner, Richard A. *Public Intellectuals: A Study of Decline*. Cambridge: Harvard University Press, 2001.

Postman, Neil. *Amusing Ourselves to Death: Public Discourse in the Age of Show Business*. New York: Penguin Books, 1985.

Potter, Clarkson N. *Who Does What and Why in Book Publishing*. New York: Birch Lane Press, 1990.

Powell, Walter W. "Adapting to Tight Money and New Opportunities." *Journal of Scholarly Publishing* 14, no. 1 (October 1982): 9–20.

————. "From Craft to Corporation: The Impact of Outside Ownership on Book Publishing." In *Individuals in Mass Media Organizations: Creativity and Constraint*, ed. James S. Ettema and D. Charles Whitney. Beverly Hills, CA: Sage, 1982.

————. *Getting into Print: The Decision-Making Process in Scholarly Publishing*. Chicago, IL: University of Chicago Press, 1985.

Prelac, Drazen, and Duncan Simester. "Always Leave Home without It: A Further Investigation of the Credit-Card Effect on Willingness to Pay." *Marketing Letters* 12 (February 2001): 5–12.

"Publish Your First Novel: Your Mac Makes It Possible." *MacAddict*, April 2001.

Quelch, J., and L. Klein. "The Internet and International Marketing." *Sloan Management Review* 37, no. 3 (1996): 60–75.

Radway, Janice A. *Reading the Romance: Women, Patriarchy, and Popular Literature*. Chapel Hill: University of North Carolina Press, 1984.

———. "Reading Is Not Eating: Mass-Produced Literature and the Theoretical, Methodological, and Political Consequences of a Metaphor." *Book Research Quarterly* 2 (Fall 1986): 7–29.

Raff, Daniel M. G. "Superstores and the Evolution of Firm capabilities in American Bookselling." *Strategic Management Journal* 21 (2000): 1043–59.

Rayner, Richard. "An Actual Internet Success Story." *New York Times Magazine*, June 9, 2002.

Reginald, R., and M. R. Burgess. *Cumulative Paperback Index, 1939–1959*. Detroit, MI: Gale, 1973.

Reichman, Henry. *Censorship and Selection: Issues and Answers for Schools*. Chicago: American Library Association and the American Association of School Administrators, 1988.

Reinstein, David A., and Christopher M. Snyder. "The Influence of Expert Reviews on Consumer Demand for Experience Goods. A Case of Movie Critics." *Journal of Industrial Economics* 53, no. 1 (March 2005): 27–51.

Rembar, Charles. *The End of Obscenity: The Trials of Lady Chatterley, Tropic of Cancer, and Fanny Hill*. New York: Random House, 1968.

Remer, Rosalind. *Printers and Men of Capital: Philadelphia Book Publishers in the New Republic*. Philadelphia: University of Pennsylvania Press, 1996.

Reskin, Barbara F. "Culture, Commerce, and Gender: The Feminization of Book Editing." In *Job Queues, Gender Queues: Explaining Women's Inroads into Male Occupations*, ed. Barbara F. Reskin and Patricia A. Roos. Philadelphia, PA: Temple University Press, 1990.

Riggar, T. F., and R. E. Matkin. "Breaking into Academic Print." *Journal of Scholarly Publishing* 22, no. 1 (October 1990): 17–22.

Robinson, Sara. "Forget E-Books." *Interactive Week*, April 2, 2001, 57–58.

Rogers, Donald. *Banned! Censorship in the Schools*. New York: Messner / Simon & Schuster, 1988.

Romano, Frank. *Digital Basics 3.0*. Cohoes, NY: Mohawk Paper Mills, 2001.

Rose, M. L. "Everything Old Is New Again: Reinventing the Publishing Model." *Poets and Writers*, 30, no. 2 (May–June 2002): 40–44.

Rose, Mark. *Authors and Owners: The Invention of Copyright*. Cambridge, MA: Harvard University Press, 1993.

Rosner, Charles. *The Growth of the Book Jacket*. Cambridge, MA: Harvard University Press, 1954.

Roth, Jill. "Digital Printing: Emerging Markets." *American Printer*, March 2002.

Rowson, Richard C. "A Formula for Successful Scholarly Publishing." *Journal of Scholarly Publishing* 25, no. 2 (January 1994): 67–78.

Ruffle, Bradley J., and Ze'ev Shtudiner. "99: Are Retailers Best Responding to Rational Consumers? Experimental Evidence." Paper available at the Social Science Research Network Electronic Library, http://papers.ssrn.com /sol13/papers.cfm?abstract _id=331466, July 2003.

Rutherford, Brett. "Print-on-Demand Here to Stay for Region's Successful Printers." *Printing News*, April 15, 2002.

Saal, Rollene. *The New York Public Library Guide to Reading Groups*. New York: Crown Trade Paperbacks, 1995.

Sabine, Gordon, and Patricia Sabine. *Books that Made the Difference: What People Told Us*. Harnden, CT: Library Professional Publications, 1983.

"Salary Survey for the Publishing Industry." *Publishers Weekly*, July 2004.

Salvaggio, Jerry L., ed. *The Information Society: Economic, Social, and Structural Issues*. Hillsdale, NJ: Erlbaum, 1989.

Salvaggio, Jerry L., and Jennings Bryant, eds. *Media Use in the Information Age: Emerging Patterns of Adoption and Consumer Use*. Hillsdale, NJ: Erlbaum, 1989.

Saxby, Stephen. *The Age of Information*. New York: New York University Press, 1990.

Schafer, Arthur. "The Market-Place and the Community." *Journal of Scholarly Publishing* 24, no. 4 (July 1993): 253–57.

Schick, Frank L. *The Paperbound Book in America: The History of Paperbacks and Their European Background*. New York: Bowker, 1958.

Schiffrin, Andre. "The Corporatization of Publishing." *Nation*, June 3, 1996, 29–33.

———. "Payback Time: University Presses as Profit Centers." *Chronicle of Higher Education*, June 18, 1999.

———. *The Business of Books: How International Conglomerates Took Over Publishing and Changed the Way We Read*. New York: Verso, 2000.

Schiller, Herbert I. *Culture, Inc.: The Corporate Takeover of Public Expression*. New York: Oxford University Press, 1989.

Schiller, Robert J. "From Efficient Market Theory to Behavioral Finance." *Journal of Economic Perspectives* 17, no. 1 (Winter 2003): 83–104.

Schlee, Edward E. "The Value of Information in Efficient Risk-Sharing Arrangements." *American Economic Review* 91, no. 3 (June 2001): 509–24.

Schmidley, A. Dianne. U.S. Census Bureau, Current Population Reports, Series p23-206. "Profile of the Foreign-Born Population in the United States: 2000." Washington, DC: U.S. Government Printing Office, 2001.

Schreyer, Alice D. *The History of Books: A Guide to Selected Resources in the Library of Congress*. Washington, DC: Library of Congress / The Center for the Book, 1987.

Scribner, Charles, Jr. *In the Company of Writers: A Life in Publishing*, New York: Scribner's, 1990.

———. *In the Web of Ideas: The Education of a Publisher*. New York: Scribner's, 1993.

Sebesta, Sam. "A Renewed View of Children's Literature." In *Inspiring Literacy: Literature for Children and Young Adults*, ed. Sam Sebesta and Ken Donelson. New Brunswick, NJ: Transaction Publishers, 1993.

See, Carolyn. *Making a Literary Life*. New York: Random House, 2002.

Segall, Jeffrey. *Joyce in America: Cultural Politics and the Trials of Ulysses*. Berkeley: University of California Press, 1993.

Server, Lee. *Over My Dead Body: The Sensational Age of the American Paperback, 1945–55*. San Francisco: Chronicle Books, 1994.

Seybold, Catherine. "The Beginnings of the University of Chicago Press." *Journal of Scholarly Publishing* 23, no. 3 (April 1992): 178–84.

Shape, Leslie T., and Irene Gunther. *Editing Fact and Fiction: A Concise Guide to Book Editing*. New York: Cambridge University Press, 1994.

Shapiro, Carl, and Hal R. Varian. *Information Rules: A Strategic Guide to the Network Economy*. Boston: Harvard Business School Press, 1999.

Shatzkin, Leonard. *In Cold Type: Overcoming the Book Crisis*. Boston: Houghton Mifflin, 1982.

Shavell, Steven, and Tanquy van Ypersele. "Rewards versus Intellectual Property Rights." *Journal of Law and Economics* 44, no. 2 (2001): 525–47.

Shealy, Daniel. "The Author-Publisher Relationships of Louisa May Alcott." *Book Research Quarterly* 3 (Spring 1987): 63–74.

Sheehy, Eugene P., ed. *Guide to Reference Books*. Chicago: American Library Association, 1986.

Sheinin, Rose. "Academic Freedom and Integrity and Ethics in Publishing." *Journal of Scholarly Publishing* 24, no. 4 (July 1993): 232–48.

Sheshinski, Eytan, and Yoram Weiss. "Inflation and Costs of Price Adjustment." *Review of Economics Studies* 44 (1977): 281–303.

Shiller, Robert J. "Stock Prices and Social Dynamics." Yale University Cowles discussion paper no. 616, 1984.

———. "Conversation, Information, and Herd Behavior." *Rhetoric and Human Behavior* 85, no. 2 (1995): 181–85.

———. "Human Behavior and the Efficiency of the Financial System." Yale University Cowles discussion paper, 1998.

———. *Irrational Exuberance*. Princeton, NJ: Princeton University Press, 2000.

Shiller, Robert J., and Pierre Perron. "Testing the Random Walk Hypothesis: Power Versus Frequency of Observations." Yale University Cowles Foundation discussion paper no. 73, December 1984. http://cowles.yale.edu/P/ab/a07/a0732.htm.

Shipp, John. "Commercial Scholarly Publishing: The Devil Incarnate or Divine Savior?" *History of Economic Review* 32 (Summer 2000): 37–45.

Shoemaker, Jack. "A Book Is a Very Serious Thing." *Journal of Scholarly Publishing* 19, no. 2 (January 1988): 91–96.

Sibly, Hugh. "Price Inflexibility in Markets with Repeat Purchasing." *Macroeconomics* 23, no. 3 (Summer 2001): 459–75.

Siegfried, J. J., and C. Latta. "Competition in the Retail College Textbook Market." *Economics of Education Review* 17 (1998): 105–15.

Siler, Jennifer. "From Gutenberg to Gateway: Electronic Publishing at University Presses." *Journal of Scholarly Publishing*, 32, no. 1 (October 2000): 9–23.

Silverman, Al, ed. *The Book of the Month: Sixty Years of Books in American Life*. Boston, MA: Little Brown, 1986.

Silverman, Franklin H. *Authoring Books and Materials for Students, Academics, and Professionals*. New York: Praeger, 1998.

Siwek, Stephen. "Copyright Industries in the U.S. Economy: The 2002 Report." Washington, DC: Economists Incorporated / International Intellectual Property Alliance, 2002.

Skillin, Marjorie, and Robert M. Gay. *Words into Type*. New York: Prentice-Hall, 1974.

Slade, Margaret. "Optimal Pricing with Costly Adjustment: Evidence from Retail Grocery Prices." *Review of Economic Studies* 65 (January 1998): 87–107.

Smith, Anthony. *The Politics of Information: Problems of Policy in Modern Media.* London: Macmillan, 1979.

———. *The Geopolitics of Information: How Western Culture Dominates the World.* New York: Oxford University Press, 1980.

Smith, Carter L., and Donald A. Hantula. "Pricing Effects on Foraging in a Simulated Internet Shopping Mall." *Journal of Economic Psychology* 24, no. 5 (October 2003): 653–74.

Smith, Eldred. *The Librarian, the Scholar, and the Future of the Research Library.* Westport, CT: Greenwood Press, 1990.

Smith, Eric H. *New Strategies to Curb Book Piracy: A Survey of the New Foreign Trade Legislation.* New York: Paskus, Gordon & Hyman, 1985.

Smith, Erin T. "Changes in Faculty Reading Behaviors. The Impact of Electronic Journals on the University of Georgia." *Journal of Academic Librarianship* 29, no. 3 (2003): 162–68.

Smith, Gordon V., and Russell L. Parr. *Valuation of Intellectual Property and Intangible Assets.* 3rd edition. New York: Wiley, 2000.

Smith, Michael, and Erik Brynjolfsson. "Consumer Decision-Making at an Internet Shopbot: Brand Still Matters." *Journal of Industrial Economics* 49 (December 2001): 541–58.

Smith, Michael D. "The Impact of Shopbots on Electronic Markets." *Journal of the Academy of Marketing Science* 30, no. 4 (2002): 442–50.

Smith, Michael D., Joseph Bailey, and Erik Brynjolfsson. "Understanding Digital Markets: Review and Assessment." In *Understanding the Digital Economy*, ed. Erik Brynjolfsson and Brian Kahin. Cambridge, MA: MIT Press, 2000.

Smith, Roger H., ed. *The American Reading Public: What It Reads, Why It Reads.* New York: Bowker, 1961.

———. *Paperback Parnassus.* Boulder, CO: Westview Press, 1976.

Smith, Tom W., and Seokho Kim. "The Vanishing Protestant Majority." NORC / University of Chicago, GSS Social Change Report no. 49, July 2004.

Smolla, Rodney A. *Free Speech in an Open Society.* New York: Knopf, 1992.

Solotaroff, Ted. "The Literary-Industrial Complex." *New Republic*, June 8, 1987.

———. *A Few Good Voices in My Head: Occasional Pieces on Writing, Editing, and Reading My Contemporaries.* New York: Harper & Row, 1987.

Solow, Robert M. "A Contribution to the Theory of Economic Growth." *Quarterly Journal of Economics Perspectives* 70 (1956): 65–94.

———. 1994. "Perspectives on Growth Theory." *Journal of Economic Perspectives* 8, no. 1 (Winter 1994): 45–54.

———. *"Learning from 'Learning by Doing': Lessons for Economic Growth."* Stanford, CA: Stanford University Press, 1997.

Solow, Robert M., Michael Dertouzos, and Richard K. Lester. *Made in America.* Cambridge, MA: MIT Press, 1989.

Solow, Robert M., James Tobin, C. C. von Weizacker, and M. Yaari. "Neoclassical Growth with Fixed Proportions." *Review of Economic Studies* 33, no. 2 (April 1966): 88.

Sorensen, Alan T. "Bestseller Lists and Product Variety: The Case of Book Sales." Working paper, Stanford University, 2004.

Sorensen, Alan T., and Scott J. Rasmussen. 2004. "Is Any Publicity Good Publicity? A Note on the Impact of Book Reviews." Working paper, Stanford University, 2004.

Spector, Robert. *Amazon.com: Get Big Fast*. New York: Harper Business, 2000.

Squires, Bruce P. "The Ethical Responsibilities of the Editor." *Journal of Scholarly Publishing* 24, no. 4 (July 1993): 214–18.

Standera, Oldrich. *The Electronic Era of Publishing: An Overview of Concepts and Technologies*. New York: Elsevier, 1987.

Starbuck, William, and John M. Mezias. "Opening Pandora's Box: Studying the Accuracy of Managers' Perceptions." *Journal of Organizational Behavior* 17, no. 2 (1996): 99–117.

Starker, Steven. "Fear of Fiction: The Novel." *Book Research Quarterly* 6 (Summer 1990): 44–59.

Steckler, Phyllis B. *Phyllis B. Steckler and the Oryx Press: A Memoir*. Tempe: Arizona State Universities Libraries, 1993.

Steele, Colin. "Phoenix Rising: New Models for Research Monograph?" *Learned Publishing* 16 (2003): 111.

Steinberg, S. H. *Five Hundred Years of Printing*. New York: Penguin, 1974.

Steinberg, Sybil, ed. *Writing for Your Life #2*. Wainscott, NY: Pushcart Press, 1995.

Stern, Madeleine B. *Books and Book People in 19th-Century America*. New York: Bowker, 1978.

Stewart, James B. "Moby Dick In Manhattan." *New Yorker*, June 27–July 4, 1994.

Stiglitz, Joseph E. "Responding to Economic Crises: Policy Alternatives for Equitable Recovery and Development." *Manchester School* 67, no. 5 (1999): 409–27.

———. "The Contributions of the Economics of Information to Twentieth Century Economics." *Quarterly Journal of Economics* 115, no. 4 (November 2000): 1441–78.

———. "Information and Change in the Paradigm in Economics." *American Economic Review* 92, no. 3 (June 2002): 460–502.

———. *Globalization and Its Discontents*. New York: Norton, 2002.

Stoll, Clifford. *Silicon Snake Oil: Second Thoughts on the Information Highway*. New York: Doubleday, 1995.

Stoughton, Mary. *Substance and Style: Instruction and Practice in Copyediting*. Alexandria, VA: Editorial Experts, 1989.

Strainchamps, Ethel. *Rooms with No View: A Woman's Guide to the Man's World of Publishing*. New York: Harper & Row, 1974.

Strong, William S. *The Copyright Book: A Practical Guide*. 5th edition. Cambridge, MA: MIT Press, 1999.

Strossen, Nadine. *Defending Pornography: Free Speech, Sex, and the Fight for Women's Rights*. New York: Scribner's, 1995.

Strothman, Wendy. "On Moving from Campus to Commerce." *Journal of Scholarly Publishing* 18, no. 3 (April 1987): 157–62.

———. "Multiculturalism at One Press: The Beacon Experience." *Journal of Scholarly Publishing* 24, no. 3 (April 1993): 144–50.

Sudhir, K. "Structural Analysis of Competitive Pricing in the Presence of a Strategic Retailer." *Marketing Science* 20 (Summer 2001): 244–64.

Sugano, Joel Yutaka, and Toshio Kobayashi. "Amazon.com E Commerce Platform: Leveraging Competitiveness Through the Virtual Value Chain." *Osaka Economic Papers* 52, no. 2 (2002): 228–58.

Sunstein, Cass R. *Democracy and the Problem of Free Speech.* New York: Free Press, 1993.

Sutcliffe, Peter. *The Oxford University Press: An Informal History.* London: Oxford University Press, 1978.

Sutherland, Zena, and May Hill Arbuthnot. *Children and Books.* Glenview, IL: Scott Foresman, 1977.

Sutton, John. *Marshall's Tendencies: What Can Economists Know?* Cambridge, MA: MIT Press, 2000.

Szenberg, Michael, and Eric Youngkoo Lee. "The Structure of the American Book Publishing Industry." *Journal of Cultural Economics* 18, no. 4 (1994–1995): 313–22.

Tebbel, John. *A History of Book Publishing in the United States.* 4 vols. New York: Bowker, 1972–1981.

———. *Between Covers: The Rise and Transformation of Book Publishing in America.* New York: Oxford University Press, 1987.

Teeter, Dwight L., and Bill Loving. *Law of Mass Communications: Freedom and Control of Print and Broadcast Media.* 10th edition. New York: Foundation Press, 2001.

Tellis, Gerald J., and Fred S. Zufryden. "Tackling the Retailer Decision Maze: Which Brands to Discount, How Much, When, and Why?" *Marketing Science* 14, no. 3 (1995): 271–99.

Tepper, Steven J. "Fiction Reading in America: Explaining the Gender Gap." *Poetics* 27 (2000): 25–75.

Teute, Fredrika J. "To Publish and Perish: Who Are the Dinosaurs in Scholarly Publishing?" *Journal of Scholarly Publishing* 32, no. 2 (January 2001): 102–12.

Thaler, Richard H. "The End of Behavioral Finance." *Financial Analysts Journal* 55, no. 6 (November–December 1999): 12–17.

———. "From Homo Economicus to Homo Sapiens." *Journal of Economic Perspectives* 14, no. 1 (Winter 2000): 133–41.

Thomas, Edward A. *The World Almanac and Book of Facts for Booksellers.* New York: World Almanac Books, 2005.

Thomas, Louis A. "Incumbent Firms' Response to Entry: Price, Advertising, and New Product Introduction." *International Journal of Industrial Organization*, no. 17 (1999): 527–55.

Thompson, Margaret E., Steven H. Chaffee, and Hayg H. Oshagan. "Regulating Pornography: A Public Dilemma." *Journal of Communication* 40 (Summer 1990): 73–83.

Thornton, Patricia H. "Institutional Logics and the Historical Contingency of Power in Organizations: Executive Succession in the Higher Education Publishing Industry." *American Journal of Sociology* 105, no. 3 (November 1999): 801–43.

———. "Personal Versus Market Logics of Control: A Historically Contingent Theory of the Risk of Acquisition." *Organization Science* 12, no. 3 (May–June 2001): 294–311.

———. *Markets from Culture: Institutional Logics and Organizational Decisions in Higher Education Publishing.* Stanford, CA: Stanford University Press, 2004.

Timko, David A. "A Study of the Book Reviewing Habits of the *New York Times*, 1950 – 2000." Master's thesis, University of North Carolina, Chapel Hill, 2001.

Tomkins, Jane. *West of Everything: The Inner Life of Westerns*. New York: Oxford University Press, 1992.

Turow, Joseph G. *Getting Books to Children: An Exploration of Publisher-Market Relations*. Chicago: American Library Association, 1979.

Tyagi, Rajeev K. "Cost Leadership and Pricing." *Economic Letters* 72, no. 2 (August 2001): 189–93.

Tzouvaras, Antonio, and Thomas Hess. "Keyword: Print-on-Demand." *International Journal of Media Management* 3, no. 1 (2001): 39–41.

U.S. Bureau of the Census. "U.S. Summary: 2000." Washington, DC: U.S. Department of Commerce, Economics and Statistics Administration, July 2002a.

U.S. Bureau of the Census. "Coming from the Americas: A Profile of the Nation's Foreign-Born Population from Latin America (2000 Update)." Washington, DC: Economics and Statistics Administration, January 2002b. http:/www.census.gov/population/www/socdemo/foreign.html.

U.S. Bureau of the Census. "Hispanic Heritage Month (2002)." CBOS-FF:15 9/3/2002 Hispanic Heritage Month 2002: 9/15-10/15/2002. Washington, DC, 2002c. Press release. factfinder.census.gov/servlet/BasicFactsServlet.

U.S. Department of Commerce, Bureau of the Census. *Book Publishers*. 2002 Economic Census Information Industry Series. Washington, DC: GPO, 2004.

U.S. Department of Commerce, Bureau of the Census. *Census of Manufactures: Newspapers, Periodicals, Books, and Miscellaneous Publishing*. Washington, DC: GPO. [Published for years ending in 2 and 7.]

U.S. Department of Commerce, Bureau of the Census. *Economic Census Information* [Book Publishing]. Washington, DC: GPO. [Published every five years.]

U.S. Department of Commerce, Bureau of the Census. *Economic Indicators*. Washington, DC: GPO. [Published annually.]

U.S. Department of Commerce, Bureau of the Census. *Statistical Abstract of the United States*. Washington, DC: GPO. [Published annually.]

U.S. Department of Commerce, Bureau of the Census. "Census Bureau Releases 1990 Census Counts on Hispanic Population Groups." Press release, June 12, 1991. Washington, DC: U.S. Bureau of the Census.

U.S. Department of Commerce, Bureau of the Census. *We, the American . . . Hispanics*. Ethnic and Hispanic Statistics Branch, Population Division. Washington, DC: U.S. Government Printing Office, November 1993.

U.S. Department of Commerce, Economics and Statistics Administration. *Income, Poverty, and Health Insurance Coverage in the United States: 2004*. Washington, DC: GPO, 2005.

U.S. Department of Commerce, International Trade Administration. *U.S. Industrial Outlook*. Washington, DC: GPO, 1999.

U.S. Department of Justice. *The Department of Justice Manual*. Vol. 6. Englewood Cliffs, NJ: Aspen, 1997.

U.S. Department of Labor. *Attorney General's Commission on Pornography: Final Report*. Vol. 1. Washington, DC: GPO, 1986.

Underhill, Paco. *Why We Buy: The Science of Shopping*. New York: Simon & Schuster, 1999.

Univision. *Annual Report 2001*. Los Angeles: Univision Communications, 2002.

Vakratsas, Demetrios, and Tim Ambler. "How Advertising Works: What Do We Really Know?" *Journal of Marketing* 61, no. 1 (1999): 26–43.

Varian, Hal. "Buying, Sharing, and Renting Information Goods." *Journal of Industrial Economics* 48, no. 4 (December 2000): 473–88.

Veliotes, Nicholas. "Copyright in the 1990s: A New Round of Challenges for American Publishers." *Book Research Quarterly* 4 (Spring 1988): 3–11.

Veronis Suhler Stevenson Communications Industry Forecast. New York: Veronis Suhler Stevenson, 1993–2005. [Published annually.]

Vitz, Paul C. *Censorship: Evidence of Bias in Our Children's Textbooks*. Ann Arbor, MI: Servant Books, 1986.

Vogel, Harold. L. *Entertainment Industry Economics: A Guide for Financial Analysis*. New York: Cambridge University Press, 2001.

Waaijers, L. "Stratum Continuum of Information: Scholarly Communication and the Role of University Libraries." *New Library World* 103, no. 4 (April 2002): 165–71.

Wakerly, Elizabeth C. "Disaggregate Dynamics and Economic Growth in Canada." *Economic Modelling* 19, no. 2 (March 2002): 197–219.

Walker, Jill Cohen. "Gutenberg's 'Gotcha'? Gee-Whiz Digital Technology Returns Book Printing to Its Short-Run Roots." *Print on Demand*, September 1999.

Walters, Ray. *Paperback Talk*. Chicago: Academy Chicago Publishers, 1985.

Waters, Lindsay. "Rescue Tenure from the Tyranny of the Monograph." *Chronicle of Higher Education*, April 20, 2001, p. B7.

Watkins, John J. *The Mass Media and the Law*. Englewood Cliffs, NJ: Prentice-Hall, 1990.

Watrous, Peter. "A Country Now Ready to Listen." *New York Times*, June 27, 1999.

Way, David. "Publishing in Libraries." *Journal of Scholarly Publishing* 29, no. 1 (October 1988): 35–38.

Webster, Edward. *Print Unchained: Fifty Years of Digital Printing, 1950–2000 and Beyond: A Saga of Invention and Enterprise*. West Dover: DRA of Vermont, 2000.

Weiler, Paul C. *Entertainment, Media, and the Law*. St. Paul, MN: West Publishing, 1997.

Weisberg, Jacob. "Rough Trade: The Sad Decline of American Publishing." *New Republic*, June 17, 1991.

Weiss, Michael J. "The Clustering of America: Target Marketing to Book Buyers." *Publishers Weekly*, November 11, 1988.

———. *The Clustering of America*. New York: Harper & Row, 1988.

Wertenbroch, Klaus, and Bernd Skiera. "Measuring Consumers' Willingness to Pay at the Point of Purchase." *Journal of Marketing Research* 39 (May 2002): 228–41.

West, James L. W., III. *American Authors and the Literary Marketplace since 1900*. Philadelphia: University of Pennsylvania Press, 1988.

Weybright, Victor. *The Making of a Publisher: A Life in the 20th-Century Book Revolution*. New York: Reynal, 1967.

Wharton, Robert, and Albert N. Greco. "Educational Publishing: Elhi and College Textbooks." In *Book Industry Trends*. New York: Book Industry Study Group, 2001.

Wharton, Robert, and Albert N. Greco. "Trade Publishing: Adult, Juvenile, Mass Market,

Book Clubs, and Mail Order." In *Book Industry Trends*. New York: Book Industry Study Group, 2003a.

Wharton, Robert, and Albert N. Greco. "U.S. Book Exports and Imports, 1997–2002." In *Book Industry Trends*. New York: Book Industry Study Group, 2003b.

Wharton, Robert, and Albert N. Greco. "Small and Independent Book Publishing: An Analysis of Sales Data." In *Book Industry Trends*. New York: Book Industry Study Group, 2004.

Whiteside, Thomas. *The Blockbuster Complex: Conglomerates, Show Business, and Book Publishing*. Middletown, CT: Wesleyan University Press, 1982.

Wicks, Jan LeBlanc, George Sylvie, C. Ann Hollifield, Stephen Lacy, Ardyth Sohn, and Angela Powers. *Media Management: A Casebook Approach*. 3rd edition. Mahwah, NJ: Erlbaum, 2004.

Williams, Frederick. *The New Telecommunications: Infrastructure for the Information Age*. New York: Free Press, 1991.

Williams, Joseph M. *Style: Toward Clarity and Grace*. Chicago: University of Chicago Press, 1990.

Willison, Ian R. "Massmediatisation: Export of the American Model." In *Les Mutations du Livre et de L'Edition dans Le Monde du XVIII e Siele A'L'An 2000, Actes du Colloque International, Sherbrooke 2000*. Quebec: Les Presses de L'Universite Laval, L'Harmattan, 2001.

Wissoker, Ken. "Scholarly Monographs Are Flourishing, Not Dying." *Chronicle of Higher Education*, September 12, 1997, p. B4.

Wolpert, Samuel, and Joyce F. Wolpert. *Economics of Information*. New York: Van Nostrand Reinhold, 1986.

Wood, Leonard A. "Demographics of Mass Market Consumers." *Book Research Quarterly* 3 (Spring 1987): 31–39.

Yosefi, Hanan. "The Convergence of Graphic Arts and Digital Print." *DocuWorld*, Fall 2000.

Young, Jeffrey R. "A University that Reveres Tradition Experiments with E-Books." *Chronicle of Higher Education*, 18 May 2001, p. A39.

Zboray, Ronald J. *A Fictive People: Antebellum Economic Development and the American Reading Public*. Oxford: Oxford University Press, 1992.

Zettelmeyer, Florian, Fiona Scott Morton, and Jorge Silva-Risso. "How the Internet Lowers Prices. Evidence from Matched Survey and Auto Transaction Data." Working paper, National Bureau of Economic Research no. 11515, 2005.

Zill, Nicholas, and Marianne Winglee. "Literature Reading in the United States: Data from National Surveys and Their Policy Implications." *Book Research Quarterly* 5 (Spring 1989): 24–58.

Zinkhan, George M. "The Role of Books and Book Reviews in the Knowledge Dissemination Process." *Journal of Marketing* 59 (January 1995): 106–8.

INDEX